CAMBRIDGE LIBRARY COLLECTION

Books of enduring scholarly value

History

The books reissued in this series include accounts of historical events and movements by eye-witnesses and contemporaries, as well as landmark studies that assembled significant source materials or developed new historiographical methods. The series includes work in social, political and military history on a wide range of periods and regions, giving modern scholars ready access to influential publications of the past.

The Monks of Westminster

For this 1916 work, Archdeacon E.H. Pearce searched through the extensive archives of Westminster Abbey to provide a list of all the known members of the monastic community until the Dissolution. Over 700 individuals are included, with all the information about them available to the author. While the list is not complete, and the use of other sources would add additional names for the early period, Pearce completed a remarkable achievement. Westminster was a substantial foundation, with an average community of 47 for the fourteenth and fifteenth centuries. About half of these, who held some office or function, are naturally better documented than ordinary monks. Scholarship was evidently valued by the abbey, although the majority of the writings evidenced were on the history of the community rather than theological or literary works. Some monks were supported at Oxford, but little is known of the education offered to the remainder.

Cambridge University Press has long been a pioneer in the reissuing of out-of-print titles from its own backlist, producing digital reprints of books that are still sought after by scholars and students but could not be reprinted economically using traditional technology. The Cambridge Library Collection extends this activity to a wider range of books which are still of importance to researchers and professionals, either for the source material they contain, or as landmarks in the history of their academic discipline.

Drawing from the world-renowned collections in the Cambridge University Library, and guided by the advice of experts in each subject area, Cambridge University Press is using state-of-the-art scanning machines in its own Printing House to capture the content of each book selected for inclusion. The files are processed to give a consistently clear, crisp image, and the books finished to the high quality standard for which the Press is recognised around the world. The latest print-on-demand technology ensures that the books will remain available indefinitely, and that orders for single or multiple copies can quickly be supplied.

The Cambridge Library Collection will bring back to life books of enduring scholarly value (including out-of-copyright works originally issued by other publishers) across a wide range of disciplines in the humanities and social sciences and in science and technology.

The Monks of Westminster

Being a Register of the Brethren of the Convent from the time of the Confessor to the Dissolution

ERNEST HAROLD PEARCE

CAMBRIDGE UNIVERSITY PRESS

Cambridge, New York, Melbourne, Madrid, Cape Town, Singapore,
São Paolo, Delhi, Dubai, Tokyo

Published in the United States of America by Cambridge University Press, New York

www.cambridge.org
Information on this title: www.cambridge.org/9781108013598

This edition first published 1916
This digitally printed version 2010

ISBN 978-1-108-01359-8 Paperback

NOTES AND DOCUMENTS

RELATING TO

WESTMINSTER ABBEY

No. 5

THE MONKS OF WESTMINSTER

CAMBRIDGE UNIVERSITY PRESS
C. F. CLAY, Manager
London: FETTER LANE, E.C.
Edinburgh: 100 PRINCES STREET

New York: G. P. PUTNAM'S SONS
Bombay, Calcutta and Madras: MACMILLAN AND CO., Ltd.
Toronto: J. M. DENT AND SONS, Ltd.
Tokyo: THE MARUZEN-KABUSHIKI-KAISHA

THE
MONKS OF WESTMINSTER

BEING A REGISTER OF THE BRETHREN OF THE CONVENT
FROM THE TIME OF THE CONFESSOR TO THE
DISSOLUTION

WITH LISTS OF THE OBEDIENTIARIES
AND AN INTRODUCTION

BY

E. H. PEARCE, M.A.
CANON AND ARCHDEACON OF WESTMINSTER

Cambridge:
at the University Press
1916

H. E. R.

DOMINO ABBATI WESTMŌN

VIRO DEO DEVOTO ECCLESIE NOSTRE NECESSARIO[1]

W. B. C.

DOMINO PRIORI

PRO SERMONIBVS IN CHORO MAGNIS RECREACIONIBVS DIGNO[2]

W. H. C.

CELERARIO ET GARDINARIO

CVIVS ARMATVRA NON POTEST ALICVI APTARI[3]

R. H. C.

THESAVRARIO

QVI PICTVRAS APOCALYPSIS IN
CLAVSTRO INFIRMITORII FIERI FACIT[4]

H. R. G.

QVI EST VLTIMVS NVNC IN CONGREGACIONE[5]

HASCE ANTECESSORVM NOSTRORVM CEDVLAS
D D
SVPPRIOR ET ARCHIDIACONVS

---

[1] p. 85.   [2] p. 153.   [3] p. 107.   [4] p. 112.   [5] p. 126.

CONTENTS

PREFACE

AN effort has been made in this volume to re-people the Convent of St Peter, Westminster, by such an examination of the records as would enable me to cite the authorities for each name included and for each statement about the bearer of the name. The Abbots are in many cases already well known in their character and their work, though much more may yet be done to make the personalities of some of them a living reality to our generation by means of the documents which survive from their time and bear their seal. But the more we know of the Abbots, the more conscious we become that the daily round of conventual doings was from their life "a thing apart," while to the Prior and monks it was their "whole existence." The material that survives in the cases of Abbot Walter de Wenlok and Abbot William Colchester shows how small a portion of each year was spent by them at Westminster. The call of the King might send them to foreign parts; the affairs of the Order or the needs of the Convent might take them to Rome or Avignon; when they were in England, they flitted about from property to property,—Laleham, Pyrford, Cleygate, Denham, Islip and Pershore,—with a monk or two in their train to act as seneschal or chaplain; and even if they were at Westminster, they mostly resided outside the precincts at their manor-house of La Neyte. So the daily existence of the Abbey depended on the Prior and his Brethren. It was time, therefore, that these should be brought out of the shadow-land in which they have been allowed to remain.

It needed some courage to undertake such a task, especially as I had had no experience in deciphering mediaeval documents when I came to live in the Abbey five years ago. But certain circumstances encouraged me. My colleagues, and more especially the Dean, were ready to give their favour to another instalment of the Westminster series. Dr Edward Scott, the Keeper of the Muniments, has never tired of allowing a beginner to draw upon his unique experience or to beg for his revision of transcripts made by a prentice hand. I had also before me the volumes already produced by the Dean of Wells, who has shown a constant interest in the continuance of his work. When I had practically completed my list of the later monks (from 1297–8 onwards), he entrusted to me a similar list drawn up by his lamented friend, the Rev. R. B. Rackham, who, if his valuable life had been spared, would have expanded his catalogue into a more adequate Register of our Benedictines than I can hope to produce. But I have been able to test my results in various ways. For instance, the Rev. H. F. Westlake, our Custodian, came upon the names of several Westminster monks in the course of a recent examination of the accounts left by the Guild of the Assumption connected with St Margaret's parish; and I was thankful to find that all of these monks were already on my list.

The Convent was clearly intended to accommodate a Prior and about 50 Brethren. I have recently noted the totals of 152 years, ranging between 1328 and 1534, and find the average number attained by the Prior and Convent to be 46·96, or roughly 47. The highest was 59, about 1400; the lowest was 32, in 1362–3, when the ravages of the Black Death were still felt. In the fourteenth century, the figures for which are by no means complete, the average was 44. In the first quarter of the fifteenth it was 49; afterwards there was a gradual decline,—48 from 1425 to 1475, 46 for the last quarter, and 44 for that portion of the sixteenth century during which the Convent was spared.

In a work which has involved the consultation of thousands of documents I cannot hope, even with the splendid help of the Cambridge Press, to escape many errors, though none of them, I hope, may be grievous. I trust that those who find them will point them out, and will pardon them for the sake of what has resulted from the investigation. Dr Scott has greatly helped in the reading of the proofs, but I must personally accept the responsibility for the indexes, only pleading that they first took shape amid the somewhat unquiet studiousness of an officers' mess and have been finished in circumstances which still compelled the *panni nigri* to yield to arms.

For myself, I can only say that, with these names and these administrative careers before my mind, I find the mediaeval Abbey no longer ghostly and unreal, but flushed with all the signs of a vigorous circulation. I feel a genuine sympathy with Thomas Elfrede who was professed as a monk here under Henry VII's Abbot and died a Prebendary under Edward VI's Dean; and who, when his will was proved, was found to have left directions that he should be buried in some spot which in his youth he had passed daily, as he and his Brethren went their processional round of prayer and praise.

E. H. P.

3 LITTLE CLOISTERS,
On the Feast of St Edward's Translation,
1916.

INTRODUCTION

IN the course of an article on *The Benedictine Abbey of Westminster* in the Church Quarterly Review, April, 1907, Dr Armitage Robinson, now Dean of Wells, laid down the lines on which investigations into the history of the Abbey can be most profitably pursued. He paid to Richard Widmore[1] a tribute, to which every searcher among the Muniments will gladly subscribe. He pointed out how much was done by his great predecessor in the Deanery, Dr A. P. Stanley, to familiarise the English people by means of wonderful word-pictures with the innumerable occasions on which the Abbey church has been the scene of stately national functions, and the present writer may venture to add himself to the number of those who, having been children when Stanley was Dean, can now trace their first impression of what Westminster means to one of his vivid addresses at the annual children's service on Holy Innocents' Day.

But Stanley, as Dean Robinson rightly insisted (*op. cit.* p. 59), "had no kind of sympathy with the monks," whether the actual denizens of our Convent or the devotees of Benedictinism in general. His heart was with the kings and queens, the courtiers and statesmen, the men of arms and of the toga, whose bodies are buried in peace here, rather than with those whose lot was to offer incense, to prevent with their orisons the dawning of the morning, to make the darkness of the Abbey to be light by burning hundreds of candles round the tombs of the mighty, and in other ways so to commend the monastic vocation to the wealthy and to the powerful that the church and its surrounding buildings were gradually helped on to completion.

Now the question which the present instalment hopes to answer may be stated somewhat on this wise. The church of St Peter being in some respects the national ecclesiastical centre, it was natural for Kings and their craftsmen to glorify it, as Professor Lethaby[2] has shown, and for Abbots and their Brethren to labour at the finances and

The nature of the inquiry.

---

[1] *A History of the Church of St Peter, Westminster, commonly called Westminster Abbey, chiefly from Manuscript Authorities.* By Richard Widmore, M.A., Librarian to the Dean and Chapter, and Author of *An Enquiry into the Time of the First Foundation of the Abbey.* London, 1751.

[2] *Westminster Abbey and the Kings' Craftsmen,* 1906.

the quarry-work of construction, as Mr Ràckham[1] has shown; but what can be gathered about the Convent on its personal side? The Abbey was the home of monks as much as its church was the oratory of Kings. The Confessor and Henry III and Richard II and Henry V and Henry VI may at certain periods have continued instant in prayer, but priests must have ministered to their liturgical necessities. If so, who were these priests? The great Dormitory, again, still stands, though it is now divided in its service to the two semi-independent societies, the Chapter and the School; but can we not re-people it with the ancient occupants of its cubicles? There remains also the northern wall of the Refectory, and a little technical ingenuity would fashion that building anew for us and restore the tables and make the *skilla* tinkle for grace or for the reading of the lection; but who in a given year sat at the tables, and what was the total muster, when the last laggard had arrived at his accustomed seat at the board? The Great Cloister, as we know, served the purposes of a common-room, a school for novices, a play-centre, and the like; the signs of these things are still there; but who were the teachers and the taught and the players of the games? To these might be added certain actuarial and hygienic considerations. Was life in the monastery marked by its brief duration, or did many seem to "pass beyond the goal of ordinance"? What evidence is there as to the incidence of disease upon a society living out its life on a system that may fairly be described as non-natural? These and many other such lines of inquiry would be satisfied if we had an adequate list of our monks with the years of their entry and their decease.

Let us reckon up what *data* we already had. The actual heads of the house at any time,—the Abbots and the Priors,—could be fairly well ascertained, the latter less completely than the former. John Flete gives information, with a certainty which we cannot now support, about the dates at which the Abbots succeeded one another, but from the middle of the eleventh century onwards there is not much question about their names. Widmore[2] gives connected records of each of them, which always bear witness to his amazing knowledge of the Muniments; and Dr Robinson[3] has further defined and diminished the uncertainties as to some of Flete's dates. Within limits, then, there is no doubt about the Abbots.

The Priors are more elusive, and no clearer witness could be borne to the thoroughness of Widmore's investigations than that which is contained in the list of Priors (some with and some without

The extent of our present information.

The Priors.

---

[1] *The Nave of Westminster*, British Academy Proceedings, Vol. IV; issued separately by the Oxford University Press. *Building at Westminster Abbey, from the Great Fire* (1298) *to the Great Plague* (1348), Archaeological Journal, Vol. LXVII, No. 267; issued separately, 1910.

[2] pp. 1—128.

[3] *Flete*, p. 140 ff.

dates), which he prints[1], and of which he truly says that "it is fuller and more exact than what has been hitherto printed." The roll of Priors is liable to addition and correction at any time, as Dr Scott proceeds with his great work of describing and indexing the Muniments. For, up to the time when the rolls of the Chamberlain or of Queen Alianore's manors begin to contain full lists, we are dependent upon the miscellaneous documents that survive,—acquittances, leases, the collection or payment of tenths, and the like; though in most cases the name of the Prior is not given, but simply the corporate title of "the Prior and Convent." As a rule, the most that we have in the way of personal touch is an initial; thus the person of William de Huntyndon [q.v.] is concealed under the description "W Prior." Let us take him as an instance of the difficulty. It happens that we possess rather more than 70 documents that refer either to him by name or to the Prior during his tenure of that office. In his case the number is largely due to the fact that he (or, as is sometimes stated, he and the Convent) was commissary in the archdeaconries of London and Middlesex to Richard de Gravesend, Bishop of London, and Bartholomew de Ferentino, Canon of St Paul's[2], the official collectors of the tenth imposed for three years by Boniface VIII. Widmore dates him as Prior in 1298, but we cannot trace his actual election, though we do know that it was by compromission[3]. Neither can we certainly date his decease. There are documents connected with the collection of the tenths which imply that he was alive in Feb. 1305. There is also a draft[4] of the protest addressed by Roger de Aldenham, after Prior Huntyndon's death, against the interference of Abbot Wenlok with the accepted custom of filling the vacancy, but the protest does not include a date. All we can show from the Muniments is that by Jul. 1307 Huntyndon's successor, Reginald de Hadham, had been both elected to the priorship by the Convent and deprived of it by Abbot Wenlok. It appears from *Flores Historiarum* (III, 129) that the election occurred on 2 Aug. 1305.

If we pass back to the twelfth century, when the business papers are more scarce, the difficulty of naming and dating the Priors is proportionately greater; often all that we know, as in the case of William Postard, is that such an one was Prior at the time of his election to the Abbacy. If, again, we pass on to the middle of the fourteenth century, we begin to have the help, such as it is, of the manorial lists and of those of the Chamberlain. In every case these lists begin with a payment of money or an assignment of clothing to Dominus Prior, but it is not till late in the fifteenth century that they give us the Prior's name. We have to detect his election by the disappearance of his name from its accustomed place in the list of monks, being careful to note that he is not included *inter mortuos*; that is, in a

---

[1] Appendix XVIII, pp. 228—9.
[2] He held the prebend of Twyford. Hennessy, *Repertorium Londinense*, p. 52.
[3] See below, pp. 73, 92.   [4] *Mun.* 9508.

little group added at the end after a slight gap. Even so, we are without
the day and the month of his election, and, failing any dated documents in
which he is styled Prior, all we can say is that he had become so by the point
of time in the autumn when the scrivener engrossed the compotus roll or
when the obedientiary with whom we are dealing balanced his accounts. In
this and in other ways it has been possible to add four names—Eadwye,
Richard Excestr', William Walsh, and Roger Blake—to Widmore's list of
Priors.

Widmore provides also a list of the Archdeacons of Westminster. He
"had no intention at first," he says, to publish this list and
The Arch-
deacons. "may have omitted some of the oldest[1]." It is a matter of
interest, indeed it is quite unique, that the Dean and Chapter
of Westminster should yearly appoint one of their number to be Archdeacon,
with the right to a place in the Lower House of the Canterbury Convocation.
But the obedientiaries' rolls make no mention of this office and our Muniments include very few documents that record its doings. The Archdeacon,
as such, had no apparent authority inside the Convent and to this day he has
no intrinsic precedence in the Chapter. Long after the courtesy adjunct of
"Venerable" had become usual in the case of other Archdeacons, it had no
place in the records of our Chapter, which speak even in May 1887 of "the
Rev. Archdeacon Farrar." The fact is that the Archdeacon of the monastery
concerned the public more than the monastery; his sphere was that of causes
matrimonial, excommunications, and the like. At the same time a right
performance of "archidiaconal functions," whatever they were, was in practice
recognised as a qualification for higher office. We learn about the earliest
known Archdeacon, Richard de Crokesley, only through his having been
such when he was elected Abbot, [16] Dec. 1246; we do not know when he
became Archdeacon nor any thing that he did as such[2]. In the same way
William Colchester [q.v.], one of the most notable of our Abbots, was certainly
Archdeacon just a month before his promotion to the highest room (10 Dec.
1386), and we can trace him at the same work in 1382[3]. Moreover, when we
examine the careers of the monks who filled this office, we find that William
de Zepeswych [q.v.] could hold the Precentorship with the Archdeaconry;
that William Colchester could be at once Archdeacon and Sacrist; John
Stowe [q.v.] Archdeacon and Almoner; John Borewell[4] [q.v.] Archdeacon and
Treasurer both of the Convent and of the Royal manors. In each of these

[1] He could have added six Archdeacons to his list, if he had examined the account-book of
Prior Walsh (*Mun.* 33289).
[2] Cf. *Flete*, p. 108.
[3] Cf. E. H. Pearce, *William de Colchester, Abbot of Westminster* (S.P.C.K. 1915), p. 41.
[4] Dr Basil Wilberforce, the late Archdeacon, presented to the Chapter a die of Borewell's
official seal, copied from an impression preserved in the British Museum (cxxi. 12). This is
handed to the Archdeacon of Westminster in Chapter at the time of his annual election, keys
being similarly delivered to the Treasurer and the Steward.

cases the responsibilities of the monastic office were considerable and the Archdeaconry would scarcely be added if its duties too were of any great weight. In Abbot Ware's time it was usual to address the Archdeacon in the cloister and in Chapter not by his title but by his name. He must get leave from the Prior to go as far as the City of London, but, being "in exteriore cura spirituali specialis domni Abbatis vicarius," he could go freely to the Palace and to other parts of Westminster in the discharge of his proper functions, leaving word that he would be absent for a time[1]. In the same way when Abbot Colchester drew up in 1407 a deed appropriating the revenues of the church at Aldenham to the purposes of his anniversary at the Abbey, he inserted an instruction that the Archdeacon of Westminster for the time being should be in direct charge of the church and should give account of the receipts[2].

Apart, then, from these three lists, containing in all about seventy-five different names spread over the long period A.D. 1000–1540, we have been left hitherto to the task of re-peopling our buildings with stray personalities discovered here or there. Camden[3], and those who came after
William Camden. him and copied his notes, have given in their lists of Abbey burials the names of a very few of our Benedictines not already included in the list of Abbots, such as William Amondesham, Ralph Selby, Thomas Brown and Robert Humfrey; but no attempt seems to have been made to check these records by reference to our official lists; for in the last case, through a misreading of the inscription, Camden gave the monk's name as Humphrey Roberts, and he has been contentedly followed in so doing by Dart[4], Neale[5], Crull, Stanley, and the rest. Again, if we turn to Abbot
The Consuetudinary. Ware's *Consuetudinary*, which is our prime authority for the manner of life of the Westminster Benedictines in the middle of the thirteenth century, we find the compiler much more concerned with the small details of the life than with the personalities, great or small, who lived it. Omitting Abbots, whom we knew otherwise, we find him including less than ten names of ordinary monks, of whom three are mentioned[6] as having taken their journey together to the Roman Court for negotiations about the church at Essewille (Ashwell).

When we pass to John Flete's History, we gather, as we should expect,
Iohn Flete. a larger amount of personal detail. For instance, a single incident, the investigation of the Abbey's traditional right to take tithe of Thames salmon[7], gives him the opportunity of recording nine

[1] *Customary of St Augustine's, Canterbury, and St Peter's, Westminster*, ed. Sir E. M. Thompson, II, 95.

[2] *Mun.* 5260 A. E. H. Pearce, *William de Colchester*, p. 16.

[3] *Reges, reginae, nobiles, &c.* (London, 1600).

[4] *Westmonasterium*, II, 15. [5] *Westminster Abbey*, II, 204.

[6] *Customary*, II, 72–3. See p. 49.

[7] *Flete*, p. 64. An examination of the names of these witnesses and the offices which they

names, of whom only one, John de Wratting, is on the list of Priors.   In
the rest of Flete's story, without reckoning the Abbots, about whom he is
frequently our only source of chronological information, we find that in all
he alludes to twenty brethren, of whom six were Priors, and that Dean
Robinson's introduction makes us acquainted quite incidentally with six
more.

A Westminster historian, who might have been expected to introduce us
to some of his companions in the Refectory, is the author of
the Chronicle of the years 1346-67, who calls himself "quidam
frater Johannes de R. monachus Westmonasteriensis," and whom
Dr Robinson[1] has finally identified with John de Redyng [q.v.].   The full
text of this interesting document has recently been edited with introduction
and notes by Professor James Tait[2], and it turns out to be entirely dis-
appointing to any one who approaches it with our present needs in view.
There is mention of four Abbots—Simon Bircheston, Henle, Langham, and
Litlington,—and of one Prior, the unfortunate Benedict de Cherteseye, but
no monk below that rank is allowed to intrude his name or concerns into
Redyng's pages.

One other chronicler raises the same expectations, even though his own
name can only be conjectured.   In a communication to the British Academy
(Proceedings, Vol. III; issued separately and entitled *An Unrecognised Westminster Chronicler*, 1381–1394), Dr Robinson has given reasons for supposing
that the continuator of the Polychronicon for those years[3] was a Westminster
monk.   This document (*op. cit.* pp. 9, 22) introduces us to John Lakyngheth
[q.v.] as the king's candidate for the Abbacy when Colchester was elected,
but it does no more to add to our knowledge of individuals.

In the mere number of monastic names we make a large advance when
we open the pages of Richard Widmore, whose thorough
examination of the Muniments has already been referred to[4].
Now, Widmore's index, if it were complete, would mean that we must
prepare for disappointment.   Apart from Abbots and Priors it includes only
eight monks, of whom five are otherwise known as chroniclers or men of
letters,—John de London, Richard Circestr', John de Redyng, Sulcard,
Warner; the legend of John Canterbery's [q.v.] great stature and of his
warlike exertions is recorded, and a notice of Ralph Selby's interment is
repeated from Camden.   But Widmore's contribution to our investigation
is much greater than is implied by his index; for he has copied from the

John de
Redyng.

Widmore.

---

held in the light of the facts given about them in the present volume leads to the conclusion that
the date of this investigation is c. 1393.

[1] Article *Simon Langham*, Church Quart. Rev., July 1908, p. 346.
[2] Manchester University Press, 1914.
[3] MSS. of Corpus Christi Coll., Camb., no. 197.
[4] For similar acknowledgments cf. J. A. Robinson, *Flete*, p. vii; R. B. Rackham, *Nave of
Westminster*, p. 4.

archives and elsewhere certain documents which contain quite a number of
names. Thus the notarial instrument[1] which records the demission of his
abbatial authority by George Norwych on 24 Nov. 1467 makes us acquainted
with Prior Millyng and twelve of his fellow-monks; and the official account
of John Islip's election 27 Oct. 1500[2] includes the most complete list hitherto
printed,—the Prior (Islip himself) and forty-three monks, of whom sixteen
are described as holding various conventual offices. Though only thirty-three
years separate these two events, there are no names common to the two
lists, for those who stood up against the misdeeds of Abbot Norwych were
naturally the older men of the community. Thus the most that we derive
even from Widmore would be about sixty names from first to last.

Stanley's want of interest in our subject has already been noted, but to
Dean Stanley. complete our survey of the authorities we may indicate the
information to be derived from him. Though he had original
authorities ready to his hand, and could have used the knowledge of
Mr Burtt, the investigator of the Muniments in his day, he dismisses the
question by saying that the names of the monks "are still more obscure[3]"
than those of the Abbots. He gives the four whose sepulture is mentioned
by Camden, including the misnamed "Humphrey Roberts" and Ralph Selby,
whom he calls "John Selby," and whom he ascribes to the sixteenth century,
whereas he died in 1420; and he adds Vertue, elsewhere dismissed (p. 342)
as "an old monk[4]," who had been laid in the West Cloister "just before the
Dissolution." Stanley goes on to mention five chroniclers, Sulcard, John de
Redyng, John Flete, Richard Circestr' and "the so-called Matthew of Westminster." He relates the story of John Canterbery's vast physique, and then
adds "two, in whose case we catch a glimpse into the motives which brought
them hither." The first of these is "Owen, third son of Owen Tudor, and
uncle of Henry VII," who "lies in the Chapel of St Blaize." It is, of course,
possible that this Owen Tudor entered our house and took another Christian
name and another surname. Stanley repeats the statement on two other
occasions[5], but neither an Owen nor a Tudor is to be found among our monks
of that or any other date. If Stanley had consulted Camden (*Reges*, &c.), he
would have seen that the son of Owen Tudor who found a home in our
house and was buried, near Abbot Litlington, "in capella Sancti Blasii qua
intratur ad Vestiarium," was called Edward, and under the head of Edward
Bridgewater [q.v.], who entered the Convent in 1465-6 and said his first
Mass three years later, I have indicated the reasons for conjecturing that
this man may be Edward Tudor. Dean Stanley's other refugee monk was

[1] Widmore, Appendix vii, p. 191 ff. = *Mun.* 5456.
[2] Widmore, Additional Instruments iii, p. 234 ff. =*Mun.* 5444.
[3] *Memorials*, p. 394.
[4] William Vertue said his first Mass in 1514-5, and may have been 46 at the Dissolution. His
death is not recorded in the rolls, but he was alive in 1535.
[5] *Memorials*, pp. 170 n.: 412.

a man of his own name, Sir John Stanley, natural son of James Stanley, Bishop of Ely. It can be shown that on 25 Jun. 1528 he executed before the ecclesiastical authorities a deed of separation "a mensa et thoro" from his wife, Margaret, with a view to ending his days as a religious in our Convent, —"ob religionis introitum." But we had no entrants between 1525–6 and 1530–1. So the Dean's story, if not discredited, is not proven[1].

So far, Stanley has added nothing to our *data* except inaccuracies; but his appendices make some slight amends, for he derived several names from the Muniments where the latter happened to suit his purposes. First, the depositions about Henry VI's choice of a burying-place[2] involve the record of three monks not hitherto mentioned, John Ramsey, William Milton, and [William] Barnell. Secondly, in his desire to see "in the close of the fifteenth century...the conventual artists[3] hard at work in beautifying the various Chapels" (p. 455), he appeals to "a Cartulary of Westminster in the possession of Sir Charles G. Young, Garter King at Arms[4]." Dean Robinson has discussed the nature of this document[5], and for our present purpose it may stand; but it must be compared with the corresponding entry in *Liber Niger Quaternus* (f. 92). It contains the name of fifteen monks, of whom two (Richard Circestr' and John Redyng, the chronicler) were already known. All of them can be traced in our compotus-rolls and elsewhere, so that the list, when it was first printed, represented a clear gain of thirteen names. What it fails to do is to illustrate Stanley's statement about the activity of the "conventual artists" at "the close of the fifteenth century." "Then," he says, "was added the Apocalyptic series round the walls of the Chapter House," the authority for which is the statement in the Chartulary that "Frater Johannes Northampton fieri fecit...picturam Apocalipsis...in Capitulo nondum completo." But John Northampton [q.v.] entered the Convent in 1372 and survived no nearer to "the close of the fifteenth century" than the year 1404. It is doubtful if John de Sutton [q.v.], who is credited with "a picture of the dedication of the Abbey" and with others "over the tomb of Sebert," ever saw even the fourteenth century, and not a monk on the list in question lived after the year 1433, except Edmund (wrongly printed "Edwardus") Kirton, who died in 1466. This loose treatment of facts[6] does not in the least detract from the picturesqueness of Stanley's method; it

[1] For John Stanley's will and the deed of separation see Archaeological Journal, Vol. xxv, pp. 72 ff.

[2] *Memorials*, pp. 600–8. *Mun.* 6389**.

[3] The document which Stanley quotes does not justify this phrase; it mostly states that the Brethren paid a certain sum to have the work carried out by unspecified artists who were probably not of the Convent; e.g. "idem Prior [R. de Merston] fieri fecit altare sancti Blasii cum pertinentiis pro c. marcis."

[4] *Memorials* (3rd ed.), Appendix, p. 640 (omitted from later editions).

[5] *Manuscripts of Westminster Abbey*, pp. 101 f.

[6] e.g. even in his 3rd edition, p. 395, n. 1, Stanley still assigned John Canterbery's appearance in armour to 1286 instead of 1386.

only illustrates the need of some accurate information about the men themselves.

Now all this time trustworthy information about the names, the standing, and the conventual careers of the Westminster Benedictines

The materials at hand.

has been within our reach,—at all events for the period (to speak roughly) between 1300 and the Dissolution; that is to say, from the time when the system arose by which an obedientiary drew up the compotus-roll of his office in the autumn, had it engrossed by a scrivener on parchment, and placed it so carefully on one side, that it is there to this day, with over 6000 others, not a few of which are duplicates.

This custom can be plainly detected towards the close of the thirteenth century. Thus the earliest compotus preserved at Canterbury

The Compotus Rolls.

is dated 1260, at Norwich 1272, at Durham and Worcester . 1278, at Ely 1291[1], and at Westminster either 1291 or 1281. The Canterbury date falls within the period of Abbot Ware's *Consuetudinary*, which, however, does not appear to concern itself with the duty of obedientiaries to render an annual account of their stewardship. On the other hand, the *Consuetudinary* of St Augustine's, Canterbury, which is based upon Ware's[2], regards the custom as so long established that it has had time to get out of hand; for in the Reformaciuncula made in his second year by Abbot Nicholas Thorn there is mention of the fact that a harmful delay was shown by the various wardens in rendering their accounts, which were being handed in to the conventual treasury at odd times[3]. The Abbot then proceeds to ordain that all the wardens were to be ready with their yearly statements immediately after St James' Day (25 Jul.), but certain other obedientiaries such as the Infirmarer and the Precentor were allowed till St Peter ad Vincula (1 Aug.). The subsequent reference to "rotulos maneriorum nostrorum vel ecclesiarum, reddituales cartas, vel scripta" shows that already the accounts were delivered in manuscript, and that there was a penalty for their improper removal. In spite, however, of Abbot Ware's indifference to the custom, it is hard to suppose that it did not prevail in some form during his period. How to account for the disappearance of the rolls is another matter; possibly the great fire[4] of 1298 is responsible to some extent; at any rate, our only rotuli[5] before that date are one which appears to be the Cellarer's of 1281-2, and one which is certainly the Chamberlain's of 1291-2, whilst we still possess the Infirmarer's roll of 1297-8, which happens to be of the greatest possible value for our present purpose.

---

[1] J. M. Wilson, *Early Compotus Rolls of the Priory of Worcester*, 1908, p. ix.

[2] Sir E. M. Thompson, *Customary*, II, p. ix.   [3] *Ibid.* I, 34.

[4] My friend the Dean of Norwich tells me that a fire in his Priory in August, 1272, similarly explains the lack of Norwich rolls from before that date.

[5] *Mun.* 18829; 18717.

For it was one of the Infirmarer's duties, laid down for him in the time of
Richard de Crokesley[1], to see that sick brethren were provided
with what they needed for their bodily sustenance "tam in
pitanciis cotidianis quam in quibuscunque rebus necessariis."
This pitancia or allowance consisted, in part, of a ferculum or mess of meat
or fish, according to the day[2]. For the purposes of the conventual accountancy
a meat-day was usually represented by three-pence and a fish-day by two-
pence. It thus became natural to record each case and the cost of maintenance
of each. Abbot Ware gives the ceremonial side of a monk's illness. He sees
him making acknowledgment in Chapter that he is not feeling well. He
hears him ask for indulgence and sympathy in the quaint formula: " Per
licenciam vestram et per licenciam conventus accepturus sum medicinam."
But the Infirmarer, having the revenues of two churches, Battersea and
Wandsworth, to account for, must be more prosaic. If Brother So-and-so
stays out of choir in the sick-room for three meat-days and three fish-days,
a charge of $9d. + 6d.$, or $1s. 3d.$, will fall upon the funds of the Infirmary[3];
and in order that there may be no difficulties with the auditor, it is necessary
that the name of each patient should be entered with the exact duration of
his sickness.

The In-
firmarer.

Now it happens that our first Infirmary rotulus gives us no fewer than
forty-nine names. Of course, the order of the names is no indication of the
status of each in the convent; for sickness is no respecter of persons; while
some of the names occur more than once and some occur many times during
the year. Fortunately we are able to get help here from an official document
preserved by the State. In the Kalendar of State Papers under date 10 Oct.
1303 there is an abstract of the letters patent in which the
King called for an investigation into the facts about the great
robbery of Crown jewels from the royal Treasury within the
Abbey. The document includes a list of the Abbot and forty-eight monks[4],
and this list, being more formal than one of Infirmary casualties, may be
expected to have regard to precedence and seniority, though it is to be noted
that Alexander de Persore, the chief culprit, comes next to Walter de
Wenlok, the Abbot. But in spite of William de Huntyndon, the Prior, not
being in his proper place, we may fairly assume that the forty-eight names
stand in some orderly sequence. Now thirty-three out of the forty-nine
names in the compotus of the 1297–8 Infirmarer appear again in the list of

The Jewel
Robbery.

---

[1] *Customary*, II, p. 243.

[2] *Ibid.* p. 235 : "habebit cotidie ..unum ferculum grossum carnis aut eciam piscis, juxta quod
diei convenit."

[3] The mode of entry is illustrated in the record of Abbot Islip ; p. 167.

[4] The list also appears in Rymer, *Foed.*, and in Dugdale, *Monast.*, I, 312. For J. Burtt's
account of the facts see G. G. Scott, *Gleanings*, pp. 282–90. The most recent study of the
incident is Professor T. F. Tout's *A Mediaeval Burglary* in the Bulletin of the John Rylands
Library, Oct. 1915 (printed separately).

1303. We can therefore start with these names in this order. That done, we shall still have sixteen names in the list of 1297–8 which have disappeared by 1303. Some of them may have been aged men in 1297–8; William de Pharindon[1] had been Pittancer twenty years earlier; Gilbert Rauel was Sacrist in 1267; Robert de Sancto Martino was a monk by about 1272 and Roger de Waleden about 1270; Simon de Gardino, who was apparently alive in 1303, but is not mentioned among the Tower prisoners, may have been omitted as a stagiarius who had ceased to be effective. On the other hand, it is natural that in the list of 1303 we should find fifteen names of Brethren who had either escaped the tender mercies of the Infirmarer in 1297–8 or who had entered the Convent in the interval.

Thus at a period when, as will be seen, the system of recording names is by no means established, we have two lists which together give us sixty-five names (including the Abbot) to start upon. Incidentally, we have picked up two others from the roll of the Warden of St Mary's Chapel for 1299–1300; for he charges himself with the cost of "sarcofagi cum cooperculis" for four Brethren deceased, of whom we already know two. Also we begin to form some notion of the extent of our problem. In 1297–8 the Infirmarer had forty-nine patients and does not say how many Brethren there were that had no need of a physician. In 1303 we have an official list of forty-nine names.

It seems best, then, to take these two large lists as the pivot of our investigation and to say something here first about the preceding period and then about the easier course of the pursuit in subsequent years.

For the period of over two centuries which separates the death of the Confessor from the year 1297–8 it has been possible to produce from the Muniments (apart from the 1297–8 list) and elsewhere the names of some 130 members of the Convent. These include fifteen Abbots, ten Priors and three Archdeacons, the great majority of whom were already on record. Of the rest, some have been found in our "Domesday" chartulary as witnesses to legal documents; some are known to have been Priors of Hurley or are actually mentioned as such in one of our documents and must have been previously monks of Westminster[2]; some appear among the Muniments as being concerned in the making of payments on behalf of the Abbot or the Convent or both; some appear only when anniversaries are granted to them and financial arrangements are being made for the maintenance of these memorials; some, as already stated, are mentioned in Abbot Ware's *Customary*; some appear as parties to one or other of the multitudinous transactions recorded in our endless bundles of acquittances, especially during the second half of the thirteenth century,

Before and after A.D. 1300.

---

[1] In this and similar cases I have of course placed monks mentioned in the 1297–8 list under such earlier date as I could find evidence for.

[2] Cf. J. Armitage Robinson, *Gilbert Crispin*, p. 32; F. T. Wethered, *St Mary's, Hurley*.

when the Abbots fell more and more into the hands of the Sienese and Florentine money-lenders.

If the result during this early period is judged to be rather meagre, it may be pleaded that it is by no means final; but as Dr Scott and I have recently examined "Domesday" for this purpose and as the indexing of the acquittances draws near its completion, the chance of adding to our list of monks gets steadily smaller.

Thus the nature of the materials in our possession for the period up to 1297–8 is such that the survival of names is conditioned by a large element of chance. A particular brother is sent by the Abbot into the City to make a tardy repayment to some Lombard financiers, and his name is perpetuated in the receipt; another is despatched to Rome upon important conventual affairs and we get to know him through the Chapter's formal record of his proctorship; a third is allowed to visit some noble lady at a time of sickness taking with him an Abbey relic calculated to effect a cure, and comes down to us as Brother Henry [q.v.], because in her gratitude, which is also her lively sense of continued favours, she writes to ask that she may retain him and the relic a little longer; yet another, such as Warner [q.v.], goes at the Abbot's bidding to perambulate, and so assert conventual possession of, a certain piece of land, and it is necessary for purposes of record that his identity should be recognised. The position roughly is that a claim may be put forward on behalf of anyone that he was of the order of St Benedict and a monk of Westminster during the twelfth or the thirteenth century, and our documents are not inclusive enough to enable us to resist the claim if we wanted to.

But when we have proceeded no great distance round the corner of 1297–8, we come upon signs of a system, which, if only all the documents had survived, would enable us to give a complete list of all our members and to reject at sight the pretences of any unlawful claimant. Long before the last survivor of the 1297–8 and the 1303 lists—it would be John de Ryngstede or Robert de Beby—had passed to his rest, other sources of information were sending forth a steady stream of names, and from their nature were bound to name all those who could rightly be included. During about thirteen years after 1303 we still have to depend upon the Infirmarer for information about the newcomers and for any idea of the pace at which death made room for them; and unfortunately we only have in that time the Infirmary lists of 1305–6 and 1309–11, and only twelve patients not hitherto known to us needed care during those three years. But in 1316 we come upon the adoption by the Chamberlain of methods that are of importance to our investigation and must therefore now be described, though they took some time to harden into a system.

With three rather vague exceptions (Ralph; Geoffrey; Walter de Bureford) we know nothing of any Chamberlain of Westminster before Henry de London, who is described in a document of 1278[1] as "nuper camerarius," and of him we know little beyond this fact. But on going

The Chamberlain. back some twelve years we can find much about the office in Abbot Ware's *Consuetudinary* and in the companion book of St Augustine's, Canterbury, from which it is at once clear that with us as elsewhere the Chamberlain was the clothier of the Convent, or rather of the Prior and Convent[2]. For at Canterbury the Chamberlain was not concerned with the equipment of the head of the house; "abbas vero," says the rule, "non comprehenditur in hac distribucione." At Westminster this plan was apparently a recent innovation[3] in Ware's time and could only be varied voluntarily and of special grace. Evidently an arrangement begun by Gilbert Crispin[4] had in more modern times been developed first by Richard de Berking and then by Richard de Crokesley, with the result that the Abbot became responsible for the replenishment of his own wardrobe. After all, he could thus please himself. Litlington's steward could purchase enough linen for four pairs of My Lord's "femoralia" for 4s. 6d. and could get the three pairs cut and made up for sixpence, but equally he could spend at his master's bidding as much as £2 on a fur coat. The Chamberlain dealt in sterner stuff, for he had at least fifty persons to clothe and to shoe, and in Abbot Ware's days he had but £88[5] a year wherewith to do it. Having, however, that income, he was bound to give careful account of his expenditure, and it is to the thoroughness of his accountancy that we owe much of our knowledge of our monks individually.

Let us take one of the Chamberlain rolls at random; it happens to be for

A year's outfit. the year 1456–7, Michaelmas to Michaelmas[6]. On the front of the roll, which bears the name of Edmund Downe, who was Archdeacon and Warden of the New Work as well as Chamberlain, and who shortly afterwards left to become Prior of Hurley, there is a full statement of receipts and expenditure. The former begin with a list of the annual charges on houses in the City of London. Each house is fully described with the name of its owner, its late owner or owners, and its street and parish, and there are 120 items on the list[7]. These charges amount to £46. 18s. 6½d. There are yearly payments or pensiones from eleven churches, of which nine are in the City of London, amounting to £8. 2s. 4d. Country property and rents bring in £26. 11s. 8d., while shops in "Grubstret" and tenements in "Langdych" take the total up to £86. 7s. 1½d., or a little less than the £88 mentioned by Abbot Ware.

---

[1] *Mun.* 5779.　　　　　　[2] *Customary*, I, 195 ff.: II, 149 ff.

[3] *Ibid.* II, 150: "Domno quidem Abbati nihil *moderno tempore* est liberaturus idem camerarius de hiis quae ad indumenta [vel] calciamenta spectant monachorum, nisi sponte voluerit de gracia speciali."

[4] Cf. J. A. Robinson, *Gilbert Crispin*, 41–4.　　　[5] *Customary*, II, 149, l. 26.

[6] The Chapter accounts are still made up yearly to 29 September.

[7] It may be noted that the roll, by no means one of the longest, measures 5 ft 9 in. × 11½ in.

When we pass on to his outlay, we find that the office is at the moment not very solvent. The Chamberlain brings forward a deficit of £13. 18s. 3¾d. which is increased at the end of the year to £16. 10s. 9¼d. But we are only concerned here with the chief item in his expenditure which is the £49. 18s. 0¾d. spent under the head of "Emptio stauri" or as we should say "on stock." The staple of this outlay is soon stated; it is a sum of £25. 10s. for the purchase of 51 sets of "panni nigri" or Benedictine habits of black serge at ten shillings a habit; evidently there was a contract price for the sup- ply of these robes, whereas the other items of the outfit were made up on the premises. Further, he buys 106¾ ells of linen cloth at 8d. an ell (£3. 11s. 2d.); 193½ yards of worsted; 52 yards of kersey; and 39 yards of "blanket." Here the sewing staff of his office finds its chance; for the linen must be made up into pairs of "femoralia,"—not such delicate underclothing, no doubt, as we saw bought for My Lord, for that cost 1s. 0½d. an ell in 1370–1, while this costs 8d. an ell in 1456–7, and we must allow for the change in the value of money in the interval as well as for the difference in price. The Chamberlain will tell us in a moment that this purchase enabled him to distribute that year 139 pairs of "femoralia" to his Brethren and himself, which works out at rather more than 5d. a pair for material alone, not reckoning "establishment charges"; Abbot Litlington's nearly a century earlier cost 1s. 3d. when made. The 52 yards' length of kersey is the amount needed to furnish the convent with "caligae," or thick socks or stockings that were almost of the stoutness of gaiters[1]; with his 39 yards of "blanket" he is to make "pedules," or loose slippers to be worn with the gaiters in winter-time; for each Brother received a pair on All Saints' Day, at Christmas and at Easter, the Prior, the Chamberlain and the Sub-chamberlain being allowed an additional pair on each occasion. In the same way, he lays in the exact number of "stragulae" (bed-blankets, at 2s. 3d. each) and of "pell' allut'" (pellicia alutaria, fur or leathern cloaks, at 2s. each) that he requires for the Brethren then under his care, allowing a double portion in each case for the Prior and the Chamberlain.

But now, having stated that he has devoted so much money to the purpose of obtaining so much material, he must still regard himself as liable for an accountant-like statement of his disposal of that material, which would be easily convertible into cash again, if he were willing to stoop to dishonesty. So, one side of his long roll being still vacant, he turns it over and gives a balance in terms of this material. He has converted his stock of linen into so many shirts (staminae) and pairs of drawers, his kersey into so many pairs of gaiters, his blanket into so many pairs of slippers, and he is possessed of a given number of habits, bed-coverings, and cloaks of skin. To make his compotus complete, he must show each Brother by name as the recipient, during the year, of his lawful share of each of these. At first, in 1316 for

---

[1] Cf. Compotus Rolls, Worcester, p. 79 (Wilson); p. 87 (Hamilton).

instance, he is content to give a list of the Brethren and to say in effect: These are the men to whom I have distributed what is their due. But in course of time the method becomes more meticulous, and in 1418–9 after a long gap in our series the names, instead of being "run on" and written in four or five lines across the roll, are arranged vertically down the left edge of it, and each name has its portions of goods entered against it under each of seven heads—abitus (= panni nigri); stragulae; staminae; femoralia; pellicia alutaria; caligae; pedules; traditional abbreviations being used in each case. Thus, if only the Chamberlain's rolls were continuous and complete, our task would be soon accomplished; it would merely be necessary to note the new names at the foot of each fresh list and the disappearance of any from their accustomed place on the rota: unfortunately there are many and grievous gaps in the series; and we must turn to other helps, if the whole of our ground is to be covered.

Happily there arose a feature in the life of the Abbey which also involved

Queen Alianore's Manors. not merely careful accountancy but also in time an exact record of the individuals concerned. On 28 Nov. 1290 died Queen Alianore of Castile, wife of Edward I. Her bounty towards the Abbey of Westminster was great and her trust in it was manifested at a time when, as the robbery of the Treasury soon showed, the honesty of some of the Brethren was lightly esteemed by the gossips of the day. Four years before her death there lay in the hands of Abbot Walter de Wenlok a very large sum. A small strip of parchment[1], dated 15 Feb. 1286, acknowledges: "summa denariorum existencium in ix saccis et i Bursa de denariorum domine Regine ccc lxiii^{li} xvii^s x^d ob q̃ " (£363. 17s. 10¾d.). Of this fund the Abbot was treasurer, with the Prior and Sub-prior as his appointed deputies.

In view of this attachment of his beloved queen to the Abbey as well as of her interment in the Confessor's Chapel, it was natural that Edward should make definite and generous provision for the maintenance of her anniversary. So by 1292 we find the convent in possession for these purposes of certain manors—"maneria pro Anniversario Regine assignata"—namely, Birdbrook, Essex; Westerham and Edenbridge, Kent; Turweston, Bucks; Knowle, Warwickshire[2]; and, shortly afterwards, Hendon, Middlesex[3].

Keeping to our subject, which is the doings of individual Brethren, we

The manorial income. find that in 1299–1300 the receivership of the manors has passed from the Abbot and his deputies to three monks chosen *ad hoc,*—Alexander de Neuporte, Alexander de Persore and Roger de Aldenham, and that in 1301 there is a Warden of these manors, Reginald de Hadham, whose name heads the compotus. For the present the information about individuals is meagre; for example, Reginald de Hadham enters in 1301–2 a "curialitas" (that is, a complimentary gift, afterwards called

---

[1] *Mun.* 23629 B.   [2] *Mun.* 1545, 25 Oct. 1292.
[3] *Mun.* 17012, 14 Oct. 1295.

xenia or exennia), " tribus capellanis celebrantibus nouas missas suas " at the rate of one shilling each; by which he means three junior monks who thus signalised their advancement to the priesthood and said their first Mass; but he does not give their names. There is also mention of a " pitancia conventus," or a gift in kind to all the Brethren, which cost 6s. 7d.; but this too is no excuse for a complete list. Again in 1301–2 there is an item— " xvi fratribus pro marcis grossis singulis assignatis x^{li} xiii^s iiii^d," but no light is thrown on the individuality of the sixteen. Still more regret arises when in 1303–4 we find a distribution of £2. 13s. 4d. "fratribus nostris incarceratis" on various occasions and a *douceur* of two shillings to those who carried the money to the Tower, without any intimation as to the number or identity of the prisoners, who were doubtless the men alleged to be guilty of pillaging the royal Treasury.

It appears that the last decade of Abbot Wenlok's somewhat litigious rule was partly occupied in contentions with the Prior and Convent with respect to the orderly distribution among the Brethren of the overplus of these manorial revenues after the anniversary had been paid for and the requisite distribution made to the poor. Just a week before his death, 18 Dec. 1307, he set his seal to a charter[1] assigning the " residuum distribucionis " for division as pittances among the Brethren and undertaking for himself and his successors to choose as Warden of the manors one of two monks proposed for the purpose by the Prior and Convent; in actual fact, he mentions the Sub-prior and Convent, presumably because Reginald de Hadham was regarded as still deposed from his priorship. This arrangement was formally renewed by Wenlok's successor, Richard de Kedyngton, also called de Sudbury[2]. But for many years it did not have the effect of producing the information that we want as to the actual recipients. In the roll of the Queen's manors for 1318–9 we have mention of three monks who received exennia on saying their first Mass, and these as being new names can be added to our list. In 1335–6 one of the new priests and four novices[3] are also additions to be noted, and there are four more in 1336–7.

Then for a generation or so we are left to rely on the record of the Infirmarer's patients and on the Chamberlain's lists, where they survive. There are years during which we get no names from either, and there are years in which we get help only from the Infirmarer, with the presumption that we still have not all the new names that we ought to have. All this time the Warden of the Queen's manors is making his yearly division of about £80 to £100 among the Prior and his Brethren, but is doing so in the lump without naming either Prior or monks.

The manorial lists.

----

[1] *Flete*, p. 118; cf. " Domesday," f. 464.   [2] *Flete*, p. 121; " Domesday," f. 464.

[3] The form used is " de nouo professi." This and other expressions—" nouicius "; " de nouo capellanus ordinatus "; " nuper professus "; " nouicius professus "—were employed at Westminster to designate the first stage of professed monkhood.

But the roll for 1369 shows us the beginnings of greater detail in the account. The Warden has thirty-six " capellani " to whom there is due a full dividend of £2. 6s. 8d. each, the sum being doubled for the Prior. In these cases he does not trouble to give the names. But there are six others, junior priests and novices, whose shares are smaller and vary from 30s. to 6s. 8d., and whose names he must needs give with the sum allotted to each. Four of these are new. The same thing happens during a period of twenty years more, from which we have twelve of the Q. Alianore rolls surviving, and the yearly average of recruits is between three and four.

At last in the compotus of 1390–1 we come upon that which we have desired. The wardens are John Lakyngheth and John Enston. The former, who had held the office and the chief responsibility since 1372,—that is, during the period which we have seen marked by a tendency to give at any rate the names of the juniors—was a Brother of recognised business capacities[1], a man useful at Parliaments, and a favourite with Richard II. Moreover, in his hands the Queen's manors had prospered. The total receipts in 1372 were £199; but in 1390–1 they rose to £300. 8s. 4½d., the actual rents, manorial and other, amounting to £243. 8s. 4½d. With this large sum the Warden was able to provide for the customary illumination round the Queen's tomb ; he bought 250 lbs. of wax (£6. 12s. 6d.), which cost 7d. for carriage from the City to the Abbey and 10s. 9¾d. for conversion into candles. The chandler's wage for the year was 10s., the candle-lighter's 3s. 4d., the bell-ringer's 5s., and each Treasurer of the manors received in this respect 3s. 4d.,—the total being £8. 8s. 10¾d. The bailiffs and rent-collectors of the manors received their wage in cloth and fur-coats, which cost £3. 9s. 3d. There were a few " establishment charges " amounting to £8. 5s. 10d. There was a distribution to the poor and to some Abbey servants of £16. 12s. 5d. The sum to be divided among the Brethren was decided, perhaps in Chapter, to be £150. 10s. Thus with an income of £300. 8s. 4½d. and an outlay of £187. 6s. 4¾d., the Warden could declare a residue of £113. 1s. 11¾d.; so the Prior agreed that John Lakyngheth, " pro bono labore suo," might retain for himself the odd £3. 1s. 11¾d. and carry forward to next year the rounder balance of £110.

Now whether we consider the amount of wax in his store or the sum of money in his coffers for distribution among the Brethren, it is

A balance in wax and in money distributed. obvious that the Warden must now begin to be more communicative as to details. He carries forward 300 or 400 lbs. of wax, beside the thirty square candles that are burning around the Queen's tomb at the moment, and he has bought, as we saw, other 250 lbs. to see him through the year. He must therefore turn over his roll and show how many pounds of wax he has found it necessary to convert into candles, so that he may carry forward a surplus stated in pounds of wax.

---

[1] See his record, under the year 1362–3.

But it is much more requisite that he should now give fuller details about his distribution of so large a sum as £150. 10s. among the Brethren. It means a dividend of £3. 10s. to each of thirty-five "fratres sacerdotes," including the Prior (entered simply as "Dominus Prior" without his name) whose share is doubled, while one of the juniors gets £3, seven get £2. 10s., and three get £1. 6s. 8d.

This, then, being a full list of the House, we are able to test our names as far as we have gone. So doing, we find that there has been only one omission. Ten places up from the end of the priests, and taking a full share, is John Borewell. The rolls of the Chamberlain for the years 1383-6, during which this monk probably joined our House, are missing. Even so, it seems as though he may have been brought in from elsewhere as a fully ordained priest, for we learn from the Infirmarer of 1386-7 that during that year he was promoted to sit by the skilla in the Refectory, and Abbot Colchester must at once have sent him to Rome, for he was there as proctor for three years up to Sep. 1390, thus excusing the Abbot his triennial visit "ad limina"; doubtless it is his return which accounts for his sudden appearance in our roll of the Queen's manors for 1390-1., By 15 Oct. 1391 he was Archdeacon and he afterwards took a prominent part in the conventual administration. Judging by the place at which his name stands in our list, we may say that he joined the Abbey after Robert Hermodesworth in 1380-1 and before William Pulburgh in 1383-4.

After this our course is clear and we can cover practically the whole ground of our investigation. For the rolls of Queen Alianore's manors are preserved almost in their entirety. There is a gap of six months in 1437-8; otherwise we only miss the roll of 1500-1. We can test our results by the Chamberlain's work, where it survives, and in due time we come to two other series of manorial rolls made out on the same lines as those of Queen Alianore. In 1394-5 John Borewell, whom we discovered just now, and Peter Coumbe, who was of note among the managers of the New Work on the nave, were associated as "Administratores Participacionis Anne Regine." Anne of Bohemia, the wife of Richard II, died at Sheen in July 1394. The King, who was unnerved by her loss, as he showed by his violence at her obsequies on 3 August, not only prepared a splendid and pathetic tomb[1] for her and for himself, but made lavish provision for the maintenance of her anniversary. Its management quickly fell into line with that of Queen Alianore's foundation, and in their second year of office, 1395-6, Borewell and Coumbe presented a full list of the monks among whom the residue was divided.

Richard II's Foundation.

It may be well to see how they settled their division. We take their second year 1395-6. They have brought forward a balance of £12. 2s. 11½d., and they receive from Richard II's Treasurer a sum of £200. As in the

---

[1] Cf. *Lib. Nig. Quat.* f. 88, b.

case of Queen Alianore's foundation, they start by paying out nearly £30 for wax to be made into candles. The Lord Chancellor, the Duchess of Gloucester, and various knights and ladies attending the anniversary, are "recreated" or regaled at a cost of £2. 9s. 10d. There has been throughout the year a weekly dole to the poor amounting altogether to £30. 6s. 8d., and the gifts on the day itself to the poor, the Abbot's servants, the virgers, and others come to £41. 8s. 8d. The outgoings would have been more by £10 if a grant of that amount to the Lord Abbot "ex consensu Prioris et seniorum" had not been deleted from the compotus with the significant comment "quia contra cartam." But, though they have expended £107. 2s. 1d. in various ways, the Wardens can still declare a dividend of twenty shillings to each "Frater Sacerdos," of whom there are thirty-nine, and to the Prior, who takes two dividends, and they can give 6s. 8d. each to six juniors. This absorbs £43 and leaves an ample surplus of £62. 0s. 10½d. The management of Queen Alianore's manors having, as we saw, adopted the principle of a full list of the recipients shortly before this date, the administrators of Queen Anne's anniversary, of whom John Borewell was the chief in each case, did the like in 1395–6, though they did not resume the practice till 1404–5.

The Distribution.

But the benefactions of King Richard II, "dead and turned to clay," did not come up to the expectations raised by him in his life. By 1404–5, the year of the next list, certain manors and lands had been legally transferred to the Convent[1],—Steventon and East Hendred, Berks; Westbury, Wilts; Northall and Downe, Middlesex; Biggleswade, Soothill, &c., Beds; and Stokenchurch, Bucks;—which produced that year only £141. 11s. 3½d., but the Wardens had only £125 to deal with altogether. They spent less on illuminations, £20 instead of £30; they distributed much less among the poor and the Abbey servants, £13 instead of £71; and they had begun to experience the manifold calls for petty outlays that fall on owners of country estates, such as the 10s. 6d. that was not scorned by the Sheriffs (vice-comites) of Buckinghamshire and Bedfordshire, though it was given "ut essent fauorabiles maneriis de Holm et Langford." Consequently, the monks' dividend must also decrease to 13s. 4d. for priests and 3s. 4d. for two "Fratres Diaconi," of whom Edmund Kirton, the future Abbot, was one. But they are faithful to the method of the list of names, on which we can henceforward rely.

Richard II's Manors.

And there was yet a third foundation of the same nature. Harry of Monmouth was a consistent benefactor of our Abbey in his life-time and he gave, as is well known, his own masterful directions for a prominent chantry-tomb[2] at the east end of the Confessor's Chapel. His funeral, carried out with a wealth of magnificent

Henry V's foundation.

---

[1] *Mun.* 7579; dated Windsor 23 Apr. 1399.
[2] Rymer, *Foed.* IX, 289.

detail that still absorbs the interest of the antiquary[1], had its natural corollary in a fund for the observance of his anniversary. In 1437 and onwards a sum of £25 was paid quarterly to the appointed "Receptor Denariorum pertinencium Anniversario Regis Henrici V^{ti},"—William Walsh, afterwards Prior, being the first. In 1445, two manors, Letcombe Regis, Berks, and Offord Cluny, Hunts, were made over to the Convent[2] in substitution for the yearly benefaction of £100, so that John Flete, who was then Receiver, appeared thereafter as "Custos Maneriorum Regis Henrici V^{ti}."

Now the annual charges upon this benefaction were not great. The largest was a distribution of £20 to the poor and of tenpence

The Distribution.

each to twenty-four poor torch-bearers on the day of the anniversary; so that when the candles and the bell-ringing had been paid for, there remained enough in the first year to make a distribution of £43. 3s. 4d. to the Brethren, most of whom received 20s. each and the Prior, as usual, 40s. Thus from the outset of this foundation we have a full list of the House, with the amount allotted to each man standing against his name; and as the date of the first rotulus may be taken to be 1 Sep. 1437, we have a convenient chronological point.

John Flete's first compotus as Warden of King Henry's manors does not differ materially from the one just referred to. It can be seen that the rental value of Offord Cluny is £28 and that of Letcombe Regis £66. 13s. 4d. On the other hand there are some expenses which were not necessary while the endowment took the easy form of a quarterly benefaction in cash from the Duchy of Lancaster. Manorial courts have to be held; the granary at Letcombe needs thatching and other repairs; scriveners and lawyers must be recompensed for the exoneration of both manors from the payment of a fifteenth for public purposes; various stewards and seneschals must receive wages in cloth and in lamb's wool garments; and as the Mayor, and Aldermen, and some of the citizens, of London became part of the regular gathering at the anniversary, it was requisite to provide a modest collation of pears and plums and cake and red and sweet wine (17s. 2d.). Still, there remained a sum of £45. 13s. 4d. to divide among the Brethren, so that the Warden of the Manors must copy the precedent set by the Receiver of the annual £100 and give on the back of his compotus a full list of the recipients.

The series of rolls is not quite so complete for either the Richard II or the Henry V foundation as it is for that of Queen Alianore;

Four parallel lists.

the first has a gap from 1463 to 1470 and the second has one from 1467 to 1473, and various single years are silent in each case. But roughly the position is this, that for the last century of monastic life at the Abbey, say, from 1437 to the Dissolution, we have four complete

---

[1] Cf. Sir W. H. St John Hope, *Funeral, Monument, and Chantry Chapel of K. Henry the Fifth*, 1914.

[2] *Mun.* 3803; 9 Jul. 1445.

lists for most of the years, the Chamberlain's, where these survive, and the lists of the three sets of manors, together with the records of the year's invalids which we can get from the Infirmarer. Apart from a few cases where confusion arises owing to a monk's change of surname, we can with comparative certainty, at any rate from 1390–1 onwards, reject the claims of any one not thus mentioned to be regarded as a Westminster Benedictine.

Having now, as we may conclude, got most of the Brethren entered by name on our list, with some feeling of assurance as to the date

A Monk's career. of their first appearance, we go on to ask about their career as members of our House. Can we detect any stages of promotion through which they passed? Can we ascertain what offices they held? Can we trace them in occupation of offices elsewhere? Is there any means of recording when they passed away?

It will be gathered from what has been said about the financial methods of the Infirmarer, that there would be no difficulty, though there might not be much profit, in drawing up a medical conspectus of each Brother's career in terms of the days that he passed each year in the sick-room. We could sometimes add a statement of the medicine he received or get a clue to the operations performed by the rude forefathers of modern surgery. But in general such a record would be scarcely worth its space. Here and there a case arises in which we like to notice such matters. John Islip, for instance, our last Abbot worth remembering, " perhaps the greatest of his line[1]," was evidently a sickly youth when he made his profession in his sixteenth year in 1480. He had an illness of nine weeks' duration in 1480–1, and another lasting six weeks in 1482–3, and he spent six weeks in the sick-room during 1483–4. But it is the man who lends interest to the fact of the sickness, which is surrounded with no particular interest of its own.

Apart from this the general rule is that, as to any individual monk, we learn from one of the manorial rolls that in the year to which the roll refers he was " de nouo professus " or that he was then " nouicius,"—not in order to record the date of his profession, but as a reason why he was in receipt only of a fraction (mostly one-third) of the dividend paid to the Brethren in general.

But from early times there arose a system of recognising the mile-stones of a monk's career by making him a gift in kind, which had

Exennia. a fixed value in money. Complimentary gifts of this sort went by various names such as " a regard," or a courtesy (curialitas), or a " refresher " (recreacio), but the technical term applied to the presents sent to the Brethren at various fixed points in their career was exennia or exhennia or exzennia, a plural form which fails, if they had only known it, to reproduce exactly the word ξένια, whereby Homer would signify the gifts,

---

[1] J. A. Robinson, *The Benedictine Abbey of Westminster*, Ch. Quart. Rev., Apr. 1907, p. 77.

chiefly of food and wine, offered by host to guest[1]. In the Canterbury *Consuetudinary* the word appears in the singular; for example, where it is laid down that four times a year the Brethren may entertain their friends and "sine aliqua contradiccione exennium a subcelerario percipere et amicis suis mittere[2]." At Worcester also the singular was in common use, as when the Cellarer spends 20s. on two oxen "pro exzennio faciendo episcopo Wygorn[3]." But at Westminster it was usual to adopt the plural form[4].

Of the two occasions on which a monk formally received exennia the earlier was that of his first Mass as a newly ordained priest, and the day was one on which it was thought meet that he should make merry and be glad with his friends. Therefore it became a custom that certain officers should send him "exennia in pane et in vino," generally to the value of 1s. 7½d. or 1s. 11½d., which when multiplied to correspond with the present worth of money seems much more than he required for his own needs. Also, as the officer in question had to account for the expense, he made an entry of it in his compotus. We are thus able to give the year in which it happened, but not (save in very rare instances) the day; for the officer has not our interest in the biography of the monk and is only concerned that his own accounts should balance for the year.

The First Mass.

The earliest instance I have found is in 1301–2 and has been already referred to[5]. Here an early compotus of Queen Alianore's manors takes credit for a "curialitas" of twelve pence to each of three priests (capellanis) "celebrantibus nouas missas suas," but it does not specify the names. The first case in which this is done is in the roll of the same manors for 1318–9, where we have exhennia given on the celebration of their first Mass to John de Ashwelle, Michael de Bridbroke and J. de Salesbury. We should have come upon the first two in later documents, but the last would have eluded us altogether, but for this mention. There are two similar cases in 1323–4 and one in 1324–5, and as there would be from two to four recruits each year, it is probable that we have not got all the entries of exennia for this period.

But what the Warden of the Queen's manors has begun may be taken up by other obedientiaries; so in 1334–5 we have the Infirmarer giving exennia on the same occasion. He may, of course, have begun before, for there is a gap of twelve years in the Infirmary rolls just before the point we

---

[1] e.g. Homer, *Il.* xi, 778:

ξεινιά τ᾽ εὖ παρέθηκεν, ἅ τε ξείνοις θέμις ἐστί.

[2] *Customary*, i, 134.

[3] Wilson and Gordon, *Early Compotus Rolls of Worcester*, p. 38.

[4] The singular was not quite unknown, however, for it will be seen under John de Tothale, 1316, that the Warden of Queen Alianore's manors spent in 1335–6 one shilling " in uno exennio empto et misso fratri J. de Tothal et sociis commorantibus...apud Hamsted." But this is a rare case. Another use of exennia was to describe the complimentary offerings made yearly to the Abbot by various donors. Cf. E. H. Pearce, *William de Colchester*, pp. 62 ff.   [5] pp. 15 f.

have reached. This time there are five monks who receive gifts at their first Mass from both the Infirmarer and the Warden of the manors. The aggravating point is that our great builder, Nicholas de Litlington, whose name now occurs for the first time as having been in the sick-room, is not one of the five, nor do we know when he was ordained priest[1].

Presently, in 1338, the Sacrist is found doing the like and may have begun long before, for the roll surviving next before this one is **Growth of the practice.** that of 1318, and in 1339–40 the newly ordained Brethren are receiving these congratulations in kind from the manors, from the Infirmarer, from the Chamberlain, and from the Warden of the Churches. Ten years later the Cellarer's rolls begin to give entries of similar gifts, and in 1356–7 he is joined by the Almoner. Thus in 1361, when Richard Excestr' celebrated Mass for the first time, he was regaled by four officers, the Warden of the Queen's manors, the Infirmarer, the Sacrist, and the Almoner, and the event cost the Convent 7s. 10d., or about £7 to £8 of our money. Before the end of the fourteenth century the number of these exennia had further increased. Robert Hermodesworth received five in 1382–3 and Roger Cretton six in 1384–5, while in 1415–6 there is a monk, Richard Parker, with seven to his credit. For in the meantime other officers have begun their series of rolls or have taken up the habit, such as the Convent Treasurer, the Warden of St Mary's Chapel, the Monk-Bailiff and the Warden of the New Work on the nave. At nine exennia, or 17s. 7½d., the custom, so far as first Masses went, appears to have reached its limit, in the case of Brother Robert London in 1497–8.

Of course its interest for us is biographical. A man's first Mass would not be said before he had reached the age of twenty-four, for **Biographical importance.** it was not till the reign of Edward IV that the monastery received the privilege,—if it was really such,—of having its clergy advanced to priest's orders as soon as they were one and twenty[2]. We can thus use the date of his first Mass to get a fair notion about the year of his birth and about the age he has reached when he first appears as a novice. To take instances which are of general interest. John Flete, the historian, who said his first Mass in 1422–3, must have been born in or about 1398–9, so that he would be two and twenty when we first come upon him in the Chamberlain's and in the manorial rolls of 1420–1; and John Islip, who, as he tells us[3], became a monk on 21 Mar. 1480, being then sixteen years of age, was under twenty-two, when he said his first Mass on 1 Jan. 1486[4]. Thus we could arrive by calculation at a rough average age for entrance into the Order.

[1] But it is known that he was professed in the reign of Abbot Curtlington (*Mun.* 5894).

[2] Widmore, p. 117–8.

[3] *Mun.* 33290; cf. J. Armitage Robinson, *The Benedictine Abbey of Westminster*, Ch. Quart. Rev., Apr. 1907, p. 67.

[4] Islip tells us (*ibid.*) that he was born 10 Jun. 1464.

The second occasion on which it became customary to give exennia was concerned with a Brother's progress as a member of the House **Promotion in the Refectory.** and was of domestic rather than ecclesiastical interest. The gift at his first Mass marked his enhanced dignity in the Sanctuary; the gift to which we now pass was a sign of his greater importance in the Refectory. In that apartment, which ran parallel with the South Cloister on its south side, the tables were arranged to suit various gradations of seniority. We can see from the rolls of the later Refectorers that there were "tabulae pro senioribus[1]," "tabulae pro mediocribus" and "mensae inferiores"; there was a "mensa pauperum" and "le Gestentable"; but the chief seats were round the "tabula presidentis." Linen is bought for the seniors' table, but "mappa de diaper pro tabula presidentis." The latter has his own ciphus, and there is a special knife known as the "cultellus prioris" or the "cultellus presidentis in refectorio." But the particular sign of the president is the skilla or skylla, the bell which he was to ring for grace or for the beginning of the lection or for other recognised incidents of meal-time, and which was an equally customary feature of other conventual houses[2]. In the days of Abbot Ware the duty of providing the bell was laid upon the Sacrist, or, as he was sometimes called, "Secretarius[3]," but in later years it fell to the Refectorer[4].

But in order to realise the duties of this president we must also turn to the thirteenth century. *Consuetudinary.* Here there are **The Refectory president.** characteristically minute directions. Of course, if the Abbot joined his Brethren in the Refectory, his lordship presided and it was necessary that he should sit with the skilla on his right hand. In his absence the president's duties devolved upon the Prior, or the Sub-prior, or the third or the fourth Prior, or some other "custos ordinis," as the case might be. Whoever he was, he was not to sit at the middle of the table, under the Majesty, but "a latere, videlicet ita quod skyllam ad dexteram habeat." This place, then, was reserved for the Prior, or some "ordinis custos, aut saltem unus ex senioribus qui primus eorum est in ordine[5]."

It would seem, however, that after Abbot Ware's time the Convent adopted the plan of promoting Brethren to this senior table more speedily,

---

[1] Sometimes called "tabulae senatorum."

[2] Du Cange, *Glossar^m*, s.v. Skella: "prope Abbatis vel Prioris sedem pendebat Scilla: unde ad Scillam sedere dicebatur, qui ad mensam Abbatis vel Prioris sedebat." Cf. *Rites of Durham*, Surtees Society (re-issue 1902), Vol. 107, p. 82. To the forms skilla, skylla, scilla, and skella Du Cange adds scala, of which he gives one instance (vol. vi, p. 178). Domesday, f. 596, furnishes another instance of the same form in a charter of Abbot Richard (i.e. Berking, Crokesley, or Ware, 1222–83) which deals with the Pitanciarius and says: "prouideat singulis diebus sex solidos ad unam bonam pitanciam coram Abbate vel alio presidente ad scalam deferendam."

[3] *Customary*, ii, 49.

[4] "Et pro factura unius noue campane pro skilla. xxii d." (Refectorer 1375–6.)

[5] *Customary*, ii, 107 f.

in order that there might never be wanting a supply of persons duly qualified
to serve the House as president at meal-times. It would not be done hastily;
some process of probation on the part of the Chapter probably preceded the
event; and therefore it was a matter for natural congratulation to a Brother,
that he should pass safely through this ordeal. The seal of his success was
that, as our rolls variously phrase it, "primo [vel nouiter, vel de nouo] sedebat
ad skillam," or "primo presidebat ad skillam," or "primo presidebat in refectorio" or simply "primo presidebat," or "primo procedebat ad skillam[1]."

My earliest record of exennia in this connexion is derived from the Queen
Alianore compotus of 1323–4, and the gift went in this case to
Peter de Wygornia who had then spent at least eighteen years
in the Convent. The Infirmarer is found adopting the practice in 1334–5,
and sending one of these compliments to Robert de Curtlington who as
Sub-prior was entitled to preside in the absence of the Abbot and the Prior,
but, presumably, had not hitherto happened to do so. With him are joined
Thomas de Wenlok, the third Prior, and John de Brichstok, the fourth Prior,
who would preside as of right, if their seniors were away. It is doubtless
due to gaps in the early rolls, more than to a lack of precision in the custom,
that there are at first very few monks whose exennia are on record both for
their first Mass and for their first session at the chief table. Thomas de
Wenlok, just mentioned, is one and Hugh de Shenegeyze (1334–5) is another;
but the number increased later, as the other officers joined in the practice at
the rate which we noted in the case of exennia for first Masses[2].

Ad skillam.

Now this custom will not act with the same chronological preciseness as
the other. The time at which a Brother must be promoted to
the president's table had no apparent laws, and the period
between the first Mass and this second promotion varied from
two or three years to fifteen or even twenty years; but from eight to ten
years may be taken as the average interval.

*Biographical
importance.*

Sometimes this promotion "ad skillam" happened very early in a monk's
Westminster career. The first thing, for instance, that we know about John
de Wratting is that he passed up to the neighbourhood of the bell in 1353–4.
There is no record of his ordination and he may have been priested before he
entered our House, but as he sat by the bell for fifty-four years, he must
have won his promotion early. On the other hand, several of the Priors
(such as Robert Whatele, who had been a priest for nearly twenty years and
had spent most of the time at Oxford, and Millyng and Fascet and Islip),
only took their seat as presidents when they had been elected Priors, while
Edmund Kirton did not attain to the position till he became Abbot,—that is,
no less than thirty-two years after his ordination.

---

[1] The phrase varied in a given year from roll to roll; cf. 1350–1, Walter de Moredon.

[2] Indeed, at a slightly greater rate, for in 1448–9 Thomas Arundel (p. 147) on his promotion
"ad skillam" received exennia from eight officers.

Negatively, the information is useful, as implying that monks who remained in the Convent for any length of time without giving the officers cause to supply them with gifts on this ground were shut out from the honour for some reason of health or incapacity or unworthiness; but we should have to pass on to about the year 1400 before the rolls survive in sufficient continuity to justify any judgment in a particular case.

There is a third event in a monk's life, which involves a date, but which cannot be classed with the other two, because its incidence was not so general. A Brother might be sent to Oxford at the expense of the convent. This became a necessary part of the Benedictine system about the year 1290, along with the foundation of Gloucester College, Oxford, at the General Chapter of the Benedictine Order, Walter de Wenlok, our Abbot, being one of the Presidents, as deputy for the Abbot of Glastonbury[1]. Our knowledge of its prevalence at Westminster from the middle of the fourteenth century onwards is due to the rolls of the Treasurers, who paid the scholars the amount granted to them annually. The first case that I have been able to find represents a system that did not last long. In 1339–40 there were two such Oxford scholars, Robert de Hamslap and Robert de Lake, and their scholarships took the form of a payment—"pro studio apud Oxoñ"—of one penny in the mark from certain obedientiaries (e.g. the Infirmarer and the Warden of the Churches). But the first case of what became the normal system is in the Treasurers' account for 1359–60 and it is given in these words: "Solut' fratri W. Zepeswych pro expensis suis apud Oxoñ una cum expensis circa domum studentium xiii[li] xiii[s] iiii[d]." For historical purposes this is ambiguous. It might imply that Zepeswych was the first Westminster scholar and that, being such, he was involved in some additional expense in providing a proper habitat for himself and those who would follow him to Oxford,—no doubt in Gloucester College. At this time Zepeswych (or Ipswich) was about twenty-seven years of age, having entered our House in 1352–3. He remained at Oxford till 1364 and on his return became in succession Archdeacon, Precentor, Sacrist, Warden of the Lady Chapel, and finally Prior of Hurley. It is of interest to note that quite late in his career at Westminster he was sent in conjunction with the Prior, Richard de Merston, to carry to Canterbury a letter from Cardinal Langham "de domo scolarium apud Oxoñ[2]."

Now, we are well supplied at this period with Treasurers' accounts and these lead us to suppose that till 1362 Zepeswych was our only representative at Oxford; but in that year he was joined by John Stowe, who in turn was joined in 1364 by Richard Circestr', who subsequently wrote the *Speculum Historiale*. Henceforward there is a place in the Treasurers' rolls at which we may confidently expect to find an entry of a payment of £10 each (it was

The Oxford students.

---

[1] Reyner, *de Antiq. Benedict.*, App., p. 54.
[2] Treasurers' roll, 1371–2.

changed about 1435 to ten marks or £6. 13s. 4d.) to each of two monks, variously entered as "existentibus Oxon," or "scolaribus Oxon," or "studentibus Oxon," or "scolaribus studentibus Oxon." There was no prescribed period for the holding of these scholarships. William Colchester, the future Abbot, held his for four years. John Farnago, who with Colchester witnessed Cardinal Langham's will at Avignon, interrupted his course for the purposes of his journey abroad, and had a further year at Oxford on his return. William de Sudbury, who lived to do our House some credit in theological scholarship, was a £10 student for at least twelve years. Thomas Merke, afterwards Bishop of Carlisle, was in residence at Oxford only from 1392 to 1394 and in his second year needed an additional gift of £10 "circa introitum ad sentencias." Robert Whatele went up at the age of about twenty-six in 1390 and remained a student till 1407, receiving a grant of £3. 6s. 8d. in 1403–4 "pro opposicione sua in scolis ibidem facienda." On his return to Westminster in 1407, he became Prior till the end of his days in 1435, and we should like to know why (if not for the special favour of Henry V) Richard Harwden stepped up before him into the Abbot's place in 1420. John Sauereye's case bears witness to the absence of system; for he said his first Mass in 1395–6, was promoted "ad skillam" ten years later, served the offices of Chamberlain, Abbot's Receiver and Seneschal, and Almoner, and then in 1415, when he was nearly five and forty, was our Oxford student for two years; was it to prepare him for the Priorship of Hurley, which he held from 1420 to 1452, if not still later? But the most Oxonian of our Oxford scholars was Edmund Kirton, who went up to the University a year before his ordination as priest, residing there almost continuously from 1407 to 1425; about 1423 he was recognised as Prior "studentium Oxon," that is, of Gloucester Hall or College. Also in fairness it must be recorded that Thomas Ruston, who was scholar from 1448 to 1456, afterwards became by his wild administration of important offices the cause of the dismal downfall of Abbot Norwych. But, speaking generally, it will be clear from the Register now compiled that a course at Oxford tended to a Brother's advancement as an ecclesiastical officer of the Convent; that is, he was more likely to be Precentor or Sacrist, than Monk-Bailiff or Cellarer.

In particular, it may be gathered from the rolls of the Sacrists that in many cases it was the Oxford scholars to whom the Monastery **The Passion-tide Preachers.** turned for preachers on Palm Sunday and Good Friday, the two great days for sermons in Benedictine houses. Millyng, for instance, came up at least five times for this special purpose, the Convent doing him honour on the last of these occasions (1476) as Bishop of Hereford. It is also evident from the items of their travelling expenses that residence at Oxford was rarely continued all the year round. In 1491 when there were four scholars, John More and his three companions rode up from the University in February, took their part in the Passion-tide sermons, returned to Oxford in May, and were brought up again to Westminster in July for the election of Roger Blake to the Priorship. Two of them, Borow and Duffeld, travelled from Oxford to Westminster in December 1492, returning to their studies in January. But Borow had to ride up once more in February to tell his colleagues that Duffeld had died at Oxford, and this time he remained in the Convent till the following May.

In 1428 the Benedictines established a hostel in the parish of St Giles, Cambridge, on the site now occupied by Magdalene College.

Students at Cambridge. This hostel, which was afterwards called Buckingham College, provided accommodation for students from various monasteries in the eastern counties, such as Croyland, Ely, Walden and Ramsey[1]. It is also on record that Abbot Millyng, who was at Oxford for eight years as one of our students, was incorporated at Cambridge in 1470–1[2]. But no connexion with Cambridge can be detected in the Treasurers' entries till 1499 when Thomas Gardener, having been for two years " scolaris studens Oxon'," appears for a short time as " studens Oxon' et Cantebrig'," and that in 1533–4 there were several "studentes Cantabrigie," some of whom had previously been at Oxford. Henry VII had added to the number of the scholars and it may be that the effect of the Lady Margaret's interest alike in Cambridge and in Westminster can be detected in this tardy modification of the ancient absorption in Oxford. Records like Foster's *Alumni Oxonienses* go to show that quite a number of these students proceeded to degrees in Divinity.

Exact information as to the end of a monk's life at Westminster is more difficult to obtain than it is in the case of his entry or his

The date of decease. promotion. If we could carry right through the history of the House the business-like thoroughness with which Prior Walsh turned his note-book[3] into a register of mortality, our trouble would be slight. We should know the hour, the day of the week and of the month, and the year of a Brother's decease; we should know where and on what day he was buried[4]. But William Walsh's delightful entries soon come to an end and, as registrar, he had neither predecessor nor follower, as far as we can tell. If, again, it had been the custom to erect some permanent memorial to all departed Brethren in the church or the cloisters or the precincts, and an earlier and equally observant Camden had gone round from time to time and copied the inscriptions, as the only Camden did for us in his *Reges*, &c., we might be better supplied with death-dates. As it is, we depend as before on the compotus rolls and on their rigid system of entry. Among these, the most certain authority for present purposes is the Infirmarer. It was his duty to pay out a sum of money, usually about 6s. 8d., for a Brother's obit;

---

[1] Cf. Willis and Clark, *Architect. Hist. of Camb.* i, xlviii. f. ; Mullinger, *Univ. of Camb.* ii, 64.

[2] " Concessa est gracia abbati Westmonasterii vt possit incorporari "; Camb. *Grace Book* A, p. 86.

[3] *Mun.* 33289.   [4] See, e.g. Cambridge, John 1418–9.

his formula being generally as follows, "et distribut' pauperibus pro anima fratris A.B." (or "pro animabus fratrum A.B., C.D."). There does not appear to be any regulation for this distribution in our *Consuetudinary*, but in that of St Augustine's, Canterbury, there are precise directions for the commendatory Mass to be said in the Infirmary Chapel[1], and this as well as the fitness of things would account for the importance of the Infirmarer as registrar of deaths. But it must be noticed that his information gives only the year (from Michaelmas to Michaelmas) in which death took place[2]; it is possible to guess from the last occurrence of the Brother's name in the sick-list at what part of the year he was taken, but it must be rough guessing.

What is surprising, in view of the directions of the *Consuetudinary*, is the absence of mortuary detail from other rolls. It was the duty of the Westminster Sacrist "monachorum sepulturas providere et jubere fieri[3]" and, as this could not be done except at the cost of labour and materials, we should expect him to charge for the items and to state the names of those whose death caused the expense. But, as far as I have observed, we do not owe to him the knowledge of a single death. At Canterbury it was the duty of the Chamberlain to provide the various cerements for the corpse, with special care that they should be new and clean[4], which again meant expense; but our Chamberlain makes no entry of such expenses. It was the duty of the Warden of the Lady Chapel,—a duty newly imposed in Abbot Ware's time[5],—to provide a resting-place for a Brother's remains; but only once, and that in the earliest document of his that we have, does the "Custos Capellae" make any entry of his costs in this respect. It is in Robert de Bures' account for 1299–1300 and is as follows: "Et in sarcofagis cum cooperculis emptis pro fratribus N. de Ware, W. de Finden, A. de Leyton, et W. de Watford xxiv[s] vi[d]." A persistence in this habit by the Warden would have spared us much investigation and more doubt. We have to rely, then, in the case of death chiefly upon the lists, whether of the Chamberlain or of the Wardens of the manors.

The officers and the dead.

---

[1] *Customary*, I, 338. On the back of a seneschal's roll, evidently of the time of Abbot Wenlok (1283—1307), I have lately found a transcript in another hand of the full liturgical directions for the unction of a Brother and for his obsequies,—"ordo visitandi infirmum," &c. (*Mun.* 6631). Allowing for local variations, such as the placing of the body before the altar of St Benedict, there is a fairly close correspondence with the Canterbury rite. No officers are concerned except the Prior and the Precentor, neither of whom kept official records of his doings. An almost identical service appears in *Missale Westm.* (ed. H.B.S., 1896) III, 1266 ff.

[2] There are tantalising cases, such as that found in the roll of the Infirmarer for 1305–6, who tells us that one of his patients, Henry de Temple, died on the Saturday after the sixth Sunday after Michaelmas; or the entry of 1334–5, which shows that Walter de Woxebrugge died on Monday, 24 Jan. 1335; but such cases are not numerous.

[3] *Customary*, II, 51.

[4] "Staminam novam, quam prius non habuit aliquis indutam, ..cucullam honestam et satis longam...." *Customary*, I, 340.

[5] *Ibid.* II, 51: "prout noviter est statutum, unicuique fratri in fata decedenti sarcophagum exhibebit."

These lists, as we saw, preserve the order of conventual precedence, and

Inter mortuos. any break in that sequence means something. Very early it comes to be realised that there is a little group out of order at the foot of the lists, sometimes running straight on, sometimes and, in later years, mostly with a space left between them and the junior novice. Some Brother who, last year, had a full share from the manors is placed this year in this little group at the end and receives the third part of a share; another Brother next to him is given two-thirds; another a twelfth; and so on. It is reasonable to suppose that these names represent the mortality of the year under review, and that the difference in the fractions of dividend assigned to them is caused by their having survived through various proportions of the said year. If the latter conclusion is conjectural, there is not much doubt about the mortuary character of this group of names; for it is confirmed by a single incident. In the list appended to his compotus of 1344–5 Hugh de Shenegeyze, the Chamberlain, inserted before the names of the last two Brethren what looks at first like the name of a monk, but proves to be the word "Mortui." I have therefore adopted the phrase "inter mortuos" to signify that a monk's name is so found; and I take it, whether in the Chamberlain's rolls or in those of the manors, to be a presumption of his decease.

But it has been puzzling to notice how often the Chamberlain seems to

The Chamber-
lain's death-
dates.

give the death a year later than it is given by the Wardens of the Manors or by the Infirmarers, where they enter the obit. I have wondered whether this is to be explained by an arrangement adopted in the eighth year of his rule by Abbot Richard de Berkyng. It meant, we are told[1], that for a year after a Westminster monk's death his corrody or allowance was to be paid by the Almoner to some suitable priest to say daily prayers and Masses for his soul throughout the year; and the Chamberlain must hand to the Almoner "omnia quae ad vesturam et calcituram fratris defuncti pertinebant, sine aliqua diminucione," for the benefit of the same priest. If this was so, the Chamberlain would be bound to include the dead Brother's name in his list one year longer than other officers did, together with the usual details of the equipment given out for him from the store.

The chief difficulty in this matter of death-dates lies in the possibility that a name may appear no more because the monk has taken his departure to some other religious house. We have the case of Edward Boteler, who received letters dimissory from Abbot Estney to enable him to join the Cluniac priory of St Milburga at Wenlock[2]. His last payment from Q. Alianore's manors is entered at the foot of the 1487–8 list, from which we should presume his death, if we had not the letters.

Thus, though there are cases in which the word "Defunctus" must be left to hover between the sense of dead to the Abbey and the sense of dead to

[1] *Flete*, p. 105, ll. 19–35.   [2] See under 1469–70.

the life that now is, it may be taken that the dates given denote in over
200 instances the actual death of the Brother in question, and that, though
the Chamberlain's method makes certainty about a given year somewhat
difficult, the margin of doubtfulness does not extend beyond twelve months.

Apart, then, from any incidental references that may be found to his
activities or his writings, these are the four chief events in a
Westminster monk's career,—his first appearance as a junior,
his first Mass, his first day as president in the Refectory, and

The Tenure of Offices.

his death.   But, if he was once drawn into the work of administration, his
career must also be described in terms of the various offices to which he was
appointed, and there is no apparent limit to the number of such offices in
a given case.   To take as our first instance the 49 Brethren serving under
Walter de Wenlok in 1297–8, it can be reckoned that 20 of these held no
office during their career, 12 held one, 5 held two, 5 held three, 5 held four,
1 held six and 1 held seven offices, at various times; but no rules can be
deduced from information so incomplete as that of the rolls of this period.
A hundred years later we can feel much more sure, though the result does
not materially differ.   In 1399–1400 the House contained 59 Brethren
serving under the Priorship of John de Wratting.   Examining the careers
of these, we get the following results: 27 did not receive any office at any
time; 6 received one office, 3 two offices, 4 three offices, 4 four offices, 8 five
offices, 2 six offices, 1 seven offices, 2 eight offices, 1 nine, 1 ten, and 1 eleven
offices.   Let us see what an extreme case meant.   The man who passed
through eleven offices was Roger Cretton.   He became a Westminster monk
in 1384–5 and he began to exercise administrative functions in 1399.   From
then till 1413 he was busy with finance and commissariat as Treasurer,
Kitchener, Cellarer, and Granger, being also for part of the time Warden of
Q. Alianore's and of Richard II's manors and Warden of the Churches.
In 1413 he became Almoner for three years; in 1416 Infirmarer and Abbot's
Receiver for two years; in 1422 (and perhaps earlier) he became Sacrist
and so remained till 1433–4.   Thus for thirty-five years, 1399–1434, with the
probable exception of the years 1414–6, 1418–22, he was never without
administrative responsibility, and never passed a year without producing
a compotus with his name at the top and a recognition "pro bono suo labore"
at the bottom.   "Infra tempus compoti mortuus est," says the Sacrist of
1433–4; he died during the time of the audit; and it must have seemed the
appropriate moment for Roger Cretton to die.

It is perhaps as well to show the last phase of this feature.   In the years
1501–4 (Michˢ to Michˢ) 20 novices were admitted to the
Convent.   Of these, 14 did not attain to office at all, 2 held
one office (that of Kitchener, a very subordinate post), 2 held

The last development.

five offices, 1 nine, and 1 twelve.   The only point of interest now is the
practical concentration of the administration in the hands of a single monk.

John Fulwell, the pluralist in question, was John Islip's right-hand man. For Islip and his predecessor, Fascet, kept the great responsibilities on their own shoulders.   For thirty-two years Islip was not only Abbot but Sacrist and Warden of the New Work and Warden of the Lady Chapel as well; that is to say, he controlled the great spending departments.   Nor did he spread the burden among his Brethren; he placed all of it in the charge first of Thomas Jaye and then of John Fulwell, the latter being his chaplain.   From 1514 to 1528 Jaye was Treasurer, Monk-Bailiff, Warden of the Churches, Warden of each set of royal manors, and Cellarer.   In May 1528, Jaye became Prior, and then all these offices passed at once to John Fulwell, who had been Granger and deputy for the Abbot as Warden of the Lady Chapel.   He became also Cellarer, Kitchener, Warden of Henry VII's foundation and (at any rate in 1528) Archdeacon.   In such a condition of things the greater part of the Brethren must have felt themselves to be mere ciphers in the administration of the House, and the end was not far off.

One more question arises.   What special care was taken of the aged?

The stagiarii.
The *Consuetudinary* makes frequent reference to the "stagiarii," the old stagers, who were too infirm to be summoned to Mass in the church or to meetings of the Chapter, and who mostly had their own special "camera" or set of rooms in the Infirmary.   Reginald Shiplake, for instance, is described as having been for the last two years of his life "stagiarius infra Infirmariam."   It is also clear from the *Consuetudinary*[1] that the Abbey had its reclusorium a short distance off, and some of our Brothers are recorded to have been "reclusi," payments being made from time to time to provide them with fuel and light in their solitude.   But in a House where manorial and other payments were made to the youngest novice it would be strange if something were not done to meet the special needs, the little creature comforts, of the aged who were infirm without being bedridden.   Yet I can find practically no trace of this being done, save under quite exceptional circumstances, and then mainly in the form of a pension for services rendered.   It will be best to set forth the facts as they may be gathered from the Register.

The earliest instance I have found is that of Richard Excestr', whose career in the Convent has some curious features.   He entered

Richard
Excestr'.
it in 1360, just before receiving priest's orders in 1361.   His promotion "ad skillam" is not recorded, but it may have taken place in or about 1371.   In 1375 he was sent to Oxford with a £10 scholarship, and he was made Prior of Westminster in 1377.   But he held this office only for five years, and seems to have resigned it in 1382, we know not for what cause.   Henceforth his place on the lists, and in Choir and in Chapter, is next to the Prior, and in whatever respects the Prior received a double portion, such as clothing or distributions of money at anniversaries, Richard

[1] *Customary*, II, 20.

of Exeter received the same till his death in 1397. This constituted his pension, and it was clearly given for services rendered in the Prior's office[1]. We may dispose, out of their proper order, of other similar cases, such as a recreation of 20s. "fratri Ricardo Harowdene nuper Abbati," paid to him after his resignation in 1440 by the Warden of King Henry V's manors, in addition, of course, to his large pension from the Abbot's portion; and the pension amounting to £5, in addition to a Prior's double portions, which was the recognition made to Thomas Arundel, when he resigned the Priorship in 1482, exactly a century after Richard Excestr' had done the like. Edmund Kirton was another Abbot who resigned his seat, receiving a pension of 200 marks, besides allowances in money and in fuel from the bounty of his successor.

We return to William Colchester, who, evidently not on account of age or infirmity, but for valuable service rendered to the corporation at home and abroad, was in receipt of a pension of six marks paid by the Treasurers out of the common funds[2]. When he was made Abbot in 1386, this pension was transferred to John Lakyngheth, then perhaps fifty years of age, whose services to the welfare of the House were hardly less signal than Colchester's, and to these six marks were added in his case the yearly profits (ten shillings) of a specified osier-bed[3]. What we may call retiring pensions begin to appear towards the middle of the fifteenth century.

William Colchester.

In 1432, William Sonewell, the Convent recluse, who as it turned out had only a few months to live, received a pension of 10s. from the Warden of the Lady Chapel, and he is the first of some two and twenty Brethren who were pensioned, as I conclude, on the same grounds of their service as obedientiaries, up to and including William Grene whose pension began in 1526–7,—an average of one pension granted every four to five years. The only proof that the pension was a recognition of administrative service is that there is no record of any others. John Ocle (1434–5) has, it is true, no such service to his credit, but he was the Convent recluse, and so needed his allowance of "fagetts" and candles and 20s. yearly. John Knolle (1498–9) is the one instance I can find of a pension (£1) being granted without the necessary reason, and he may have been an invalid or he may have held an office or offices of which there is no surviving record; the former is more probable, as he was only about forty-five years of age when pensioned, and died soon after. Against this apparent exception we must set the care with which it is stated[4] that a regard of 4s. 4d. given to John Norton (1473–4) was granted "causa debilitatis hac vice

Good-service pensions.

---

[1] Cf. E. H. Pearce, *William de Colchester*, pp. 42, 49–51.
[2] See his record in the Register and cf. E. H. Pearce, *William de Colchester*, p. 47.
[3] See 1362–3, Lakyngheth, John, where the references are given.
[4] Roll of Q. Alianore's manors 1501–2.

tantum," and on the other hand that Magister Richard Southbroke's pension[1] was "pro quadam annuitate sibi concessa ad terminum vite"; for Norton held no offices, while Southbroke was Precentor for at least eighteen years. It is sufficient to specify that among the twenty-two who appear to have been pensioned for services rendered William Chertsey was in office almost continuously from 1445 to 1483, and Richard Charing from 1483 to 1524.

There remain two cases which seem to lie outside this pension scheme and to be due to special circumstances. Magister Ralph Selby entered the Convent in 1398–9, after a busy career in the broader life of the Church of England. He is stated[2] to have been Prebendary and Sub-dean of York (1386); Archdeacon of Buckingham (1392); and Archdeacon of Norfolk (1398). What his age was, and why, being still in the last-named office, he entered our House, it is not possible to decide. He may have been a personal friend of Abbot Colchester, who would be glad to have among his Brethren an experienced jurist. The doggrel on Selby's tomb in the south Ambulatory called him[3]

Ralph Selby.

> Doctor per merita, praepotens lege perita,
> Legibus ornatus, a regibus et veneratus;

but he was also assured of a welcome within our walls as being one of the executors of John de Waltham, Bishop of Salisbury, and as having had his part in founding an anniversary for that royal favourite, which brought no small gain to the Brethren. It would be, perhaps, on these grounds that at his first appearance on our lists (Q. Alianore, 1398–9; Chamberlain, 1399–1400), Ralph Selby was given precedence next to the Prior. But it is not so clear why in 1402–3 the Treasurer, who says that he acted under the capitular authority of the Abbot, Prior and Convent, should have begun paying to Selby the large annual pension of £4, which continued till he died, like Abbot Colchester, in 1420.

The other case was that of a monk who also had connexions with the outside world and who entered the monastery about five years before Selby's death. John Stokes who said his first Mass in 1417–8 was absent from the Convent from about 1421 to 1436, and his appointments at St Stephen's College, Westminster, and at St Paul's Cathedral are noted in the Register[4]. Like Selby he was Magister, and during his absence from the House he may have been conferring services upon it which justified the exceptional treatment extended to him. At all events in 1449–50, the year of his decease, the Treasurers began to pay a sort of post-mortem pension of £20 on his behalf, and the Sacrist in 1450–1 a pension of £2. 13s. 4d., such amount in each case to be payable for five years. As the Infirmarer of 1450–1 enters an expenditure of 20s. "pro debitis magistri Johannis Stokys de collegio sancti Stephani," it is legitimate to conclude

John Stokes.

---

[1] Roll of the New Work 1445–6.   [2] Widmore, p. 112.
[3] Camden, *Reges*, &c.   [4] See 1415–6, Stokes, John.

that the Convent shouldered the obligations which Stokes left unsettled at his death. The pension given to Bishop Merke (p. 116) is equally exceptional.

This, then, is our catalogue of "obscure names." Let us admit the obscurity for a moment in order that the names may be discussed merely as names which throw light on the system of monastic nomenclature. We may deal first with the concluding forty years of the Convent's life as a period distinct in its methods, when a name was not infrequently given to conceal rather than to indicate. Christopher Godehappes and John Godeluke, Richard Jerome and William Ambrose, Humfrey Charite and John Grace, John Felix and William Faith, William Hope and T. Veryty are specimens of the names "in religion" that mark these closing years; and the custom reached its height in 1533–4, when out of seven novices only Robert Barnards seems real; the rest are shadows,— Chrysostom, Ambrose, Patience, Veryty, Jerome, Mercye. Even to the last we find some whose style recalls the earlier local names,—John Yslyp (for a name-sake of the great Abbot joined the House in 1536–7, and like him was quickly committed to the Infirmarer's care), Robert Lyncoln, Armigel Hurley, Henry Winchester. But a number of names, perhaps about half, are formed to the last on the simple English plan,—William Penne, Thomas Chamberleyn, Edmund Brice.

The names.

The main point is that in the years with which our record opens we are faced with a plan of naming the Brethren to which there are very few exceptions, such as W. Capes and Henry Payn, who might have been so entered yesterday. The essential thing is a Christian name; indeed, in some early cases that is all we know. Robert, the Prior (+ 1085) and Brother Edward who appears first in 1317, the year of his decease, did not attain to a local name worthy of the notice of the documents which mention them. Then there is "Dan Henri," who carried some healing relic[1] to the Countess of Gloucester and Hertford and who needs no other designation, as far as the lady's letter is concerned. If we knew more, it might be possible to identify him, say, with Henry of Colchester [q.v.], who was Warden of the Lady Chapel and therefore a man of some experience in the matter of relics. Yet the system was so sound that there are only some fifty-four for whose surnames or place-names we are left lamenting,— none of them later than 1317.

Christian names.

The Christian names are an interesting study. Only seven Brethren bear St Peter's name, four of them before 1300; though perhaps we ought to include the thirteen Simons as paying at least an indirect compliment to the Apostle. There is no use of Paul as a Christian name. It may be thought that the Confessor's memory and the perpetual glory of his shrine

---

[1] The Norman-French letter of the Countess (*Mun.* 9323) speaks merely of "la relique," without specifying its nature. Probably it was the girdle of the Virgin, which seems to have been in the special keeping of the Sacrist (*Customary*, II. 49).

and the continuance of his name in the royal House would all cause Edward
to appear frequently on our list; but it is in fact much less in evidence than
Edmund, appearing only five times. The first of these is in 1317 and the
rest occur in and after 1447–8.

The fact appears to be that from its quite early years the Convent was
predominantly English; after 1300 there are scarcely any names that even
look foreign. So the prevalence of certain names followed the English habit.
Richard and Robert run a neck and neck race down the centuries and have
about fifty each to their credit at the close. Henry claims a posse of 21.
But John and William outpace all comers, with 154 and 103 respectively.
In fact 451 monks out of the 706 were called either John or William or
Thomas or Richard or Robert or Henry. Surnames must have been a real
necessity in a year such as 1458–9 when four out of six novices were called
John. Two monks, again, came about the same time from Holbeach; each
of them is John Holbech.

We pass to the surnames and arrive at some inevitable results. For
the surname being an indication of origin and London having
the largest population, it follows that a considerable number of
our Brethren were called de London or, simply, London. As far
as can be ascertained, there were thirteen of these, the latest appearing
among the novices of 1494–5. But, as John is the most frequent Christian
name, it will also follow that John of London is the most common combina-
tion. There are four monks in all so named, but, as they are well spread
over the list, the similarity creates no confusion; indeed a fifth John London,
1435–6, considerately changed his name to John Daunt, as if to insist that
he had a patronymic, as well as a place-name.

Surnames or place-names.

Admitting that London as a place of origin is in a class by itself, we go
on to notice that the towns of Reading (though never so written) and of
Wenlock are a fair second. Each gave us six of our Brethren. Two of the
Reading men were called John, of whom the chronicler was the elder. It
would be interesting to arrive at the reason why these Berkshire folk were
thus drawn to the Abbey, which had no obvious connexion with their town
either as landlord or otherwise.

To sum up our results, we may note that between 1049 and the surrender
of the Monastery in 1540 we have here the names and careers
of 706 Westminster Benedictines. Of these

The numbers.

14	joined	during the	11th century
43	„	„	12th „
130	„	„	13th „
230	„	„	14th „
198	„	„	15th „
91	„	„	16th „
706			

For reasons already stated, our *data* for the 13th century (and still more for the 11th and the 12th) are incomplete, but we may conclude that we lack about seventy names. For, passing by the 14th century, when the total of admissions was swollen by the many vacancies due to the ravages of the Black Death, we come to see from the complete record of the 15th century that the average of admissions to the Order at Westminster was about two each year.

If anybody asks in conclusion by what means the House was recruited, the answer is not easy to give. There are some exceptions which must still not be taken as proving rules.

Method of recruiting.

Thus, there are apparently no strict limits of age. A single paper[1] records the profession in 1501 of Thomas Jaye, afterwards Prior, and three of his Brethren, with their ages at the time of their profession. Jaye's age cannot be deciphered, but the other three were aged seventeen, twenty-one, and nineteen respectively. John Islip[2] has told us that at his admission he was in his sixteenth year. Such variations at a given period hardly suggest that vacancies were supplied chiefly from the Convent schools; for the tendency in such case would be to adopt a normal age for passing from the one to the other. But the Almoner's rolls refer to the instruction of the "pueri cantantes" and of the "scolares" and of the "pueri Elemosinarie," and it is not to be supposed that these three seminaries (if they must be spoken of as three) were without their effect on the *personnel* of the Monastery. On the other hand, we are by no means devoid of instances of men who on their admission were of an age for priest's orders, and we have one or two cases, e.g. Ralph Selby, in which long service had already been rendered to the Church outside.

Neither was there any restriction of the privileges of the House to men born in lawful wedlock. For Thomas Pomeray, whose name first appears in 1421–2, was the son of a nobleman, but not by his wedded wife. We only know of this bend sinister through a Papal dispensation, which was not necessary to secure his admission, but was requisite before he could hold office in the Convent. It was granted in 1437, and Pomeray became Cellarer, probably in 1439; he was certainly appointed to the important offices of Treasurer and Monk-Bailiff in 1440; his other posts and his pension prove that he was held in high honour[3].

Nor, whatever may have been the general rule, was it at all difficult for a monk to be received into the Abbey from another House or even another Order. Testimonials passed, for instance, in 1354 in favour of one Roger de Pydele, of Waltham, Holy Cross[4], which satisfied Abbot Langham that he was worthy of admission to our Convent, though it is practically certain that he did not join it. But in

From other Orders.

---

[1] *Mun.* 12890 v.   [2] *Mun.* 33290; see p. 167.   [3] p. 138.
[4] *Mun.* 6667.

Litlington's time we have the case of Robert Wynewyk[1], a canon of the Gilbertine or Sempringham Order, who was released by the Master of his Order on 10 Jan. 1367, the said Master receiving from Convent funds by command of the Abbot a consideration of ten marks or £6. 13s. 4d. in respect of the transference. The payment is a strange one, especially as Wynewyk was not used by the Convent except as Warden of the Lady Chapel for a brief period.

It follows that on occasion our own monks could pass hence to another confraternity. From the lack, which I have occasionally indicated, of direct evidence of death, I incline to believing that this was not an infrequent event. But we have the clear case of the letters dimissory written in English by Abbot Estney to the Prior of the Cluniac House of St Milburga Wenlock[2], with which Westminster had ancient affinity from the days of Abbot Walter de Wenlok. Estney states that Edward Boteler, the monk in question, whose interesting attainments he fully describes, desires "to be dismissed out of our obedience" and "to be a brother of your place and your obedience."

Still, taking the system as a whole, we are in no doubt as to what it meant. Young men were accepted in their boyhood and became, **From the Abbey lands.** in most cases, members of the House for life; and it is not difficult to realise how they were selected. The Abbots were untiring in their journeys of inspection and of ceremony through the estates belonging to the abbatial portion. The Treasurers and the Monk-Bailiff went their factorial rounds through the manors belonging to the Convent's portion. In so doing they came to learn of youths with an apparent vocation for claustral life. A comparison of the place-names in our list with the record of the towns and villages situate in or near the property of the Convent will show that this was the normal method of recruiting. Those who occupied the stalls in the Choir of old time, like the crowds who throng to its services to-day, came from many parts of England. Then, as now, King Henry III's fabric was a truly national centre for the worship of the Lord, who fulfils Himself in various ways.

[1] p. 110.

[2] Cf. p. 163; the letter is fully transcribed by J. Armitage Robinson in *Manuscripts of Westminster Abbey*, p. 12.

A REGISTER OF
THE MONKS OF WESTMINSTER

NOTE.

1. The figure at the head of each name or set of names signifies the year in which the monk joined the Convent as a novice, or otherwise. Sometimes this can only be given approximately, e.g. c. 1092; sometimes it is evident that the date of joining must be earlier than the first known date, e.g. + 1049.

2. The names of those who became Abbots are printed in spaced capitals, e.g. **CRISPIN, Gislebert**; the names of those who became Priors are printed in solid capitals, e.g. **CLARE, Osbert de.**

3. The conventual offices held by a monk are given in monastic Latin. The documentary authority for each statement is generally added in round brackets. Such authority consists of

    (*a*) a separate document among the Muniments, e.g. (*Mun.* 2001);

    (*b*) a compotus-roll of some obedientiary, whose title is given in English according to the names used on the boxes in which they are contained, together with the year in question; e.g. Laurence de Benflet (p. 72), Precentor 1297–8 (Infirmarer) signifies that this monk is so described in the Infirmarer's roll for that year;

    (*c*) an entry in the great Chartulary called Domesday; e.g. (Domesday f. 493), or (Domesday f. 493 b), if the reference is to be found on the dors. of the folio;

    (*d*) an entry in the miscellany called Liber Niger Quaternus, e.g. (*Lib. Nig. Quat.* f. 125 b).

Where no authority is added, it may be assumed that the roll of the obedientiary for the year in question may be consulted, e.g. Chalk, William de (p. 66), Custos Maner^m Regine Alianore 28 Mai. 1302—17 Apr. 1305 signifies that the authority is the rolls of Q. Alianore's manors for the period specified.

4. Quotations from the documents are given as they stand, except that, for convenience, the customary abbreviations are disregarded.

5. In cases where it is possible that an office was held longer than can be proved from the documents, the sign ? + is used; e.g. Coggeshale, Walter de (p. 125) Celerarius ? + 1416–7 ? + signifies that the office was possibly held both before and after the year specified.

6. Each form of a surname is included, that which stands first being on the whole the most prevalent[1]. Some occasional variations in the Christian name are also noted.

+1049

EDWIN.
    Monachus Westm.
    Abbas 1049—12 Jun. 1071 (J. Armitage Robinson, *Flete*, p. 140).

Alwold.
    Donum quod Alwoldus de porta sancti Botulphi eis dedit, quando monachus ibi effectus est…[time of Edwd Confess^r] (Domesday f. 98).

---

[1] The majority of the names have some variants; Islip has no less than fourteen.

+1065

Ralph.

Camerarius. Witnessed Edward the Confessor's charter 28 Dec. 1065, of which *Mun.* XXI is a copy, dated 2 Mar. 1314 and witnessed by John de Butterle [q.v.].

c. 1071

GEOFFREY, Galfridus.

Abbot of Jumièges.

Appointed Abbot of Westminster c. 1071 by the Conqueror who removed him on the advice of Lanfranc and sent him back to Normandy in disgrace c. 1075 (cf. J. Armitage Robinson, *Flete*, p. 141).

c. 1076

VITALIS.

Abbot of Bernay, a cell of Fécamp.

Appointed Abbot of Westminster by the Conqueror on the advice of Lanfranc (v. letter in Widmore, p. 180) c. 1076 (1073, *Flete*, p. 84; but see Robinson's note, p. 141).

Received from the Conqueror a confirmation of the grant of the manor of Dodinton [Doddington, Lincs.] with Thorpe (Domesday f. 500 b).

Defunctus 19 Jun. 1085 (1082, *Flete*, p. 84); sepultus in australi parte claustri...ad pedes abbatis Gervasii (p. 85).

Sulcard.

Wrote a Chronicle of the Abbey, which he dedicated venerabili viro et semper dei servo domino Abbati Vitali. It is frequently quoted or referred to by Flete, who calls him monachus egregie litteratus (p. 83). For the substance and character of his story cf. J. Armitage Robinson, *Flete*, pp. 3–11.

Camden (*Reges*, etc.) includes Sulcardus monachus et cronographus among those buried in locis ignotis ecclesiae. *Flete*, p. 83, says he was finally buried in the Chapter House.

+1085

ROBERT.

Prior.

Witnessed Abbot Gilbert's enfeoffment of a knight c. 1085 (Domesday f. 79) and a charter (*ibid.* f. 124). For a discussion of the date of the enfeoffment see J. Armitage Robinson, *Flete*, p. 141; *Gilbert Crispin*, p. 38.

Appointed Abbot of St Edmundsbury 1102; consecrated by Anselm 15 Aug. 1107. Died 16 Sep. 1107.

1085

CRISPIN, Gislebert or Gilbert.

Son of William Crispin, a Norman noble (d. 8 Jan. 1074), and the lady Eva de Montfort his wife (d. 22 Jan. 1099). Entered the abbey of Bec as a boy and was there when Anselm joined it. At the age of about 34, was sent by Anselm to Lanfranc at Canterbury, c. 1079.

Abbot of Westminster 1085–1117 (1082–1114, *Flete*, p. 87), by the influence of the Conqueror at the instigation of Lanfranc, being about 40 when appointed.

Received from William the Conqueror a grant of land at Pyrford c. 1085–7 (*Mun.* XXIV).

In his time c. 1085–6 Geoffrey de Mandeville, Sheriff of London and

Middlesex, founded the priory of Hurley as a cell of Westminster, and Gilbert was present at the dedication of the church (*Mun.* 2001).

He completed the Cloister before 1100 and probably "built the Abbot's *camera* (or *capella*, or perhaps both) over the locutory."

Presided at the opening of the Confessor's tomb 1102.

Gave a corrody to the Nuns of Kilburn (*Lib. Nig. Quat.* f. 125 b).

Granted lands to the priory of Greater Malvern consensu communi capituli (Dugdale, *Monasticon*, III, 448); possibly the foundation of the priory also belongs to his time.

Died 6 Dec. 1117; buried in the South Cloister at the feet of Abbot Vitalis (*Flete*, p. 87).

Was "remembered on his anniversary [7 Dec.], for having extended the *camera*, making assignment for the clothing of eighty monks." (Customary, II, p. 149; cf. *Mun.* 1497, which is a confirmation by Henry III of his ordinances in this last matter.)

His extant writings are Vita Herluini; Disputatio Judaei cum Christiano; de Simoniacis; de Spiritu Sancto; and five minor pieces (Brit. Mus. Add. MS. 8116). See J. Armitage Robinson, *Gilbert Crispin*, 1911.

c. 1085
HERBERT, Herebert.

Witnessed Abbot Gilbert's enfeoffment of a knight (Domesday f. 79).

Probably = Herbert, a Norman (*Flete*, p. 87), who became Almoner and in Jan. 1121 was made Abbot; possibly he may have come with Gilbert Crispin from Bec.

Received a grant of privileges from Peter of Cluny, papal legate, 1121 (Domesday f. 387).

Mun. 3435 appears to be a 13th century copy of his grant of money for the services of the High Altar in the Abbey church from the church of St Margaret, from the church at Denham, and from his own purse (see Brit. Mus. Harl. Ch. 84, F. 46).

For the foundation of the nunnery at Kilburn in his time see *Lib. Nig. Quat.* f. 125.

For date of death, 3 Sep. ? 1136, see J. Armitage Robinson, *Flete*, p. 142.

William.

Witnessed Abbot Gilbert's enfeoffment of a knight (Domesday f. 79).

? Identical with William a monk mentioned in the mortuary roll of Abbot Vitalis of Savigny who died 16 Oct. 1122 (J. Armitage Robinson, *Gilbert Crispin*, p. 27).

Nicholas.

Witnessed Abbot Gilbert's enfeoffment of a knight (Domesday f. 79).

c. 1092
Hugh.

Along with Warner [q.v.] he perambulated the lands which Abbot Gilbert gave to the priory of Greater Malvern.

Warner.

? = Warnerius, a monk of Bec c. 1070 (Porée, *Histoire du Bec*, I, 629).

Along with Hugh, another monk, he perambulated the lands which Abbot Gilbert gave to the priory of Greater Malvern (J. Armitage Robinson, *Gilbert Crispin*, pp. 31, 33).

A senior monk of Westminster, present at Ely at the translation of St Etheldreda, St Withburga and two other saints 1107 (cf. J. Armitage Robinson, *Osbert of Clare*, Ch. Quart. Rev. Jul. 1909, p. 346, n. 2).

For his writings see Widmore, p. 22; Pits, p. 191.

c. 1095
Maurice.

Mentioned in mortuary roll of Abbot Vitalis of Savigny (J. Armitage Robinson, *Gilbert Crispin*, p. 27, 31). Probably = Mauricius subdiaconus sancti Wulstani Wigorniensis episcopi, who became a monk of Westminster when the Bishop died c. 1095 (Osbert de Clare, *Life of St Edward*, Brit. Mus. Add. MS. 36737 f. 147).

Witnessed a charter of Abbot Herbert [c. 1121–36] (Domesday f. 124).

+ 1121
CLARE, Osbert de.

Prior ? + 1121. Not elected Abbot in succession to Gilbert Crispin [q.v.], apparently on account of Henry I's interference. Sent to Ely (Epp. XII; XIX), either in disgrace or on an official visitation before 1123.

Kept the Feast of the Conception of the Virgin Mary (? at Westminster) in 1127 or 1128 (Ep. VIII).

Was again at Westminster as Prior 1134. Took a prominent part in the foundation of the Nunnery of Kilburn (*Lib. Nig. Quat.* f. 125).

Wrote a Life of St Edward, 1138. Started for Rome 1139 with a commendatory letter to the Pope from King Stephen in order to promote the canonization of St Edward. This was refused for lack of sufficient testimony, with the result that Osbert again fell into disgrace at Westminster and ceased to be Prior. *Flete* (p. 92) says that Abbot Laurence (1158) sent Prior Osbert de Clare to Rome where the canonization of St Edward was granted by Alexander III at Anagni, 7 Feb. 1161; but there is no known authority for using Osbert's name in this connexion. [See J. Armitage Robinson, *Westminster in the Twelfth Century*, Ch. Quart. Rev. Jul. 1909.]

c. 1121
EADWYE.

Prior under Abbot Herbert (Domesday f. 124).

Philip.

Witnessed a charter of Abbot Herbert (Domesday f. 124).

1122
Riculf.
Turstin.
Turkill.
Ægelward.

Mentioned in mortuary roll of Abbot Vitalis of Savigny who died 16 Oct. 1122 (J. Armitage Robinson, *Gilbert Crispin*, p. 27).

c. 1130–4
Godfrey.

Was sent to Rome to inform Innocent II [1130–42] that Gilbert the Universal, Bishop of London [1128–34], had intruded into Westminster Abbey, celebrating Mass on the feast of St Peter and St Paul and claiming jurisdiction (Domesday f. 1 b). ? = Godfrey, the Sacrist, p. 53.

c. 1137
GERVASE.

Natural son of King Stephen.

Amalricus frater Abbatis witnessed a charter about Hendon (Domesday f. 124) and, together with Ralph, another brother, a charter about land in the City (*ibid.* f. 493 b).

Abbas 1137 (?)–1157 (?). His deposition probably took place between Apr. 1157 and Aug. 1158; see J. Armitage Robinson's note in *Flete*, p. 143. Res loci illius [Westminster] juveniliter dissipavit (John of Hexham's Continuation of Simeon of Durham, Rolls Series, II, 329 f.).

In his time the Abbot and Convent assigned 8s. yearly to the Precentor from Roinges [White Roothing], Essex, for the repair of the books in the library (*Manuscripts of Westminster Abbey*, p. 1; *Mun.* 1172 A).

Sepultus in australi parte claustri...ad pedes abbatis Willelmi de Humez (*Flete*, p. 91).

Lobbe, Goderic.

Gave to the Abbey the church of St Agnes [Aldersgate] and its tenures with his body on the day that he became a monk of the Abbey. The gift is referred to by Abbot Gervase in a grant of the same church to St Martin-le-Grand (Domesday f. 477).

Thus Lobbe died in or before 1157.

Capes, W.
Brancun, Roger. } Witnessed a grant of Abbot Gervase to William de
Hairun, Richard de. } Wenduna (*Mun.* L).

Ansgode.

A frequent witness to charters, often with Richard de Bissea [q.v.], in time of Abbot Gervase (*Mun.* 32668; Domesday f. 493 b, &c.).

+1141

Æiric.

Prior de Hurley ante 1141 (*Mun.* 3551).

Lefric.

William of Malmesbury's Miracles of the blessed Virgin Mary (contained in a Brit. Mus. MS.—Cleop. C. x. f. 142—of the late twelfth century) includes a story headed de quodam monacho. It relates that quidam monachus Westmonasteriensis Lefricus nomine fuit qui abbatiam Certesii dum eadem abbatia erat sine abbate multis modis ut eandem abbatiam haberet quesivit. He obtained his wish, but was removed by the King to Holme. Later he returned to Chertsey, was taken suddenly ill, and by the mercy of the blessed Virgin received the Holy Sacrament before his death. This story was told to the compiler of the treatise by Ædric, Prior of Chertsey.

There is no record of any Abbot of Chertsey called Lefric and no trace of any such monk at Westminster. If he existed at all, the middle of the twelfth century would be a possible date.

c. 1148-57

Bissea, Richard de.

Witnessed a notification from Abbot Gervase (c. 1137–57) to R. [Robert de Chesney] Bishop of Lincoln (1148–66) about an appointment to Islip church in that diocese (*Mun.* 15183).

John.

Witnessed *Mun.* 15183, next to Richard de Bissea.

HUGH.

? = Hugo, nouicius monachus (Domesday f. 493 b, where he witnessed a charter of Abbot Gervase next to Richard de Bissea).

Prior.

Abbot of St Edmundsbury 1157 (Dugdale, *Monasticon*, III, 104).

Died 1180 (*ibid.*).

c. 1157

William.

Prior de Hurley c. 1157 (*Mun.* 3750*).

ELIAS, Helias.

Prior (*Flete*, p. 143); witnessed a charter of Abbot Gervase, no date (*Mun.* 17311).

Witnessed a charter (*Mun.* 32670, Domesday f. 316 b) of the whole Convent along with Osbert de Clare during the vacancy caused by the deposition of Abbot Gervase (c. 1157), and before the appointment of Abbot Laurence (1158).

c. 1158

LAURENCE.

His parents had an anniversary at the Abbey on 28 Jan. (*Mun.* 8579). He had a nephew John (Domesday f. 649).

Abbas 1158 (?)–11 Apr. 1173. (For a discussion of the dates given in *Flete*, p. 91 f., see Armitage Robinson's note, p. 143.)

With the consent of the Chapter he granted the church of Sawbridgeworth to the altar of St Peter for the maintenance of a lamp ante corpus Christi; the rents to be paid and payments made by the monk who was Abbot's proctor or factotum, and the payments to include special wine and pittance for the Convent on the day set apart for the anniversary of the Abbot's father and mother, 28 Jan. (*Mun.* 8579). The grant of Alexander III confirming this is dated Anagniae VII Id. Feb. (7 Feb.) [1161]; cf. Domesday ff. 382, 570 b.

Sepultus in australi parte claustri ad pedes Gisleberti abbatis (*Flete*, p. 94). Was commemorated at Durham on 3 Apr. (Liber Vitae, Surt. Soc. p. 142).

ALQUIN, Alequin.

Prior "in the time of Abbot Laurence or between 1159 and 1175" [?1158–73] (Widmore, p. 228).

Was commemorated at Durham on 21 May (Lib. Vit. p. 143).

Wyndesore, Wind', Peter de.

A charter of Abbot Laurence (Domesday f. 368) mentions petrus de Wind' monachus nuper ecclesie nostre as having possessed a house in the City of London, in Piscaria. The longer form of the name is given in the margin.

Roger.

Infirmarius.

Mentioned in a grant of Pope Alexander III about the assignment of the churches of Battersea and Wandsworth to the Infirmary [ad sustentacionem monachorum de Infirmaria iuxta capellam sancte Katerine] in the time of Abbot Laurence (Domesday f. 570 b). The date, Anagniae VII Id. Jul., is the same as that of Alexander III's Bull for the Confessor's canonization in 1161.

c. 1161

Thomas.

Celerarius.

So named in a list of persons indebted to William Cade, a financier of Henry II's time, who is found witnessing documents 1161–8, &c. Thomas owed him £100 in conjunction with William Cape, who may be identical with Brother W. Capes [q.v.] (Eng. Hist. Rev. 1913, p. 227).

Walter.

Sacrista 1161.

This appears from a charter in the Sacrist section of Domesday (f. 382), the grant being made at Anagni 7 Feb. (as above). The title of Sacrist is omitted after his name, but it may be safely assumed.

? = Walter de Rokersbure, who appears in the Durham Liber Vitae, f. 57 p. 94 among the nomina monachorum ad succurrendum, and is there described as monachus Westmonasterii. The script is of the 13th century, but if W. de R. = Walter the Sacrist, he would be contemporary with Abbot Laurence and Alquin [q.v.], the other Westminster names in the Durham list.

+1169
Rocella, John de.
> Prior de Hurley ?—c. 1169 (*Mun.* 2222; where he witnessed the confirmation of a grant of land).

+1170
Seger, William.
> Prior de Hurley c. 1170–3 (*Mun.* 2280, which is a grant from Abbot Laurence [*d.* 1173] to him as Prior and to the Convent of Hurley of the church of Easthampstead, Berks).

+1173
A R U N D E L [Papilon], Ralph de.
> ? = Radulfus monachus, a witness (Domesday f. 293).
> ? = Radulfus camerarius Abbatis who witnessed a grant by Abbot Walter 29 Sep. 1176 (*Mun.* LII).
> ? = Radulfus de Arundel who witnessed an undated charter connected with the Almonry, but is not described either as frater or as monachus (Domesday f. 465 b; cf. f. 324). He was probably Almoner (v. infra).
> Prior de Hurley ? 1173–1200. Gave the priory some lands in Little Waltham to support his anniversary at Hurley (*Mun.* 2229).
> Abbas 30 Nov. 1200—23 Jan. 1214. *Flete*, p. 99, gives 1201, but see J. Armitage Robinson's correction (*ibid.* p. 144). *Mun.* 5788 describes May 1209–May 1210 as the ninth year of his benediction, which is not of much assistance, but inclines in favour of 1200.
> For his letter conferring benefits on Robert Mauduit, King's Chamberlain, in return for benefactions to St Mary's Chapel see Domesday f. 507 b.
> Islip Manor was restored to the Abbot and Convent by King John 1 Nov. 1204 (*Mun.* 15160).
> Was deposed 23 Jan. 1214 (Flor. Hist. II, 147) by Nicholas, Abbot of Waltham, fracto sigillo ipsius in capitulo.
> *Mun.* 4961 implies that provision was made for him in his retirement out of the manors of Sunbury and Teddington.
> Defunctus 12 Aug. 1223; sepultus in navi ecclesiae (*Flete*, p. 100).
> Leland (*Collectanea*, IV, 48, 49) noted among the contents of the Convent library
>> Sermones Radulphi Eleemosynarii Prioris de Hurteley

and added that the book was begun under Abbot Laurence and completed after his death with a dedication to Abbot Walter (cf. M. R. James in *Manuscripts of Westminster Abbey*, p. 23).

1175
WALTER.
> Prior of Winchester.
> Abbas 1175 (Flor. Hist. II, 88); July 1175 (Ralph de Diceto, Rolls Ser. I, 401; 404).

His brother, Alexander, witnessed a writing about knight-service (Domesday f. 293).

His nephew, Walter de Donitona [? Downton, Wilts; cf. Kitchin, *Obedientiary Rolls of Winchester*, p. 13], witnessed a charter of his (Domesday f. 485).

Granted the manor of Pertune [Perton, Staffs] to Hugh de Nunante [Nonant], Bishop of Coventry, for his life for 40s. a year 2 Feb. 1190 (Domesday, f. 468).

Defunctus 27 Sep. 1190 (?1191, *Flete*, p. 96; see Robinson's note, p. 144). For his anniversary, 27 Sep., see Domesday f. 464; *Flete*, p. 96.

RICHARD.
    Prior.
Martin.   } Witnessed deeds in Abbot Walter's time (Domesday f. 293, f. 324).
Alexander.

c. 1189

MOLESHAM, Mulesham, Mullesham, Mulsam, Robert de.
Precentor (*Mun.* 17323; Domesday ff. 509 b; 546; 551 b). *Mun.* 17323 = Domesday f. 552, which is witnessed by Odo the Goldsmith, is a quit-claim of Simon de Gaiola, or Gayola, who can be dated 1197–8 by means of *Mun.* 17080.

Custos altaris b. Marie (*Mun.* 23638 dors.; time of Odo the Goldsmith); procurator altaris (Domesday f. 509 b).

Prior c. 1189–97.

One of his leases was witnessed by Dnus Willelmus Eliensis domini Regis Thesaurarius; i.e. William de Longchamp Bishop of Ely, 1189–97 (*Mun.* 17326; Domesday f. 547 b).

? = R. dictus Prior...mentioned in a charter of Abbot Arundel's time (Domesday f. 602 b; *Flete*, p. 99).

There was an assignment of 100 s. for his anniversary, 9 Dec., of which 20 s. were for a provision of bread for the poor on the Feast of the Conception of the Virgin Mary, that being the vigil of his anniversary (Customary, ii, 92).

+1191

POSTARD, William.
Witnessed, as Prior, a confirmation by Abbot Walter; no date (*Mun.* 2270).

Abbas, 9 Oct. 1191 (cf. Ralph de Diceto, ii, 100; Flor. Hist. ii, 106).

Granted to the Convent his vill of Parham, retaining the advowson of the church there, toto conventu...assistente...et...pro beneficio isto gratias omnimodas...referente (*Mun.* 4064).

Assigned to the Infirmary an annual payment of 21 marks from the churches of Ocham [Oakham] and Hameldone [Hambleton] (Domesday f. 578).

Consented to the erection by the Bishop of Exeter [Henry Marshall] of a chapel on some land bought for the use of the Bishops of Exeter from Geoffrey Picot and situate in Langedich, Westminster, on the Abbey's estate; the consent was given on condition that there be no prejudice thereby to the rights of the Abbey or of St Margaret's chapel [1194–8] (*Mun.* 17312).

Defunctus [? 4 Mai] 1200 (Flor. Hist. ii, 122; *Flete*, p. 98, gives 1201).

Sepultus in australi parte claustri ante cymbalum (*ibid.* and Robinson's note, pp. 22–4).

For his anniversary see *Flete*, p. 98; Domesday f. 578. The latter, which only gives "William, Abbot," in its text, has a note interpreting this as

Postard but then correcting the interpretation to Humez. If the identification with Postard is correct, he had a brother Arnulf and a nephew Nicholas.

c. 1·191

Philip. }
Adam.   }   Capellani et monachi nostri.   (So named in a charter of Abbot
Gilbert. }   William [Postard]; Domesday f. 650.)

+ 1193

Geoffrey.

Gaufridus Camerarius witnessed a grant of an annual rent from the churches of Oakham and Hambleton to the Pittancer of the Convent, c. 1193—1205 (Domesday f. 649 a, b).

1199

James.

James the Cellarer was attorney for Abbot Postard in a suit about the church of Parham in Sussex, 1 Nov. 1199 (*Mun.* 4036; Domesday f. 578. The date is preserved in the latter). He is not called Frater in the document but he probably was one.

+1200

Robert.

Prior de Hurley c. 1200–1 (cf. F. T. Wethered, *Last Days of Hurley Priory*, p. 11).

1214

H U M E Z , de Humeto, William.

Monk of Caen and Prior of Frampton, Dorset, a cell of St Stephen, Caen.
His brother Alexander (Domesday f. 470 b).

Abbot, 4 May 1214 (Flor. Hist. II, 147). He is mentioned in a charter which was certified at New Sarum 15 May 1214 (Domesday f. 473 b).

Was blessed by William de St Marychurch, Bishop of London, 25 May, 1214 (Flor. Hist. II, 148).

For his assignments for his anniversary, for observing the translation of St Edmund [9 Jun.], and other purposes, see *Mun.* 32354; Domesday f. 120 b.

Made an agreement with Hugh [de Northwold] Abbot of St Edmundsbury for a confederation of the two Convents (*Mun.* 17315*).

Made a composition with the Prior and Convent of Greater Malvern securing his right to approve their choice of a Prior, to visit their house yearly with not more than 20 horses in his train, to receive at Westminster the professions of their monks, and to have the use on certain conditions of his hospice at Powick Manor [1216-18] (*Mun.* 32628; Domesday f. 574).

Issued a grant of full spiritual benefits from the Abbey and its cells to all who contributed to the cost of the new Lady Chapel—noui operis apud Westm. in honorem matris virginis inchoati—c. 1220 (Domesday f. 507 b).

For the award in the dispute between the Bishop of London [Eustace de Fauconberg] and the Dean and Chapter of St Paul's of the one part and our Abbot and Convent of the other part, 1222, see *Mun.* 12753 and cf. Widmore, p. 37.

Defunctus 20 Apr. 1222 (*Flete*, p. 102).

Sepultus in australi parte claustri...ad caput abbatis Gervasii (*ibid.*; and cf. Robinson's note, p. 23).

+1219

BERKING, Berkyng, Richard de.

His mother's name was Lucy, and her anniversary was on 25 Feb. (Domesday f. 375–6).

Prior + Jun. 1219 (Domesday f. 615 b).

Abbas (electus post 20 Apr.) 1222—23 Nov. 1246.

Honorius III issued a mandate 7 Jul. 1222 to the Abbot of St Albans and the Abbot of Waltham to examine his election and confirm it if canonical (Kal. Pap. Reg. I, 88).

Received benediction from Peter des Roches, Bishop of Winchester, 18 Sep. 1222 (Flor. Hist. II, 176).

Consiliarius specialis Henrici III; baro scaccarii principalis; Angliae thesaurarius (*Flete*, p. 103).

Received from Gregory IX a faculty to give the first tonsure on solemn festivals 10 Dec. 1228 (Kal. Pap. Reg. I, 121) and an indult to give episcopal benediction at masses, vespers, and matins 23 May 1246 (*ibid.* 225).

Had a dispute with the Convent about the application of the rents of certain manors,—a settlement being brought about by the Bishops of Wells, Salisbury and Chichester, and confirmed by Gregory IX 7 Jul. 1227 (*Mun.* 5683***).

Came to an arrangement with Roger Niger, Bishop of London, as to jurisdiction, visitation, procurations, &c., in the matter of the Nuns of Kilburn Priory; dated in capella apud Fuleham 21 Jul. 1231 (*Mun.* 4843; LIV).

Received a royal grant entitling the Convent to have eight stags yearly against the feast of St Peter ad Vincula from the herd in Windsor Forest 16 Jul. 1235 (*Mun.* 1517).

Abbot Richard, who granted an indulgence to all who would contribute to the repair of the cell of St Bartholomew, Sudbury,—in favillam et cinerem redacte,—(*Mun.* 20768) was probably de Berking (cf. its phrase minister humilis with the same as used by him, Domesday f. 375 b).

Defunctus 23 Nov. 1246 (Flor. Hist. II, 314); sepultus ante medium altaris in capella beatissimae Mariae virginis in tumba marmorea decenter ornata (*Flete*, p. 106).

For his anniversary see Domesday f. 376; *Flete*, p. 107; and for his assignment of land outside Estgrave Wood [Kensington] for the illumination of St Mary's Chapel see *Mun.* 4868; Domesday f. 566 b.

In ii candelabris factis de nouo ad pedes Abbatis de B. vi^d. 1298–9 (St Mary's Chapel).

Et pro i petra marmorea pro tumba Abbatis R. de B. c^s. 1397–8 (*ibid.*).

+1221

Stanford, William de.

Prior de Hurley c. 1221 (*Mun.* 474; 2185).

+1231

Le Gras, Richard.

Son of William le Gras (v. infra).

Richard [de Berking], Abbot, and the Convent granted him an anniversary on 28 Feb. for the souls of his father William and other relations. Out of lands acquired for the purpose at Stevenage, Herts, &c., he made provision for a refection of wine and a pittance to be provided on the day, which after his decease was to be changed to that of his death (*Mun.* 5399*).

Prior of Hurley Sep. 1231 (*Mun.* 20619; Domesday f. 595 f.)—27 Feb. 1236 (*Mun.* 2028).

Abbot of Evesham 1236. Died in Gascony 8 Dec. 1242 (Dugdale, *Monasticon*, II, 6).

1234

William.

Proctor of Abbot Berking in a suit against William Mauduit, Trinity term, 1234 (Domesday f. 91 b).

? = Willelmus Infirmarius [v. William, p. 53], mentioned in an exchange of land belonging to the Infirmary (Domesday f. 571 b).

1235

Ayswelle, Theobald de.

Proctor for Abbot Berking in a suit at Chelmsford 3 Feb. 1235 (Domesday f. 617).

Prior of Hurley ?.1247 (F. T. Wethered, *Last Days of Hurley Priory*, p. 11). Still Prior 1 May 1255 (*Mun.* 7605).

+1239

Sancto Albano, Hugh de.

Celerarius. Went to Rome on 'the business of the church of Essewille [Ashwell] (Customary, II, 72–3).

Cf. Kal. Pap. Reg. I, 181, 17 Ap. 1239, which shows that the Bishop of Lincoln had refused to induct the Abbot and Convent to the church of Aiswelle [Ashwell] and had excommunicated them. They appealed to the Pope through Hugh, Richard de Crokesley, and others, and were successful.

Hermodesworthe, Reginald de.

Celerarius forinsecus (Customary, II, 72–3).

Maleth, John de.

Went to the Roman Court on the business of the church at Essewille [Ashwell] (Customary, II, 72–3).

C R O K E S L E Y, Crokele, Crockele, Richard de.

(Magister; Flor. Hist. II, 320.)

Went to the Roman Court c. 1239 on the business of the church at Essewille [Ashwell] (Customary, II, 72–3).

Went to Gascony 1246 (? 1242) with Brother Normannus to carry the Virgin's girdle to Henry III and his Queen (*ibid.* xviii; 73).

Archidiaconus ?—1246.

Abbas [? 16] Dec. 1246; eodem die quo...sanctus Edmundus canonizatus est (Flor. Hist. II, 320; *Flete*, 108, 144).

Was sent to Germany by Henry III 1247 (Flor. Hist. II, 335).

Sopita est discordia quae fuerat inter Abbatem Westm. et eius conventum rege procurante 1252 (*ibid.* 379). The quarrel was concerned with a composition made with the Prior and Convent by Abbot Berking and was settled through the withdrawal of three articles, 16 Aug. 1252 (*Mun.* 5956).

Faculty issued to him, as Papal Chaplain, and to his successors by Alexander IV to grant dispensations from the observance of the Benedictine statutes, except where dispensation is forbidden by the rule, 22 Apr. 1255 (Kal. Pap. Reg. I, 316).

His anniversary ordained c. 11 Jun. 1256 (*Mun.* 5405, 5400; Domesday f. 115 b).

Defunctus 17 Jul. 1258 apud Wyntoniam; sepultus in capella sancti Edmundi quam ipse construxerat. [This was afterwards pulled down and Crokesley's body was removed to the Chapel of St Nicholas.] (*Flete*, p. 110.)

+1240

Glovernia, Glouernia, Gloucestre, Ralph de.

Custos fabrice capelle b. Marie 28 Oct. 1240 (Domesday ff. 559 b, 560).

Procurator noui operis et custos altaris gloriose Virginis Marie (*Mun.* 17396). There are some fifteen deeds relating to the property of the Chapel in his time; only one bears a date, Oct. 1246—Oct. 1247 (*Mun.* 17155 B); so he may have served under Abbot Berking and Abbot Crokesley.

Had two hanging lamps burning day and night in the Chapel, which were removed by order of Henry III, who substituted one large wax candle (Customary, II, 92).

Ordinance of Abbot Richard [? Berking; ? Crokesley] as to the uses to which R. de G. was to put a rent acquired for the Chapel (*Mun.* 17335).

+1242

Lyra, Lyre, John de.

Celerarius 1246 (? 1242) (Customary, II, 73).

Elemosinarius (*Mun.* 1862); et hostilarius (Domesday f. 466).

Prior de Hurley c. 13 Oct. 1267 (Domesday f. 315); c. 27 Mai. 1274 (*Mun.* 2180).

Suttone, Geoffrey de.

Celerarius exterior, 1246 [? 1242] (Customary, II, xviii, 73).

Perhaps = Galfridus monachus, who was Proctor for Abbot Crokesley in a suit about estates at Thorpe, Rutland, 12 Nov. 1253 (Domesday f. 600 b).

Prior de Hurley 1258 (F. T. Wethered, *op. cit.* p. 11).

Resigned before 13 Oct. 1267, corporis valetudine pressus et senio fessus (Domesday f. 315).

Normannus.

Went with Richard de Crokesley to Henry III and his Queen then in Gascony, taking the Virgin's girdle, 1246 [? 1242] (Customary, II, xviii, 73).

1245

LEWESHAM, Philip de.

Appeared in the King's Court at Westminster before the justices, Easter term, 1245, as agent for Abbot Richard [de Berking] (*Mun.* 16743).

Prior ? + 11 Jun. 1253—Aug. 1258.

There is a royal grant by Henry III to Philip, Prior of Westminster, and his successors, that his chamber called Longa Camera shall not be seized for the King's use nor given up to any one upon any kingly visit, except with the Prior's consent; dated Windsor, 11 Jun. 1253 (*Mun.* 1568). In Customary, II, 133, there is a reference to Prior Philip having made a window in the kitchen ob causam scaccarii longae camerae clarificandae in suos usus sumptu regio renovatae; which may allude to the same Long Chamber and the same royal grant.

Abbas Aug.—Oct. 1258 (*Flete*, p. 144. Robinson prefers the account of Matthew Paris, who says that Lewesham died at home, to that of Flete, p. 113, who says that his death was caused by the journey to Rome for confirmation).

The Convent borrowed from Florentine merchants a sum of 600 marks in order to procure Philip's election to the Abbacy on the death of Richard de Crokesley, 1258. But Philip died, munere benedictionis nondum optento. Therefore Richard de Ware, the incoming Abbot, raised the question whether the loan was repayable; and after mediation this was settled in the affirmative Nov. 1259 (*Mun.* 12802).

Of this sum 300 marks were due to the Papal Camera and 300 to the Cardinals; there were also 60 marks due to various creditors. In Feb. 1262 the Pope annulled the bond to the Camera (Kal. Pap. Reg. I, 376).

+ 1246

PETER.

Elemosinarius (before John de Lyra; Domesday f. 466, 467 b).
Prior under Richard de Crokesley (*Flete*, p. 109; Flor. Hist. II, 321).
Defunctus c. 1246; sepultus in capella hospitum (*ibid.*).

MAURICE.

Precentor ?—c. 1246.
Prior c. 1246. (*Flete*, p. 109, quoting from Flor. Hist. II, 321, calls him virum approbatum and says that he was made Prior by Richard de Crokesley soon after his election as Abbot.)

Bedeford, William de.

Sacrista 1247 (Domesday f. 354 b; also f. 351 a, b).

Juhele.

Senescallus Abbatis.
(Witnessed a quit-claim, shortly after Ralph de Glovernia ceased to be Warden and Proctor of St Mary's Chapel [1247 +]; Domesday f. 552.)

+ 1257

Tailard, William.

Sacrista (Domesday f. 373 b—a lease containing the name of Abbot Richard, either de Crokesley or de Ware). In Kal. Pap. Reg. I, 345 there is an indult to William Gailard (*sic*), monk of Westminster (who had already been dispensed on the ground of illegitimacy), to enable him to be promoted to the offices and dignities of his Order, 13 Jun. 1257. His appointment as Sacrist would follow, and, as Abbot Crokesley lived till 17 Jul. 1258, there was time for it to happen in his life.

W A R E , Wara, Richard de.

Acted as Proctor to Abbot Crokesley Jun. 1257 (*Mun.* 1202).
Abbas per viam compromissi electus (*Flete*, p. 113) Dec. 1258—8 Dec. 1283.
Appointed a Papal Chaplain 11 Mar. 1259 and permitted to borrow 1000 marks for promoting the business of the Convent in Rome 13 Mar. 1259 (Kal. Pap. Reg. I, 364).
Borrowed 1000 marks from Florentine merchants 20 Mar. 1259 (*Mun.* 12800). Also incurred responsibility for 600 marks borrowed in order to secure the election of Philip de Lewesham as Abbot 1 Nov. 1259 (*Mun.* 12802). This led to a long suit with Carlinus Guiberti of Florence (*Mun.* 12806; 12826, &c.), in the course of which the Abbot was sentenced to be suspended from celebrating divine service, 23 Nov. 1266 (*Mun.* 12835). On 11 Sep. 1282 the merchants stated their demand as (i) the repayment of the 1000 marks, (ii) damages for non-payment at the rate of 1 mark for each 10 marks for each period of two months (*Mun.* 12854). Ware died before the suit ended.

Was engaged in clearing Tiddesley Park, his peculiar near Pershore, from many rights of commonage acquired by residents in Birlingham and elsewhere; no dates (*Mun.* 22450–22511).

For the part taken by Ware in the compilation of the Customary, 1266, see Sir E. M. Thompson's ed. (Hen. Brad. Soc.) 1904, II, p. vii—ix. The only known reference to it in the Muniments is Domesday ff. 639–40, dated 1307–8.

Gold, precious stones, and jewels belonging to the Confessor's Shrine and other valuables of the Abbey were handed to Henry III for his pressing needs, the King pledging himself to restore them within 16 months; 1 Jun. 1267 (*Mun.* 9464). They were all restored to the Abbot and Convent 10 Feb. 1269 (*Mun.* 9465).

For his expenses in a progress through the manors Nov.—Dec. 1275 see *Mun.* 24489.

The claim of the Bishop of Worcester [Godfrey Giffard] to exercise visitatorial rights over the Priory of Greater Malvern was successfully resisted, 1282—5 Nov. 1283 (*Mun.* 32633–43).

Was sent by Edward I, along with Edmund, Earl of Cornwall, and another to Northampton to attend a Provincial Assembly of the Clergy 26 Jan. 1283 (Wilkins *Conc.* II, 92; J. Armitage Robinson, Ch. Quart. Rev. Oct. 1915). The royal letter called him Abbas Westmonast. thesaurarius noster.

Charters of his anniversary 14 Dec. 1265 (Domesday f. 592); 29 Dec. 1271 (Domesday f. 591 b; *Flete*, p. 115 f.).

Defunctus 8 Dec. 1283; sepultus...ante magnum altare in plano pavimento porphyritico ex parte boreali (*Flete*, p. 115. Cf. W. R. Lethaby, *Westminster Abbey and the Kings' Craftsmen*, p. 348).

c. 1258–83

ELIAS, Elyas.

Prior during the reign of Abbot Ware.

There are some 26 documents during this period which mention the Prior as party to transactions. Only one (*Mun.* 16753) gives the name, Elias, and this is undated; see also Domesday f. 614 b.

Fundur, Foundour, Fundour, John le.

An anniversary, with two copes and a special pittance, was endowed for him by Thomas de Stratford, le Brazur (dictus le Brewere) in Abbot Ware's time. Both Thomas and he were alive at the time of the endowment, which is not dated (*Mun.* 1075, 1076).

Was a frequent witness of documents with Odo the Goldsmith.

Witnessed the resuscitation of a drowned child, along with Bacinus [q.v.].

Hen. III

Henry.

Was sent to Caerleon (Kaerlion) with a relic for the healing of Maud de Clare, Countess of Gloucester and Hertford. *Mun.* 9323 is a letter dated 8 July, in which the countess apologizes to the Prior and Convent for retaining their brother Dan Henri so long in her train. The wife of Richard de Clare, 8th Earl of Clare, 7th Earl of Gloucester, and 6th Earl of Hertford (d. 1262), was called Maud.

Stanes, Gregory de.

Known only through grants of rents from Aldenham, Herts, to support his anniversary; no dates (*Mun.* 4470, &c.; Domesday f. 460).

The monk called Gregory who was Proctor for the Abbot and Convent in a money transaction with H. Abbot of St Geneviève, Paris, 1231, 1234

(*Mun.* 12796, 12797) may have been either Gregory de Stanes or Gregory de Tayleboys or neither.

Colecestr', Colecestria, Henry de.
>Procurator operis b. Marie (Domesday f. 509).
>Supprior (*ibid.* f. 510 b).
>Mentioned in a charter about property in St James's Street, time of Odo and Edward the Goldsmiths (*ibid.* f. 530 b).

London, Stephen de.
>Procurator altaris b. Marie.
>Mentioned in a deed of gift to St Mary's Chapel, time of Odo the Goldsmith (*Mun.* 17442; Domesday f. 532 b).

Hurley, Hurleya, Walter de.
>Procurator altaris b. Marie.
>Mentioned in a deed of gift to St Mary's Chapel, time of Odo the Goldsmith (*Mun.* 17442; Domesday f. 532 b).

Tayleboys, Taillebois, Gregory de.
>His anniversary endowed (Domesday ff. 460 b, 461); time of Odo the Goldsmith.
>Nuper Elemosinarius (*ibid.*).

Tayleboys, Taileboys, Robert.
>Grant of rents from Aldenham, Herts, to support his anniversary; no date (*Mun.* 4506); grant of a rent charge in Westminster for same purpose; no date; time of Odo the Goldsmith (Domesday f. 460 a, b). The grantor, Ralph de Bosco, is the same as in the case of Gregory de Stanes [q.v.]. R. T. was then dead.

William.
>Infirmarius.
>Mentioned in an exchange of land belonging to the Infirmary; no date (Domesday f. 571 b). See William, 1234 (p. 49).
>? is he to be identified with William, monk of Westminster, Henry III's "beloved painter" c. 1240–80 ? (cf. Lethaby, p. 259).

Godfrey.
>Sacrista.
>Concerned as such in a grant of land witnessed by Odo the Goldsmith (Domesday f. 357).

Bureford, Walter de.
>Camerarius.
>Mentioned as such in a grant of rent ad usus vesture monachorum (Domesday f. 493; no date; Odo the Goldsmith, a witness).

Tyteburste, Simon de.
>Concerned in the payment of a rent in Langedich, Westminster, in the time of Abbot Richard [? Berking, ? Crokesley] (*Mun.* 17339; Domesday f. 459).

Wautone, Ralph de.
>Custos altaris b. Marie (he let a tenement in Tothill Street in the time of Abbot Richard [? Berking, ? Crokesley]; Domesday ff. 523, 527).

Bacinus.
>Elemosinarius.
>Mentioned with the two following, and also with John le Fundur, William de Pharindon and William de Hasele [q.v.], as witnesses of the record of the drowning and resuscitating of a boy in the time of Henry III; described as tunc elemosinarius Westmon. Bodleian; Ashmole MS. 842, f. 80 b.

Cademan, Gilbert }. Witnesses with Bacinus (supra).
Hampton, William de

Baunc, Walter de.
Custos capelle b. Marie (Domesday f. 525).

Innocentibus, Robert de.
Concerned in a grant of land at Charing to St Mary's altar, being then Hostillar—tunc hospitarius (Domesday f. 538 b).

Sancta Katerina, Simon de.
Infirmarius.
Sole mention in a quit-claim made ·to the Infirmarer for the burning of a candle before the image of St Katharine in the Infirmary chapel; no date; witnesses of the time of Hen. III (Domesday f. 582). As Simon paid the consideration for the quit-claim, it may be assumed that he was then Infirmarer.

+1260

Marleberge, Thomas de.
Archidiaconus 2 Apr. 1260 (*Mun.* 12805).

1260

London, Walter de.
Mentioned in an acquittance (*Mun.* 12805) as Capellanus Abbatis [R. de Ware] 2 Apr. 1260.
Ballivus 9 Jun. 1271 (*Mun.* 4479).
Prior de Hurley ? + 3 Sep. 1279 (*Mun.* 2124)—4 Jun. 1285 ? + (*Mun.* 2327).
Probably identical with W. de L. who appears in the Infirmarer's roll 1297–8, and was in the sick-room for a short time May 1306 (Infirmarer).

Sutton, Suthone, John de.
Abbot Ware's Proctor in a suit 11 Ap. 1260 (*Mun.* 12806; Domesday f. 591); c. 14 Apr. 1266 (*Mun.* 12832, where he is called John the Sacrist).
Ballivus ?1260 (*Mun.* 12807); c. 15 Oct. 1269 (*Mun.* 28792).
Proctor with Richard de Waltham in a loan to the Abbot from Dando Aldebrandi the Sienese, c. 6 Dec. 1271 (*Mun.* 12841).
Camerarius 1277; 1278 (*Mun.* 5869; 5779).
Sacrista Mar. 1266 (*Mun.* 12832; Domesday f. 593); 1282–7 (*Mun.* 28803; 28822).
Witnessed the formal handing over of Abbot Ware's jewels to Abbot Wenlok c. 24 Aug. 1284 (*Mun.* 9467).
Was publicly excommunicated by Archbishop Peckham in the course of his dispute with the Abbot and Convent about visitatorial rights over the priory of Greater Malvern, a cell of Westminster, 1285–9 (*Mun.* 22929–42). Honorius IV "contradicted" the excommunication; and the Papal document, being ignored by the Archbishop, was formally laid upon his Grace's arm 15 Feb. 1287 (*Mun.* 22930).
Tenens locum Abbatis ipso Abbate [Wenlok] in partibus transmarinis existente, c. 26 Mai 1286 (Domesday f. 500).
Last mention 19 Oct. 1289 (*Mun.* 22932).
In a list of benefactors to the chapels of the Abbey church it is stated: Frater J. S. fieri fecit picturam Dedicacionis ecelesie Westm. cum censuris scriptis ad Altare sancti Pauli Et similiter picturam ad tabulam regis sancti Seberti. There is no other John Sutton among our monks and his inclusion in this roll of benefactors is open to the suspicion arising from his date being

much earlier than those of the rest (*Lib. Nig. Quat.* f. 92 b). But his name may have been still legible on his gifts when the list was made.

1261

Micheham, Micham, Walter de.
Along with Robert de Warton [q.v.], received from Florentine merchants an acquittance for 200 marks, out of 760 marks borrowed by Abbot Ware, c. 24 Feb. 1261 (*Mun.* 12811); along with Walter de London [q.v.], for a further sum of 200 marks, 1 Mar. 1262 (*Mun.* 12814).

Warton, Robert de.
See **Micheham, Walter de.**

Wratting, Wrattingge, Wrottinge, Wrottyng, Jordan de.
Born c. 1238; professed c. 1261 (*Mun.* 9497).
Camerarius Mar. 1296 (*Mun.* 28998).
Granator 1297–8; 24 Feb. 1303—24 Jun. 1304 (Treasurer).
Liberat' fratri Jordano pro denariis acquietandis xxiiii^{li} 1301–2 (Q. Alianore, *Mun.* 23631 c).
Thesaurarius 15 Nov. 1301 (*Mun.* 29100); 24 Mai. 1302 (*Mun.* 29115); 24 Feb. 1303—24 Jun. 1305 (Treasurer).
Pitanciarius 19 Mai. 1301 (*Mun.* 29081).
Imprisoned in the Tower c. 10 Oct. 1303.
Supprior 1304 (Domesday f. 417 b).
Auditor compoti Maneriorum Regine Alianore 30 Nov. 1304 (Domesday f. 417 b); custos, 31 Dec. 1305; 8 Apr. 1306 (*Mun.* 29189; 29193). A marginal note, Domesday f. 421, says that a charter there copied was still in his keeping.
Diem clausit extremum 27 Feb. 1323 (Infirmarer; he had apparently been bedridden since Mich^s 1320).

c. 1263

HUNTYNDON, Huntyngdon, Huntedone, Hontyndon, William de.
Born c. 1240; professed c. 1263 (*Mun.* 5024; 5022).
? Archidiaconus 1292 (so Widmore, p. 229; Walter de Huntyndon [q.v.] was Archdeacon, Easter 1290).
Prior ? 1298 (Widmore, p. 228); per viam compromissi canonice electus (*Mun.* 9508; no date).
The Prior and Convent were appointed collectors in the Archdeaconries of London and Middlesex of the tenth imposed by Boniface VIII towards the relief of the Roman Church (*Mun.* 5821, &c.). About 70 documents relate to this collection; none of them gives the Prior's full name; a few give W. Prior, and of these the earliest is *Mun.* 29102, 30 Nov. 1301.
Imprisoned in the Tower 10 Oct. 1303; the official list (Rymer, *Foedera*) neither calls him Prior nor gives him precedence.
His name and office occur in *Mun.* 5024, where his age is stated together with his evidence about Abbey tithes at Lower Halliford, Middlesex, 1303.
There is reference to his death in *Mun.* 9508 which is not dated.
Alive 23 Feb. 1305 (*Mun.* 5816; cf. Flor. Hist. III, 129).

Waltham, Richard de.
Born c. 1240; professed c. 1263 (*Mun.* 9497; 5024).
Abbot Ware's Proctor for the repayment of a debt c. 6 Dec. 1271 (*Mun.* 12841); generally associated with John de Sutton [q.v.] in Abbot Ware's business.

An elector of Abbot Wenlok 1283 (Kal. Pap. Reg. I, 472).

In charge of manor of Oakham before 1297 (*Mun.* 23630).

Imprisoned in the Tower c. 10 Oct. 1303.

Gave evidence about Abbey tithes at Lower Halliford, Middlesex, 1303 (*Mun.* 5024).

Auditor compoti Maner^m Regine Alianore 30 Nov. 1304 (Domesday f. 417 b).

The Treasurer 1304–5 paid him £10 on account of 40 marks due to him for tithes of Battersea Church sold to him ad opus conventus.

Protested against the deprivation of Prior Hadham 4 Sep. 1307 (*Mun.* 9499 B).

Was in the sick-room from Mar. 1309 till 5 Nov. 1311, when payment of his pittance ceased as if he were dead (Infirmarer).

c. 1266

SANCTO PAULO, John de.

Custos altaris b. Marie.

Gave one of the principal albs to St Mary's Chapel (*Mun.* 23180).

Prior (*ibid.*).

Secured funds for providing graves for deceased Brethren,—xxii s. yearly (Customary, II, 93).

Haseley, Hasele, William de.

Supprior ?—?

Witnessed during Hen. III's reign the resuscitation of a drowned child, along with Bacinus the Almoner [q.v.].

Hugo de Balsham, Bishop of Ely, issued an indulgence for prayers in the Abbey church ad tumulum fratris W. de Hasele quondam supprioris eiusdem monasterii; apud Wyuelingham [Willingham] 3 May 1283 (*Mun.* 6680; cf. *Flete*, p. 75).

Completed Abbot Ware's Customary (*Flete*, p. 114, quoting from Richard Sporley [q.v.]: et felicis memorie frater Willelmus Haseley in hoc opere laborans ad finem debitum perduxit anno 1266).

In the library of St John's College, Oxford, there is a late 13th century MS. of Bonaventura, sermons, &c., ex procuratione fratris Will. de Hasele (cf. *Manuscripts of Westminster Abbey*, p. 25).

Pharindon, Perendon, Peryndon, Perndona, Peredone, William de.

Precentor c. Domin. in Ramis Palmarum 1266 (Domesday f. 593).

Witnessed during Hen. III's reign the resuscitation of a drowned child, along with Bacinus, the Almoner [q.v.].

Pitanciarius 7 Dec. 1278 (*Mun.* 5779).

Infirmarius 1286 (Domesday f. 500).

In the sick-room all 1297–8 (Infirmarer).

Fanelore, Richard de.

Was about 57 years of age and had been 37 years a monk 1303 (*Mun.* 5024); so was born c. 1246 and professed c. 1266.

Elemosinarius ante 1293 (*Mun.* 18962*).

Statement of the rents of the Convent manors in tempore fratris R. de F. 1293–4 (*Mun.* 6190).

Probably Convent Treasurer 1293–5 ? + (*Mun.* 28947; 28964; 28982).

Infirmarius 1297–8.

Thesaurarius Abbatis Jun. 1296 (*Mun.* 29006); Nov. 1297—Mai. 1298 (*Mun.* 24255).

Imprisoned in the Tower c. 10 Oct. 1303.

Gave evidence about Abbey tithes at Lower Halliford, Middlesex 1303, he having been formerly for two years warden of the manor (*Mun.* 5024).

Auditor compoti Maner^m Regine Alianore 30 Nov. 1304 (Domesday f. 417 b).

An elector of Abbot Kedyngton 26 Jan. 1308 (*Mun.* 5424, where he is called Fanerole).

Was in the sick-room 24 Jul. 1309—Palm Sunday 1311 (Infirmarer).

Rauel, Rauel', Reuel, Gilbert.

Sacrista c. 13 Dec. 1267 (*Mun.* 14270; Domesday f. 589 b).

Sub-custos capelle b. Marie 30 Nov. 1298—30 Sep. 1299; socius custos 1299–1300 (St Mary's Chapel).

Was in the sick-room from Palm Sunday to 3rd Sunday after Easter 1298 (Infirmarer).

Not included in the list of those imprisoned in the Tower Oct. 1303.

Stanes, Reginald de.

Pitanciarius 1267 (Domesday f. 503).

Sancto Bartolomeo, Peter de.

Witnessed a deed c. 13 Dec. 1267 (*Mun.* 14270 ; Domesday f. 589 b).

1270

Waleden, Walenden, Roger de.

Roger the Refectorer witnessed a deed, 25 Dec. 1270 (Domesday f. 457). Refectorarius 1278 (*Mun.* 5779).

Pitanciarius; custos ecclesie de Ocham [Oakham] c. 15 Aug. 1286 (*Mun.* 20624).

Intravit cameram 18 Nov. 1297 (Infirmarer; he was still there 29 Sep. 1298 ; medicine ii s. iiii d.). No further mention.

+1272

Sutton, Suttone, Sotton, Philip de.

Held a court at Harpenden c. 8 Dec. 1272 (*Mun.* 8937).

Celerarius 19 Apr. 1281—29 Sep. 1282; 1284-5.

Imprisoned in the Tower c. 10 Oct. 1303.

Infirmarius 1305-6.

Thesaurarius 25 Nov. 1307—29 Sep. 1308; 29 Sep. 1310—4 Apr. 1311.

Ballivus 1307 (*Mun.* 29234); 1312 (*Mun.* 29334); 1318 (*Mun.* 29383); 1319 (*Mun.* 29401).

Was appointed, with Abbot Curtlington's leave, to be seneschal to Walter de Istelepe, clerk, 8 Apr. 1322 (*Mun.* 6005).

Senior monk, next to Prior, 1328-9 (Chamberlain) ; no further mention.

c. 1272

{Sancto Martino, Robert de.
{Marttin, Martyn.

Fifty years of age and 35 years in the Order 22 Aug. 1307 (*Mun.* 9497); so was born c. 1257 and professed c. 1272.

Not included in the list of those imprisoned in the Tower Oct. 1303.

Protested against Prior Hadham's deprivation 4 Sep. 1307 (*Mun.* 9499 B).

Defunctus 17 Jun.—29 Sep. 1317 (Almoner).

1275

Triffeld (? Driffield), J. de.

Sole mention as receiving a payment in the business of Abbot Ware's manors 1275 (*Mun.* 24489).

Labanke, W.

Engaged on Abbot Ware's business at Bourton, Glouc., 1275 (*Mun.* 24489).

Wodeham, John de.

Abbot Ware's Proctor in a protest against the exaction of certain tenths in the City of London; in die veneris proxima ante dominicam qua cantatur quasi modo geniti [i.e. the introit for First Sunday after Easter] 19 Apr. 1275 (*Mun.* 5842).

Concerned, along with Alexander de Persore [q.v.], in obtaining a loan for Abbot Wenlok 1284 (*Mun.* 28801).

Proctor for the Abbot and Convent at the Roman Court, Aug. 1285 (*Mun.* 22942); 1290 (*Mun.* 22942*).

London, Simon de.

Proctor for Abbot Ware in the matter of an exchange of land in Westminster Nov. 1275 (Domesday f. 381 b).

Wycumbe, Wicumbia, Adam de.

Abbot's Proctor in protests against exaction of tenths for the Holy Land, 29 Jun. 1275 (*Mun.* 5868).

Precentor 25 Mai. 1277 (*Mun.* 5869).

Archidiaconus 21 Mar. 1278 (*Mun.* 6684); 7 Dec. 1278 (*Mun.* 5779); c. 26 Mai. 1286 (Domesday f. 500); c. 21 Sep. 1288 (*Mun.* 28832).

Excepted from the absolution from excommunication pronounced in favour of the Prior and other Brethren in the matter of W. de Pershore, the apostate Franciscan friar, 11 Jul. 1291 (*Mun.* 6391).

Died after Michaelmas 1293 (*Mun.* 18962*).

London, Henry de.

Camerarius Oct. 1275 (*Mun.* 5835).   Alive 1284 (*Mun.* 25583).

c. 1276-7

Bures, Robert de.

In 1307 was over 50 years of age and had been 31 years in the Order (*Mun.* 9497); thus became a monk c. 1276-7, having been born before 1257.

Made payments for W. de Wenlok, Abbot-elect, on the way through Kent, when starting for Rome for confirmation, 6 Feb. 1284 (*Mun.* 9241).

Received absolution in the matter of the apostate Franciscan Friar, W. de Pershore, 11 Jul. 1291 (*Mun.* 6391).

In expensis fratris Roberti de Bures pro se et equo suo per duas vices de Lalham et Piriford usque Westm. vii d. 1291-2 (Abbot's Steward).

Custos capelle b. Marie 30 Nov. 1298—30 Sep. 1301.

In expensis custodis missi ad Regem pro negotiis ecclesie xxii d.   In expensis eiusdem spaciantis apud Padinton cum sociis propter infirmitatem suam ii s. 1299-1300 (St Mary's Chapel).

Imprisoned in the Tower c. 13 Oct. 1303.

Item solut' fratri R. de B. pro ii peliubus acquietandis impignoratis in Ciuitate Lond. per fratrem Rogerum de Bures ante incarceracionem suam pro expensis factis in visitacione Archiepiscopi 1304-5 (Treasurer).

Was one of Prior Hadham's witnesses against Abbot Wenlok 22 Aug. 1307 (*Mun.* 9497).

1278

COLEWORTH, Coleworthe, Culeworth, Coleword, John de.
Sacrista 7 Dec. 1278 (*Mun.* 5779).
Prior ? + 31 Dec. 1283 (Domesday f. 638)–1295 (*Mun.* 9499 A dors.).
He was Prior at time of Richard de Ware's death and Walter de Wenlok's election.
Mentioned in the formal absolution of the Convent from Archbishop Peckham's excommunication in the matter of William de Pershore, the apostate Franciscan friar, 11 Jul. 1291 (*Mun.* 6391).
A messuage in Eye, Westminster, assigned to his anniversary (Domesday 327 b, 328).

Hanyngton, Hanynton, Haninton, Haniton, William de.
Proctor in a claim for absolution from excommunication for non-payment of Papal tenths 7 Dec. 1278 (*Mun.* 5779).
Bond for a loan lent by him 3 Jun. 1284 (*Mun.* 28044).
Supprior 2 Feb. 1286 (*Mun.* 23628, which contains his statement of receipts from Q. Alianore's manors); c. 26 Mai. 1286 (Domesday f. 500).
Abbot Wenlok made him one of his substitutes as Queen's Treasurer along with the Prior 15 Feb. 1286 (*Mun.* 23629).
Alive 1290–1 (*Mun.* 26145).

Neuporte, Newport, Alexander de.
Custos capelle Virginis 1278 (*Mun.* 5779).
Custos Maner^m Regine Alianore 18 Feb. 1297 (Kal. Pat. Rolls, Ed. I 235).
Et iii s. x d. fratri A. de N. ad liberandos homines nostros incarceratos apud Hereford 1297–8 (*Mun.* 19838).
For his journey to Scotland with W. de Chalk [q.v.] 1302–3, see *Mun.* 23638.
Imprisoned in the Tower c. 10 Oct. 1303.
Prior de Hurley 1305–9.
Specially deputed to see that money granted for the building of St Katharine's Chapel in the Infirmary—operi capelle b. Katerine in infirmitorio dicti monasterii construende—was so applied c. 29 Jun. 1311 (*Mun.* 6227).

Lokeleya [Lockley], William de.
Precentor 7 Dec. 1278 (*Mun.* 5779).

Pelham, Richard de.
Hostillarius 7 Dec. 1278 (*Mun.* 5779).

Dorkecestre, Geoffrey de.
Witnessed the record of the absolution of a testamentary executor who had been contumacious and had been excommunicated by Adam de Wycumbe [q.v.], Archdeacon, 21 Mar. 1278 (*Mun.* 6684; *Lib. Nig. Quat.* f. 124).

1282

Waledene, Henry de.
Gardinarius [time of Abbot Ware] (Domesday, f. 624).
Witnessed a charter with Richard de Fanelore in camera eiusdem loci prioris ipso presente 1 May 1282 (Domesday f. 246).
Camerarius c. 26 Mai. 1286 (Domesday f. 500).
Last mentioned as in the sick-room, end of Aug. 1298 (Infirmarer).

+1283

WENLOK, Walter de.

Son of William le espicer (apothecary), who was buried, by 1298, in the graveyard of St Milburga's Priory, Wenlock, and of Agnes la specere, his wife (Domesday f. 407).

For various orders concerned with his mother's comfort cf. *Mun.* 31506, 31540; the bailiff at Islip to provide fish on three days for her and her two damsels, Sep. 1297 (*Mun.* 31363).

Had a sister for whom he provided 8 ells of cloth and the rent of her lodging Apr. 1307 (*Mun.* 31479; 31494). The Abbot's Treasurer (*Mun.* 24257) paid £4 in exequiis sororis domini, 1306–7; so her death may be placed during the summer of 1307.

Had a niece (neptis) Alice, presumably the daughter of the sister beforementioned, who stayed with him at a cost of 13s. 14 Sep.—21 Dec. 1307 (*Mun.* 24260); perhaps after her mother's funeral.

Had a nephew, William, whom he educated [et cuidam pauperi scolari informanti nepotem domini apud Oxon. xii d. (Abbot's Steward 1298–9)] and clothed (*Mun.* 31556), and nominated to the benefice of St Magnus, London Bridge, 14 Apr. 1300 (Domesday f. 478 b).

Other relations—Roger de Prestindene (nostre parent) and Cristine de Evesham (nostre cosyn); cf. *Mun.* 31347; 31368; the latter may be identical with nostre cosine for whom he paid 5d. a week for her maintenance to Dame Ysabele de Compton, Lady of Stodleye [Studley, Warwickshire], 8 Sep. 1297 (*Mun.* 31366).

Abbas per viam compromissi electus 31 Dec. 1283 (*Flete*, p. 116).

The Convent borrowed 250 marks from Sienese merchants for the expenses of his election and confirmation 11 Feb. 1284 (*Mun.* 12878). For heavy borrowings at this time, over 1000 marks, see *Mun.* 12879–83.

The Papal Bull for his confirmation cost £233. 6s. 8d. (*Mun.* 28811). For his journey to Italy 6 Feb.—20 Mar. 1284 see *Mun.* 9241. Martin IV who confirmed him ordered the Bishop of Ostia to give him the benediction 8 May 1284 (Kal. Pap. Reg. I. 472).

Magister Robert and Magister Adam de Phyleby were his agents at the Roman Court pro arduis ecclesie sue Westmon' negociis expediendis c. 1 Nov. 1284 (*Mun.* 9436).

Had a contention with Archbishop Peckham about the right of visitation of the priory of Greater Malvern 1285 (*Mun.* 22942; 32644); 1289 (*Mun.* 22929–32).

Subrogatus fuit...in officio Thesaurarie Domine Alienore, 15 Feb. 1286 (*Mun.* 23629 A).

Edward I issued a grant that on a vacancy in the Abbacy the Crown would seize only that portion of the temporalities which was assigned to the Abbot, 18 Feb. 1286 (*Mun.* 5438).

His statute about Divine Service, 19 Jun. 1287, is given in Domesday f. 641 b. At that date he was in Orleans.

Assigned the manor of Amwell, Herts, for the support of the Convent Cellarer in accordance with an intention expressed by Abbot Ware, 21 Dec. 1288 (*Mun.* 4241).

Made progresses through the manors 1289–91 (*Mun.* 9252–3; 9242).

For the controversy about W. de Pershore, the apostate Franciscan Friar, 1290–5, see *Mun.* 6386–97; cf. Monumenta Franciscana, Rolls series, II, 31–62. The Proctor of the Abbot and Convent challenged the action of the Bishop of London (Richard de Gravesend) in excommunicating them throughout the city of London and carrying off the oblations belonging to them in the church of St Laurence in "Chandlewycstreete," 17 Feb. 1290 (*Mun.* 12783).

Presided over the General Chapter of the Benedictines at Abingdon, in place of the Abbot of Glastonbury, 1290 (Reyner, *de Antiq. Benedict.* tract. II, p. 39).

The Abbot was abroad in 1291; he was in Paris 20 May (*Mun.* 6389) and there is a letter from him dated Seintrie, near Corboil, 29 May (*Mun.* 31276).

By command of Edward I, Wenlok delivered the heart of Henry III to the Abbess of Fontevraud [Fontevrault] in the Abbey Church c. 10 Dec. 1291 (*Mun.* 6318 B).

Received from Edward I a grant of manors [Birdbrook, Essex; Westerham and Edenbridge, Kent; Turweston, Bucks; Knowle, Warwickshire] to maintain Q. Alianore's anniversary, &c. 25 Oct. 1292 (*Mun.* 1545); Hendon, Middlesex, was added 14 Oct. 1295 (*Mun.* 17012).

Rebuilt the hall of his manor-house at Denham, 1297 (*Mun.* 3434).

Edward I requested the prayers of the Abbot and Convent for the success of his expedition against the King of France 7 Aug. 1297 (*Mun.* 12201).

Edward I nominated him with others as suitable for the Bishopric of Ely, 1298 (Flor. Hist. III, 298).

On 10 Oct. 1303, Wenlok and 48 monks of Westminster, being then prisoners in the Tower of London, were ordered to be tried on a charge of breaking into the Royal Treasury at Westminster and carrying off property to the value of £100,000 (Rymer, *Foedera*, I, part ii, p. 959).

Mordon church, near Merton, Surrey, was appropriated to the Abbey in its distresses, incendio nuper ex pallacio regali casualiter exorto quod vestrum nobile monasterium quasi funditus destruxit; 7 May 1300 (*Mun.* 1863).

Member of the King's Council on Scottish affairs at the New Temple, 15 Sep. 1305 (Flor. Hist. III, 124).

For his dispute with the Convent about the election to the Priorship 1304–7, see under R. de Hadham and cf. *Mun.* 9508 A, 9499 B–E.

He finally confirmed the compositions made by his predecessors with the Prior and Convent, 16 Aug. 1307 (*Mun.* 5671) and sealed in Chapter a dispensation about the distribution of the residue of Q. Alianore's money, 18 Dec. 1307 (*Lib. Nig. Quat.* f. 106 b; Domesday f. 464).

Spent 40s. on a new carriage ad opus Principis (? Edw. II) 6 Jul. 1307 (*Mun.* 31490).

Defunctus in manerio suo de Pireforde 25 Dec. 1307 (Flor. Hist. III, 140). In expensis circa sepulturam domini una cum factura tumbe sue et retentione familie sue post sepulturam per vii dies... £70. 13s. 7¾d. (Abbot's Treasurer).

His tomb was to the south of the High Altar, "exactly in front of the sedilia, which were probably his work" (Lethaby, p. 348).

News of his death was brought to Edward II at Wye by W. de Chalk, H. de Bircheston, and R. de Coleworth [q.v.] 10 Jan. 1308 (Kal. Pat. Rolls 1307–13, p. 34).

After his death £1000 of his money came into the hands of the party, headed by A. de Persore [q.v.], who were promoting the election of Abbot Kedyngton. They gave a bribe of £100 to Piers Gaveston to secure his support (*Mun.* 5460).

Alanus.

Alanus monachus was Proctor for Abbot Richard [? Ware] in an agreement about commonage of pasture at Thames Ditton (Domesday f. 468 b).

Several times in the sick-room 1297–8 (Infirmarer); no surname or place-name given.

1284

Persore, Persora, Perschore, Persouer, Persouere, Alexander de.
Accompanied Wenlok to Rome when he went for confirmation as Abbot 6 Feb. 1284 (*Mun.* 9241).
Employed in getting loans for Abbot Wenlok 6 May 1284 (*Mun.* 28801).
Drew up account of the Abbot's hospice at Pyrford 1286 (*Mun.* 24491).
Sacrista 1288 (*Mun.* 24495).
Custos hospicii Abbatis 29 Sep. 1289—Sep. 1290.
Paid for land purchased for the Abbot's mother 1290 (*Mun.* 28852*).
Abbot Wenlok's Proctor at the Roman Court, where he made a compromise about the apostate Franciscan friar, W. de Pershore, against which compromise the Abbot appealed 20 May 1291 (*Mun.* 6389). A. de P. had returned to Westminster 2 May (*Mun.* 23638 dors.; cf. 31276).
Elemosinarius c. 14 Feb. 1293—18 Jun. 1294 (*Mun.* 18963 A).
Receptor Abbatis Jun. 1296—Mai. 1298 (*Mun.* 29006; 24255).
Journeyed to Rome and stayed there (R. de Hadham [q.v.] being with him till c. 20 Jul.), c. 19 May 1298—c. 24 Feb. 1299 (*Mun.* 9243, 9244, 9246, 9250); returned with W. de Chalk [q.v.] 22 Apr.—2 Jun. 1299 (*Mun.* 9249).
Obtained in Rome an indulgence for prayers for his soul and for that of Thomas de Lenton [q.v.] 18 Jul. 1298 (Domesday f. 403; *Flete*, p. 75).
Helped to draw up a state of Q. Alianore's manors 1299–1300 (*Mun.* 23630).
Imprisoned in the Tower c. 10 Oct. 1303; for his special guilt in the matter of the robbery of the Royal Treasury in (?) Apr. 1303, see G. G. Scott, *Gleanings*, pp. 282–90.
Frequently engaged on the Abbot's business 1306, 1307 (*Mun.* 31439; 31499).
Precentor 1311 (*Mun.* 29313).
Archidiaconus 24 Aug. 1311 (*Mun.* 9505). No further mention.

Gardino, Simon de.
Proctor for the Abbot and Convent at the time of Abbot Wenlok's election and confirmation; his bond in 250 marks dated at the New Temple 11 Feb. 1284 (*Mun.* 12878).
Mentioned in the absolution concerning William de Pershore, 11 Jul. 1291 (*Mun.* 6391).
Not included in the list of those imprisoned in the Tower, Oct. 1303.
In the sick-room during most of 1305–6 (Infirmarer).

Lyminstre, Lymmstr', Adam de.
Payment from Fering manor, Essex, 1284 (*Mun.* 25583).
Along with Adam de Wycumbe and Robert de Parham [q.v.] attended at the banking house of some Sienese merchants in London to repay a loan of 100 marks due from Abbot Wenlok 2 Mar. 1285 (*Mun.* 28809, where all that can be deciphered of his name is Ade de Leo...).
Made payments for the Abbot's household expenses c. 12 Mar. 1287 (*Mun.* 31273).

1285

Watford, Watforth, William de.
The Abbot of St Albans was ordered to hear the complaint of the Abbot and Convent of Westminster that accusations of immorality had been made falsely against W. de W. 15 Jul. 1285 (*Mun.* 22942 (4)).
Thesaurarius 1297–9 (*Mun.* 29025; 29065). One of his tallies containing

£37. 10s., found after his death, was delivered to Prior Hadham, 9 Jun. 1306 (*Mun.* 5777).

Defunctus 1299–1300 (St Mary's Chapel).

Parham, Perham, Robert de.

2 Mar. 1285 (*Mun.* 28809). See Adam de Lyminstre.

Defunctus post 29 Sep. 1293 (*Mun.* 18962*).

1286

HADHAM, Reginald or Renald de.

Proctor for the Abbot and Convent at the Roman Court 1286 (*Mun.* 28821). With the Abbot at Pyrford, Jan. 1288 (*Mun.* 24492).

Along with Ralph de Mordon [q.v.], he was Proctor for the Prior and Convent on the one part against Abbot Wenlok on the other part in a formal protestation made at the Bishop of London's house c. 10 Aug. 1295, to the effect that the Prior and Convent made payment to the Cardinals or Nuncios then in England only out of courtesy—solum ob reuerentiam dictorum dominorum per viam curialitatis (*Mun.* 9499 A).

For the expenses of his journey to Rome and back 19 May—20 July 1298 see *Mun.* 9244 ; 9250.

In curialitate facta fratri R. de H. et sociis suis spaciantibus apud Hamstede viii d. 1297–8 (St Mary's Chapel).

Constantly engaged on Abbot Wenlok's manorial business 1293–1305 (*Mun.* 31285, &c.).

Elemosinarius 18 Jun. 1294—24 Jun. 1305 (*Mun.* 19841).

Pitanciarius 19 Mai. 1301 (*Mun.* 29082).

Custos Maner^m Regine Alianore 30 Nov. 1301—29 Mai 1302.

Custos Gardini Conventus Westm. apud la Charring 1302 (*Mun.* 5701).

Refectorarius 24 Feb.—29 Sep. 1303 (Treasurer ; also *Mun.* 29143).

Imprisoned in the Tower c. 10 Oct. 1303.

Custos capelle b. Marie ?—11 Jun. 1304 (*Mun.* 23180).

Sacrista 29 Sep. 1303—24 Jun. 1305 (Treasurer).

Receptor denariorum Abbatis 1304–5 (Treasurer). Solut' fratribus R. de H. et R. de Aldenham [q.v.]...pro quadam contribucione concessa eidem domino Abbati [Wenlok] in Capitulo generali pro fratre W. de Persora iiii^ll xix^d q. (*ibid.*).

Prior 2 Aug. 1305 (Flor. Hist. III, 129).

Solut' Ricardo de Reding apotecario pro cura tibie Prioris iii s. vi d. 1309–10 (Treasurer).

By 14 Jul. 1307 (*Mun.* 9499 E) he was deprived of his Priorship by Abbot Wenlok and, together with his adherents in the Convent, made formal protest against this action at the General Chapter of the Benedictines at Oxford in domibus Prioris et monachorum 21 Sep. 1307 (*Mun.* 9499 D). The question turned on a composition between the Abbot on the one part and the Prior and Convent on the other as to division of the temporal and spiritual properties of the Abbey (*Mun.* 9497). The case was decided in Prior Hadham's favour 17 May 1308 (*Mun.* 9496), and on 14 Jul. (*Mun.* 12777) a King's mandate was issued calling upon the Prior and Convent to obey Roger le Brabazon, Chief Justice, and four others who were to inquire into the controversies.

Hadham placed on record a grant of Edward I to the Abbot and Convent, dated 18 Feb. 1286, that at a vacancy in the Abbacy the Crown shall seize, not the entire temporalities of the Abbey, as heretofore, but only the Abbot's portion ; 29 Dec. 1307 (*Mun.* 5438).

For his correspondence with Proctors at Avignon about Abbot Kedyngton's election, to which he was opposed, see *Mun.* 5460.

Indulgence of 40 days' pardon for those who say the Pater Noster and the Ave Maria for his soul here and hereafter 10 Oct. 1315 (*Mun.* 6668).

Witnessed the notarial instrument recording the Papal attempt to enforce repayment of an old debt of 8000 florins, 23 Feb. 1318 (*Mun.* 9458).

Was alive 21 Dec. 1318 (*Mun.* 5710).

Lenton, Lyntone, Thomas de.
Engaged on Abbot Wenlok's business ad reparacionem wallorum 25 Mar. 1286 (*Mun.* 31271).

Senescallus Abbatis [Wenlok] 1289 (*Mun.* 24497)–1292 (*Mun.* 31277).

A. de Persore [q.v.] obtained an indulgence for prayers for his own soul and for that of T. de L. cuius corpus in cimiterio Westm. est humatum ; Rome, 18 Jul. 1298 (Domesday f. 403).

+1287

Wenlok, Wanlok, Reymund de.
Custos hospicii Abbatis [Wenlok] 1287 (*Mun.* 24492); 1291 (*Mun.* 28882).

Proctor for the Convent in all suits, &c. 12... (*Mun.* 9521; the rest of the date torn away).

Edward I ordered his Treasurer to pay to R. de W., monk of Westminster, 46s. 8d. for making three marble columns round the Shrine of St Edward, 1290 (Liberate Roll 18 & 19 Edw. I; cf. G. G. Scott, *Gleanings*, p. 136).

Made payments to the King for tenths from the Abbot's estates 1296–7 (*Mun.*·31314; 31338).

Sacrista 1 Jan. 1297 (Domesday f. 374)—21 Nov. 1299 (Kal. Pat. Rolls, Ed. I, 479); 1301, 1302 (*Mun.* 29077 ; 29120).

Appointed as such by Edward I to assist in a search for treasure believed to be buried in the church of St Martin in the Fields, 21 Nov. 1299 (Kal. Pat. Rolls Ed. I, p. 479).

Ballivus 24 Feb. 1303—24 Jun. 1305 (*Mun.* 19841).

Imprisoned in the Tower c. 10 Oct. 1303.

Solut' per manus fratris Reymundi ballivi Archidiacono Surr' pro induccione ecclesie de Mordon vi s. viii d. 1304–5 (*ibid.*).

In expensis fratris Reymundi et suis (sic) euntium apud Wiz (?) cum litteris Regine anno...xxxi° xxxiii s. 1302–3 (*Mun.* 23638).

Held a manorial court at Wheathampstead, Herts, 22 Jul. 1307 (*Mun.* 8939).

+1288

Henle, Henleya, John de.
Receptor Abbatis 1288 (*Mun.* 24253).

In a mutilated precept of Abbot Wenlok (*Mun.* 31394) there is an order to pay a yearly pension to Dom J. de H., procurator of...16 Feb. 1306.

Mordon, Morton, Ralph de.
Capellanus Abbatis c. 1 Aug. 1288 (*Mun.* 28829) 28 Mai. 1289 (*Mun.* 28837).

Custos hospicii Abbatis 29 Sep. 1288—20 Mar. 1289 (*Mun.* 24495).

Absolution in the matter of W. de Pershore, the apostate Franciscan friar, 11 Jul. 1291 (*Mun.* 6391).

Proctor with Reginald de Hadham for the Prior and Convent in proceedings against Abbot Wenlok Feb. 1295 (*Mun.* 9499 A).

Imprisoned in the Tower c. 10 Oct. 1303.

Protested against Prior Hadham's deprivation 4 Sep. 1307 (*Mun.* 9499 B).

In albo vino pro tibia R. de M. ii d. (Infirmarer 1309–10).

Short illness Aug. 1310 (Infirmarer); no further mention.

Depedene, Nicholas de.⎫ Received gifts from Abbot Wenlok Nov. 1288
Beremundeshe, R. de. ⎭ (*Mun.* 24495).

Cornwell, Cornewell, Henry de.
Payment to him by Abbot Wenlok pro emendacione domorum apud Birchurst. Feb. 1289 (*Mun.* 24495).
Ill for about 6 weeks from 17 Sep. 1311 (Infirmarer); no other mention.

1289
Trompeltone, W. de.
In vi vlnis Rosset pro fratre W. de T. xii^s. Oct. 1289 (*Mun.* 24493(2)).

c. 1290
Bures, Roger de.
Proctor of the Abbot and Convent in the appeal against Archbishop Peckham in the matter of the alleged Franciscan friar, William de Pershore, 7 Oct. 1290 (*Mun.* 6386; cf. Monumenta Franciscana, Rolls series, ii, 33, 56).
Dudum Archidiaconus 6 Mai. 1293 (*Mun.* 5991, where he is described as executor to John de Pyuelesdon, Canon of St Paul's).
In expensis fratris R. de B. et Gerini uersus Scociam x^{li} 1300–1, 1301–2 (*Mun.* 23631 f.).
Imprisoned in the Tower c. 10 Oct. 1303 and detained there after the release of the rest.
Solut' magistro Henrici de Greneford substituto fratris R. de B. in visitacione Archiepiscopi...post incarceracionem predicti fratris...x^s 1303 (Treasurer).
Along with Henry de Bircheston [q.v.] he produced before two Papal Nuncios a bull of Alexander IV [7 Nov. 1256] in favour of the Convent's refusal to pay procurations to any Nuncio below the rank of Cardinal, 25 Mar. 1306 (*Mun.* 12737).
Mentioned in a commission dated Poitiers 2 Nov. 1307 (*Mun.* 6679). Was at Avignon in 1308 opposing the confirmation of Abbot Kedyngton (*Mun.* 5460).

Huntyndon, Walter de.
[It is possible that the compiler of Domesday wrote Walter instead of William f. 156 b, but Walter occurs also in the margin of f. 156 a; v. William de Huntyndon.]
Archidiaconus 1290 (Domesday f. 156).

Colecestr', Colecestre, Colecestria, Thomas de.
Made a payment to the Nuns of Kilburn 18 Oct. 1290 (*Mun.* 4860).
For his expenses on various journeys to "Funtaynes," &c., see Abbot's Steward ? 1290, *Mun.* 24500.
In expensis eiusdem et fratris Alexandri de Persore euntium versus Episcopum Londinensem iii s. v d. ob. 1291–2 (Abbot's Steward, *Mun.* 24501).
In expensis fratris Thom. de Colec' et Magistri W. de Bray apud Northampton ad capitulum generale et commorantium ibidem per quinque dies una cum expensis fratris T. usque Westm' xiii^s (*ibid.*).
Paid £30 on account for spices for the Abbot 25 Feb. 1293 (*Mun.* 28925).

Ware, Nicolas de.
Mentioned in the compotus of the manor of Amwell, Herts, 1290–1 (*Mun.* 26145).
Richard, son of Geoffrey Pistor, made a grant to the Convent to support a lamp in St Dunstan's Chapel in the sub-hostelry, Westminster, and for an anniversary within 15 days after 13 Oct. for himself and brother N. de W.

(*Mun.* 17507 ; Domesday f. 455 b : not dated, but N. de W. was apparently still alive when it was drawn up).

Prior of St Bartholomew, Sudbury (*Mun.* 20858).

Defunctus 1299–1300 (St Mary's Chapel).

1291–2

Berking, Jordan de.

Drew up accounts of tithes at Staines, Nov. 1291—Nov. 1292 (*Mun.* 26675).

Paid Abbot Wenlok some tithe from Oakham, 26 Apr. 1302 (*Mun.* 29111).

Hereford, Richard de.

Received vi^d from the Chamberlain 17 Sep. 1292 by command of the Prior (*Mun.* 18717).

+1293

Wenlok, R. de.

Only known through the Almoner's payment of 6s. 8d. die sepulture fratris R. de Wenlok c. 14 Feb.—30 Sep. 1293 (*Mun.* 18962*). Reymund de Wenlok [q.v.], who was commonly entered as Brother Reymund, survived till 1307.

1293

Chalk, Chalke, William de.

Made a payment from the Abbot's [Wenlok's] chest c. 6 Dec. 1293 (*Mun.* 28947); 23 May 1297 (*Mun.* 29027).

In Rome with Alexander de Persore [q.v.] on the business of Longdon and Mordon churches 4–22 Apr. 1299 ; their expenses, *Mun.* 9249.

Custos Maner^m Regine Alianore 28 Mai. 1302—17 Apr. 1305.

For his journey to Scotland with Alexander de Neuporte [q.v.] 1302–3, see *Mun.* 23638.

Item fratri W. de C. pro sumptibus suis versus Carliol' vi^{li} xiii^s iiii^d 1307 (Abbot's Treasurer) ; Chalk made a second journey to Carlisle the same year at a cost of £8. 13s. 4d. for which the Abbot paid, 5 Mar. 1307 (*Mun.* 31473 ; 31479). Parliament met there 20 Jan. 1307.

Four days' travelling with J. de Butterle [q.v.] on Abbot Wenlok's business, 27 Aug. 1307 (*Mun.* 31497).

In denariis liberatis fratri W. de C. pro expensis suis eundo apud Norhampton cum exennio [a gilt cup and a flagon costing £4. 12s.] misso domino Petro de Gaueston, xl^s 1307 (Abbot's Treasurer).

Nominated attorney to Abbot Kedyngton during his absence at the Roman Court 28 Mar. 1313 (Kal. Pat. Rolls, 1307–13, p. 562). Was one of those who bribed Piers Gaveston to support Kedyngton's cause (*Mun.* 5460).

Supprior 1318 (*Mun.* 9458).

Elemosinarius 1321–2.

In i mappa et i manutergio emptis pro W. de Chalk [in the sick-room] iii^s 1328–9 (Chamberlain). No further mention.

1293–4

Elinton, Elintone, Elynton, Elyngton, Laurence de.

Made a payment for Abbot Wenlok 1293–4 (*Mun.* 25921), and was attached to his Hospice 1295–8 (*Mun.* 31290, &c.).

? Capellanus Abbatis 1296 (*Mun.* 28992 : dan Laurens son chapelein).

In expensis fratris L. de E. euntis apud Waltham ad prouidendum hospicium pro domino xiii^d 1306–7 (Abbot's Treasurer).

Superintended the enlargement of Abbot Wenlok's hall at Denham 25 Apr. 1297 (*Mun.* 3434; cf. R. H. Lathbury, *History of Denham*, p. 93). In sururgia L. de E. ii^s 1305–6 (Infirmarer).

In i mappa et i manutergio emptis pro Laurencio de Elinton [in Infirmary] iii^s viii^d (Chamberlain 1328–9). No further mention.

1296

Wenlok, Wenlak, Wenloc, John de.

Engaged on the business of Abbot Wenlok's manors from Jul. 1296 (*Mun.* 31324). Probably some relation of the Abbot; perhaps the son of his sister (cf. *Mun.* 31494).

Imprisoned in the Tower c. 10 Oct. 1303.

Elemosinarius 21 Sep. 1301 (*Mun.* 29092); 1305–7 (*Mun.* 24256–7).

By the Abbot's order he received 11*s.* 8*d.* each week pro participacione Regine [Alianore] 22 May—1 Aug. 1306 (*Mun.* 31420).

Frequently in the sick-room 1320–1, 1322–3 (Infirmarer).

Fratri J. de W. cum sociis suis spaciantibus apud Hamstede ii^s 1323–4 (Q. Alianore).

1297

Butterle, Butterleya, Butterleye, Botterle, Buterleia, Buterleye, Buturle, John de.

Made payment on behalf of Abbot Wenlok c. 18 Oct. 1297 (*Mun.* 29029).

Senescallus hospicii Abbatis 1298–9.

Custos capelle b. Marie 24 Feb.—28 Sep. 1303 (Treasurer).

Imprisoned in the Tower c. 10 Oct. 1303.

In vino misso fratri J. de B. in die quo factus erat custos ordinis vi^d 1305–6 (Infirmarer).

Made payments for Abbot Wenlok to various members of the Royal Household 3 Jun. 1306 (*Mun.* 31427).

Item fratri J. de B. ad opus fratris Cardinalis xx^s (Abbot's Treasurer); for the precept for this payment see *Mun.* 1649, 20 Jul. 1306.

Camerarius 25 Nov. 1307—24 Jun. 1308.

Four days' travelling with W. de Chalk [q.v.] on Abbot Wenlok's business 27 Aug. 1307 (*Mun.* 31497).

The Hampstead portion of the Camb. Univ. MS. Kk. 5. 29, "extenta maneriorum," was written coram fratre Johanne de Buterleye, 7 Nov. 1312 (cf. *Manuscripts of Westminster Abbey*, p. 102).

Thesaurarius 1313.

Suggested with 5 other monks [? by the Abbot] as a possible Prior of Greater Malvern, ? 1314 (*Mun.* 32645).

Precentor 1318 (*Mun.* 9458).

Was Abbot Curtlington's Proctor to render account of the biennial and triennial tenths 24 Apr. 1318 (*Mun.* 5748).

Vicar-General of the same at a visitation of the Hospital of St James, Westminster, 2 Oct. 1320 (*Mun.* 17119).

No mention after 1328–9 (Chamberlain).

Warfeld, Warefield, Warfend, Adam de.

Made payment in behalf of Abbot Wenlok c. 18 Oct. 1297 (*Mun.* 29029).

Senescallus hospicii Abbatis 1298–9.

Power of attorney to receive seisin of Deerhurst manor for Abbot Wenlok Aug. 1299 (*Mun.* 32692).

Sacrista 24 Feb.—29 Sep. 1303 (Treasurer; *Mun.* 19839).

Imprisoned in the Tower c. 10 Oct. 1303. For his alleged guilt as chief burglar of the Royal Treasury, 24 Apr. 1303, see T. F. Tout, *A Mediaeval Burglary*, 1915, p. 13.

Defunctus in die veneris 25 Mar. 1306 (Infirmarer; he had been ill since the account began, at Michaelmas 1305).

1297-8

[The names given under this date appear in the Infirmarer's list of Mich⁸ 1297—Mich⁸ 1298; they are entered in the order of the official list of the prisoners in the Tower, c. 10 Oct. 1303; cf. Rymer, *Foedera*.]

Dene, Thomas de, de la.

Perhaps identical with Thomas de Dene, Abbot Wenlok's Lardenarius at Denham 31 Dec. 1295 (*Mun.* 28991).

Thesaurarius 1299 (*Mun.* 29066); 1301 (*Mun.* 29083, &c.).

Imprisoned in the Tower c. 10 Oct. 1303.

An elector of Abbot Kedyngton 26 Jan. 1308 (*Mun.* 5424).

Custos feretri sancti Edwardi (so described in an early marginal note, Domesday f. 384).

Sacrista 1 Aug. 1311 (*Mun.* 4615).

Elemosinarius ante 1317 (*Mun.* 18964).

Short illness Sep. 1323 (Infirmarer); no further mention.

Notelle, Notele, Nottele, John de.

One John de Nottele was a witness at Westminster 24 Mar. 1297 (*Mun.* 17482) and on several other occasions.

In curialitate facta fratri J. de N. decumbenti [in Infirmaria] viᵈ 1299–1300 (St Mary's Chapel).

Imprisoned in the Tower c. 10 Oct. 1303.

Protested against Prior Hadham's deprivation 4 Sep. 1307 (*Mun.* 9499 B).

Alive 12 Nov. 1307 (*Mun.* 6679).

Cherring, Robert de.

Imprisoned in the Tower c. 10 Oct. 1303.

Short illness Mar. 1311 (Infirmarer); no further mention.

Henle, Henlegh, Henleye, Henleia, Simon de.

Camerarius 1298 (*Mun.* 29053); 1299 (*Mun.* 29061-2); 1300 (*Mun.* 29071); 1301 (*Mun.* 29088); 1302 (*Mun.* 29128); 29 Sep. 1303—24 Jun. 1304 (Treasurer: Liberat' fratri S. de H. pro mandato die cene xxxˢ. In the previous roll this payment was made to the Chamberlain); 1312-4 (*Mun.* 29331; 29348).

Imprisoned in the Tower c. 10 Oct. 1303.

Suggested with 5 other monks [? by the Abbot] as a possible Prior of Greater Malvern ?1314 (*Mun.* 32645).

In a letter from Richard de Walsham [? the attorney of the Convent: *Mun.* 19839] to Roger de Aldenham [q.v.] there is reference to some words spoken at St Bartholomew's Hospital on the Tuesday after St Hilary's Day by Dan Simond Henle, by which the Abbot had been grievously damaged and for which the speaker would probably be fined; no date; perhaps Abbot Kedyngton's character was in question (*Mun.* 9507).

Prior of St Bartholomew, Sudbury, 1323 (*Mun.* 20848-9).

Arkesdene, Harkesdene, Walter de.

Thesaurarius 1299 (*Mun.* 29066), 1301 (*Mun.* 5879), 1302 (*Mun.* 29113).

Imprisoned in the Tower c. 10 Oct. 1303.

Solut' fratri W. de A. pro quadam cuppa argentea eidem impignorata pro denariis mutuatis ab eodem pro curialitate facta in Turri ut fratres soluerentur de compedibus vi^s viii^d 1304–5 (Treasurer).

Camerarius 1306–7 (*Mun.* 29201, 29236).

Protested against Prior Hadham's deprivation 4 Sep. 1307 (*Mun.* 9499 B).

Alive 1308 when he took part in the opposition to Abbot Kedyngton's confirmation (*Mun.* 5460).

Rye, Henry de la, de, or atte.

Thesaurarius 1297 (*Mun.* 9453).

Imprisoned in the Tower c. 10 Oct. 1303.

Quondam Refectorarius (Treasurer) 1304–5 [as such he had been obliged to pawn some silver goblets belonging to the Refectory, one of which the Treasurer recovered for 16*s.*].

Custos capelle b. Marie c. 11 Jun. 1304–?

Procurator capelle 1 Mai. 1305 (Domesday f. 563 b).

Protested against Prior Hadham's deprivation 4 Sep. 1307 (*Mun.* 9499 B).

Infirmus 1322–3 (Infirmarer).

Lalham, Adam de.

Item fratri A. de L. ad opus Juratorum pro Roysia la Marescal...12*s.* 11$\frac{3}{4}$*d.* 1297-8 (*Mun.* 19838).

Imprisoned in the Tower c. 10 Oct. 1303.

Was in the sick-room for much of the autumn 1310, and again when the Infirmarer's account closed, Easter 1311 ; no further mention.

London, John de.

Imprisoned in the Tower c. 10 Oct. 1303.

Protested against Prior Hadham's deprivation 4 Sep. 1307 (*Mun.* 9499 B).

Opposed the confirmation of Abbot Kedyngton 1308 (*Mun.* 5460).

Request from the Archdeacon of London's commissary to the Archdeacon of Westminster to publish the excommunication of Brother J. de L. dictus le Beuere for some crime committed within the Archdeacon of London's jurisdiction 28 Mar. 1310 (*Mun.* 6047).

Entered the sick-room 2 Sep. 1310 and was still there 4 Feb. 1311, when his name is dropped without a statement but with a presumption of his death (Infirmarer).

In uno clisterio ad opus J. de L. xviii^d (*ibid.*).

See *Dict. Nat. Biog.* s.v. John Bever, or of London.

Witteneie, Wytteneie, Wynteneye, John de.

Fratri Johanni de Witten' et Willelmo le Rous precepto capituli pro inquisicionibus procurandis xx^s 1303 (Treasurer).

Imprisoned in the Tower c. 10 Oct. 1303.

Granator 1304–5 ; 1327–8 (Treasurer).

Thesaurarius 1306–7 (Abbot's Treasurer) ; 1313 (*Mun.* 29339, 29342).

Sacrista 25 Nov. 1307—29 Sep. 1308 (Treasurer) ; 10 Dec. 1318—14 Oct. 1320 ? + (*Mun.* 17575).

Custos Maner^m Regine Alianore 25 Mar. 1315—30 Nov. 1319 (*Mun.* 5752).

No mention after 1328–9 (Chamberlain).

Middelton, Robert de.

Imprisoned in the Tower c. 10 Oct. 1303.

Was in the sick-room as infirm during most of 1305–6 (Infirmarer).

Coleworth, Colworth, Culeworth, Colewordе, Richard de.

Imprisoned in the Tower c. 10 Oct. 1303.

Thesaurarius Conventus 1306–7 (Abbot's Treasurer).

Proctor at Rome with Richard de Beby [q.v.] for Abbot Kedyngton's confirmation (*Mun.* 5453).

Engaged with William de Curtlington [q.v.] in Abbot Kedyngton's sequestration of his manors for a debt of 8000 florins to the Papal Court 21 Oct. 1313 (*Mun.* 22533).

Prior de Hurley ? + 29 Sep. 1320—13 Sep. 1336 ? +.

Aldenham, Roger de.

Drew up a state of Q. Alianore's manors 1299–1300 (*Mun.* 23630); Lady Day 1305 (*Mun.* 23640).

Imprisoned in the Tower c. 10 Oct. 1303.

Thesaurarius 24 Feb. 1303—24 Jun. 1305.

Sub-collector of Papal tenths 23 Oct. 1303 (*Mun.* 12327).

Receptor denariorum Abbatis 1304–5 (Treasurer).

Made inventory of St Mary's Chapel before 11 Jun. 1304 (*Mun.* 23180).

On the death of William de Huntyndon, he made a formal protest against the effort of Abbot Wenlok to interfere with the accepted customs of election to the vacant Priorship (*Mun.* 9508 A). The Abbot's excommunication of him was quashed Nov. 1308 (*Mun.* 9494).

After Richard de Kedyngton's election as Abbot, Roger de Aldenham appeared before the Pope at Avignon by a proctor to allege that the Abbot-elect was not free from certain faults (Kal. Pap. Reg. II, 65). In *Mun.* 5460, which is a contemporary copy of letters from R. de A. and W. de Bolton [q.v.], who were engaged on this business at Avignon, it is stated that R. de A. dignus est aureola martirii ut pote pro iusticia vestra iam diu agonizans.

It appears from a letter written to him by Richard de Walsham (no date; but during Simon de Henle's [q.v.] lifetime) that Brother Roger was apt to be in difficulties with the Exchequer (*Mun.* 9507).

He and his brother Gilbert were collectors of the tenth imposed within the confines of the Archdeaconries of Essex and Colchester (*Mun.* 31750; no date).

No certain mention after 1308.

Braybroke, William de. [J. de; *Mun.* 23631 c.]

Imprisoned in the Tower c. 10 Oct. 1303.

Defunctus in die Martis 13 Sep. 1306 (Infirmarer).

Reding, Rading, Robert de.

Imprisoned in the Tower c. 10 Oct. 1303.

Item fratri R. de R. et Gerino pro expensis suis versus Eboracum pro redditibus de Wiche [Wick, near Pershore] iiii^{ll} xvii^s 1303 (Treasurer).

Protested against Prior Hadham's deprivation 4 Sep. 1307 (*Mun.* 9499 B).

Wrote a chronicle in continuation of the *Flores Historiarum* from 1299 to 1326 (?), which is copied in Brit. Mus. Cotton MS. Cleopatra A XVI; cf. James Tait, *Chronica Johannis de Reading*, Manchester, 1914, p. 2, 4–8; J. Armitage Robinson, *Simon Langham*, Ch. Quart. Rev. July, 1908, p. 346 ff.

Defunctus 17 Jun.—29 Sep. 1317 (Almoner, whose evidence must prevail against the mention of 1326, above, if the identification is to stand; cf. T. F. Tout, *Eng. Hist. Rev.* Jul. 1916, pp. 450–64).

Cruce, la Croys, la Croix, Peter de.

Imprisoned in the Tower c. 10 Oct. 1303.

There is a mandate from Abbot Wenlok for the delivery of wheat to Dan Peter de la Croys de Pere to make bread for the Abbot's sister c. 28 Mar. 1306 (*Mun.* 31401).

Was associated with Roger de Aldenham [q.v.] in his suit against Abbot Wenlok, Nov. 1308 (*Mun.* 9494).

Defunctus 17 Jun.—29 Sep. 1317 (Almoner).

Payn, Pain, Henry.
Celerarius 29 Sep. 1303—24 Jun. 1304 (Treasurer).
Imprisoned in the Tower c. 10 Oct. 1303.
Thesaurarius 24 Jun. 1304—24 Jun. 1305 (Treasurer).
Thesaurarius Abbatis 13 Dec. 1305—24 Dec. 1307 (*Mun.* 24256).
Sacrista 1305 (*Mun.* 31391); 1306 (*Mun.* 29192).
Supprior c. 25 Jul. 1307 (*Mun.* 31492).
An elector of Abbot Kedyngton 26 Jan. 1308 (*Mun.* 5424), and one of those who bribed Piers Gaveston to support the Abbot's confirmation (*Mun.* 5460).
Alive 21 Apr. 1310 (*Mun.* 9456).

Bircheston, Bercheston, Burston, Byrcheston, Henry de.
Imprisoned in the Tower c. 10 Oct. 1303.
Camerarius 24 Jun. 1304—24 Jun. 1305.
Protested against Prior Hadham's deprivation 4 Sep. 1307 (*Mun.* 9499 B).
Solut' Henrico Costhard pro catehenis fratrum H. de B. et W. Almali incarceratorum in palacio domini Regis iiii^s viii^d 1307-8 (Treasurer).
An elector of Abbot Kedyngton 26 Jan. 1308 (*Mun.* 5424), but a prominent opponent of his confirmation (*Mun.* 5460).
Infirmarius 1309-11.
Custos Maner^m Regine Alianore 1309-10; 8 Dec. 1318—30 Sep. 1325; was still holding this office 7 Dec. 1334, when he handed it over to Simon de Bircheston (*Mun.* 23668).
Was in the sick-room continuously 1309-11.
Sacrista 30 Sep. 1317—10 Dec. 1318.
Defunctus in Infirmaria 29 Dec. 1334 (Infirmarer).

Asshewelle, Aswelle, Guido, Guydo, or Gwydo de.
Imprisoned in the Tower c. 10 Oct. 1303.
Protested against Prior Hadham's deprivation 4 Sep. 1307 (*Mun.* 9499).
Granator 1307-8; 1310-1 (Treasurer).
Thesaurarius 1311-3 (*Mun.* 29303-44).
Alive 4 Apr. (Palm Sunday) 1316 (*Mun.* 23644).

Beby, Bebi, Bibi, Bybi, Byby, Robert de.
Imprisoned in the Tower c. 10 Oct. 1303.
An elector of Abbot Kedyngton 26 Jan. 1308 (*Mun.* 5254); and proctor at Rome for his confirmation (*Mun.* 5453).
Helped to draw up a state of the manors of Westminster 1312-3 (*Mun.* 9298).
Visited the Cardinals at Valence with Abbot Curtlington after his election, 15 Jul. 1315 (*Mun.* 5463-6).
Proctor at Avignon for Abbot Curtlington's confirmation 30 Oct. 1316 (Kal. Pap. Reg. II, 132).
Custos ecclesie de Ocham [Oakham] 1321-9 (*Mun.* 20339-45).
xii^d dat' uno garcioni eunti cum littera domini Abbatis [W. Curtlington] fratri R. de B. apud parliamentum de Northampton 1327-8 (Treasurer).
In expensis dicti fratris R. et J. de Tothale [q.v.] missis (*sic*) apud Notingham pro corpore Regis defuncti [Edward II] petendo...cum iiii equis per xxi dies iiii^{li} x^s 1327-8 (*Mun.* 20344).
Some idea of the amount of travelling done by the officials of the Convent may be gathered from a record of his expenses 1334-5 circa renouacionem vnionis ecclesie de Langedon [Longdon, Worcs.]. At Michaelmas 1334 he was at the Court of the Bishop of Winchester. He spent 31 days, up to All Saints, in a journey through Uxbridge, Islip, Pershore, Longdon, Berkeley, Bristol, Tewkesbury, and Gloucester. He then started upon an inquisicio

dampnorum domorum, 3 Nov., and during 27 days visited Windsor, Oxford, Campden, Worcester, Pershore, Longdon, and Chipping Norton. On 13 Dec. he proceeded on the business of Longdon to Hartlebury, this occupying 12 days. On 22 Jan. 1335 in company with Dominus John de Shoreditch (cf. *Dict. Nat. Biog.*) he set out for Alvechurch, taking six horses and being absent 21 days; again to Alvechurch 16 Mar., 17 days; again to Longdon 30 Ap., 32 days; on 29 Jun., 10 days, pro autumpno ordinando et feno vendendo; and on 8 Sep., 12 days (*Mun.* 21262).

Elemosinarius 1335–6.

Item in porcionibus fratrum R. de B. et J. de Aysshwelle [q.v.] exeuntium cum zona beate Marie in partibus transmarinis cum Regina pregnante per xxiii septimanas 4 Jul.–13 Dec.[1] xlvi^s. Item in ii paribus braccarum nouarum emptis pro fratribus R. de B. et J. de Aysshwelle transfretantibus cum Regina et cum zona b. Marie xviii^s. Item in i pari botarum de allutt' pro fratre R. de B. ii^s ii^d. Item liberat' eisdem pro expensis eorum ultra mare...x^{li} 1338 (Sacrist).

Was sent to invite the Abbot of St Albans to Abbot Henle's funeral 4 Nov. 1344 (*Mun.* 5467 A).

Indult to choose confessor 26 Jan. 1345 (Kal. Pap. Reg. III, 159).

Alive 28 Jan. 1349 (*Mun.* 29834); no further mention.

Benflet, Beneflete, Beneflet, Laurence de.

? Capellanus Abbatis [W. de Wenlok] 1296 (*Mun.* 28992: dan Laurens son chapelein; more probably Laurence de Elinton [q.v.]).

Precentor 1297–8 (Infirmarer); 1304 (Domesday f. 417 b).

Imprisoned in the Tower c. 10 Oct. 1303.

Entered the sick-room 2 Jul. 1306 and was still there at Michaelmas (Infirmarer); no further mention.

Temple, Henry de.

Imprisoned in the Tower c. 10 Oct. 1303.

Defunctus in die sabbati 12 Nov. 1305 (Infirmarer).

Wantyng, Wanting, Wanetyng, Waleting, Walething, Henry de.

Thesaurarius 1297–8 (*Mun.* 19838); 1298 (*Mun.* 29056); 1299 (*Mun.* 29065).

Imprisoned in the Tower c. 10 Oct. 1303.

No mention after 1328–9 (Chamberlain).

London, James de.

Defunctus 17 Jun.–29 Sep. 1317 (Almoner).

London, Robert de.

In the sick-room for a short time Easter 1298 (Infirmarer).

Witteney, Henry de.

In the sick-room 2–11 Nov. 1397 (Infirmarer). No other mention.

Stanes, John de.

In the sick-room almost continuously Nov. 1297—Aug. 1298 (Infirmarer).

Pistor, John.

Several periods in the sick-room, May, Jun. 1298 (Infirmarer); no further mention.

Chicelden, Chyselden, Thomas de.

Custos capelle b. Marie ante 30 Nov. 1298 (*Mun.* 23179).

---

[1] Philippa of Hainault landed at Antwerp with Edward III Jul. 1338, went on with him to Coblenz and then returned to Antwerp, where her son Lionel, afterwards Duke of Clarence, was born 29 Nov. 1338.

Segesber', Thomas de.
Was at the Roman Court with A. de Persore [q.v.] Jul. 1298 (*Mun.* 9243).

1299-1300

Finden, W. de.
The sole mention of him and of A. de Leyton (v. infra) is by the Warden of St Mary's Chapel who entered the cost of their sarcofagi cum cooperculis. Defunctus 1299–1300 (St Mary's Chapel).

Leyton, Lechton, Aleyn de.
There is a precept of Abbot Wenlok to his provost of Eye to repay to Dan Aleyn de Lechton some wheat lent by him to the Abbot's hospice; no date (*Mun.* 31526). Defunctus 1299–1300 (St Mary's Chapel).

1303

Salopia, John de.
Imprisoned in the Tower c. 10 Oct. 1303.
Exonerated together with Abbot Curtlington and other monks for violence done to William de Wycoumbe in the Abbey 28 Jun. 1326 (*Mun.* 5699).
Last mention 1328–9 (Chamberlain).

Lichefeld, Licheffeld, Lycheffeld, Lychesfeld, Thomas de.
Imprisoned in the Tower c. 10 Oct. 1303.
Very frequently in the sick-room 1305–6, 1309–10, 1310–11 (intervening Infirmary lists are missing); no further mention.

KEDYNGTON, Kedynton, Kidinton, Kydington, Kydinton, de; dictus de Sudbury; Richard.
[The form employed by Prior Hadham in announcing K's. election to the Pope is Ricardus de Kydinton dictus de Sudbury (*Mun.* 5453; cf. Domesday f. 409 b). On the other hand, the notarial announcement of Curtlington's election (*Mun.* 5463) uses the form Ricardus de Sudberia dictus de Kidinton.]
Imprisoned in the Tower c. 10 Oct. 1303.
Abbas, per viam compromissi, 26 Jan. 1308 (*Flete*, p. 121); the electors being R. de Fanelore, Thomas de Dene, Henry de Bircheston, Henry Payn, W. de Almaly, R. de Beby, and Kedyngton himself (*Mun.* 5424).
The expenses of his confirmation at Avignon for himself and his two Proctors (for their appointment see *Mun.* 5453) necessitated a loan of £300 21 Apr. 1310 (*Mun.* 9456).
After Kedyngton's election the Pope was appealed to by Roger de Buiyns, Prior of Sudbury, on the ground that he ought to have been summoned to take part in it, while Roger de Aldenham [q.v.] asserted by his proctor that the Abbot-elect was not free from certain faults. It is clear from *Mun.* 5460 (no date, except Trinity Sunday) that there was bitter opposition to this election on the part of a section of the Brethren, especially Prior Hadham, Henry de Bircheston (one of the electors), Walter de Arkesdene, John de London, Guido de Asshewelle, Philip de Sutton and, with less decision, Roger de Bures [q.v.]. They sent Roger de Aldenham and Walter de Bolton [q.v.] to Avignon as their Proctors in 1308. The other party, led by A. de Persore, W. de Chalk, and Henry Payn [q.v.], gave a bribe of £100 to Piers Gaveston out of Wenlok's money; so the efforts of the opponents were directed to secure the influence of the Queen (Isabella of France), of her father, the King of France, and of her uncle, Charles of Valois, and they hoped to do this through Henry de Lacy, Earl of Lincoln. Their action was based on infamia et insufficiencia Electi. Clement V (at Avignon, Jan. 1310) issued a mandate

to the King to inquire into Kedyngton's merits and to appoint him, if found worthy (Kal. Pap. Reg. II, 65). The King restored the temporalities 25 Apr. 1310 (Kal. Pat. Rolls 1307–13, p. 225).

The Papal mandate for Kedyngton's benediction was issued 23 Jul. 1310 (Kal. Pap. Reg. II, 71).

Royal letters allowing him to nominate Proctors on going beyond seas 25 Aug. 1311 (Kal. Pat. Rolls 1307–13, p. 385).

For his deed authorising the distribution among the brethren of the residue of the profits of Q. Alianore's manors, 1311, see *Mun.* 5672; Domesday f. 441; *Flete*, p. 121 f.

In July 1313 the Pope issued a mandate to distrain the proceeds of the Abbot's manors in Worcestershire to satisfy a debt of 8000 florins owing from the Abbot to the Roman Church (Kal. Pap. Reg. II, 118). Of this sum 7000 florins were due to the Papal Camera and 1000 to the College of Cardinals. Kedyngton paid off 5500 florins and John XXII remitted the balance to Abbot Curtlington (*ibid.* p. 209). See *Mun.* 9459, which is the Papal absolution from the interdict upon the Abbey, 12 Dec. 1320, and *Mun.* 9460, 8 Jan. 1321, which is a release from the debt (see Curtlington, W. de).

There is a letter from him to Prior R. de Hadham, dated from Pyrford, 1 Aug., no year, to say that he was taking medicine and had business which prevented his presence when the Convent met to elect to the benefice of Aldenham, and to request them to present in due form Mag^r Richard de Gloucestria (*Mun.* 4495).

Letters of protection on going beyond seas to the Roman Court were issued to him, 28 Mar. 1313 (Kal. Pat. Rolls 1307–13, p. 562).

Defunctus 9 Apr. 1315 (*Flete*, p. 122; *Mun.* 21067 says he died on "Hockeday," i.e. the second Monday or Tuesday after Easter Tuesday).

Sepultus...ante magnum altare in inferiori pavimento ubi cereus paschalis solet stare ex parte...australi (*Flete*, p. 122).

WANETYNG, Wantyng, Wantynghe, Wanting, John de.

Imprisoned in the Tower c. 10 Oct. 1303.

Suggested [? by the Abbot] as a possible Prior of Greater Malvern ? 1314 (*Mun.* 32645).

Attended Abbot Curtlington when he visited the Cardinals at Valence for confirmation in his office, 15 Jul. 1315 (*Mun.* 5463–6).

Proctor at Avignon for that Abbot's confirmation 30 Oct. 1316 (Kal. Pap. Reg. II, 132).

Thesaurarius 1318 (*Mun.* 29390); 1319 (*Mun.* 29405).

Custos ecclesie de Ocham ante 1320 (*Mun.* 20339).

Infirmarius 1320–1, 1322–3.

Prior ?+25 Jun. (*Lib. Nig. Quat.* f. 81 b) 1325–7 (a new Prior "R" was elected in 1327–8; *Mun.* 19845).

CURTLINGTON, Curtlyngton, Curtlinton, Curlinton, Kertlingtone, Kirtlintone, William de.

Imprisoned in the Tower c. 10 Oct. 1303.

Was attached to Abbot Wenlok's Hospice Aug. 1306; 1307 (*Mun.* 31449; 31492).

Assigned the Abbot's manors in Worcestershire, Gloucestershire and Warwickshire in mortgage to the Papal Nuncio for 8000 florins in behalf of Abbot Kedyngton; dated in domo decanatus sancti Pauli London : 21 Oct. 1313 (*Mun.* 22533); 2804 florins had been repaid by 18 Oct. 1314 (*Mun.* 9457).

Abbas, per viam Spiritus sancti electus [i.e. by acclamation of the whole Chapter], 24 Apr. 1315—11 Sep. 1333 (*Flete*, p. 122 f.).

Visited the Cardinals at Valence for confirmation 15 Jul. 1315 (*Mun.* 5463–6).

Election confirmed by John XXII at Avignon 30 Oct. 1316 (Kal. Pap. Reg. ii, 132).

Received the temporalities from the King c. 25 Jan. 1317 (*Mun.* 8428).

Visitation by him of the Hospital of St James, 1317 (*Mun.* 17117). For his ordinances and injunctions thereabout, 13 Jul. 1319, see *Mun.* 17118.

Was much concerned at reported indiscipline in the Priory of Greater Malvern c. 1318 (*Mun.* 32646–7).

The Papal Nuncio (Rigaud de Asserio) threatened him with excommunication and sequestration of his manors for non-payment of the above-named debt of 8000 florins; but the Crown anticipated matters by seizing the same revenues for a debt; see notarial instrument dated in the chapel of the hospice of the Dean of St Paul's, 22 Feb. 1318 (*Mun.* 9458). Rigaud, then Bishop of Winchester, gave a release from this debt 8 Jan. 1321 (*Mun.* 9460).

Summons to him and the Convent under the Privy Seal to provide carriages for the expedition of Edward II against the Scots; it was necessary, it says, auoir grant foison de cariage pour cel voiage; dated Nottingham 16 Aug. 1318 (*Mun.* 12192).

Further request for 60 oaks for "verges" of engines, lances, quarrels, etc., from the wood at Bubewell [? Bubnell, Derbyshire], to aid Edward II in his expedition against the King of France who was trying to rob him of his Duchy of Guienne; dated Ravensdale, Derbyshire, 2 Jan. 1325 (*Mun.* 5430).

Granted a pension of 5 marks to his nephew John de Curtlington, clerk; this was discontinued by Abbot Henle (*Mun.* 5894).

Defunctus 11 Sep. 1333 (*Flete*, p. 123); sepultus in australi parte ecclesiae ante altare sancti Benedicti...versus vestibulum divertendo (*ibid.*).

Woburne, Wobourn, Woubourne, Thomas de.

Imprisoned in the Tower c. 10 Oct. 1303.

Protested against Prior Hadham's deprivation 4 Sep. 1307 (*Mun.* 9499 B).

Short illness Christmas 1310 (Infirmarer); no further mention.

Glaston, Glastingber', Gleston, Glestonia, William de.

Imprisoned in the Tower c. 10 Oct. 1303.

Protested against Prior Hadham's deprivation 4 Sep. 1307 (*Mun.* 9499 B).

Last mention 1328–9 (Chamberlain).

Wygornia, Wigornia, Wircestre, John de.

Imprisoned in the Tower c. 10 Oct. 1303.

Proctor for the Abbot and Convent in the delivery of a challenge to the official of the Archbishop of Canterbury; dated in publica via Regia de Chepe 17 Jul. 1312 (*Mun.* 12749).

Suggested with five other monks [? by the Abbot] as a possible Prior of Greater Malvern ? 1314 (*Mun.* 32645).

Thesaurarius 1316 (*Mun.* 29362); 1321 (*Mun.* 28810).

Camerarius 20 Mar.—6 Jul. 1316.

Elemosinarius 17 Jun. 1317—28 Sep. 1319.

Short illness 31 Oct. 1322 (Infirmarer); no further mention.

Almaly, William de.

Imprisoned in the Tower c. 10 Oct. 1303.

Took part in a view of the inventory of St Mary's Chapel c. 11 Jun. 1304 (*Mun.* 23180).

Protested against Prior Hadham's deprivation 4 Sep. 1307 (*Mun.* 9499 B).

Incarceratus in palacio dni Regis (v. Henry de Bircheston, supra) 1307–8 (Treasurer).

An elector of Abbot Kedyngton 26 Jan. 1308 (*Mun.* 5424), but an opponent of his confirmation (*Mun.* 5460).

In the sick-room four times during 1309–10 (Infirmarer); no further mention.

Ryngstede, Ringstede, John de.

Imprisoned in the Tower c. 10 Oct. 1303.

? Gardinarius 1327–8 (Treasurer). Et de lx^s xi^d recept' de ffre J. de Ryngstede de terra locat' in Gardino Conventus. Et de viii^{li} recept' de fruct'...et de xviii^s vii^d rec' de arbor' vend' in predicto gardino per predictum fratrem J. de R. (*ibid.*).

Infirmarius 1333–5 ; 1339–41 ; 1344 ; 1347–8.

Elector of Abbot Henle 1333 (Kal. Pap. Reg. ii, 410).

Elector of Abbot Bircheston, being then Infirmarer, 1344 (Kal. Pap. Reg. iii, 182).

No mention after his own compotus as Infirmarer, 1347–8.

1305–6 (Infirmarer)

Boklond, Adam de.

In the sick-room all 1305–6 (Infirmarer); no further mention.

Scrowest, John de.

Short illness Jul. 1306 (Infirmarer); no further mention.

Wygornia, Wygorn, Wircestre, Peter de.

Ad skillam 1323–4 (Q. Alianore).

Harleston, Harston, Harletona, Harlet', William de.

[Harston and Harleton, Cambridgeshire, are different villages; but it is improbable that there would be monks called William de Harleston and William de Harleton at the same time for fear of confusion. The identity is fairly settled by *Mun.* 28810; 29362.]

Thesaurarius 1316 (*Mun.* 29362); 1319 (*Mun.* 29405); 1321 (*Mun.* 28810).

Custos ecclesie de Ocham ante 1320 (*Mun.* 20339).

Custos capelle b. Marie 29 Jan. 1325 (*Mun.* 17587).

Camerarius 1326–7.

Elemosinarius 31 Mai. 1328—23 Feb. 1329.

Defunctus 30 Sep. 1334 (Infirmarer).

Dadington, Dadyngton, Dadinton, Dadintone, John de.

Gift of 5*s.* to Sacrist 1338.

Ill at Easter 1340 for a fortnight (Infirmarer); no further mention.

Blythe, Blithe, Robert de.

Protested against Prior Hadham's deprivation 4 Sep. 1307 (*Mun.* 9499 B).

R. de B. diem clausit extremum die Jovis 23 Dec. 1322 (Infirmarer; he had been ill since 1 Nov.).

1306–7

Knolle, W. de.

Item in vi olnis de russeto pro fratre W. de K. pretio olne ii^s vi^d xv^s (Abbot's Treasurer, 1306–7; *Mun.* 24257).

Abbot Wenlok issued a precept for payment of 20*s.* to him for underclothing purchased by him for the Abbot; no date (*Mun.* 31541).

+ 1308

Salopia, Salop, Ranulph de.

Camerarius 1308 ; c. 18 Oct. 1311 (*Mun.* 29261 ; 29316).

Thesaurarius 1311-2 (*Mun.* 29303, &c.).

Solut' Ad. de Sar' pro debitis fratris R. de S. de tempore quod fuit ballivus precepto domini Abbatis in persolucionem iiii[li]. (Chamberlain 1328-9).

Bolton, Walter de.

One of the letters transcribed in *Mun.* 5460 was written by him from Avignon c. 1308 to the Prior [Hadham], Henry [de Bircheston], Gwydo [de Asshewelle] and Philip [de Sutton], the party opposed to the election of Abbot Kedyngton. He was then staying with a Cardinal, who was supporting this party, and to whom he paid 10*d.* a day for the keep of his horses and two florins a week for the board of himself and his colleague. In the course of the letter he upbraided the Prior for being, with others, *plus solito tepidi in causa sancta que suum et suo tempore effectum habebit*; and he praised by contrast the zeal of Roger de Aldenham [q.v.]. A letter, evidently written at the Abbey, describes him as *nuncius specialis in Curia qui precessit viam parare in agendo et Cardinales cum aliis amicis procurare* (*ibid.*).

1309-10 (Infirmarer)

Istelep, J. de.

In the sick-room most of 1310-11 (Infirmarer); no further mention.

Cherlton, Cherltone, Henry de.

Short illness Dec. 1322 (Infirmarer); no further mention.

Langeberwe, Langeber', Langeborwe, Henry de.

H. de L. diem clausit extremum die sabbati 13 Sep. 1321 (Almoner).

Hurle, Hurlle, H. de.

Short illness Apr. 1310 (Infirmarer); no other mention.

? 1314

Cotes, Gilbert de.

Suggested with 5 other monks [? by the Abbot] as a possible Prior of Greater Malvern ? 1314 (*Mun.* 32645).

Westbury, Westburi, Ralph de.

Suggested with 5 other monks [? by the Abbot] as a possible Prior of Greater Malvern ? 1314 (*Mun.* 32645).

Ballivus 1322; 1323; 1326-7 (*Mun.* 29444; 29446; 29447; 29457; 29459; 29466; 29473).

Concerned in a grant of property at Hendon 25 Jun. 1325 (*Lib. Nig. Quat.* f. 81 b).

? + 1314-5

Biburi, Beburi, Bybury, Byburi, J. de.

In expensis...J. [de Witteneie] et J. de B. euntium per maneria predicta pro bosco vendendo, 56*s.* 3*d.* c. 1315 (Q. Alianore, *Mun.* 23643).

Elemosinarius 1320-1; 1325 (*Mun.* 27216); et Ricardo de Chyriton pro debitis fratris J. de B. c[s] (Almoner 1321-2).

Liberat' fratri J. de B. pro episcopo Winton [J. de Stratford] pro i dolio vini misso eidem episcopo de exennio iiii[li] xiii[s] viii[d] 1328-9 (*Mun.* 20345).

1316 (Chamberlain)

Tothale, Tothal, Tuthale, Tuthele, John de.

In surgeria fratris J. de T. v[s] 1320-1 (Infirmarer).

Refectorarius ? —1327 (*Mun.* 9468).

An elector of Abbot Henle 1333 (Kal. Pap. Reg. ii, 410).

Pro expensis fratris J. de T. ad cartas confirmandas ad Curiam Regis c^s 1334–5 (Q. Alianore's manors; *Mun.* 23667).

In uno exennio empto et misso fratri J. de T. et sociis commorantibus cum benedictione apud Hamsted i^s 1335–6 (*Mun.* 23669).

Sacrista ?—17 Feb. 1338 : decedente de officio sacriste Westm. ad prioratum de Hurlee (*Mun.* 19620). Among the items handed over by him to his successor was sigillum de officio sacriste.

Prior de Hurley 17 Feb. 1338–49.

Went abroad on the King's business 1347 (*Mun.* 3787).

Alive 11 Nov. 1349 (*Mun.* 2016). Probably died of the Plague (cf. J. Armitage Robinson, *Simon Langham*, Ch. Quart. Rev. Jul. 1908, p. 342).

Hardmed, Hardmede, Nicholas de.

Mandate to the rectors of St Magnus and St Margaret, Bridge Street, to excommunicate certain persons unknown, who, instinctu diabolico succensi, had laid violent hands on Fr. N. de H. 30 Jul. 1320 (*Mun.* 6675).

No mention after 1328–9 (Chamberlain).

Kirkele, Kyrkele, J. de.

Curtlington, Curtlinton, Kertlington, Kyrtelington, Robert de.

Visited the rectory of Longdon, Worcestershire, and made a list of various goods after the death of a rector; no date (*Mun.* 21253).

Solut' fratri R. de K. pro hospicio domini Abbatis...vi^{li} xiii^s iiii^d 1329–30 (*Mun.* 20349).

Ad skillam, Supprior, 1334–5 (Infirmarer).

Thesaurarius 1337–40 (*Mun.* 20354).

Sacrista 17 Feb.—29 Sep. 1338 ?+; he " initiated the repair of the nave " (R. B. Rackham, *Building at Westminster Abbey* 1298–1348, pp. 272 ff.).

Defunctus 1344–5 (Chamberlain).

1317

Edward.

Defunctus 17 Jun.—29 Sep. 1317 (Almoner).

1318

Pershore, Persore, John de.

Professed Sat. 6 Oct. 1318, with five others during High Mass at the Abbey church by Petrus Bononiensis, Bishop of Corbavia[1], under a commission issued by Abbot William de Curtlington at Islip 1 Oct. (*Mun.* 9325, which is the Bishop's report dated from the House of the Friars Minors, London).

No mention after 1328–9 (Chamberlain).

Cotes, Robert de.

Professed Sat. 6 Oct. 1318 (*Mun.* 9325).

In surgeria Roberti de Cotes iiii^s iiii^d 1320–1 (Infirmarer).

No mention after 1328–9 (Chamberlain).

Woxebrugge, Woxebruge, Woxebrugg, Walter de.

Professed Sat. 6 Oct. 1318 (*Mun.* 9325).

Thesaurarius 1327–8 ; 1329–33.

Custos ecclesie de Ocham 1329–33 (*Mun.* 20348, &c.).

Die dominica 2 Oct. 1334 W. de W. post prandium cum aliis fratribus deuillauit ad capiendum aerem (Infirmarer 1334–5).

---

[1] Suffragan Bishop of London; died and was buried at the Greyfriars, London, 1331; cf. C. L. Kingsford, *The Grey Friars of London*, p. 72; Stubbs, Chron. Ed. i, Ed. ii, i, xci.

Nuper coquinarius 1345 (*Mun.* 29692).
Defunctus in Infirmaria, die Lune, 24 Jan. 1335 (Infirmarer).

Abindon, Abinton, Abyndon, Richard de.
Professed Sat. 6 Oct. 1318 (*Mun.* 9325).
Custos feretri sancti Edwardi (3rd quarter) 1338 (Sacrist).
Elector of Abbot Bircheston 1344 (Kal. Pap. Reg. III, 182).
Stagiarius 1358–9, with pittance of 17*s.* 2*d.*; 1359–60, with pittance of 30*s.* 10*d.* (Infirmarer).
Defunctus ? 26 Mai. 1360 (Infirmarer): 1359–60 (Treasurer).

Papworth, Papeworth, Hugh de.
Professed Sat. 6 Oct. 1318 (*Mun.* 9325).
Thesaurarius 25 Mar. 1333 (*Mun.* 29527).
Indulgence for prayers for his soul granted at Avignon 28 Feb. 1334 (Domesday f. 407 b, 408 a; cf. *Flete*, p. 75).

Payn, Pain, John.
Professed Sat. 6 Oct. 1318 (*Mun.* 9325).
Thesaurarius Maner^m Regine Alianore 1334–42; quondam custos (Domesday f. 409 b).
Custos feretri sancti Edwardi 1338 (2nd quarter); gift of 5*s.* to Sacrist 1338; custos 1346–7 with stipend of 20*s.* (Sacrist).
Liberat' J. P. pro scolaribus inueniendis ad scolas ix^s viii^d 1339–40 (Chamberlain).
Exhennia facta fratribus commorantibus apud Hendon, viz. fratri J. P. cum sociis suis xviii^s 1339–40 (Infirmarer);...per festum Assumpcionis b. Marie ii^s (Warden of the Churches).
Last mention Mar. 1348 (Infirmarer).

1318-9

Ashwelle, Asschewelle, Aysshwelle, Aysthwell, Essewell, John de.
Prima Missa 1318–9 (Q. Alianore).
Custos capelle b. Marie 1 Oct. 1328 (*Mun.* 29477).
Custos ecclesiarum de Ashwelle Stanes et Ocham [Oakham] 1334–43.
Along with R. de Beby (q.v.), accompanied Queen Philippa to Antwerp with the girdle of the B. Virgin, 1338 (Sacrist). John de Mordon [q.v.] took charge of Oakham dum custos erat in partibus transmarinis (*Mun.* 20354).
Elemosinarius ?—31 Mai. 1339; 24 Jun.—28 Sep. 1349; 1351–2 (Treasurer; *Mun.* 27229 A).
Thesaurarius 10 Aug. 1343 (*Mun.* 29658).
Pitanciarius 1343 (*Mun.* 29653, 29671).
Refectorarius ?—17 Oct. 1344 (*Mun.* 9468*).
Elector of Abbot Langham, being then Cellarer, 1349 (Kal. Pap. Reg. III, 339).
Indult to choose a Confessor 4 May 1351 (Kal. Pap. Reg. III, 378).
Coquinarius ante 1335 (*Mun.* 33333); 1351–2; 1356–7 (Treasurer).
Celerarius et Gardinarius 1355–61?+.
Infirmarius 1354–7.
Granator 1355–9; 1360–1.
Defunctus 1368–9 (Infirmarer).

Bridbroke, Bridebroke, Brydebroke, Michael de.
Prima Missa 1318–9 (Q. Alianore).
In surgeria fratris M. de B. xii^d•(Infirmarer 1320–1).
Refectorarius 1327–8 (Treasurer).

Camerarius 1328–31 (*Mun.* 29497).

In expensis camerarii et Johannis de Tothale existentium...apud Windlesore una cum ballivo et aliis seruientibus...xxiii^s 1328–9 (Chamberlain).

In feno empto pro equo camerarii quem tenuit ex mutuo W. de Bridebroke per annum ix^s 1328–9 (*ibid.*).

Last mention Feb. 1335 (Infirmarer).

Salesbury, J. de.
Prima Missa 1318–9 (Q. Alianore).

? + 1319-20

Atte Heyg, Hegge, Richard.
Elemosinarius 1319–20 (*Mun.* 27203).
Ballivus de Padyngton 1320–1 (*Mun.* 18965*).

1320-1 (Infirmarer)

Clare, Richard de.
No mention after 1344–5 (Chamberlain).

Logardin, Logwardin, Logwardyn, Lugwardin, Lugwardyn, William de.
In surgeria fratris W. de L. ii^s 1320–1 (Infirmarer).
Granator 1327–8 (Treasurer).
Sacrista ante 1338 (*Mun.* 19621).
In Chamberlain's list 1328–9 ; no further dated mention.

Castel, Castell, Castro, John de.
Ad skillam 1324–5 (Q. Alianore).
Frequently ill during 1334–5 ; deuillauit cum domino Abbate Oct. 1334, Apr. 1335 (Infirmarer).

Harleston, Harlestone, Nicholas de.
Solut' Thome de Waledene apoticario pro Nicholao de Harlestone... 30s. 8½d. 1328–9 (*Mun.* 20345).
Was continuously in the sick-room from 1350 till his death.
Had a camera in the Infirmary 1351–2 (Infirmarer; where his medicines are also entered).
Defunctus 24 Jun. 1357 (Infirmarer) ; 1356–7 (Almoner).

Pireford, Pirrefordde, Pyreford, Pyrford, Simon de.
An elector of Abbot Henle 1333 (Kal. Pap. Reg. II, 410).
Celerarius 1334–7 ; 1343–4.
Gardinarius 1336–7.
Thesaurarius 1337–8 (*Mun.* 20354) ; 1344–5.
Indult to choose confessor 11 Aug. 1349 (Kal. Pap. Reg. III, 327).

Hampslap, Hamslape, Hamslep, Hamselap, Hanslap, Robert de.
On 6 Feb. 1326 Thomas de Greynhull and two others quitclaimed to Abbot Curtlington, Fr. R. de H. and all fellow-monks all actions and especially the violence done to them in the Abbey on 1 Aug. 1324 (*Mun.* 5707; cf. 5717 ; 31771).
Custos ordinis 1326–7 (Chamberlain).
Proctor for repayment of a loan at Avignon to Florentine merchants, 3 May 1331 (*Mun.* 12889).
Precentor 1332 (*Mun.* 29524).
Thesaurarius Maner^m Regine Alianore 1334–7.
Sacrista ante 1338 (*Mun.* 19620).
Camerarius ante 1338 (*Mun.* 29567).

Soluͭ' fratribus R. de H. et R. de Lake pro studio apud Oxoñ, 3s. 8¾d. 1339-40 (Infirmarer; the payment was made up of one penny in the mark from the goods of the Infirmary and the rectories of Wandsworth and Pershore. The other obedientiaries paid at the same rate; e.g. the contribution of the Warden of the Churches was 8s. 9d. Mun. 20355). This seems to be the earliest mention of such students from Westminster.

Elector of Abbot Bircheston, being then Magister nouiciorum, 1344 (Kal. Pap. Reg. III, 182).

Last mention 1347–8 (Infirmarer).

Wenlok, Wanlok, Wenlak, Thomas de.
Prima Missa 1323-4 (Q. Alianore).
Ad skillam, tertius Prior, 1334–5 (Infirmarer).
At Hendon in 1334–5 (Infirmarer).
Camerarius 16 Feb. 1338—16 Feb. 1339.
Witnessed at St Albans the notarial instrument recording a suit between the Abbot and Convent of Westminster about a pension of one mark due to them from the rector of St Alban, Wood Street, 7 Dec. 1338 (Mun. 13352, a parchment 18 ft 2 in. × 1 ft 4 in.).
Short illness Sep. 1348 (Infirmarer); no further mention.

Titeberst, Titeburst, Tytburst, J. de.
Porrexit apud Hamstede Sep. 1340 (Infirmarer).
Last mention 1344–5 (Chamberlain).

1321-2

Brackele, Brakkele, R. de.
Received a payment from the Almoner 30 Nov. 1321—29 Sep. 1322 (Mun. 18966).
Thesaurarius 1327–8.
No mention after 1328-9 (Chamberlain).

1322-3 (Infirmarer)

Wynton, Winton, Wynchester, Wyncestre, Wyntonia, Richard de.
Prima Missa 1323-4 (Q. Alianore).
Ballivus 21 Dec. 1339 (Mun. 29577); 20 Dec. 1340 (Mun. 29604); 1343–5. Quondam ballivus 20 Mai. 1346 (Mun. 4504).
Revestiarius 1346–7 (Sacrist; but as he only gives the initial R. there is possibility of confusion with Robert de Wynton [q.v.]); stipend xˢ.
For his alleged complicity in a raid on Moulsham, Essex, 1344, see under Thomas Henle.
No certain mention after 1344–5.

Northalle, Hugh de.
Refectorarius 1327–8 (Treasurer).
In the sick-room all 1347–8 (Infirmarer); no further mention.

Brightwell, Brigthewelle, Brihtwelle, Brithewell, Brittewell, Britwell, Bryhtwell, Philip de.
Son of William and Agnes (Domesday f. 407 b) of West Brightwell, Berks, in the diocese of Sarum.
Indulgence for prayers for his soul and those of his parents, granted at Avignon 28 Feb. 1334 (Domesday f. 407 b; Flete, p. 75).
Drew up with Robert de Curtlington [q.v.] a view of Q. Alianore's manors

when Simon de Bircheston took over the wardenship from Henry de Bircheston [q.v.] 7 Dec. 1334 (*Mun.* 23668).

Several brief illnesses early in 1348; returned to the choir Saturday before Palm Sunday (12 Apr.); no further mention.

1324-5

Mockyngge, Mokynge, Mokkynghe, Thomas de.
Prima Missa 1324–5 (Q. Alianore; *Mun.* 23664).
Not in Chamberlain 1328–9.
Stayed out of the choir 3 Nov. and entered the sick-room 7 Nov. 1334, remaining there till his death; in surgeria fratris T. de M. xii^d (Infirmarer 1334–5).
Defunctus in die sabbati 18 Feb. 1335 (Infirmarer).

1328-9 (Chamberlain)

Bures, Ad. de.
The sole mention of him is among nomina habencia caligas estiuales, i.e. those to whom the Chamberlain supplied light gaiters for summer, 1328–9. He was not given panni nigri that year.

Somerset, T.
Sole mention, Chamberlain 1328–9.

Twynyng, Twynnyng, Twynnyngge, Twenyngh, Tweninge, Walter de.
Ad skillam 1337–8 (Q. Alianore).
Novus custos ordinis 17 Feb.—29 Sep. 1338 (Sacrist).
In cuppyng pro Waltero Twynyng (he was in the sick-room all this year) 1347–8 (Infirmarer).
Had a camera in the Infirmary 1351–2 (Infirmarer). No further mention.

Brichstok, Briggestoke, Brixtoch, Brixtok, John de.
Journey to Oakham with R. de Beby, the custos, Jan. 1328 (*Mun.* 20346).
Ad skillam, quartus Prior, 1334–5 (Infirmarer; Q. Alianore; Oakham Church: pro tempore quo fuit ordinis custos).
At Hendon in 1334–5 (Infirmarer).

Sancto Neoto, Sant Neot, John de.
Nouiciis ultimo professis et fratri J. de s. N. x^s 1336 (Q. Alianore).

Lardene, Larderne, Richard de.
·An elector of Abbot Henle 1333 (Kal. Pap. Reg. II, 410).
Gift of 6s. to Sacrist 1338.
Defunctus 1344–5 (Chamberlain).

Staunton, Stauntone, Stanton, William de.
[William de Staunton Harecourt, *Mun.* 15698.]
Ad skillam 1337–8 (Q. Alianore; Oakham Church).
Custos feretri (first quarter) 1338 (Sacrist).
Novus custos ordinis 17 Feb.—29 Sep. 1338 (Sacrist).
Elemosinarius 31 Mai.—29 Sep. 1339; 1340–1; 29 Sep.—28 Oct. 1342.
Refectorarius 1344–5 (half-year; Treasurer).
Elector of Abbot Bircheston 1344 (Kal. Pap. Reg. III, 182).
Celerarius et Gardinarius 1346–7; 29 Sep. 1348—25 Mar. 1349.
Thesaurarius 1346 (*Mun.* 4504; 26145**; 29746).
Indult to choose confessor 14 May 1349 (Kal. Pap. Reg. III, 311; but this may have arrived too late to be of service, as the Cellarership fell vacant 25 Mar., and the presumption is that Staunton died of the Pestilence; cf. J. Armitage Robinson, *Simon Langham*, Ch. Quart. Rev. July 1908, p. 342).

WAREWIK, Warewyco, Warrewyco, Simon de.

Prior ? + 1334–46. (The Infirmarer made several gifts to "Prior Simon," beginning 23 Oct. 1334.)

In exhennio facto domino priore (sic) commoranti apud Belacis [Belsize] pro aere capiendo 1334–5 (Infirmarer).

Gift of 3s. to Sacrist (de priore iii^s) 1338.

Apparently the only document which bears his name as Prior is *Mun.* 15698, which he witnessed as such in the chapel of St Thomas, que dicitur locus antecapitularis iuxta chorum, 1341.

Indult to choose confessor 29 Aug. 1344 (Kal. Pap. Reg. iii, 159).

Had ceased to be Prior at the time of the drawing up of the Chamberlain's list 8 Dec. 1346—29 Sep. 1347.

BIRCHESTON, Bercheston, Birston, Burston, Brigeston, Simon de.

[The spelling of John de Redyng's Chronicle is "Byrchestone."]

Celerarius 1331–3 ; Gardinarius 1332–3.

Was ill in the sick-room 1334, returning to the choir on Sunday 2 Oct. ; et per preceptum domini Abbatis subtrahebatur illo die (Infirmarer 1334–5).

Custos novi operis 1341–4.

Custos maner^m Regine Alianore 8 Dec. 1334—29 Sep. 1344. For the visus compoti, on his taking over the manors from Henry Bircheston, see *Mun.* 23668. On the back of his first roll as such is a Norman French letter which he wrote as "gardeyn de la Knolle" to the Sub-prioress and nuns of Henwode about a vacancy in their headship (*Mun.* 23669). The roll of 1339–40 (*Mun.* 23680) may serve to indicate what was required of him in the way of supervision. He went with Benedict de Cherteseye to Birdbrook on 17 Oct., returning on the 28th ; to Turweston on 5 Dec., returning on the 13th ; to Turweston again and on to La Knolle on 10 Feb., returning on 4 Mar. ; and with Frs. Beby and Charleton for a tour of all the manors, which lasted from 14 Sep. to 20 Oct., and cost xx^s for the three. For his expenses at assizes held for the Abbot at Knolle and other manors Sep. 1344 see *Mun.* 590.

Abbas die Mercurii in vigilia sancti Martini 10 Nov. 1344 (*Mun.* 5467 A, where the expenses of the vacancy and the election are recorded).

Redyng's Chronicle (ed. Tait, p. 108) says : qui locum illum aere alieno tam propria superfluitate [quam] fraude familiarium atque parentum vastatione nimis oneratum reliquit. *Flete* (p. 131) records that his successor, Simon Langham, paid debts incurred by Bircheston to the amount of 2200 marks.

Issued a commission to his Prior, Simon Haumodesham [q.v.] and to Robert his Sub-prior (? Hampslap) to punish the Prior of Greater Malvern for contumacy 13 Dec. 1346 (*Mun.* 32653).

Prior Haumodesham contended against him successfully for the right of presentation to the church of Turweston, Bucks, 1347 (*Mun.* 7672).

Defunctus apud Hamstede...in magna pestilencia 15 Mai. 1349. He had executed a grant on 4 May (*Mun.* 20867).

Sepultus...in claustro ante introitum locutorii domus capitularis iuxta ostium dormitorii sub lapide marmoreo (cf. *Flete*, pp. 128–130).

His anniversary was on St Martin's Day (*ibid.*; and Domesday f. 67) and in the deed arranging for it he left money for the new work on the cloister and locutorium.

Torinton, Torynton, Torryntone, John de.

[Totington, *Mun.* 32652.]

Precentor 1341 (*Mun.* 15698).

Short illness Jun. 1348 ; no further mention.

Arderne, Arderderne, Robert de.

Coquinarius ante 1335 (*Mun.* 33333).

Thesaurarius reddituum de Esthampstede 1334–5 (Cellarer).

No mention after 1339–40 (Chamberlain).

HENLE, Thomas de.

Thesaurarius 1330; 1332; 1333 (*Mun.* 29483; 29522–3).

Abbas Sep. 1333—29 Oct. 1344. (Papal dispensation, because he had come to the Pope without the necessary letters, and benediction as Abbot, Avignon, 23 Jan. 1334 (Kal. Pap. Reg. ii, 410).)

Exonerated the Prior and Convent from paying a yearly due of 30 oak timbers from their wood at Hendon, 6 Oct. 1333 (*Mun.* 5408).

Established a claim to jurisdiction over the Hospital of St James in the parish of St Margaret; for his visitation of it, 3 Aug. 1334, cf. *Mun.* 17121.

Gave a pastoral staff with a carving of the Salutation in the crook (*Flete*, p. 126).

Licence to him and the Convent to hand over the advowson of St Laurence, Candlewick Street, to the Warden and chaplains of John Pulteney's new chapel, 16 Jan. 1335 (*Mun.* 13794).

Was requested by Edward III to have the remains of his brother, John of Eltham (d. 1336), removed from the place of sepulture to a more fitting place "entre les roials" in St Edmund's Chapel; 24 Aug. 1339 (*Mun.* 6300**).

First President of the General Chapter of the Benedictines (under the constitutions of Benedict XII) at Northampton, 10 Jun. 1338; also in 1340 (*Lib. Nig. Quat.* f. 89; Reyner, *de Antiq. Benedict.* tract ii, p. 39).

The middle section (1325–45) of the chronicle in Cotton MS. Cleopatra A xvi (ed. Tait, p. 86 f.) calls him vir perfectae religionis, devotus, simplex, justus, misericors.... It refers to raids at Pershore, and Tait (*op. cit.* p. 87) notes an allegation that in 1344 Henle and Richard de Wynton [q.v.] had invaded the estate of Sir John del Isle at Moulsham, Essex, and carried away many valuables (Kal. Pat. Rolls 1343–5, p. 281).

Defunctus in die Veneris 29 Oct. 1344.

Sepultus...in inferiori pavimento ante magnum altare, ubi cereus paschalis solet stare, ex parte...boreali (*Flete*, p. 126).

For the expenses of his funeral on 4 Nov. and the cost of his tomb, £8. 13s. 4d., see *Mun.* 5467 A.

He initiated and provided money for the rebuilding of the Cloister,—a work which lasted from 1344 to 1365 (*Mun.* 23453; cf. R. B. Rackham, *Building at Westminster Abbey* 1298–1348, p. 276 f.).

?+1333

LITLINGTON, Litlyngton, Littlynton, Lytlyngton, Litleton, Lyttel-tone, Nicholas de.

The first mention of him in the rolls is in the Infirmarer's 1334–5, when he was at Hendon for change of air; but there is a letter to him (*Mun.* 5894) which, speaking of Abbot Curtlington, says: sub cuius regula benedictionem suscepistis habitus et religionis monachalis; i.e. he was professed before 11 Sep. 1333.

Son of Hugh and Joan (*Mun.* 32660).

Thesaurarius 1344–5; 1350–1 (*Mun.* 9290).

Custos temporalium Abbatis tempore vacacionis (on Abbot Henle's death) 29 Oct. 1344 (*Mun.* 5467 A). It is stated in the middle section of the Cotton MS. Cleopatra A xvi, that at this time he redeemed the temporalities for the Convent from the Queen, to whom Edward III had granted them at the vacancy (cf. *Flete*, p. 134; Widmore, p. 102). This has been questioned (cf.

Tait, *Chronicon J. de Reading*, p. 88); but his activity at the vacancy as shown by *Mun.* 5467 B points to his being the most likely person in the Convent to succeed in the effort.

In 1346 he obtained for the Convent a royal grant dated at Calais forgiving the escapes of all prisoners to the time then present for whom the Abbey gate-house had been made responsible (Tait, *op. cit.* p. 103).

Custos maner^m Regine Alianore 15 Ap. 1349—29 Sep. 1350.

Granator 1349–50.

Receptor vel custos ecclesiarum 1349–50.

Elector of Abbot Langham c. 27 May 1349 (Kal. Pap. Reg. III, 339).

In 1349 the King conceded to him the profits arising during the vacancy caused by Bircheston's decease (cf. Tait, *op. cit.* pp. 109, 243, and J. Armitage Robinson, *Simon Langham*, Ch. Quart. Rev. Jul. 1908, p. 347).

The favour thus shown to Litlington probably gave rise to the rumour (Joshua Barnes, *History of Edw. III*, p. 910) referred to by Robert Glover (1544–88), Somerset Herald, that he was the natural son of Edward III (cf. Tait, *op. cit.* pp. 233–4). But as Litlington was probably at least 22 in 1334–5 and Edward III was born in 1312, it is equally possible that he was the King's twin-brother.

Prior 1350 (probably by 18 Nov., *Mun.* 1575)–1362.

Indult to choose confessor 12 Feb. 1351 (Kal. Pap. Reg. III, 410).

Abbot Langham and the Convent granted him an anniversary, 20 Mar. 1360 (*Mun.* 5406–7), to be kept on St Nicholas' Day (6 Dec.) according to the custom of Prior Robert's [de Molesham] anniversary; it being agreed that from the rent of the manor of la Hyde and of lands at Knightsbridge and of marsh-land at South Benfleet (which N. L. had acquired for the Abbey at his own cost) there should be a distribution of 6s. 8d. to the poor, a pittance of 13s. 4d. for the Convent, and a recreation of 3s. 4d. for the Boy Bishop and his companions.

Abbas 7–14 Apr. 1362—29 Nov. 1386.

The royal licence to the Convent to elect a successor to Abbot Langham bore date 7 Apr. (*Mun.* 5417) and directed them to choose a man deo deuotus ecclesie vestre necessarius nobisque et regno nostro vtilis et fidelis. The election was announced to Innocent VI by Edward III in a letter dated Windsor 14 Apr. 1362 (*Mun.* 5402*).

The temporalities were restored 11 Dec. 1362 (*Mun.* 5420).

23 Oct. 1366, the Abbot and Convent received a royal licence, in which he was described as N. de L. nuper Prior Westm., to assign lands for a chantry for his and his parents' souls at Westminster (*Mun.* 1566).

He also founded an anniversary for himself and his parents Hugh and Joan every 26 Sep. at the Priory of Greater Malvern, with a recreation of 20s. for the Prior and brethren ut labor confratrum...die anniversarii...eo micius tolleretur (*sic*) 25 Jul. 1382 (*Mun.* 32660).

Royal licence to receive grant of the manor of Chelcheheth [Chelsea] 23 Jun. 1367 (*Mun.* 4799).

Privilegiorum Abbatum et conventuum ordinis Cisterciensis in Anglia conseruator et iudex per sedem Apostolicam deputatus 1371 (*Mun.* 6000).

Licence to act as attorney for Edward le Despenser versus partes transmarinas profecturus 12 May 1373 (*Mun.* 9509).

For his correspondence with Cardinal Langham and others at Avignon c. 1373–7 see *Mun.* 9231–9 and cf. J. Armitage Robinson, *Simon Langham*, Ch. Quart. Rev. July 1908, pp. 357–63.

For further detail as to his building operations see R. B. Rackham, *Nave of Westminster*, pp. 6–8.

Et in iiii ulnis panni linei emptis pro femoralibus domini [Abbatis, N. L.]

faciendis iiii^s vi^d Et pro factura dictorum femoralium vi^d 1370–1 (Abbot's Steward).

Et in diuersis medicinis emptis pro domino apud London...per magistrum W. Tankeruyl, xviii^s viii^d et...apud Oxon. mense Augusti...x^s iiii^d 1370–1 (*ibid.*).

Et in una furura de Beuere empta pro domino xl^s vi^d 1372–3 (*ibid.*).

Grant to him by W. Bromle [q.v.], Prior of Hurley, of an anniversary in festiuitate sancti Nicholai episcopi (6 Dec.) for himself and his parents, in consideration of a gift of £40 and other benefits, with an expenditure of 15s. yearly; 26 Mar. 1374 (*Mun.* 5399).

Papal faculty to him to dispose of his moveable property by will 1 Apr. 1375 (Kal. Pap. Reg. IV, 203).

Assigned to the Abbot's portion the property purchased by him in Pyrford, Denham, Sutton (? Sutton-under-Brailes, Warws.), and Staines, worth 25 marks, and the reversion of the manor of Birlingham 9 May 1378 (*Mun.* 5408).

Gift of 48 trenchers, 2 chargers, 24 salt-cellars, weighing 104 lbs., for daily use in the Refectory; 24 trenchers, 12 salt-cellars and 2 chargers, weighing 40 lbs., to be used at "recreations" (probably meat-meals) in the Misericorde; each piece to be marked with N & L coronatis, N. scilicet pro Nicholao et L. pro Lytlyngton, with an allowance of 10 marks to repair any losses or breakages in the set; a set of silver-gilt plate for the Abbot for the time being, similarly engraved and with a similar allowance; direction that daily after meals the Ebdomadarius magne misse, or whoever says grace, is to add Anima Nicholai Abbatis et anime omnium fidelium defunctorum...requiescant in pace Amen, 9 May 1378 (*Mun.* 9470–1; cf. *Lib. Nig. Quat.* f. 85 b).

His gifts to the Misericorde also included a small ciphus murrenus, a cloth (mappa) of old Norfolk work of small value, and a towel (togella) of Norfolk work 8 yards long (*Mun.* 6628).

For an account of his military service in 1386 see under John Canterbery (*Lib. Nig. Quat.* f. 87).

In a now mutilated letter in Norman-French he explained to Richard II that through "age et feblesse" he could not come "en propre persone" and bring "le noble relik lanel seint Edward" (St Edward's ring) ? 1386 (*Mun.* 9474).

He transacted business in the Vestry and received an oblation juxta summum altare in loco suo solito...videlicet in presbiterio ibidem 13 Oct. 1386 (*Lib. Nig. Quat.* f. 88 b).

Defunctus in manerio de la Neyte, hora prandendi, 29 Nov. 1386 (*Lib. Nig. Quat.* f. 86). Sepultus ante ostium vestibuli et ante medium altaris sancti Blasii episcopi (*Flete*, p. 137; i.e. at south end of south transept). Camden (*Reges*, &c.) says: in capella sancti Blasii qua intratur ad Vestiarium; but he apparently could not identify the tomb.

For details and distribution of his effects after death see *Mun.* 5446; they included armour, bows and arrows, and catapults, and among the payments were 48s. for the two Oxford scholars, T. Merke and W. Pulburgh [q.v.], and £4. 8s. 10d. priori studentium Oxon. pro capella ibidem construenda.

The Infirmarer 1443–4 enters among the effects of St Katharine's Chapel: item i magnum portiforium ex dono Nicholai Abbatis incipiens ii^o folio ris ciuitas iusti[1].

For the cost of making the Litlington Missal 1383–4 see *Manuscripts of Westminster Abbey*, pp. 7–8.

---

[1] Dr Frere kindly identified this for me as [uocabe]ris ciuitas iusti, Isaiah i. 26, being part of a lesson for the 1st Sunday in Advent.

1334-5 (Infirmarer)

Maidenheth, Maidynhethe, Maydenhitthe, Maydenhoeth, Maydenhooth, John de.
Prima Missa 1335-6 (Q. Alianore).
Short illness 5-9 Jan. 1348; was again in the sick-room when the Infirmarer closed his list 28 Sep. 1348.
Indult to choose confessor 15 Mar. 1350 (Kal. Pap. Reg. III, 328).

Dumbeltone, Dombeltone, Dompletone, Doumbulton, Dumbulton, William de.
Granator 1338 (*Mun.* 26262)-1341 (*Mun.* 26894).
Elemosinarius 21 Oct. 1342—29 Sep. 1344 (and apparently till 1349, cf. *Mun.* 18980).
Elector of Abbot Bircheston 1344, being then Almoner (Kal. Pap. Reg. III, 182).
Elector of Abbot Langham May 1349, being then Almoner (*ibid.* 339).
Defunctus, 1349 (before 24 Jun., during the Pestilence; *Mun.* 18980).

HAUMODESHAM, Aumodusham, Hamondesham, Simon de.
Prior 1346 (? + 13 Dec.)-1349.
Commission from Abbot Bircheston to Simon the Prior and Robert (? Hampslap) the Sub-prior to punish and correct Brother Thomas de Legh, Prior of the Cell of Greater Malvern, for disobedience and contumacy, 13 Dec. 1346 (*Mun.* 32653).
Defunctus 1349 (before 10 Apr. and during the Pestilence; cf. J. Armitage Robinson, *Simon Langham*, p. 341).

Staunton, Reginald de.
In surgeria fratris Regenaldi de Staunton iii⁵ 1334-5 (Infirmarer).
Last mention 1346-7 (Chamberlain).

Morton, William de.
Prima Missa Sep. 29—8 Dec. 1334 (Infirmarer; Q. Alianore).
? inter mortuos 1346-7 (Chamberlain).

Abindon, Abyndon, Nicholas de.
Prima Missa 8 Dec. 1334—29 Sep. 1335 (Infirmarer; Q. Alianore).
In 1341-2 was still receiving from the manors at the same rate as the three ultimo professi (*Mun.* 23683).
Short illness Jun. 1348 (Infirmarer); no further mention.

Campeden, Campedene, Adam de.
Prima Missa 8 Dec. 1334—29 Sep. 1335 (Infirmarer; Q. Alianore).
Custos capelle b. Marie 1336; 1344 (*Mun.* 17622; 17634).
Refectorarius 25 Mar.—29 Sep. 1345 (Treasurer).
Not mentioned after 1346-7 (Chamberlain).

Shenegeyze, Shenegeye, Shengeye, Shynegeye, Schynghe, Syngheye, Hugh de.
Prima Missa 8 Dec. 1334—29 Sep. 1335 (Q. Alianore); 1334-5 (Infirmarer).
Custos vestibuli 17 Feb.—28 Sep. 1338 (Sacrist).
Ad skillam 1338-9 (Q. Alianore).
Camerarius 31 Mai. 1344—31 Mai. 1345; 20 Dec. 1346—29 Sep. 1347.
Sacrista ante 1346-7 (*Mun.* 19622).
Last mention, in his own Chamberlain roll 1346-7.

Henle, Henelee, Henlee, John de.

Prima Missa 8 Dec. 1334—29 Sep. 1335 (Q. Alianore); 1334–5 (Infirmarer).

Thesaurarius Abbatis ? + 22 Jan. 1341 (*Mun.* 26894)—17 Nov. 1342.

No mention after 1344–5 (Chamberlain).

Okyngton, Okynton, Okenton, John de.

Prima Missa 8 Dec. 1334—29 Sep. 1335 (Q. Alianore); 1334–5 (Infirmarer).

Pelham, William.

At Hendon, to take the air, in 1334–5 (Infirmarer).

Visit of inspection to Q. Alianore's manors with Simon de Bircheston and Robert de Beby [q.v.], 1341–2 (*Mun.* 23686)

No mention after 1344–5 (Chamberlain).

1335

Mordon, John de.

His place in the list is just before those who celebrated their first Mass in 1334–5.

Custos capelle b. Marie in vigilia Pasche, 15 Apr. 1335 (*Mun.* 17621).

Thesaurarius maner^m Regine Alianore 1339–42.

Sacrista 25 Mar. 1341 (*Mun.* 15698); 1344; 1351–3 (St Mary's Chapel; New Work); 1354–5 ?+.

Elector of Abbot Bircheston, being then Sacrist, 1344 (Kal. Pap. Reg. III, 182).

Custos novi operis (with Simon de Bircheston) 1341–4; (alone) Apr.— Nov. 1344; 1349–65 (the Treasurer 1362–3 paid him £10 pro nouo opere claustri); also 1377 (*Mun.* 9498). For the work done by them, cf. R. B. Rackham, *Building at Westminster Abbey* 1298–1348, pp. 272 f.

Ballivus 1345–7.

Precentor 1349 (Warden of the Churches).

Elector of Abbot Langham, May 1349 (Kal. Pap. Reg. III, 339).

Indult to choose confessor 11 Aug. 1349 (Kal. Pap. Reg. III, 327).

Proctor for Prior Benedict de Cherteseye [q.v.] during his absence at the Papal Court, 31 Aug. 1350 (*Mun.* 9515; cf. J. Armitage Robinson, *Simon Langham*, Ch. Quart. Rev. Jul. 1908, p. 344).

Supprior 1351–2 (Cellarer).

Ad skillam 1351–2 (Infirmarer; Cellarer; St Mary's Chapel).

Thesaurarius 29 Sep. 1351—1 Aug. 1352; 1356–7.

In expensis J. Mordon et J. Palterton [master mason] euntium ad quarr' ad ordinandum de eadem ad utilitatem ecclesie per ii dies et una nocte (*sic*) 1352–3 (New Work; where frequent mention is made of such visits).

Infirmarius 1357—25 Jan. 1379. Rebuilt the Infirmary under Abbot Litlington's direction (*Mun.* 19345, &c.).

In expensis J. Mordon semel hoc anno existentis apud Wendlesworth ii^s 1366–7; surgical treatment of his tibia xlvi^s 1374–5 (Infirmarer).

Defunctus (?25) Jan. 1379 (Infirmarer; *Mun.* 19355).

As he was Infirmarer at the time of his death, he was probably buried in St Katharine's Chapel. His successor paid to Henry Welton sacerdoti celebranti in capella beate Katerine pro anima fratris J. M. a stipend of 40s., which implies a weekly Mass for the rest of 1378–9 (*Mun.* 19357).

Frater J. M. fieri fecit Tabulam (c^s) Altaris beate Katherine cum pictura (x^{li}) eiusdem et ii ymaginibus (xv^{li} $\overline{sm}$ [i.e. in all])...fieri fecit ymaginem Crucifixi et beatorum martirum Thome et Edmundi cum pictura superioris tabule ibidem (*Lib. Nig. Quat.* f. 92 b).

1335-6

London, Adam de.

Prima Missa 1335-6 (Q. Alianore).

Forty days' indulgence for those who pray for his soul and those of his parents, &c., or who visit the Abbey church on specified feasts, or who say three Aves on bended knee at the sound of the curfew; Avignon 25 Oct. 1342 (Domesday f. 408; *Flete*, p. 75).

Six brief illnesses at intervals in 1347-8 (Infirmarer); no further mention.

CHERTESEYE, Certese, Certeseye, Chertese, Benedict de.

De novo professus 1335-6 (Q. Alianore).

Prima Missa 17 Feb.—28 Sep. 1338 (Sacrist); 1337-8 (Queen Alianore; Oakham Church).

Camerarius + 1346-7. In debitis solutis de tempore fratris Benedicti de Chertes' nuper camerarii ibidem lxxii^s iii^d (Chamberlain 1346-7).

Celerarius et Gardinarius 25 Mar.—28 Sep. 1349.

Elector of Abbot Langham May 1349 (Kal. Pap. Reg. III, 339).

Indult to choose confessor 11 Aug. 1349 (Kal. Pap. Reg. III, 327).

See his story in J. Armitage Robinson, *Simon Langham*, Ch. Quart. Rev. July 1908, pp. 342-5.

Prior (after c. 27 May, when Langham was elected Abbot) 1349-50 (had ceased to be Prior 18 Nov. *Mun.* 1575).

Appointed Richard de Redyng and John de Mordon to be his Proctors (*Mun.* 9515) during his absence at Avignon about the appropriation of the churches of Sawbridgeworth and Kelvedon. But he went to Rome for the sake of the great indulgences of 1350, the year of Jubilee, and not having received the leave of the Abbot to go there, he forfeited his place as Prior. The Pope at Avignon issued a grant 18 May 1351 (Kal. Pap. Reg. III, 384) authorising him to return to his place in the Chapter. But already, 18 Nov. 1350, a royal licence had been issued to the Convent to prosecute him for pawning its goods without its consent (*Mun.* 1575), and in this he was described as nuper priorem (cf. *Mun.* 8593-4).

At Avignon in 1351, on his return from Rome, he obtained (i) an indult for a confessor, 12 Feb. (Kal. Pap. Reg. III, 410; where he is still described as claustral Prior); (ii) leave to contract a loan of 800 florins to pay his expenses at the Papal Court, 17 Apr. (*ibid.* 396); (iii) the renewal of the appropriation of Sawbridgeworth and Kelvedon, 5 May (*Mun.* Bk 3, p. 78; Kal. Close Rolls 1349-54, p. 405).

He was not restored to his Priorship again, but in due course was granted a camera in the Infirmary: et in ii clauibus ad cameram B. de Certeseye factis vi^d 1356-7 (Infirmarer); and a pension of 33s. 4d., which was paid to him in 1351 and 1352, but not in 1353 (Treasurer). So he died between 24 Jun. 1352 and 24 Jun. 1353; but his camera was still called by his name in 1356-7 and probably the keys were wanted for a new tenant.

Lake, Robert de.

De novo professus 1335-6 (Q. Alianore).

Prima Missa 17 Feb.—28 Sep. 1338 (Sacrist); 1337-8 (Q. Alianore; Oakham Church).

Gift of 2s. to Sacrist 1338.

Solut' fratribus R. de Hampslape [q.v.] et R. de L. pro studio apud Oxon. 3s. 8¾d. 1339-40 (Infirmarer).

Thesaurarius 1346 (*Mun.* 4504; 26145**).

Precentor 22 Nov. 1346 (*Mun.* 29752).

Several brief illnesses in 1347-8 (Infirmarer); no further mention.

Crendon, Crendone, John de.

De novo professus 1335–6 (Q. Alianore).

Prima Missa 17 Feb.—28 Sep. 1338 (Sacrist); 1337–8 (Q. Alianore; Oakham Church).

Thesaurarius Abbatis 25 Dec. 1343—4 Apr. 1344 (*Mun.* 24254).

Sacrista 1346–7.

Custos temporalium Abbatis tempore vacacionis 30 Oct. 1344—26 Mar. 1345 (*Mun.* 5467 A).

Was in correspondence with a prelate who had ordered a marble tombstone for himself, which Crendon was obtaining from the quarry patronised by the Abbey at Corfe Castle; scriptum apud Westm. die sabbati in festo sancti Thome apostoli [21 Dec.? 1364]; see *Mun.* 12205 with J. A. R.'s manuscript notes as to the date and possible destination of the letter.

Defunctus 1368–9 (Infirmarer).

Raundes, Richard.

De novo professus 1335–6 (Q. Alianore).

Not in Chamberlain's lists 1344–5; 1346–7.

In instrumento tangente R. R. iii^s iiii^d Nov. 1344 (*Mun.* 5467 B).

Placed last, as if deceased, in Chamberlain 1355–6.

1336–7

Charleton, Cherlton, Robert de.

De novo professus 1336–7 (Q. Alianore).

Prima Missa 25 Dec. 1339—25 Mar. 1340 (Infirmarer); 1339–40 (Chamberlain; Q. Alianore; Warden of the Churches).

No mention after 1346–7 (Chamberlain).

Flete, William de.

De novo professus 1336–7 (Q. Alianore).

Prima Missa 1340–1 (Q. Alianore).

Custos capelle b. Marie 29 Sep. 1351—8 Apr. 1352.

Ad skillam 1 Aug. 1353—29 Sep. 1354 (Cellarer).

Coquinarius 1356–7 (Treasurer).

Precentor 1361–4 (Treasurer).

No mention after 1364–5 (Chamberlain).

Borwell, Borewell, Burwell, Edmund de.

De novo professus 1336–7 (Q. Alianore).

Prima Missa 25 Dec. 1339—25 Mar. 1340 (Infirmarer); 1339–40 (Q. Alianore; Chamberlain; Warden of the Churches).

Elector of Abbot Bircheston 1344 (Kal. Pap. Reg. III, 182).

Custos ordinis de nouo 30 Sep. 1348—25 Mar. 1349 (Cellarer).

Indult to choose confessor 17 Apr. 1349 (Kal. Pap. Reg. III, 310).

Walingford, Walyngfford, Wallingford, Wallyngford, John de.

De nouo professus 1336–7 (Q. Alianore).

Prima Missa 25 Dec. 1339—25 Mar. 1340 (Infirmarer); 1339–40 (Q. Alianore; Chamberlain; Warden of the Churches).

Porrexit apud Hendon per licenciam Prioris Aug. 1340 (Infirmarer).

Ad skillam 1349–50 (Cellarer).

Camerarius 1350–1 (Treasurer).

Pro tibia sua curanda xii^d 1354–5 (Infirmarer).

Custos capelle b. Marie 1356–7 (Chamberlain); 1357–8 (Treasurer).

No mention after 1364–5 (Chamberlain).

+1339-40

Redyng, Redyngge, Richard de.
[The following is the first mention of him, but he would scarcely become Chamberlain till he had been about ten years in the Convent.]
Camerarius 1339-43 (*Mun.* 29647, 29652); in the Chamberlain's roll 1344-5 he is referred to as nuper camerarius, receiving as such a double allowance of panni nigri.
Granator 1346-7.
Custos capelle b. Marie 1348-51.
Indult for confessor 4 May 1351 (Kal. Pap. Reg. III, 378).
Proctor for Prior Benedict de Cherteseye during his absence at the Papal Court 1350, with John de Mordon [q.v.] (*Mun.* 9515).
Made the first account of the rents of Sir John Shoreditch 1352-4.
Celerarius 1354-5.
Solut' fratri R. R. x^s sibi concessos de gracia domini Abbatis et Prioris pro camera a retro attingente de anno quo fuit apud Sudbury 1357-8 (Treasurer). This may mean that he held the Priorship of Sudbury for a short time like John Lucas [q.v.].
Additional payments to the washerman propter debilitatem fratris R. de R. 1366-7 (Infirmarer). No further mention.

1339-40 (Infirmarer and Chamberlain)

Combroke, Conbrok, Comebrok, Thomas de.
Subsacrista 17 Feb.—28 Sep. 1338 (Sacrist).
Custos capelle b. Marie 1346-7 (Sacrist).
Celerarius et Gardinarius 1349-50; 1350-1 (*Mun.* 9290).
Granator 1350-1 (*Mun.* 9290).
Thesaurarius et Ballivus 1350-1.
Prior de Hurley 1352-63.
He was still a monk at Hurley, 3 Sep. 1372 (*Mun.* 3601).

Gisors, J.
No mention except as receiving outfit 1339-40 (Chamberlain) and as being ill for a few days Jul. 1340 (Infirmarer).

Wynton, Wincestr', Wynchestre, Robert de.
Prima Missa 25 Dec. 1339—25 Mar. 1340 (Infirmarer); 1339-40 (Chamberlain; Q. Alianore; Warden of the Churches).
Revestiarius 1346-7 (Sacrist; the entry is R. de Wynton, and this may be Richard de Wynton [1322-3], but the office was usually given to juniors).
No mention after 1346-7 (Chamberlain; Sacrist).

Redyng, Redyngg, Redingh, Radingh, John de.
Prima Missa 1341-2 (Q. Alianore).
Custos ordinis de nouo 30 Sep. 1348—25 Mar. 1349 (Cellarer).
Elector of Abbot Langham, May 1349 (Kal. Pap. Reg. III, 339).
Indult for a confessor 11 Aug. 1349 (Kal. Pap. Reg. III, 327).
Infirmarius ?+1350-3?+.
Thesaurarius et Celerarius 1 Aug. 1353—29 Sep. 1354.
Helped to compile a list of the Regalia 17 Jul. 1359 (*Mun.* Coron. III; cf. *Flete*, ed. J. A. Robinson, pp. 19-20).
Refectorarius 1360-1 (Treasurer).
Custos reliquiarum 1363-4 (Sacrist).
Frater J. R. senior fieri fecit clausuram Altaris sancte Trinitatis [in Nave, southwards] pro xx^li (*Lib. Nig. Quat.* f. 92 b).

Defunctus 1368–9 (Infirmarer).

Almost certainly the author of the chronicle of the years 1346–67, the concluding portion of the chronicle of 1299–1367 contained in Brit. Mus. Cotton MS. Cleopatra A xvi. For the identification, which is due to Dr Armitage Robinson, cf. his article *Simon Langham*, Ch. Quart. Rev. Jul. 1908, pp. 346 ff. The Chronicle has been edited by Professor James Tait, Manchester Univ. Press, 1914. Redyng calls himself "monachus...nomine tantum non conversatione perfecta, litera vacuus et ingenio, plus relatione vulgari quam propria consideratione seu literis magnatum instructus (Tait, *op. cit.* p. 99).

LANGHAM, Simon de.

Son of Thomas, who was buried in the Abbey Church (J. Armitage Robinson, *Simon Langham*, Ch. Quart. Rev. July 1908, p. 340).

Probably a native of Langham in the diocese of Lincoln, a village in the Abbey's Rutlandshire property; he bequeathed to the church of Langham unum vestimentum de plunket cum altari eiusdem sectae (*Mun.* 9225).

An elector of Abbot Bircheston, 1344 (Kal. Pap. Reg. III, 182).

Proctor for the Abbot [S. Bircheston] at the General Chapter of the Benedictine Order at Northampton 1346 (*Lib. Nig. Quat.* 91).

Prior 10 Apr. 1349 (Cleop. A xvi, f. 190 b).

Abbas 27 Mai. 1349, electus per viam compromissionis (*Flete*, p. 130). The electors were John de Ashwelle, Nicholas de Litlington, William de Dumbeltone, John de Mordon, John de Redyng, Benedict de Cherteseye and Richard de Merston.

Election confirmed at Avignon by Clement VI 20 Jul. 1349 (Kal. Pap. Reg. III, 339); benediction received from Arnald, Bishop of Sorra, before 26 Jul. (*ibid.* 337).

Indult to choose confessor 11 Aug. 1349 (*ibid.* 327).

For the method of raising money for the expenses of this visit by selling the Abbey jewels and ornaments, value £315. 13s. 8d., see *Lib. Nig. Quat.* f. 80; Robinson, *op. cit.* p. 341.

Installed 7 Sep. (Cleop. A xvi, f. 190 b).

Temporalities restored to him by Edward III at Gloucester 8 Sep. (*Mun.* 5416).

Consented, with the Convent, to the statutes of the Dean and College of St Stephen, 8 Dec. 1355 (*Mun.* 18431).

Redyng's Chronicle (ed. Tait, p. 127) notes that Langham was prominent in his attentions to de Périgord and Capocci, the two Cardinals who arrived on a peace mission in Jul. 1357, and suggests the motive ut forte nomen sibi acquireret ac beneficia pinguiora.

Granted an anniversary to Nicholas Litlington, then Prior, 20 Mar. 1360 (*Mun.* 5406–7).

Received royal grant of two stags from Windsor Forest 1 Mar. 1362 (*Mun.* 1529).

During twelve years, he paid off debts accumulated by Abbot Bircheston to the amount of £2200 and other charges (cf. Robinson, *op. cit.* p. 348).

For his gifts to the Monastery see *Flete*, pp. 130–2; e.g. he obtained of Nicholas de Gaugeria a serjeantcy in the Cellary of Westminster for £80 ad utilitatem conventus; he acquired for his anniversary and for the well clothing of the brethren the manor of Thomas Bidek[1] and le Fryth in Finchley (*Mun.* 4818). His personal generosity was shown, nihil a conventu in xeniis [presents of money or in kind] extorquens, sed ea eis integraliter

[1] Et in diuersis expensis factis circa placitum manerii de ffynchesle et la ffrith inter nos et Thomam Bedyk motum ixˢ iiᵈ (Treasurer 1375–6).

relaxans. He took nothing from the profits of Q. Alianore's manors (cf. p. 19), sed semper fatebatur et dicebat portionem conventus nimis fuisse exilem.

The statement that as Abbot he demanded no exennia is supported by the evidence of the account-rolls. The Chamberlain, the Almoner, the Sacrist, the Infirmarer, the Wardens of the Queen's manors, the Treasurers, and the Warden of St Mary's Chapel all omit any such payment during his Abbacy, though they include it in the cases of his predecessor and his successor. One, the Warden of St Mary's Chapel, keeps up the heading in exenniis missis domino Abbati, and adds nil hoc anno.

On 29 Jun. 1358 he gave the Prior and Convent a garden called Burgoyne or le Bourgoigne, which formerly belonged to the portion of the Abbot, but was taken away by Edward II, and afterwards restored (Robinson, op. cit. p. 351; Lib. Nig. Quat. f. 77).

Treasurer of England, 21 Nov. 1360.

Consecrated Bishop of Ely, 20 Mar. 1362, in succession to Thomas de Lisle, who had died at Avignon. Royal letter for election of another Abbot, dated Windsor 7 Apr. 1362 (Mun. 5417).

Chancellor of England, 19 Feb. 1363.

Archbishop of Canterbury, 24 Jul. 1366; enthroned, Lady Day, 1367.

Cardinal Presbyter of St Sixtus 23 Sep. 1368.

Dean of Lincoln and Prebendary of Brampton; Treasurer of Wells and Archdeacon of Wells and Taunton; Prebendary of Wistow in York Minster and Archdeacon of the West Riding.

His effect on the Abbey customs appears (i) in his direction in full Chapter that St Dunstan's Day should be celebrated in quinque capis; (ii) in his grant to Prior Nicholas Litlington of an anniversary on St Nicholas' Day (6 Dec.); (iii) in his decree (1352) that a loving cup should be served to the brethren on the day of St Edward's Deposition (5 Jan.) by the Almoner and on the day of St Edward's Translation (13 Oct.) by the Custos feretri. The Almoner generally included under petty expenses an entry pro speciebus et vino ad potum caritatis in festo deposicionis sancti Edwardi.

Et pro campano pulsando contra adventum domini Cardinalis xx^d 29 Sep.— 30 Oct. 1371 (Sacrist); i.e. he came to keep the feast of St Edward's Translation.

Et dat' hominibus domini Cardinalis apud Denham iiii^{li} v^s 1371–2 (Steward of Abbot's Household).

Mun. 9224* is a receipt from the Strozzi, Florentine bankers in London, for 2000 florins repayable to the Cardinal at Avignon, dated 14 Dec. 1372.

Leased all his benefices in England to William Palmere, Canon of Derby, for 1360 marks, 2 Jan. 1373 (Mun. 9223*); for his letter to Abbot Litlington about this money, 15 Apr. [1374], see Mun. 9237.

Et solut' cuidam pro missali misso a domino Cardinali precepto domini Prioris iiii^{li} 1375–6 (Treasurer).

For a list of the books which came to the Convent by his bequest see Manuscripts of Westminster Abbey, p. 4 f.

J. Bokenhull [q.v.] wrote to Litlington 9 May 1375 from Avignon to say that Langham was giving £200 yearly from his benefices in England to promote the New Work on the nave (Mun. 9239). See also Robinson, op. cit. pp. 361–3.

Gregory XI borrowed from him 6000 florins ut...ecclesie bona et iura in partibus Italie defendamus; Avignon 13 Jan. 1376 (Mun. 9230).

Died at Avignon 22 Jul. 1376, three or four days after being, dum sedit in collatione sua post prandium, subito paralysi percussus (Chron. Angl., Rolls Series, p. 339; Robinson, op. cit. p. 363 n.).

His will (Widmore, pp. 184–191; Mun. 9225).

His goods were received at the Abbey by Richard Excestr' [q.v.] from the hands of John Draper who had brought them from Avignon; 11 Mar. [1378]. They included silver gilt plate; a chalice; a thurible; i tabula volubilis argentea et deaurata cum ymaginibus interius inscriptis; iiii nouacule [razors] de quibus timeo ne rubigo eas consumat. Also books such as Memoriale decreti Johannis; quattuor nouiter scriptos de sanitate et de pace; Compilatio theologie cum aliis libris in uno volumine contentis; Scolastica historia; Ysidorus de summo bono. Also his large silver seal (*Mun.* 6604).

There are lists of his benefactions to the Abbey (*Mun.* 9225*; 9226), and receipts from the Prior of Canterbury (*Mun.* 9221*) and the Prior of Ely (*Mun.* 9224) for the vestments delivered to them by the Abbot and Convent in accordance with the will, 1379–80.

In diuersis expensis factis circa interracionem domini Cardinalis— £96. 15s. 5½d. 1387–8 (Treasurer).

Three Oxford students—Thomas Colchester, J. Sandon, and William Pulburgh—returned to the Convent for the ceremony, expenses 26s. 8d. (*ibid.* Cf. Robinson, *op. cit.* p. 364).

The Refectorer 1387–8 entered a payment of viii^d to the washerman pro mappis ad exequias domini Cardinalis accommodatis lauandis.

Acquittance to the Abbot and Convent from Henry Yeuele and Stephen Lote, citizens and masons, for £20 in part payment of the cost of making the Cardinal's tomb 26 Nov. 1394 (*Mun.* 6318).

1341–2

Thorgaston, Twrgastone, Thomas de.
Prima Missa 1341–2 (Q. Alianore).
Elector of Abbot Bircheston 1344 (Kal. Pap. Reg. III, 182).
Had brief illnesses, from which he recovered, in 1347–8 (Infirmarer).
No further mention.

1344–5 (Chamberlain)

Bray, R.
Not mentioned after 1346–7 (Chamberlain).

Blaston, Blastone, Ralph de.
Last mentioned in respect of a brief illness in Nov. 1347 (Infirmarer).

Pik, Pike, Pyk, Peyk, Thomas.
Solut' fratri Thome Pik pro O Sapiencia [= 16 Dec.] xx^s 1348 (Cellarer Sep. 1348—Mar. 1349; for the custom of making payments in respect of these O's which is rarely referred to in our documents, cf. Kitchin, *Compotus Rolls, Winchester*, pp. 61–2, &c.; Hamilton, *Compotus Rolls, Worcester*, VIII, IX; Wilson, ditto, p. 82).
Thesaurarius (? Conventus; ? maneriorum) Apr.—Sep. 1349 (Q. Alianore; *Mun.* 23692).
Mandate to the Bishop of London and others to carry out in his case the ordinances touching apostates who desire to return to their order, 4 Sep. 1353 (Kal. Pap. Reg. III, 515).
Coquinarius 1356–7; 1380–2 (Treasurer).
Archidiaconus 5 Apr. 1372; 12 Oct. 1373 (*Mun.* 5995, 5975).

Swyneforde, W.

Horniton, John de.
First Mass 1344–5 (Chamberlain, who enters domino Johanni de Horniton).

He and John de Redyng were custodes ordinis together in 1349 at some date after 25 Mar. (*Mun.* 18837); and received exennia, 4*s.* 4*d.*, quando primo sederunt ad mensas in refectorio (*Mun.* 23692).

1346-7 (Chamberlain)

Carsalton, Kersalton, John de.
Prima Missa 1347–8 (Infirmarer).

Murymouth, Murimout, Meremouthe, Mérymough, John.
First Mass 1347–8 (Infirmarer).
Indult to choose confessor 11 Aug. 1349 (Kal. Pap. Reg. III, 327).
Reclusus, ? – 1393–4.
Frater J. M. reclusus fieri fecit picturam Altaris sancti Benedicti pro xxvi^s viii^d (*Lib. Nig. Quat.* f. 92 b).
Defunctus 1393–4 (Infirmarer).

Crassyngham, Kersingham, John de.
Prima Missa 1347–8 (Infirmarer).

Vinterie, Vyntrie, John de.
Prima Missa 1347–8 (Infirmarer).

Clifton, Clyftone, Henry de.
Prima Missa 1347–8 (Infirmarer).

MERSTON, Merstheton, Richard de.
Prima Missa 1347–8 (Infirmarer).
Elector of Abbot Langham May 1349 (Kal. Pap. Reg. III, 339).
Thesaurarius 1350–4; 1357–62.
Granator 1350–1.
Ballivus ? + 1352–6 ? +.
Custos ecclesiarum 1353–4 (*Mun.* 20359).
Instituted a perpetual vicar to Kelvedon and took possession of that church 30 Jun. 1356 (*Mun.* 1015; 1020; 1021).
Custos maner^m Regine Alianore 1357–62.
Took possession of the church at Sawbridgeworth 18 Jun. 1361 (*Mun.* 8598. There is a statement of his legal and other expenses therein in the Treasurer's roll 1360–1; cf. J. Armitage Robinson, *Simon Langham*, Ch. Quart. Rev. Jul. 1908, p. 344).
Prior c. Apr. (*Mun.* 5402*) 1362–76?
In expensis domini Prioris usque Calies pro cardinali [Langham] et redeundo et alia vice usque...Cantuar' pro eundo et redeundo xl^s 1370–1 (Treasurer). This was the time at which the Cardinal with his colleague John de Dormans, "Cardinal of Beauvais," was engaged in France on a fruitless Papal mediation between the French and English Kings.
In expensis domini prioris et Willelmi Zepiswich equitantium uersus Cantuar' cum una littera domini Cardinalis pro domo scolarium apud Oxōn xvi^s 1371–2 (Treasurer).
In expensis domini prioris et ballivi equitantium uersus Sudburgh pro manerio ibidem videndo precepto domini Cardinalis vi^s x^d (*ibid.*).
For his journey to Avignon, Oct. 1376, to take delivery of Langham's effects, see *Mun.* 9232, which is a letter to Abbot Litlington signed vester deuotus orator R. Merston P. Westm. *Mun.* 9233 shows that he and John Bokenhull [q.v.] intended to go thence to Rome.
John Lakyngheth [q.v.] was appointed receiver of his estate; the account begins 14 Sep. 1376, which would be about the date at which the Prior started for Avignon; and it ends 24 Jun. 1377. But it gives no date of the

Prior's death. There are payments for his anniversary and for a house with which it was endowed, but such arrangements were not seldom made in a man's life-time. There is a reference to expenses incurred on the Prior's affairs after his return—post recessum[1] suum—and he was evidently alive at Christmas 1376. His death is implied in Lakyngheth's payments to the brief-writer (breuiator) for carrying round the mortuary rolls and to the chaplain for saying Mass for his soul in St Katharine's Chapel. Out of his residuary estate £20 were given by order of Abbot Litlington towards the cost of the Novum Opus, and £6. 13s. 4d. ad opus muri lapidei inter cameram domini Abbatis et gaolam clericorum (*Mun.* 9498).

R. M. prior fecit Crucifixum...in Claustro iuxta sedem magistri Nouiciorum pro xx marcis...altare sancti Blasii...pro c. marcis (*Lib. Nig. Quat.* f. 92 b).

Hertwelle, Herwell, Hugh de.
Prima Missa 1347–8 (Infirmarer).
In cuppyng pro...H. de H. iii^d 5–9 Mai. 1348 (Infirmarer, who says he went back to the choir). No further mention.

Biritone, Biryngtone, Richard de.
Prima Missa 1347–8 (Infirmarer). No further mention.

Warfeld, Warfelde, Warefel, Warefeld, Walter de.
Prima Missa 1347–8 (Infirmarer).
Ad skillam xii kl. maii = 20 Apr. 1351 (Infirmarer).
Coquinarius 1353–4.
Elemosinarius 5 Apr. 1355—29 Sep. 1361. [As such, he built five shops, which were bringing to the Almoner a rental of 5s. each in 1396–7.]
Thesaurarius 1356–72.
Granator 1361–71 (Treasurer).
Celerarius ?+1362–77?+. [For his work on the gates of Tothill and on Abbot Litlington's new house, cf. J. Armitage Robinson, *The Abbot's House at Westminster*, pp. 11, 18–20; *Mun.* 18858–9.]
For his accounts of the manor of la Hyde 1363 see *Mun.* 27069.
Sacrista 23 Jun. 1363—28 Sep. 1364.
Infirmarius 25 Jan. 1379—28 Sep. 1383.
Entertained Thomas Preston [q.v.] while he worked at the Litlington Missal, 1382–3 (Treasurer).
Defunctus 1383–4 (Infirmarer).

Tourseie, Tourseye, Torsye, Toruseie, William de.
Prima Missa 1347–8 (Infirmarer).
Coquinarius 1350–2 (Treasurer; *Mun.* 9290).
Thesaurarius maner^m Regine Alianore 1351 (*Mun.* 29856).
W. T. mittebatur apud Hurleie...iiii^d Nov. 1352 (Infirmarer).
Ad skillam 1354–5 (Infirmarer).
Solut' surgico pro fratre W. T. causa infirmitatis sue xx^s 1356–7 (Infirmarer).
Defunctus 1357–8 (Treasurer).

1349–50

Mordon, Moordon, William de.
Prima Missa 1349–50 (Cellarer).
Ad skillam 1362–3 (Infirmarer: fratri W. de Mordon primo presidenti: Chamberlain; Cellarer; St Mary's Chapel; Treasurer, but there deleted:

---

[1] The Dean of Wells doubts if " recessus " can be thus interpreted and believes that " from this journey [to Rome] the Prior never returned " (*op. cit.* p. 363).

Almoner has in exhenniis emptis pro fratre Waltero Mordone [q.v.] sedenti ad skillam de nouo, but Walter is evidently meant for William).

Camerarius 1364–5; 1366–71?+ (Treasurer).

Collector of Abbey rents in Wood Street 1364–71.

Sacrista 29 Sep. 1372—30 Nov. 1377; 1384—17 Nov. 1385 (Treasurer).

Elemosinarius 1382–5 (Abbot's Treasurer); 28 Sep.—24 Nov. 1387.

Infirmarius 29 Sep. 1387—19 Aug. 1391.

Defunctus 19 Aug. 1391. In pitancia Willelmi Litlyngton custodis infirmarii post mortem W. M. videlicet a xix° die Augusti usque ad festum sancti Michaelis. In distribucione pauperibus die sepulture W. M. vi^s viii^d (Infirmarer 1390–1).

Bokenhull, Boukenhull, Bukenhull, John.

Prima Missa 1349–50 (Cellarer).

A long illness in the summer of 1352; medicine administered, to the value of £1. 10s. 11d. (Infirmarer).

Ad skillam 1354–5 (Infirmarer; Sacrist).

Thesaurarius maner^m Regine Alianore 1357–62.

Helped to compile list of Regalia 17 Jul. 1359 (*Mun.* Coron. III; cf. *Flete*, pp. 19–20).

Precentor 1360–1; 1368–9?+ (Treasurer); 1372–4 (Warden of the Churches).

Sacrista 1361–2 (Treasurer).

Custos capelle b. Marie ?–1369.

Was sent to Rome in 1375–6 in order to obtain from the Curia a conseruacia (v. Du Cange, s.v.), his expenses being £3. 6s. 8d. and the costs about £10 (Treasurer; *Mun.* 9234–5 show that the "reservation" was obtained).

For letters from and to him during his business at Avignon 1375–6 see J. Armitage Robinson, *Simon Langham*, Ch. Quart. Rev. Jul. 1908, pp. 358–362; *Mun.* 9231–3; 9236; 9239.

Indult for confessor 3 Mar. 1375 (Kal. Pap. Reg. IV, 204).

He was one of Cardinal Langham's executors and received a legacy of 150 florins (*Mun.* 9225) pro expensis suis.

In *Mun.* 9233, a letter from him to Abbot Litlington, dated Avignon, 6 Nov. 1376, he said that the Pope had graciously made provision for the Priory of Deerhurst to be granted to him; but there was a rival candidate; so he prayed the Abbot pro eo penes dominum Regem et alios proceres Regni sic mediare ut idem filius vester...possit officialiter consequi quod intendit.

It may be assumed that he was successful, as there is no further mention of him at Westminster.

Hampton, J.

Prima Missa 1349–50 (Cellarer).

He was ill in Nov. 1350 (Infirmarer, who records his medicines) but returned to the choir. No further mention.

1350–1

Moredon, Walter de.

Prima Missa, kl. maii. (1 May) 1351 (Infirmarer).

Ad skillam 1355–6 (nouiter ad skyllam sedentis: Infirmarer; primo procedenti ad skillam: Chamberlain; de nouo sedenti ad skillam: Almoner; Cellarer).

Elemosinarius 1361–3. Built five shops, from each of which the Almoner received 6s. 8d. rent, and ten shops rented at 10s. each (1396–7).

Defunctus 1363–4 (Almoner).

Skilton, Skiltone, J.

Frequently in the Infirmary this year; for medicine administered to him see *Mun.* 19331. No further mention.

Solers, R.

Was frequently in the Infirmary from this year onwards; for medicines administered to him see *Mun.* 19331–2.

Et pro j clistore facto pro fratre R. S. per ordinacionem phisici xii^d 1356–7 (Infirmarer). No further mention.

Piriton, Perington, Puriton, Puryton, Pyrtton, Pyrytone, Thomas.

First Mass 1350–1 (Infirmarer).

Ad skillam, custos ordinis, 1361–2 (Infirmarer; Q. Alianore; Sacrist; Almoner).

Defunctus, 1375–6 (Infirmarer).

Nassington, J.

The only mention of him is in the Infirmarer's list of 1350–1, when he was ill for most of August 1351 and c. 27 Aug. arripuit iter uersus priorem.

1351-2

London, John de.

Prima Missa 1351–2 (Infirmarer; Cellarer).

Elemosinarius (before Easter) 1355 (*Mun.* 18981).

Coquinarius 1360–1 (Treasurer).

Custos capelle b. Marie 17 Apr. 1362 — 29 Sep. 1364.

Refectorarius 1363–7 (Treasurer).

Thesaurarius maner^m Regine Alianore 1372–5.

In surgeria pro tibia J. London xl^s: et pro eadem tibia cuidam mulieri pro eodem J. L. x^s 1374–5 (Infirmarer).

Custos hostillarie intrinsece 28 Sep. 1372 (*Mun.* 30066).

Defunctus 1375–6 (Infirmarer).

Grantham, W.

W. G. rediit ad Abbatem apud Denham 16 Jul. 1352 (Infirmarer).

No other mention.

Colcestr', Colchestr', Richard de.

Granator 29 Sep. 1351—1 Aug. 1353.

Celerarius 28 Sep. 1351—1 Aug. 1352.

Defunctus 1356–7 (Almoner).

1352-3

Ledrede, Leddrede, Lethered, William.

For dyadragant', diapemdion, and other remedies administered to him at a cost of xxii^d, see Infirmarer 1352–3.

Was infirm and in receipt of additional pittance in 1377.

Defunctus Jun. 1381 (having been in the sick-room for one year and 38 weeks from Michaelmas 1379; Infirmarer).

Zepeswych, Zepeswyk, Zepiswich, Zeppeswych, Zepuswych, Ipswyk, Ypeswich, Ypiswich, William de.

Non professus, Mar. 1353 (Infirmarer).

Prima Missa 1356–7 (Infirmarer; Almoner; Chamberlain).

Studens Oxon. (£10) 1359–64: Solut fratri W. Z. pro expensis suis…una cum expensis circa domum studentium xiii^{li} xiii^s iiii^d 1359–60 (Treasurer).

Archidiaconus 19 Oct. 1366; 2 Mar. 1367 (*Mun.* 5989; 1262). In *Mun.* 5987 W. de Z. ordinarius Abbatis Westm. ad omnes clericos de quibus cunque criminibus irretitos claimed to have a convicted horse-thief handed over to him tanquam clericum c. 25 Jan. 1370; so he was probably still Archdeacon.

Precentor 1364-7 ? + (Treasurer).

Sacrista 29 Sep. 1370—30 Oct. 1371.

Custos capelle b. Marie 1373-4 ? +.

Prior de Hurley 1377 (8 Oct. *Mun.* 3600)-1400 (15 Sep. *Mun.* 3590).

Eodem tempore [1391] Prior et Conventus de Hurley supplicant domino Regi vt pro reuerentia domine Edithe sororis sancti Regis Edwardi Confessoris ibidem sepulte Et quia dictus locus in multis aggrauatur videlicet de inundacione fluminis Thamisis de domibus ruinosis de moris tenentium suorum de onere hospitalitatis sue et quod modice sunt dotati placeat eidem domino Regi appropriare eis Ecclesiam de Warefeld Sar' diocesis... (*Lib. Nig. Quat.* f. 88).

Norton, Hogonorton, Thomas de.
Infirmus Mar. 1353 (Infirmarer).

Solut' fratri T. N. pro expensis apud Oxon. xxvi⁸ viii⁴ 1358-9 (Treasurer; but this is not the phrase used of a scolaris studens).

Ad skillam 1358-9 (Infirmarer; Sacrist; Q. Alianore).

No mention after 1364-5 (Chamberlain).

1353-4

WRATTING, Wrattynge, Wrothinge, Wrottingh, Wrottyngh, John de.
Ad skillam 1 Aug. 1353—29 Sep. 1354 (Cellarer).

Camerarius 1355-7; 1359-61 (Treasurer). In his time one pannus was divided between two brethren, to each according to his stature. Et ista erat consuetudo antiqua (*Lib. Nig. Quat.* f. 80).

Collector of Abbey rents in Wood Street 1355-62.

Thesaurarius 1362-71; ballivus 1365-71.

Custos ecclesiarum 1366-7 (*Mun.* 20361).

Custos maner^m Regine Alianore 1369-70

Prior 1382-1407. Gave evidence as such about the tithing of the Thames salmon (*Flete*, p. 64).

Et dat' duobus pueris ludentibus in Misericordia precepto domini Prioris iii⁸ iiii⁴ 1385-6 (Treasurer).

Et cuidam Nich° ludenti ad organa precepto domini Prioris xxvi⁸ viii⁴ 1387-8 (Treasurer).

Was granted custody of the temporalities 16 Dec. 1386 after Abbot Litlington's death on payment of 800 marks yearly to the Crown till the next Abbot was duly elected (*Mun.* 5425).

Et in surgeria pro domino priore hoc anno iii⁸ iiii⁴ 1400-1 (Infirmarer).

Defunctus 1407-8 (Infirmarer; probably about Michaelmas 1407 as he received no manorial payment for 1407-8).

It seems from *Mun.* 9500 that in 1405 his administration gave some cause for complaint; it was then 52 years since he had been promoted ad skillam and he must have been over 80. A protestation on his behalf was read in his absence to the Chapter in which he referred to his iam grauis senectus propter metum mortis et corporis mei cruciatum et alium iustum metum qui cadere possit in constantem virum. He was afraid, he said, that the Abbot and Convent might eject him, and so he affirmed ad hec sancta dei euangelia his adherence to the regulations and customs of the Convent. Evidently he was not ejected (cf. E. H. Pearce, *William de Colchester*, p. 70).

1354-5

Bampton, John.

In i quart' vini albi empto pro tibia J. B. nouicii lauanda,...cuidam surgico propter ordinacionem phisici communis ad curandum quemdam morbum in tibia J. B. x⁸ 1354-5 (Infirmarer).

Prima Missa 1356-7 (Infirmarer; Chamberlain; Almoner).

Custos capelle b. Marie 1359-61 (Treasurer).

Fratri J. B. precepto domini [Litlington] xx⁸ 1371-2 (Abbot's Steward).

Defunctus 1375-6 (Infirmarer).

Walkelyn, John.

Nouicius 1354-5 (Infirmarer).

Prima Missa 1357-8 (Infirmarer; Cellarer); 1358-9 (Q. Alianore).

Hereford, Herford, Robert de.

Nouicius 1354-5 (Infirmarer).

Prima Missa 1359-60 (Almoner; inserted in 1360-1 by the Infirmarer as having been omiss' in anno precedente).

Ad skillam 1369-70 (Infirmarer; Treasurer; St Mary's Chapel).

Precentor 1382-4 (Treasurer; Warden of the Churches).

Frater R. H. fieri fecit picturam Natiuitatis Domini in Claustro juxta hostium hostillarie uersus cameram Prioris pro xx marcis (*Lib. Nig. Quat.* f. 92 b).

Defunctus 1383-4 (Infirmarer).

Circestr', Richard.

Nouicius 1354-5 (Infirmarer, who notes a three days' illness).

Prima Missa 1361-2 (Infirmarer; Q. Alianore; Almoner).

Scolaris Oxon. 1364-5 ?+ (Treasurer).

Ad skillam 1365-6 (Almoner; Cellarer).

Precentor 1374-6 (Warden of the Churches).

Custos capelle b. Marie 1382-3 (Chamberlain).

Refectorarius 1387-91 (*Mun.* 19508); 1395-8.

Drew up an inventory of the Vestry, 1388 (ed. Dr Wickham Legg)..

Three days' illness and some surgery Aug. 1389 (Infirmarer).

Author of *Speculum historiale de gestis regum Angliae* (edited by Prof. J. E. B. Mayor, Rolls Series, 1869) bks. i and ii before 1376; bk iii, time of Richard II (cf. J. Armitage Robinson, *An Unrecognised Westminster Chronicler*, p. 12).

Licence to visit Rome and other places was granted to him by Abbot Colchester, 21 Dec. 1391 (*Mun.* 6663) with a testimonial to his morum honestas, vite puritas, sincera religionis obseruancia.

Gave evidence, as primus senior, about the tithing of Thames salmon (*Flete*, p. 64).

Frater R. C. fieri fecit picturam (xl⁸) tabule altaris sancte Helene[1] et ymaginis beate Marie pro iiii marcis (*Lib. Nig. Quat.* f. 92 b).

Gave new towels (togella) to the Misericorde (*Mun.* 6628).

Defunctus (? Jan.) 1400 (Infirmarer); inter mortuos 1400-1 (Chamberlain).

1355-6 (Chamberlain)

Paxton, Geoffrey.

Refectorarius 1359-60; 1361-3 (Treasurer).

No mention after 1364-5 (Chamberlain).

Leycestr', Richard.

[Walter de Licestria, a monk of Westminster, who received an indult for

---

[1] Probably in the nave, next to Holy Cross altar. Lethaby, p. 353.

a confessor 11 Aug. 1349 (Kal. Pap. Reg. III, 327), must be a distinct person, unless we assume a Papal error in his Christian name. No such monk is mentioned in our documents.]

No mention after 1356–7 (Chamberlain).

Waltham, Hugh.

Prima Missa 1356–7 (Infirmarer; Almoner; Chamberlain).
Defunctus 1359–60 (Treasurer).

Warewyk, Warwyk, John.

Defunctus 1361–2 (Treasurer).

Bromle, Bromlee, Bromlegh, Bromley, Bromleye, William.

Ad skillam 1361 (Q. Alianore); 1360–1 (Infirmarer; Almoner; Cellarer).
Coquinarius 1359–60 (Treasurer).
Sacrista 1362–3 (Treasurer).
Frater W. B. fieri fecit picturam frontis Altaris sancti Nicholai pro xl^s. Idem...picturam ymaginum sanctorum Laurencii et Nicholai. (*Lib. Nig. Quat.* f. 92 b.)
Prior de Hurley 1365–75.
Granted an anniversary at Hurley to Abbot Litlington 26 Mar. 1374 (*Mun.* 5399; *Lib. Nig. Quat.* f. 106).
In 1384 one frater William Bromlee was renter (redditor) of the House of the Holy Trinity, London (*Mun.* 30189).

Lakyngheth, Lakingheth, William de.

Sacrista 31 Jul. 1356—28 Sep. 1360.
Defunctus 1360–1 (Treasurer).

1356-7 (Chamberlain)

Arundel, John.

Ad skillam 1358 (Q. Alianore); 1357–8 (Infirmarer; Cellarer).
Helped to compile list of Regalia, 17 Jul. 1359 (*Mun.* Coron. III; cf. *Flete*, pp. 19–20).
Defunctus 1360–1 (Treasurer).

Staneford, Stanford, J.

Item uno nouicio vz. J. Stanford j pellicia alutaria 1356–7 (Chamberlain).
Prima Missa 1365–6 (Cellarer; probably Almoner[1]).
In expensis fratris Willelmi Colcestr' et aliorum secum equitantium usque Douere et alibi pro Johanne Stanford querendo et inquirendo xl^s 1375–6 (Treasurer; but without the term fratris the identification is doubtful).
Alive 1375–6, and still entered at the end of the list (Q. Alianore, *Mun.* 23703).

1360

EXCESTR', Richard.

His corrodium of one shilling a week was paid by the Treasurer from Mich^s 1360 (*Mun.* 19855).
Prima Missa 1361 (Q. Alianore); 1361–2 (Infirmarer; Sacrist; Almoner).
Scolaris Oxon. (£10) ?+1375–6?+ (Treasurer).
Gave a large ciphus murrenus to the Misericorde (*Mun.* 6628) and mappe mensales to the Hostillar (*Mun.* 9480).
Prior 1377–82. (He resigned, and in the Chamberlain's roll 1382–3 and thereafter he was entered next to the new Prior as receiving a double or Prior's

---

[1] The Almoner of this year records the Primae Missae of *seven* brethren without giving names; probably Staneford, Canterbery, Farnago, W. Litlington, Coumbe, W. Witlesford, and Giffard.

portion of clothing, &c.   Similarly he received a double or Prior's pittance on the anniversaries of Richard de Berking, Litlington and others.   He was also granted a life pension of 4 marks; his first surviving quarterly receipt 5 Oct. 1383, *Mun.* 30180; last, 6 Jul. 1396, *Mun.* 30310.)

Received from John Draper the goods of Cardinal Langham, which had been conveyed from Avignon, 11 Mar. [1378] (*Mun.* 6604.   Ista...deposuit... in thesauraria in quadam cista cum aliis donis domini nostri Cardinalis. Et erunt ibi usque aduentum magistri T. de Southam.

Defunctus 1396–7.   [The Treasurer paid him his allowance as ex-Prior at Mich[s] 1396 but not at Easter 1397.]

Mun. 6603 contains a full list of his furniture and effects as they existed in his rooms at his death (cf. E. H. Pearce, *William de Colchester*, pp. 49–51); a statement of how they were assigned or disposed of; and the expenses of his funeral and tomb-stone.

1360–1

Somerton, Richard.
   Defunctus 1360–1 (Treasurer).

1361–2

Stowe, John.
   Prima Missa 1361 (Q. Alianore); 1361–2 (Infirmarer; Almoner).
   Scolaris Oxon. (£10) 1362–7 (Treasurer).
   Ad skillam 1367–8 (Almoner; Cellarer).
   Thesaurarius maner[m] Regine Alianore 1369–70.
   Camerarius 1372–4 (*Mun.* 1909).
   One of the three Proctors for the Convent in the suit with the Dean and College of St Stephen 10 Dec. 1378 (*Mun.* 18441); 20 Dec. 1387 (*Mun.* 18450).
   Custos capelle b. Marie ante 1382 (*Mun.* 23188).
   In expensis fratrum J. S. et Johannis Lakynghethe cum v hominibus equitancium uersus Sarum et ibidem commorancium per v septimanas tempore parliamenti ibidem pro negociis domini Abbatis et conuentus prosequendis et expediendis...£7. 19s. 4d. 1383–4 (Treasurer; the Abbot paid Stowe £3. 13s. 9d.).
   Elemosinarius 24 Nov. 1387—20 Nov. 1411.   Built three shops, the rentals of which went into the Almoner's receipts.
   Archidiaconus 24 Jun. 1388 (*Mun.* 5979: in which he sent to dominus William, priest of St Margaret's, a notice of maior excommunicacio against John Broke, skinner, for non-payment of a debt of one mark sterling).
   Defunctus 1412–13 (Infirmarer); nuper defunctus 29 Sep. 1413 (Treasurer).

Staunton, Robert.
   Prima Missa 1361 (Q. Alianore); 1361–2 (Infirmarer; Almoner).
   Gave a large ciphus murrenus to the Misericorde (*Mun.* 6628).
   Defunctus 1375–6 (Infirmarer; the first of seven Brethren who died during this year,—a sixth part of the Convent).

Honyngton, Honyngtone, Richard.
   Prima Missa 1361–2 (Infirmarer; Almoner; Sacrist).
   Refectorarius 1368–70 ?+ (Treasurer).
   Custos capelle b. Marie 1369–70.
   The Hostillar of 1400 was still using mappe mensales de linea tela which were partly his gift (*Mun.* 9480).
   Elemosinarius 1371–5.   Drew up a rental of the Almonry 1371 (*Mun.* 18995).

Solut' fratri R. H. pro uno missali domini [Litlington] emendando xxviii⁸ iiii^d 1372–3 (Abbot's Steward).

Sacrista 30 Nov. 1377—28 Sep. 1383.

Thesaurarius et ballivus 1383–7.

Custos ecclesiarum 1383–7.

Celerarius 1387–93 ? + (Treasurer).

Granator 1386–90 ; 1391–4.

Defunctus 1394–5 (Infirmarer).

COLCHESTER, William.

Son of Reginald and Alice of the parish of St Nicholas, Colchester (*Mun.* 3571).

Prima Missa 1361–2 (Infirmarer ; Sacrist ; Almoner).

Scolaris Oxon. 1366–70 (Treasurer).

Ad skillam 29 Sep.—30 Oct. 1371 (Sacrist) ; 1371–2 (Infirmarer ; Treasurer) ; 1372–3 (repeated in Sacrist).

In expensis fratris W. C. et duorum valettorum emissorum usque North-amtone ad generale capitulum, xx⁸ 1371–2 (Abbot's Steward).

Among the receipts of the Sacrist 1372–3 is £2 from W. C. de oblacione comitisse de March ad zonam beate Marie ; there is in the same compotus a charge of £6. 16s. 8d. for the two horses bought for this journey and of 13s. 4d. for Colchester's personal expenses.

Custos hospicii Abbatis [N. Litlington] 1373–4 ? +.

Thesaurarius 1375–6.

Coquinarius 1375–6 (Treasurer) ; repaired the Convent kitchen (*ibid.*).

Was sent abroad by the Convent 10 Jun. 1377—22 Nov. 1379 to Avignon and Rome in the matter of the suit against the Dean and College of St Stephen and subsequently in that of the murder of Robert Hawley. For his expenses and law-costs, see *Mun.* 9256 ; for John Farnago's [q. v.] outlay on his behalf at Avignon 24 Jul.—19 Aug. 1377, see *Mun.* 9228 ; for letter of commendation which he took with him from William Courtenay, Bishop of London, see *Mun.* 12731. At Avignon he witnessed probate of Cardinal Langham's will and other documents 14 Aug. 1377 (*Mun.* 9225, 9223*). His letter from Rome, 20 Nov. 1377, *Mun.* 9240.

Archidiaconus 1382 (*Mun.* 18478 D) ; 9 Nov. 1386. As such, he possessed a flock of over 300 sheep, which were leased to a Westminster butcher c. 9 Nov. 1386 (*Mun.* 5984).

Was granted by the Abbot and Convent a camera, with that part of the garden which belonged to the Lady Chapel ; a pension of 6 marks ; and a senior's corrody, 25 Sep. 1382 (*Lib. Nig. Quat.* f. 86 b). For two of his receipts for the pension see *Mun.* 30181, 30196 ; it was paid till Christmas 1386.

Granator 1380–2.

At Rome 1382–3 (Chamberlain, who noted that W. C. et W. Halle non habuerunt habitus hoc anno quia...fuerunt Rome).

The Pope during this visit "provided" him to the Priorship, *vice* R. Excestr' ; Colchester received the royal pardon for any prejudice or contempt caused to the Crown by such action ; signed by John Waltham, afterwards Bishop of Salisbury ; fee to the Hanaper ; 2 Jan. 1384 (*Mun.* 9503).

Sacrista 1383–4 (Treasurer).

Et solut' fratri W. C. pro expensis suis usque Curiam Romanam et ibidem commorando pro negociis conuentus prosequendis et expediendis c⁸ 1384–5 (Treasurer).

Et solut' fratri W. C. pro diuersis negotiis in Curia Romana prosequendis et expediendis per manus domini Prioris x^li et in uno equo empto pro eodem W. desuper equitando usque Curiam Romanam iiii^li 1385–6 (Treasurer).

Abbas 10 Dec. 1386 (*Lib. Nig. Quat.* f. 86).

Mun. 5431 is a petition to Richard II from the Prior and Convent in French to give his consent to the election of " Daunz William Colchestre un de lours commoignes en abbe et pastoure " and to make formal announcement of it to the Pope. The election was made per viam compromissi, in spite of the King's desire to have John Lakyngheth [q.v.] elected (cf. J. Armitage Robinson, *An Unrecognised Westminster Chronicler*, pp. 16, 22).

Received Abbot Litlington's armour, Jan. 1387 (*Mun.* 5446).

Richard II gave to St Edward's shrine quoddam jocale solempne. Anulum videlicet aureum cum quodam lapide precioso vocato Rubyo valoris ut fertur c^{ll} et amplius 14 Nov. 1388 (*Lib. Nig. Quat.* f. 86 ; cf. f. 108 b).

Et dat' cuidam homini venienti de sorore domini a Cantabrege xii^d 1389–90 (Abbot's Steward).

Was absolved from his triennial visit to the Roman Court as being represented by his Proctor, John Borewell [q.v.], 19 Sep. 1390 (*Mun.* 6664).

For the gifts of the Abbot and his brethren to the Roman Court for the year of Jubilee, 1390, see *Lib. Nig. Quat.* f. 92.

Went abroad on the King's business 22 Dec. (*Polychronicon* IX, 264) 14 Dec. 1391 (*Lib. Nig. Quat.* f. 87 b) ; Et dominus Rex suscepit eum et omnia bona sua in proteccione sua.

Royal licence to appropriate the church of Aldenham to the maintenance of an anniversary of Richard II in the Abbey church every 16 Jul. in quo die coronabamur, 18 Aug. 1391 (*Mun.* 4499).

Received from Richard II the alien priory of Stoke by Clare, on condition of paying £100 yearly to the Novum Opus, 12 Nov. 1391 (*Mun.* 6226).

Was one of the Presidents of the General Chapter of Benedictines, c. 7 Jul. 1393 (*Lib. Nig. Quat.* f. 90).

Received Richard II's grant of £200 a year for an anniversary for Queen Anne and himself, 9 Aug. 1394 (*Mun.* 5257).

£20 paid towards the cost of Cardinal Langham's tomb, 1394 (*Mun.* 6318).

Mandate to him and the Bishop of Salisbury and the Abbot of Waltham on petition of Richard II to correct and reform the statutes, customs, &c. of the collegiate Chapter of the Chapel in Windsor Castle 15 Mar. 1393 (Kal. Pap. Reg. III, 456).

For his ordinance about the better maintenance of the Lay Brothers of the Almonry see *Lib. Nig. Quat.* f. 85.

Assigned the church at Aldenham to the Prior and Convent for the maintenance of his anniversary every 29 Jun., with a pittance for the brethren and a distribution to the poor 1 Dec. 1397 (*Mun.* 4515). A further indenture to the same end, 3 Dec. 1407 (*Mun.* 5260 A).

Received grant of Richard II's manors ; Windsor 23 Apr. 1399 (*Mun.* 17016).

Assented to a lease being granted to Geoffrey Chaucer of a tenement in the garden of the Lady Chapel, 24 Dec. 1399 (*Mun.* LVII).

Royal licence for an anniversary for himself and his parents, to be maintained by the Prior and Convent of St Botolph, Colchester, in their chapel of St Katharine and in the parish church of St Nicholas, with gifts to the canon-chaplain who said the memorial Mass, the vicar of St Nicholas, the poor, and the prisoners in Colchester Castle, and for the repair of his parents' tomb, 20 May 1406 (*Mun.* 5259).

Went abroad, 1407 (*Mun.* 1676).

Endowed an anniversary for himself and his parents, Reginald and Alice, and Thomas Merke [q.v.], Bishop of Carlisle, in the Priory of St Mary, Hurley, 5 Oct. 1411 (*Mun.* 3571).

Presided alone at the General Chapter of Benedictines at Northampton, 6 Jul. 1411 (*Lib. Nig. Quat.* f. 90).

Granted an anniversary every 18 Sep. for John de Waltham, Bishop of Salisbury, 15 Jul. 1412 (*Mun.* 5262 A).

xxxiii^{li} liberat' domino Abbati de assensu domini prioris et seniorum pro certis ecclesie negociis in curia romana expediendis, 1412–3 (New Work).

Dat' domino Abbati xv^{li} pro diuersis infortuniis accidentibus in maneriis suis annis precedentibus et precipue anno presente 1412–3 (Q. Alianore).

In expensis domini ac familie sue eundo uersus Cales ac portagio et batellagio domini usque nauem videlicet die dominica die lune die martis ac etiam expensis J. Sandon J. Stowe [q. v.] ac partis familie redeundo uersus London...iiii^{li} xii^s (*Mun.* 24544, undated).

In batillagio domini quando comedit apud Lambhyth cum Archiepiscopo viii^d 1413–4 (Abbot's Treasurer).

Solut' pro anniversario domini Abbatis apud Colcestre xlvi^s viii^d 1413–4 (Abbot's Treasurer).

In i noua charyet cum vi equis in eadem ultra i per dominum Abbatem et cum toto harnes' ad dictam charyet et equos pertinentes empta et data domino Regi in transitu suo in ffranciam cum stipendio i valetti i garcionis i pagetti ad dictam chariet cum panno empto pro liberata eorum una cum custibus eorundem et equorum predictorum per iii septimanas ante exitum domini Regis in ffranciam hoc anno xxxiii^{li} xii^d 1414–5 (Treasurer).

Attended the Council of Constance, 1414.

The Warden of the Queen's Manors paid him lvi^s viii^d for entertaining dominum imperatorem et magnates 1415–6 (? the Emperor Sigismund who landed at Dover, May 1416; cf. J. H. Wylie, *Henry V*, p. 67).

Et solut' appotecario London pro glistore et electuario confort' pro domino tempore infirmitatis sue xvi^s viii^d 1416–7 (Abbot's Receiver).

As collector of the triennial contribution of $\frac{1}{2}d$. in the mark imposed on Benedictine houses at the General Chapter at Northampton, 1414, it was his duty to pay for the cost of loans to the Abbot of St Edmundsbury and the Prior of Worcester, the Benedictine delegates (£12. 13s. 4d.); the charges of lawyers retained by the Order at Constance (£23. 6s. 8d.); the gifts made to messengers sent home by the delegates (£4. 3s. 4d.). His accounts survive for 1417 (*Mun.* 12395) and 1420 (*Mun.* 12397). In the latter year he paid 13s. 4d. to a monk of York predicanti in Anglico in ecclesia omnium Sanctorum Northampton; £10 to a monk of Worcester for a journey to Constance and back; and gifts to the two men who followed him in the Abbacy, Richard Harwden and Edmund Kirton.

Et dat' seruienti principalis Baronis portanti noua de captione ciuitatis Rothemagensis, 1417–8 (Abbot's Receiver).

Defunctus, ? Oct. 1420. (The roll of Q. Alianore's manors 1419–20 gives the names of 12 Brethren deceased that year, and adds: hii omnes moriebantur hoc anno una cum domino abbate et fratre Thoma Peuerel. This might mean that he died before Mich^s, but his anniversary was in Oct. (*Mun.* 5262 B). The royal licence to elect a successor (*Mun.* 5440) was dated 12 Nov. 1420.) Buried in the chapel of St John Baptist.

In writing to Colchester about the respect in which he was held, and employing what cannot wholly be dismissed as the language of flattery, Thomas Merke, Bishop of Carlisle, said: vident etenim vestram soliditatem, que rara virtus est modernis diebus et illo specialius in vobis confidunt (*Mun.* 9240*).

For a longer account of his career see E. H. Pearce, *William de Colchester, Abbot of Westminster* (S.P.C.K. 1915).

Somerton, Somertone, John de.

His early record is obscure; in his own list as Chamberlain 1362–3 he stands between R. Staunton and J. Lakyngheth, which would make 1361–2 his year of entrance. If so, he must have come from another house, having been about nine years in priest's orders, and being old enough to become custos ordinis at once.

Ad skillam, custos ordinis, 1361–2 (Infirmarer; Sacrist; Almoner; Q. Alianore).

Camerarius 1362–4.

Sacrista 1364–5 ? +.

Elemosinarius 1370–1.

Refectorarius 1372–3 (*Mun.* 19503).

Gave a large ciphus murrenus to the Misericorde (*Mun.* 6628).

Defunctus 1375–6 (Infirmarer).

1362-3 (Chamberlain)

Lakyngheth, Lakynghethe, Lakynghith, Lakynghuth, Lakynghuthe, John.

Custos hospicii Abbatis [N. Litlington] 28 Sep. 1362—26 Oct. 1371 (cf. J. Armitage Robinson, *An Unrecognised Westminster Chronicler*, p. 16).

Thesaurarius Abbatis 1363–4; 1371 (for his business with the bailiff at Denham cf. R. H. Lathbury, *History of Denham*, pp. 418, 433; for his outlays at the manors of Eybury and la Neyte 1368–70 cf. *Mun.* 26923 B; 26924 B).

Thesaurarius 1371–81; 1382–3 (Abbot's Treasurer); 1387–92 (*Mun.* 4219).

Custos ecclesiarum 1372–7; 1381–3; 1387–92.

Custos maner^m Regine Alianore 1372–92.

"Outcelerarius" (= celerarius extrinsecus) 1373 (*Mun.* 32587*); 1379 (*Mun.* 17699, which is a record of the prison gear which he handed over to Robert Norton, janitor et custos Gaole domini Regis, viz. various stocks, chains, "lynkes," fetters, a large iron "bolte" or fetter called "Saintpetrysbotes," shackles, manacles, padlocks, and iron bolts with "crampounz").

Ballivus 1373 (*Mun.* 32587*)–83 (*Mun.* 3227); 1387–92.

As an instance of his work as Bailiff see *Mun.* 31778 :—

Ceste endenture tesmoigne que Harry atte Watere de Croydone et Johan Dobeneye de Strethame ount venduz a danz Johan Lakyngheth moigne de Westm. et Baille xl^ml [40,000] de Teyll pur x^li dargent pris le m^l v^s. Et...lez auaunditz...deyuent faire et carier les auaunditz xl^ml de Teill tanque a Westm. a le Stone Wharf nomme le mille flete...parentre cy et le comencement de le mois de Juyn proschein ensuant apres la date du cestes, 6 Dec. 1390. The indenture states that these manufacturers are bound by a penalty of £20 to deliver the tiles. Their bond also survives, bearing the same date (*Mun.* 28116).

Receptor denariorum fratris Ricardi Merstone nuper Prioris 14 Sep. 1376—23 Jun. 1377 (*Mun.* 9498).

Proctor for the Convent in the suit against the Dean and College of St Stephen 16 Dec. 1378 (*Mun.* 18441); 20 Dec. 1387 (*Mun.* 18450).

Celerarius 1382–7 (cf. *Lib. Nig. Quat.* f. 145 b).

Granator 1382–6.

In expensis fratrum Johannis Stowe et J. L. cum v hominibus secum equitancium uersus Sarum et ibidem commorancium per v septimanas tempore parliamenti ibidem pro negociis domini Abbatis et conuentus prosequendis et expediendis...vii^li xix^s iiii^d 1383–4 (Treasurer).

Custos temporalium Abbatis [at Litlington's decease and during the vacancy] 29 Nov. 1386—11 Sep. 1387 (*Mun.* 5462; 5468; 5446).

Was strongly pressed upon the Convent by Richard II as Litlington's successor, in preference to W. Colchester (Robinson, *op. cit.* p. 22).

Pension of £4 in succession to Colchester as from Easter 1387 (Treasurer), and also 10s. yearly for life, being the profits of an osier bed growing on a croft called le Eldcurtell "on a little island where the Church House now stands" (Cellarer 1387–8; Robinson, *op. cit.* p. 17). For his pension-receipt to Christmas 1395 see *Mun.* 30301.

Received a double, or Prior's, share at the anniversary of John Blokley 1391–2 (*Mun.* 18525).

In uno medico conducto ad videndum statum fratris J. L. iii⁸ iiiiᵈ 1392–3 (Infirmarer). As he was not an inmate of the sick-room, it is probable that he succeeded to Colchester's camera.

Defunctus ante festum Pasche 1396 (Treasurer); 1395–6 (Infirmarer).

Before he ceased to be Treasurer, he "inspected the account rolls of all the officers of Westminster and set them at their true annual value," in order to find out what sums were available for the Novum Opus (*Lib. Nig. Quat.* f. 85 b; cf. f. 140).

The Hostillar of 1400 was still using mappe mensales de linea tela which were partly his gift; J. L. also gave two ciphi murreni, six silver salt-cellars weighing iiiiᵒᶻ xᵈʷᵗ "de troye," one silver piece with cover, weighing xviiᵒᶻ vᵈʷᵗ, and a considerable stock of crockery and furniture, all of which survived in 1400 (*Mun.* 9480).

Hervyngton, Heruynton, Herwynton, William de.

Must have been above the usual age at entering and probably already a priest.

Elemosinarius 1363–8 ? +. Built four shops from which in 1386–7 the Almoner received rentals of 13s. 4d. No further mention.

Canterbery, Canterbury, Canturbury, Canntbery, Cannterbery, Canntbury, Cauntabery, Caunterbury, John.

Prima Missa 1365–6 (Cellarer; probably Almoner).

Ad skillam 1373 (Q. Alianore); 1372–3 (Cellarer).

Granator 1378–80; 1397–1400.

Celerarius ? + 1379–82; 11 Nov. 1397—15 Aug. 1400.

Infirmarius 1383–7; 1391–7.

Refectorarius 1383–4 (Treasurer).

1386. Rex Francie apparatum suum fecit super mare veniendi in Angliam. Sed vento contrario existente de dei misericordia mare introire non est permissus. Et sic post longas expensas ibi factas ad partes suas rediit cum suis confusus. Hiis diebus apparauit se Nicholaus Abbas Westm' cum duobus monachis scilicet J. C. et Johanne Burghe in omni armatura de communi assensu capituli quia licitum pugnare pro patria vt ad custodiam super ripam maris cum curribus et equitibus properarent. Sed tandem cassato dei nutu Regis Francie negocio vt superius dictum totus apparatus [? suus] et fratrum domi remansit. Verumptamen cum postea armatura fratris J. C. esset London exposita vendicioni, non est inuentus aliquis cui armatura ipsa posset aptari. Erat enim dictus Johannes tante longitudinis et magnitudinis in statura tam in tibiis et femoribus quam in aliis eciam corporis membris quante vix aliquis aut nullus in Regno Anglie fuerat estimatus (*Lib. Nig. Quat.* f. 87).

The Treasurer 1386–7 included among his expense forinsece—solut' fratri J. C. pro armatura emenda precepto domini prioris viˡⁱ (*Mun.* 19874).

Proctor for the Convent in the suit against the Dean and College of St Stephen, 20 Sep. 1387 (*Mun.* 18450).

Supprior 1387–8 (*Mun.* 18521).

In diuersis expensis factis per fratrem J. C. equitantem per vices hoc anno uersus dominum Regem pro negociis ecclesie expediendis xxix^s xi^d ob. 1387–8 (Treasurer).

Collector of Abbey rents in Wood Street 1390–1.

Senescallus hospicii Abbatis [W. Colchester] 16 Nov. 1390—29 Sep. 1391.

For his gift of mappe mensales de linea tela to the Hostillar cf. *Mun.* 9480.

Et pro surgeria fratris J. C. xxvi^s viii^d 1393–4 (Infirmarer).

Et in batillagio fratrum J. C. et Ricardi Merlawe euntium usque Ducem de Gloucestre [Thomas of Woodstock] cum exennio sibi facto de panno aureo eundo et redeundo vi^s 1393–4 (*Mun.* 18527).

Defunctus 15 Aug. 1400 (*Mun.* 18882); 1399–1400 (Infirmarer). Sepultus 18 Aug. 1400 (*Mun.* 18883).

Attached to *Mun.* 18883 is a statement of his effects and their distribution and of the expenses connected with his illness and burial, which amounted in all to £6. 14s. 9d. The expenses began on Friday 13 Aug. and include meat, fish, and wine for the brethren; hire of candelabra and two wax candles and their carriage by water (7s. 5d.); a piece of marble, with the carriage and laying of it (55s. 4d.); and a brass plate inscribed with verses, cum dicti imagine super predictam petram (13s. 4d.).

1363-4 (Chamberlain)

Stokton, Stoghton, Hugh.

In 1369 he was still receiving from Q. Alianore only ⅟₇th of the portion paid to a priest. No further mention.

Farnago, Farnego, Farnygho, Farnyghow, Farnyngho, John.

Prima Missa 1365–6 (Cellarer; probably Almoner).

Scolaris existens Oxon. (£10) 1368–9; 1371–2? +; 1378–9 (Treasurer).

Ad skillam 1374 (Q. Alianore); 1373–4 (Infirmarer; Almoner; Cellarer; St Mary's Chapel).

At Avignon 14 Aug. 1377 he was witness with William Colchester [q.v.] to Cardinal Langham's will (Widmore, p. 191; *Mun.* 9225); for details of his expenses see *Mun.* 9228.

William de Colchester (at Rome, 20 Nov. 1377) addressed a letter to him at Westminster as an alternative to the Prior [R. de Merston] who was dying or dead at the time (*Mun.* 9240).

Thesaurarius maner^m Regine Alianore 1380–3.

Refectorarius 1384–5 (Treasurer). As such he gave evidence about the tithing of Thames salmon (*Flete*, p. 64).

His last appearance in any surviving list is in Chamberlain 1382–3; but he was paid by the Treasurer 1384–5 pro caseo emendo et aliis necessariis, being then Refectorer. No further list till 1390.

Litlington, Litlyngton, Lytlynton, Littelyngton, Litelton, William.

Prima Missa 1365–6 (Cellarer; probably Almoner).

Refectorarius 1373–6? +.

Ad skillam 1380–1 (Infirmarer; Treasurer; Warden of the Churches).

Precentor 1384–7 (Treasurer).

Custos capelle b. Marie 1387–8 (*Mun.* 18521); 29 Sep. 1388—25 Nov. 1389.

Camerarius 1389–92 (Treasurer); 1392–3; 1393–7 (Treasurer). Gave evidence as such about the tithing of Thames salmon (*Flete*, p. 64). In his time each brother received one pannus integer, 6 "quarters" in width and 11½ yards in length, each pannus costing 10s. (*Lib. Nig. Quat.* f. 80).

Infirmarius 19 Aug.—28 Sep. 1391; 1397–1413?+.

The Infirmarer made payments for surgical treatment for him in 1366–7 (pro tibia curanda hoc anno xx^s), in 1374–5 (for the same, £4), in 1400–1 (for his arm), in 1403–4, and 1405–6. In the case of the last three payments, vi^s viii^d each, he was himself Infirmarer.

Nuper defunctus 1414 (Q. Alianore; i.e. he probably died shortly before the audit of 1413–4; his own compotus as Infirmarer to Mich^s 1414 does not survive).

Coumbe, Combe, Cumbe, Peter.

Prima Missa 1365–6 (Cellarer; probably Almoner).

Existens Oxon. (£10) 1369–72?+ (Treasurer).

Ad skillam 1375–6 (Infirmarer; Treasurer).

Custos ecclesiarum 1377–81; 1399–1401.

Thesaurius maner^m Regine Alianore 1378–80.

Thesaurarius 1380–5; (et Ballivus) 1399–1401.

Coquinarius 1380–5 (Treasurer; cf. *Flete*, p. 64).

Archidiaconus 27 Mar. 1383 (*Mun.* 18447—a notarial declaration of the decision of the Roman Curia in favour of the Abbot and Convent of Westminster in the dispute with the Dean and College of St Stephen).

Sacrista 17 Nov. 1385—25 Nov. 1399; 1411–3 (Treasurer; New Work).

It fell to him as Sacrist to render the first account for the provision of round and square candles for the tomb of Queen Anne at the command of Richard II, from whose Treasurer he received 800 lbs. of wax, 1394–5 (*Mun.* 23970 B).

As Sacrist he received xxxii^s yearly, at the rate of iiii^s for each of the eight principal feasts, ex noua ordinacione domini Willelmi [Colchester] nunc Abbatis, 1393–4 (Warden of the Churches).

He made frequent journeys to Purbeck and Reigate to procure marble and stone; e.g. in expensis sacriste versus Purbyk xlv^s ii^d ob. 1395–6 (New Work).

Custos Novi Operis 29 Sep. 1387—25 Nov. 1399. [His "great work was the purchase and placing of the marble pillars" in the nave; cf. R. B. Rackham, *Nave of Westminster*, pp. 8–12.]

Proctor for the Abbot and Convent in the suits against the Dean and College of St Stephen 10 Dec. 1378 (*Mun.* 18441); 20 Dec. 1387 (*Mun.* 18450). He acted as sub-executor of the Bishop of Penna and published sentence against the Dean and College who had contumaciously continued to celebrate the divine offices 7 Jul. 1393 (Kal. Pap. Reg. IV, 463).

Administrator participacionis Anne Regine (with John Borewell) 1394—7 Jun. 1399.

Custos capelle b. Marie 1395–8?+; 1401 (*Mun.* 18535)–1403; 1407–8; 1410.

Thesaurarius maner^m Regine Alianore 1378–80; custos 1399–1400.

He destroyed the tomb of Abbot Richard de Berking (cf. *Flete*, p. 106).

Was entered at his usual place in the manor rolls 1421–2, and for his outfit in 1422–3 (Chamberlain); inter mortuos, 1423–4 (Chamberlain); so probably died 1422–3.

Witlesford, Wittlesford, Wytlesford, William.

Prima Missa 1365–6 (Cellarer; probably Almoner).

Scolaris Oxon. (£10) 1370–1 (Treasurer). The Steward of the Abbot's Household of this year gave him viii^s viii^d in recessu suo versus Oxon.

Precentor 1376–82 (Treasurer; Warden of the Churches).

Gave a parva tabula cum duobus trestallis to the Misericorde (*Mun.* 6628).
Defunctus 1381–2 (Infirmarer).

Redynge, Redyngg, John, Junior (T. Redyngg in Chamberlain 1363–4).
Prima Missa 1367–8 (Almoner; Cellarer).
Defunctus 1375–6 (Infirmarer).

Warewyk, Warrewyke, Warwike, Thomas.
Defunctus 1382–3 (Infirmarer).

Denham, Roger.
Prima Missa 1367–8 (Almoner; Cellarer).
Defunctus 1384–5 (Infirmarer).

Giffard, Gyffard, J.
Prima Missa 1365–6 (Cellarer; probably Almoner).
Last mention 1382–3 (Chamberlain).

1366–7

Wynewyk, Wynwike, Wonewyk, Robert.
Canon of the Gilbertine or Sempringham Order; a general release in
respect of his transference to Westminster was sealed by the Master of the
Order 10 Jan. 1366(7) (*Mun.* 31775).
Solut' magistro de Scherpyngham precepto domini Abbatis pro fratre
R. W. canonici dicti magistri, vi^{li} xiii^s iiii^d 1366–7 (Treasurer).
Custos capelle b. Marie 1376 (*Mun.* 17690, a lease dated 12 Oct.; in
Mun. 23188 he is mentioned as having held the office between J. Holbech
and J. Stowe).
Defunctus 1383–4 (Infirmarer).

1369 (Q. Alianore)[1]

Holbech, Holbeche, John.
Prima Missa 1369 (Q. Alianore); 1368–9 (Infirmarer).
Camerarius 1375–9 (Treasurer; Refectorer).
Custos capelle b. Marie (*Mun.* 23188; between 1374 and 1382).
Defunctus c. Jan. 1411 (Infirmarer; he had been treated with diuersis
emplastris,—ii^s iii^d).

Witlesford, Wittelesford, Wittlesford, Wytlesford, Wytlisford, John.
Nouicius 1369 (Q. Alianore).
Ad skillam 1375–6 (Infirmarer; Treasurer).
Thesaurarius maner^m Regine Alianore 1375–7.
Thesaurarius 1378–9.
Coquinarius 1378–9 (Treasurer).
Last mentioned, seventh below W. Witlesford (Chamberlain 1379–80).

Merlawe, Merlowe, Marlowe, Richard de.
Prima Missa 1370–1 (Infirmarer; Cellarer; Almoner; Treasurer).
Custos vestibuli 1377 (*Lib. Nig. Quat.* f. 81).
Camerarius 1379–80; 1382–3; 1383–7 (Treasurer; Refectorer); 1389
(*Mun.* 27824); 28 Sep. 1400–5 Aug. 1401. *Mun.* 27824 gives details about
manor-courts held by him as Chamberlain 1380–9 at Headley, Surrey.
Senescallus hospicii Abbatis 1380–3; 29 Dec. 1387—16 Nov. 1390 (cf.
R. H. Lathbury, *History of Denham*, p. 458).

[1] It may be assumed, unless otherwise stated, that the rest of the names appear first in the
lists attached to the manor-rolls (Q. Alianore; Richard II; Henry V) of the years specified.

Among the purchases he made from Litlington's executors 1387 were 17 bows, a sheaf of "catapults" and 13 sheaves of other missiles (*Mun.* 5446).

Collector of Abbey rents at Westminster and Wood Street 1391–4.

Ad skillam 1391–2 (Infirmarer; Cellarer).

Coquinarius 1391–7 (Treasurer).

Refectorarius 1392–4 (Chamberlain; Treasurer).

Custos capelle b. Marie 1392–3.

Thesaurarius et Custos ecclesiarum 1393–7.

For his visit with a present to the Duke of Gloucester 1393–4, see John Canterbery (*Mun.* 18527).

Granator 1394–7.

Celerarius et Gardinarius 1396—11 Nov. 1397.

Indult for confessor 28 Sep. 1398 (Kal. Pap. Reg. v, 148, where the name is given as Marlowe. On the same date there was a similar indult issued to William Merlawe, monk of Westminster, but no monk of that name was in the Convent at the time).

From 1400 onwards he was in the sick-room frequently and for long periods :—Solut Johanne Lethe mulieri pro diuersa medicina facta pro fratre R. M....iii^s iiii^d et...ii medicis...pro dicto R. vi^s ii^d (1408–9). In 1409–10 he spent 172 days in the sick-room, receiving altogether the sum of £2. 13s. 2d. in pittance. In 1411–2, when he was laid up from October to May,—Solut diuersis medicis pro diuersis medicinis plastris surripp' [? syrops] et unguentis pro fratre R. M. viii^s vii^d.

Defunctus, c. Mai. 1412 (Infirmarer).

Adelard, Athelard, Hathelard, Alard, Robert.

Camerarius 1380–1 (Treasurer).

Coquinarius 1380–1 (Treasurer).

Ad skillam 1382–3 (Infirmarer; Q. Alianore; Chamberlain; Sacrist; Warden of the Churches).

Thesaurarius maner^m Regine Alianore 1383–7.

Custos reliquiarum 1385–6 (*Mun.* 18519).

Hostillarius 22 Dec. 1400–? (*Mun.* 9480).

Defunctus 1418 (half-share, 1417–8, Q. Alianore); inter mortuos 1418–9 (Chamberlain).

Twiford, Twyford, Richard.

Ad skillam 29 Sep.—30 Nov. 1377 (Sacrist); 1377–8 (Infirmarer).

Defunctus 1380–1 (Infirmarer).

1372

Peuerell, Peverel, Thomas.

Prima Missa 1373 (Q. Alianore); 1372–3 (Cellarer).

Was levite at the Mass during which Robert Hawley was murdered in the choir 11 Aug. 1378 (*Lib. Nig. Quat.* 88 b, 89).

Ad skillam (Infirmarer; Q. Alianore; Chamberlain; Sacrist; Warden of the Churches).

Magister nouiciorum 1388–9 (*Mun.* 24538 A).

Collector of Abbey rents at Westminster and Wood Street 1390–1419.

Helped to make the screen for the chapel of St Thomas (Stanley, *Memorials*, p. 640; Lib. Nig. Quat. f. 92 b).

Supprior ?—? (Camden, *Reges*, &c.).

Defunctus 1419–20 (Q. Alianore; see entry of Abbot Colchester's death; Chamberlain); nouiter defunctus, 1418–9 (Richard II; i.e. at the time of the compotus; his name is deleted from the list of payments).

Camden (*Reges*, &c.) includes Thomas Peuerell, Sub-prior, among those buried in locis ignotis ecclesiae.

Cleangre, Clehungre, Cleungre, William.

Prima Missa 1373 (Q. Alianore); 1372–3 (Cellarer).

Custos capelle b. Marie 1384–5 (Abbot's Receiver); 1386–7 (*Mun.* 18520); 29 Sep.—23 Nov. 1387; 5 Nov. 1389—29 Sep. 1390; 29 Sep.—9 Dec. 1391; 1393—4 ?+.

Thesaurarius 1387–8.

Coquinarius 1389.

So named on a parchment in which he has left his statement of the cost of providing the Convent with the customary pancakes (*Mun.* 27968) :—

Expense facte per fratrem Willelmum Clehungre coquinarium Westm. circa flacones ordinatos confratribus et liberatos monasterio prout consuetudo monasterii antedicti per xiiii dies annuatim exigit, videlicet a die pasche usque diem sancte Trinitatis hoc anno regni regis Ricardi secundi xii^{mo} ut patet per omnes parcellas.

Lac	In primis in cxxvi lagenis lactis pretio lagene i^d	x^s vi^d
Butirum	Item in iii lagenis iii quartis butiri pretio lagene ii^s iiii^d	viii^s ix^d ob.[1]
Oua	Item in v DCCC xvi oua pretio c. x^d	xlviii^s v^d q^u
Sal	Item in i p^o grossi salis per idem tempus iii^d	iii^d
	Summa totalis	lxviii^s xi^d ob q^u

Defunctus Oct. 1395 (Infirmarer).

Borw, Borough, Borugh, Burgh, Burghe, John.

De nouo capellanus ordinatus 1373 (Q. Alianore).

Prima Missa 1374 (Q. Alianore); 1373–4 (Almoner; St Mary's Chapel; Cellarer).

Was deacon and was in the act of reading the Gospel at the Mass when Hawley was murdered in the choir 11 Aug. 1378 (*Lib. Nig. Quat.* f. 88 b, 89).

Refectorarius 1380–1 (Treasurer); 1385–7 (*Mun.* 19506).

Precentor 1387–1418 (Treasurer; Warden of the Churches).

Indult for plenary remission 21 Mar. 1398 (Kal. Pap. Reg. v, 126).

Defunctus 1418–9 (after being 134 days in the sick-room; Infirmarer).

Vincent, Vyncent, Simon.

Defunctus 1375–6 (Infirmarer).

Northampton, John.

Prima Missa 1375–6 (Treasurer).

Provided the Doom-picture in front of the Chapter House; the Apocalypse-picture inside it (£4. 10s.); the Calendar and other pictures in the Cloister near the door of the church (£2. 10s.); and, along with John London [1378–9], the picture for the altar of St John Baptist's Chapel (*Lib. Nig. Quat.* f. 92 b; Stanley, *Memorials*, 3rd ed. pp. 640–1).

Was in the sick-room for five weeks, Dec. 1403—Jan. 1404: in surgeria pro fratre J. N. vi^s viii^d (Infirmarer).

Defunctus (? Jan.) 1404 (Infirmarer).

---

[1] In the body of the bill he entered the total cost of butter as viii*s*. ix*d*. ob, but when he carried it to the margin, he altered it to ix*s*. iiii*d*. ob.

1373

Sudbury, Sudberi, Sudbery, Sudebury, William de.

Diaconus 1376 (Q. Alianore).

Prima Missa? 1376–7[1].

Scolaris Oxon. (£10) ? + 1375–87 (Treasurer).

Fratri W. S. ad soluendum ad generale capitulum et pro expensis suis xvi^{li} v^s 1385–6 (Treasurer).

Solut' fratri W. de S. veniendo de Oxoñ predicando [on Palm Sunday and Good Friday] et redeundo xxvi^s viii^d 1386 ; 1387 (Sacrist). In Dec. 1386 he returned from Oxford for Abbot Colchester's election (Treasurer).

Proxy for the Convent in the suit against the Dean and College of St Stephen, 20 Dec. 1387 (*Mun.* 18450).

Refectorarius 1391–2 ; 1400–11.

Et fratri W. S. ad soluendum ad generale capitulum et pro expensis suis xvi^{li} v^s...pro expensis suis illic eundo ibidem commorando et inde redeundo xl^s 1386–7 (Treasurer).

Rex Ricardus scripsit litteram specialem domino pape Vrbano sexto pro privilegiis Westm. confirmandis per eundem papam quam litteram fecit frater W. S. Bachalarius in Theologia que sigillata est apud Wyndesore, 1 Sep. 1389 (*Lib. Nig. Quat.* f. 88).

In expensis frat. W. S. equitantis usque Cantuar' pro colloquio habendo cum priore ecclesie XPI ibidem pro causa tangente domum scolarium in Oxoñ ...xiii^s x^d 1391–2 ; 1392–3 (Treasurer).

In expensis fratrum Johannis Burghwell [q.v.] et W. S. equitantium usque Wyndesore et ibidem existentium per vii dies pro tractatu inter dominum Abbatem et conuentum Westm' et capellam sancti Steph. 1^s iiii^d 1391–2 (Treasurer).

Thesaurarius 1392–3.

Thesaurarius maner^m Regine Alianore 1392–3.

Indult for plenary remission 26 Feb. 1398 (Kal. Pap. Reg. v, 122).

Indult to possess for life any books, jewels, money, or other goods, provided that they be preserved for the monastery and finally converted to its use 4 May 1399 (*ibid.* 197) ; he being then S. T. B.

Leland noted two tabulae or indices of his in the Convent Library,— super Lyram ; super libros sancti Thomae de Aquino (M. R. James, *Manuscripts of Westminster Abbey*, p. 23). See also the note on his writings in J. Armitage Robinson, *An Unrecognised Westminster Chronicler*, p. 14.

Richard Circestr' described him as venerabilis vir et in sacrae theologiae pagina eleganter doctus, *Speculum*, III, 3, p. 26.

Not mentioned after 1414–5 (Q. Alianore ; Richard II), and then in his usual place.

Enston, Eynston, Eyneston, Eygneston, John.

Diaconus 1376 (Q. Alianore).

Prima Missa? 1376–7 (Infirmarer).

Ad skillam 1380–1 (Infirmarer ; Treasurer ; Warden of the Churches).

Thesaurarius 1385–7.

Coquinarius 1385–7 (Treasurer).

Thesaurarius maner^m Regine Alianore 1390–1.

Custos capelle b. Marie 9 Dec. 1391—29 Sep. 1392 (*Mun.* 23191) ; 8 Dec. 1400—29 Sep. 1401.

Camerarius 1397–1400 (Treasurer ; Refectorer).

Defunctus Nov. 1409 (Infirmarer).

---

[1] The Infirmarer entered exennia for first Masses (1*s.* 4*d.* each) to three Brethren not named ; probably W. Sudbury, T. Enston, and J. Braynt.

Braynt, Braynte, Brentt, Brente, Breynte, John.

Diaconus 1376 (Q. Alianore).

Prima Missa ? 1376–7 (Infirmarer).

Ad skillam 1388–9 (Infirmarer; Sacrist; Warden of the Churches; St Mary's Chapel).

Thesaurarius 1391–3.

Coquinarius 1391–3 (Treasurer; Chamberlain; Sacrist). As such, he gave evidence about the tithing of Thames salmon (cf. *Flete*, p. 64). Also he received iiii[s] yearly for each of the five principal feasts ex noua ordinacione domini Willelmi [Colchester] nunc Abbatis, 1392–3 (Warden of the Churches).

Thesaurarius maner[m] Regine Alianore 1393–1401. In a paper slip (*Mun.* 23726 B) he calls himself Custos cere Regine Alianore and gives an account of his outlay in candles, &c. 28 Nov. 1396—29 Nov. 1397.

Defunctus 1418–9 (obit in Infirmarer; bedridden 28 Sep.—12 Dec. ? + 1417; a 3 weeks' illness in the autumn of 1418; probably died before Xmas 1418); inter mortuos 1418–9 (Chamberlain).

1373-4 (Almoner)

Cranlye, T.

In expensis factis circa fratrem T. Cranlye, qui habitum recepit monachalem...xxx[s] 1373–4 (Almoner).

[It is not certain, in view of the exceptional character of this entry, that he was actually a member of the Convent.]

1375

Halle, William.

Prima Missa 29 Sep. 1378—25 Jan. 1379 (Infirmarer); 1378–9 (Treasurer).

At Rome with William Colchester [q.v.] 1382–3 (Chamberlain).

Thesaurarius maner[m] Regine Alianore 1387–8.

Defunctus Sep. 1389 (Infirmarer, 1388–9, who records an illness of 5 weeks in Aug. and Sep. and the usual distribution in die sepulture eius).

London, Bartholomew.

Prima Missa 29 Sep. 1378—25 Jan. 1379 (Infirmarer); 1378–9 (Treasurer).

Defunctus 1393–4 (Infirmarer). Et solut' abbreuiatori portanti cedulas de morte fratris Bartholomei precepto domini Prioris x[s], 1393–4 (Treasurer).

Asshwell, Asshewell, Assewell, William.

Prima Missa 1381–2 (Infirmarer; Q. Alianore; Warden of the Churches).

Bought from the executors of Abbot Litlington a sheaf of arrows, Jan. 1387 (*Mun.* 5446).

In surgeria solut' Johanni Brademoor pro fratre W. A., vi[s] viii[d]; the illness lasted through August and September 1402 (Infirmarer).

Refectorarius 1413–4 (Treasurer).

Entered in his usual place, 1413–4 (Q. Alianore); no later mention.

1376

Chereton, Cheriton, Cheryngton, Cheryton, Chiriton, Chiryton, Chyryngton, Nicholas.

Prima Missa 29 Sep. 1378—25 Jan. 1379 (Infirmarer); 1378–9 (Treasurer).

Ad skillam 1384–5 (Infirmarer; Q. Alianore; Warden of the Churches).

Last mentioned 1391–2 (Q. Alianore) in his usual place.

Colchester, Colcester, Thomas.

Diaconus 1377 (Q. Alianore).

Prima Missa 29 Sep. 1378—25 Jan. 1379 (Infirmarer); 1378–9 (Treasurer).

Studens apud Oxon. (£10) 1380–8?+ (Treasurer). Recalled for Wm Colchester's election, 1386–7, and for Cardinal Langham's interment 1387–8 (*ibid.*).

Was described as tunc Oxon. when the Brethren made their gifts to the Pope for the year of Jubilee 1390 (*Lib. Nig. Quat.* f. 92).

Pomfrett, Pomfreyt, Pontfreyt, Poumfrett, Poumffreyt, Pounfreyd, Pountfrett, Thomas.

Prima Missa 1381–2 (Infirmarer ; Q. Alianore ; Warden of the Churches).

Defunctus Jan. 1396 (Infirmarer ; as he was ill for 61 days in Dec. 1395 and Jan. 1396, his death may be placed c. 31 Jan.).

1378-9

Palgrave, Richard.

Was a priest by 1390–1 (Q. Alianore), his place being ˙next after R. Whatele [q.v.] whose first Mass was in 1388–9 ; if that is the correct date for Palgrave's ordination, he must either have entered the Convent very young or have been ordained late in life. The Chamberlain 1392–3 entered him last, after R. Birlyngham, but Q. Alianore of the same year put him three places higher, after W. Sonewell. Such indecision is unusual.

Defunctus Jan. 1399 (Infirmarer) ; inter mortuos 1399–1400 (Chamberlain).

Stratton, J.

He received from Q. Alianore's manors 1378–9 at the same rate as the deacons, but was not entered as such.

Last appearance by name 1382-3 (Chamberlain).

London, John.

Prima Missa 25 Jan.—29 Sep. 1379 (Infirmarer) ; 1378–9 (Treasurer).

Ad skillam 1386–7 (Infirmarer ; Sacrist ; Warden of the Churches).

Thesaurarius maner^m Regine Alianore 1388–90 ; 1391–3.

Custos Misericordie ?—9\Dec. 1391 (*Mun.* 6628).

Custos feretri ?—? ; as such, gave evidence about the tithing of Thames salmon (*Flete*, p. 64).

Along with John Northampton [q.v.] he provided the picture for the altar of St John Baptist's chapel (*Lib. Nig. Quat.* f. 92 b ; Stanley, *Memorials*, 3rd ed. p. 641).

Solut' priori minoris Malvernie pro mensa fratris J. L. viz. pro xli septimanis per septimanam xx^d lxviii^s iiii^d. Pro expensis eiusdem Johannis et familie sue per viam de Westm. versus Malverniam et in denariis traditis xv^s iiii^d 1401–2 (*Mun.* 24413).

Absent 1416–9 (Q. Alianore).

Reclusus 1424–5 ; cccc fagetts pro recluso xiii^s iiii^d 1426–7 (Treasurer).

Defunctus c. 1428 (entered in his usual place, as senior monk, next to the Prior, 1427–8, Q. Alianore) ; inter mortuos 1428–9 (Chamberlain).

1379-80

Sandon, John.

Subdiaconus 1379–80 (Q. Alianore).

Prima Missa 1381–2 (Infirmarer ; Q. Alianore ; Warden of the Churches).

Came up from Oxford for Cardinal Langham's interment, 1387–8 (Treasurer) ; he was not one of the two scholars, but his name is inserted over their names.

Ad skillam 1390–1 (Infirmarer ; Sacrist ; Warden of the Churches).

Indult to hold a benefice with cure of souls, 21 Jul. 1398 (Kal. Pap. Reg. v, 159).

Refectorarius 1398–1400 (Treasurer).
Last mentioned in his usual place 1412–3 (Q. Alianore).

Toneworth, Tonworth, Tonworthe, Tonneworth, Tunworth, Ralph.
Prima Missa 1382–3 (Infirmarer; Chamberlain; Q. Alianore; Sacrist; Warden of the Churches).
Vestiarius ?—? Gave evidence as such about the tithing of Thames salmon (cf. *Flete,* p. 64).
Sacrista 25 Nov. 1399—22 Nov. 1411 (Treasurer).
Custos Novi Operis 1400—22 Nov. 1411 (cf. R. B. Rackham, *Nave of Westminster,* pp. 12—13).
Custos capelle b. Marie 1411–6.
Et solut̃ fratri R. T. pro recompensacione facta sibi pro dampno in camera archidiaconi dum dominus Abbas [W. Colchester] jacuit ibi viˢ viiiᵈ 1417–8 (Abbot's Treasurer). It is fair to presume from this that he was Archdeacon, but there is no other evidence.
Infirmarius 1418–9.
Defunctus 1419–20 (Q. Alianore); inter mortuos 1420–1 (Chamberlain).

Forde, B.
No panni nigri were issued to him 1382–3 because he was cum croisoria (Chamberlain).
Last mentioned 1384–5 (Q. Alianore), when he was paid 30s., a priest's share being 70s.; he may have been sub-deacon at the time.

Merke, Merk, Merks, Thomas.
In Chamberlain 1379–80 and 1382–3 his precedence is between N. Chereton and T. Pomfrett, which suggests that he may have joined the Convent in 1376. Was entered by Chamberlain 1379–80; 1382–3; but not in the list of those who made Jubilee contributions 1390 (*Lib. Nig. Quat.* f. 92).
Item dat' famulo prioris de Ely conducenti dominum [W. Colchester] per viam de Ely vii die Octobris [1388] per fratrem T. M. xiiᵈ (Abbot's Steward).
Dat' T. M. et Johanni Sandon [q.v.] pro gaudiis viˢ viiiᵈ 1388–9 (*ibid.*).
Studens Oxon. (£10) 1392–4 (Treasurer).
Solut' fratri T. M. studienti Oxonie pro expensis suis factis circa introitum ad sentencias xˡⁱ 1392–3 (Treasurer).
In expensis T. M. et R. Whatele [q.v.] venientium de Oxon erga festum Natalis Domini et redeundo xxˢ 1393–4 (*ibid.*).
Was granted a pension of £20 by the Abbot, Prior, and Convent 1395–6 (Treasurer); same sum paid 1396–7 episcopo Karliolensi; and in 1397–8 £3. 6s. 8d. in plenam solucionem pensionis sue.
Bishop of Carlisle before 23 Apr. 1397 (Stubbs, *Registrum,* 2nd ed. p. 83).
There is a letter from him to Abbot Colchester, signed vester obedientiarius T. C. [Carliol.], endorsed per Thomam Merke, and dated 2nd Sunday in Advent, without year, in which he asked the Abbot to foster a cause of the Warden of Merton Hall in the Roman Curia (*Mun.* 9240*).
Defunctus 1410 (Stubbs, *Registrum,* p. 83). In 1411 (5 Oct.) when Abbot Colchester made a covenant with the Prior of Hurley for the celebration of his own anniversary there, he stipulated that memorial should be made of his parents and of Thomas Merke (*Mun.* 3571).

1380-1

Coggeshale, Coggeshalle, John.
Diaconus 1381–2 (Q. Alianore).
Prima Missa 1382–3 (Infirmarer; Chamberlain; Sacrist).
Defunctus 1385–6 (Infirmarer).

Hermodesworth, Hermondesworth, Hermodiesworth, Hermerdsworthe, Hermundesworth, Hermysworthe, Robert.

Diaconus 1381–2 (Q. Alianore).

Prima Missa 1382–3 (Infirmarer; Chamberlain; Q. Alianore; Sacrist; Warden of the Churches).

Solut' Magistro Galfrido phisico venienti per iiii^{or} vices ad videndum fratrem R. H. vi^s viii^d 1393–4 (Infirmarer).

For his evidence about the tithing of the Thames salmon cf. *Flete*, p. 64.

Custos capelle b. Marie 29 Sep. 1398—8 Dec. 1400. As such, he granted a lease of a house to Geoffrey Chaucer in 1399 (*Mun.* lvii).

For his gifts towards the new Choir-book, 1398–9, cf. *Manuscripts of Westminster Abbey*, p. 9.

Ad skillam 29 Sep.—8 Dec. 1400 (St Mary's Chapel); 1400–1 (Infirmarer; Chamberlain; Cellarer; Warden of the Churches); 1401–2 (Almoner).

In surgeria pro fratre R. H. pro pede iiii^s vii^d 1406–7 (Infirmarer).

Thesaurarius maner^m Regine Alianore 1405–10; Ricardi II et Anne 1406–9.

In attendance upon Abbot Colchester at the General Chapter of the Benedictines, Northampton, 6 Jul. 1411 (*Lib. Nig. Quat.* f. 90 b).

Defunctus 28 Sep.—12 Dec. 1417 (Infirmarer).

One of the few Brethren of whose family relationships there is any trace. In *Mun.* 27805, 27806, he has left accounts, drawn up with the same care as were his balance-sheets as an obedientiary, of his administration of some property belonging to his sister Alice. They are dated 1 May 1399 and 31 Oct. 1405, and the later repeats some of the matter contained in the earlier.

Alice had handed to him a sum of £2. 13s. 4d. in 1399; there was also 3s. 4d. paid at Christmas as rent of an acre of land let to the vicar of Hermodesworth (= Harmondsworth, Middlesex), from which it may be assumed that Robert's place-name was genuine; also Alice had delivered 2s. to him near the church of St Magnus [by London Bridge]. So he had to account for £2. 18s. 8d. in all.

It appears that Alice had come to London in 1398 and that the expenses of her journey and of her residence in the house of John de Bury in veter' piscar' London [Old Fish Street] came to 16s. 8d. Robert had bought for her three yards of green cloth at 2s. 6d. a yard and three yards of linen to line this garment (pro viridi toga duplicanda) at 6d. a yard, and he had paid a tailor 2s. 8d. to make it; also a cape against the Feast of All Saints, when the weather was getting cold, costing 3s. 4d. By the Feast of the Purification she needed another dress, this time of russet at 2s. 4d. a yard, and trimmed with fur for 5s. The total was made up of various sums handed to Alice, closing with one of 6s. 8d. given her by the hand of John Sakeuille, baker, of London, to whom she was married after her arrival in London.

Evidently the affairs of this modest estate were not settled without difficulty. For there comes in another person, Matildis, wife of Thomas Goyland and sister of Alice; she was now deceased, but Alice held that the widower was responsible for his wife's debts.

Matildis had received 20s. for 2 quarters of wheat at Hermodesworth; 11s. 5½d. for barley; 10s. for malt; 8s. for a heifer; and 1s. 8d. for an ewe with her lamb; total £2. 11s. 1½d. Her husband therefore had to account for these items. The 11s. 5½d. and the 10s. were handed, he says, to Alice in London in the presence of persons named; the heifer was delivered to Margaret her servant; the ewe had been a gift from Alice to her sister Matildis before her departure for London; as for the lamb, it afterwards perished on the shore (in marina). There remained the 20s. for the wheat;

13*s*. 4*d*. of this had been paid with the assent of Alice to her servant Margaret
and the remaining 6*s*. 8*d*. was more than represented by various utensils
which had been allotted to Alice out of Margaret's effects; viz. 4 brazen
pots, 6 brazen pans, 2 chargeturis [? chargers] with 6 plates, 6 tin salt-cellars,
6 silver spoons, 1 small crystal goblet, 2 silver bracelets, 2 cloths, 3 cushions,
one wash-basin, one iron tripod, one gridiron, one iron firefork, besides one or
two bedspreads with a tester, 2 blankets, 2 pairs of sheets, and one pair of
large amber beads,—the whole valued at £5.

Thus it would seem that Alice Sakeuille had her money's worth.   Brother
Robert added a memorandum of gifts that he had made over and above what
was required of him :—clothing bought for the wedding of John and Alice
26*s*. 8*d*.; six capons given to them on the same day 3*s*. 4*d*.; a small red box
with lock and key 3*s*. 4*d*.; a leathern skin (i pell' de Cordowana) 1*s*. 8*d*.; and
four capons on All Saints' Day, 2*s*.

1382-3

Bury, David de.
Only appears, last but one, in the Chamberlain's list of this year.

1383-4

Borewell, Bourwell, Burghwell, Burgwell, Burwell, John.
Was not entered in Chamberlain 1382-3, after which there is a gap in the
series; but his place in Chapter was next before W. Pulburgh (*Lib. Nig. Quat.*
f. 92).   Probably entered the Convent as a priest.

Ad skillam 1386-7 (Infirmarer; Sacrist; Warden of the Churches).

Abbot Colchester's proctor at the Roman Court for three years, 20 Dec.
1387 (*Mun*. 18450) to Sep. 1390 (*Mun*. 6664; *Lib. Nig. Quat.* f. 87, f. 92)
and the Convent's representative in the suit against the Dean and College of
St Stephen.

Archidiaconus 4 Oct. 1391; 12 Jul. 1393 (*Mun*. 28117; 28120).   For
his appointment of an apparitor 10 Oct. 1391, see *Mun*. 5981.   A die of his
seal, the gift of Dr Basil Wilberforce, Archdeacon, 1900-16, is now handed
to each holder of the office on appointment yearly.

For his business at Windsor 1391-2 see Sudbury, William.

Custos ecclesiarum 1392-3; 1397-9; 1401-3.

Thesaurarius et Ballivus 1393-8; 1401-3; 1405-9.

Custos maner^m Regine Alianore 1393-9; 1400-3.

Administrator participacionis Anne Regine 28 Sep. 1394—7 Jun. 1399;
custos maner^m Ricardi II et Anne 7 Jun. 1399—29 Sep. 1403.   In expensis
fratris Johannis Burwell et aliorum equitancium usque Steuyngton [Steven-
ton, Berks.] mense Aprilis pro curia cum visu tenenda manerio et stauris
ibidem superuidendis xxvi^s iiii^d ob. 1401 (*Mun*. 23978).

Celerarius et Gardinarius 1400—13 Nov. 1401; 1406-8 (*Mun*. 30376*).

Granator 1399-1401; 1404-9.

Coquinarius 1405-9.

For a letter addressed by Abbot Colchester from Cologne ? 1408 to him
and Peter Coumbe, see *Mun*. 1653; cf. E. H. Pearce, *William de Colchester*,
pp. 77-9.

Defunctus 1409-10 (Infirmarer).

Pulburgh, Pulborugh, Pulborgh, Polborough, William.
Subdiaconus 1385-6 (Q. Alianore).
Prima Missa 28 Sep.—24 Nov. 1387 (Almoner); 1386-7 (Sacrist; Warden

of the Churches; St Mary's Chapel); 1387–8 (Infirmarer); in Q. Alianore 1386–7 he is mentioned among the sacerdotes de nouo celebrantes.

Studens Oxon. (£8. 16s.) 1387–93 (Treasurer); recalled for Cardinal Langham's interment 1387–8 (Treasurer).

Ad skillam 1393–4 (Infirmarer; Sacrist; Warden of the Churches; St Mary's Chapel).

Thesaurarius 1397–8.

In attendance on Abbot Colchester at the General Chapter of the Benedictines, Northampton, 6 Jul. 1411 (*Lib. Nig. Quat.* f. 90 b).

Prior de Hurley 1416–7.

Barton, Robert.

Subdiaconus 1385–6 (Q. Alianore).

Prima Missa 23 Sep.—24 Nov. 1387 (Almoner); 1386–7 (Q. Alianore); 1387–8 (Infirmarer; Sacrist; Warden of the Churches; St Mary's Chapel).

Was accused to the Pope by his rivals (emulis) of improper conduct— supping with monks and secular persons of both sexes, talking alone with a woman, and going out at night to avenge himself (ad vindicandum se). Was imprisoned and sentenced to lose his vote, distributions, and place at table. Mandate for his restoration after due penance 21 Jan. 1395 (Kal. Pap. Reg. IV, 523).

He received his Q. Alianore portion regularly up to Mich[s] 1395, but in the compotus of 1395–6 his name is deleted in its ordinary place and instead of receiving 70s. he was put among the juniors who received 50s.; in 1396–7 30s. instead of 70s.; in 1397–8 he was restored to his place and a full share.

Defunctus 1416–7 (Infirmarer; Q. Alianore).

Derteford, J.

No mention of his exennia for First Mass; was apparently in priest's orders by 1387–8 (Q. Alianore).

Was not included in the list of those who made offerings to the Roman Court in the year of Jubilee, 1390 (*Lib. Nig. Quat.* f. 92).

Last mention 1393–4 (Q. Alianore) in his usual place.

1384-5

Feryng, John.

De novo professus 1384–5 (Q. Alianore).

Prima Missa 1385–6 (Q. Alianore).

Ad skillam 1391–2 (Infirmarer; Cellarer; Warden of the Churches).

Collector of Abbey rents in Westminster and Wood Street 1399–1400.

Senescallus hospicii Abbatis [W. Colchester] 1400–2.

Hostillarius ?—22 Dec. 1400 (*Mun.* 9480, which states the goods which he handed to his successor).

Custos capelle b. Marie 1403–7.

Camerarius 1404–8.

Prior de Hurley 1409—14 Jun. 1415 (*Lib. Nig. Quat.* 82 b). As such gave the charter for the anniversary of Abbot Colchester 5 Oct. 1411 (*Mun.* 3571).

Thesaurarius maner[m] Regine Alianore; Ricardi II et Anne 1416–7.

Refectorarius 1418–9.

Collector of Abbey rents in Westminster and Wood Street 1419–22.

Infirmarius 1421 (Treasurer)–1431.

Gave 10 marks to maintain a lamp constantly burning before Cardinal Langham's tomb (Stanley, *Memorials*, 3rd ed. p. 641; *Lib. Nig. Quat.* f. 92 b).

Defunctus 1431–2 (deleted from Q. Alianore and Richard II of that year); inter mortuos 1432–3 (Chamberlain).

Snellyng, Snellynge, Smellyng, John.

De novo professus 1384–5 (Q. Alianore).

Subdiaconus 1385–6 (Q. Alianore).

Bought a sheaf of arrows from Abbot Litlington's executors Jan. 1387 (*Mun.* 5446).

Prima Missa 28 Sep.—24 Nov. 1387 (Almoner); 1386–7 (Q. Alianore); 1387–8 (Infirmarer; Sacrist; Warden of the Churches; St Mary's Chapel).

Indult for plenary remission 23 Jan. 1399 (Kal. Pap. Reg. v, 231).

Was in the sick-room 44 days during Oct. and Nov. 1411; in uno homine conducto ad custodiendum fratrem J. S. per xliiii dies et noctes...capiente per diem et noctem ii^d (Infirmarer).

Defunctus c. Nov. 1411 (Infirmarer).

Wyk, Wyke, Wik, Richard.

De novo professus 1384–5 (Q. Alianore).

Prima Missa 1386–7 (Infirmarer; Q. Alianore; Sacrist; Warden of the Churches).

Ad skillam 1392–3 (Infirmarer; Chamberlain; Cellarer; Sacrist; Warden of the Churches; St Mary's Chapel).

Defunctus Jan. 1399 (Infirmarer; having been in the sick-room almost continuously since Jul. 1398).

Preston, Thomas.

De novo professus 1384–5 (Q. Alianore).

Prima Missa 1386–7 (Infirmarer; Q. Alianore; Sacrist; Almoner; Warden of the Churches).

Tunc apud ffolstone [? Folkestone], 1390 (*Lib. Nig. Quat.* f. 92).

Ad skillam 1394–5 (Infirmarer; Sacrist; Almoner; Warden of the Churches).

The probable writer of the Litlington Missal; if so, he was the guest for two years of Walter de Warfeld [q.v.], before formally joining the Convent (cf. Robinson, *Manuscripts of Westminster Abbey*, p. 8).

Defunctus 1419–20 (Q. Alianore; Richard II, which says nuper defunctus, i.e. at the time of the audit).

Cretton, Critton, Curton, Cyrton, Kyrton, Kirton, Kritton, Roger.

De novo professus 1384–5 (Q. Alianore).

Prima Missa 28 Sep.—24 Nov. 1387 (Almoner); 1386–7 (Q. Alianore); 1387–8 (Infirmarer; Sacrist; Warden of the Churches; St Mary's Chapel).

Custos Misericordie 9 Dec. 1391 (*Mun.* 6628).

Ad skillam 1395–6 (Infirmarer; Almoner; Sacrist; Warden of the Churches; St Mary's Chapel).

Collector of the Abbey rents in Westminster and Wood Street 1396–7; 1400–4.

Thesaurarius 1399–1408.

Coquinarius 1399–1400.

Celerarius 13 Nov. 1401—29 Sep. 1406; 25 Jun. 1410 (*Mun.* 30381).

Granator 1402–3; 29 Sep. 1409—19 Nov. 1413.

Custos maner^m Regine Alianore 1403–8.

Ballivus ? + 1404.

Custos maner^m Ricardi II et Anne 1403–6; Thesaurarius 1406–7.

Custos ecclesiarum 1403–8.

Elemosinarius 1411–2 (*Mun.* 18551); 1413–4; 1431–3.

Infirmarius 29 Sep. 1416—12 Dec. 1417.

Receptor Abbatis 1416–8.

The collector of Westminster rents paid lix^s vii^d pro quadam summa pendente in lite inter R. C. et W. Sonewell [q.v.] 1416–7 (*Mun.* 18560).

Sacrista ?+1422–33.

Compiler of the Black Paper Register, which forms part III of *Liber Niger Quaternus* (cf. J. Armitage Robinson, *Manuscripts of Westminster Abbey*, p. 96 f.).

Indult to choose confessor 16 Apr. 1421 (Kal. Pap. Reg. VII, 332).

With John Sauereye [q.v.], he made and dedicated the altar of St Michael, St Martin, and All Saints, and also the screen of the same chapel (£10) (Stanley, *Memorials*, 3rd ed. p. 640; *Lib. Nig. Quat.* f. 92 b).

Defunctus 1434. (Infra tempus compoti mortuus est: Sacrist 1433–4; i.e. probably before Christmas 1434; inter mortuos, 1433–4, Richard II; deleted from Q. Alianore.)

Belden, Beldene, Beldone, William.

De novo professus 1384–5 (Q. Alianore).

Prima Missa 28 Sep.—24 Nov. 1387 (Almoner); 1387–8 (Infirmarer; Sacrist; Warden of the Churches; St Mary's Chapel).

In the sick-room for four periods 1410–1; solut' pro diuersis emplastris et unguentis pro fratre W. B. ii^s vi^d (Infirmarer).

Defunctus 28 Sep.—1 Dec. 1420 (Infirmarer); 1419–20 (Q. Alianore; Richard II: nuper defunctus, i.e. at the time of the audit).

1385–6

Crendon, Crandon, Crundon, John.

Prima Missa 28 Sep.—24 Nov. 1387 (Almoner); 1386–7 (Q. Alianore); 1387–8 (Infirmarer; Sacrist; Warden of the Churches; St Mary's Chapel).

Et in surguria pro fratre J. C. iii^s Oct. 1395 (Infirmarer).

Ad skillam 28 Sep.—13 Nov. 1401 (Cellarer); 1401–2 (Infirmarer; Warden of the Churches).

Mentioned in his usual place, Q. Alianore, 1414–5, but not afterwards; probably left the Convent.

1386–7

WHATELE, Whately, Whatley, Whetele, Whetelee, Whetle, Whetley, Whetleye, Watele, Robert.

[Wrongly transcribed as "Bathley" in Kal. Pap. Reg. IX. 2.]

De novo professus 1386–7 (Q. Alianore).

Prima Missa 1388–9 (Sacrist; Warden of the Churches; St Mary's Chapel; probably Infirmarer[1]).

Studens Oxon. (£10) 1390 (*Lib. Nig. Quat.* f. 92)–1407 (Treasurer).

Et solut R. W. venienti a Oxñ erga festum Pasche [probably to preach the Palm Sunday and Good Friday sermons] xx^s, 1399–1400 (Sacrist).

Et solut...in persolucionem vi^{li} xiii^s iiii^d sibi concess' per dominum priorem et conventum pro opposicione sua in scolis ibidem facienda lxvi^s viii^d 1403–4 (Treasurer).

He received a further grant of £10 by instalments in addition to his £10 a year, 1405–7 (Treasurer).

Prior 1407–35.

---

[1] Infirmarer 1388–9 entered exhennia missa vii^{tem} nouis presbiteris primo celebrantibus missas. These seven would be Whatele, Holbech, Amondesham, Bassyngbourne, Botkesham, Merston, and Sonewell.

Ad skillam, Prior, 1407–8 (Infirmarer; Almoner; Sacrist; Warden of the Churches; St Mary's Chapel).

Indult to choose confessor 12 Nov. 1411 (Kal. Pap. Reg. VI, 335); being then S. T. M.

Magister R. W. theologus was in attendance upon Abbot Colchester at the General Chapter of the Benedictines at Northampton 6 Jul. 1411 (*Lib. Nig. Quat.* f. 90).

Received Henry V's royal licence to the Prior and Convent to elect an Abbot in place of W. Colchester; dated 12 Nov. 1420 (*Mun.* 5440).

Indult for portable altar 10 Apr. 1421 (Kal. Pap. Reg. VII, 333); he being then S. T. P.

Defunctus 1435, between Mich⁸ and 17 Dec. (obit in *Mun.* 23034, Treasurer); inter mortuos, 1435–6 (Chamberlain).

Holbech, Holbeche, John.

De novo professus 1386–7 (Q. Alianore).

Prima Missa 1388–9 (Sacrist; Warden of the Churches; St Mary's Chapel; probably Infirmarer).

Defunctus 1430–1 (Infirmarer).

1387-8

Amondesham, Amondysham, Amotesham, Agmondesham, Agmunde-sham, Agmotesham, Augmotesham, Amodsam, William.

Prima Missa 1388–9 (Sacrist; Warden of the Churches; St Mary's Chapel; probably Infirmarer).

Ad skillam 1395–6 (Infirmarer; Almoner; Sacrist; Warden of the Churches; St Mary's Chapel).

Camerarius 1401–4 (Treasurer).

Scolaris Oxon. (£10) 1405–12 (Treasurer).

Sacrista 1413–4 (Treasurer).

Archidiaconus 6 Nov. 1414 (*Mun.* 5988, in which he was nominated with two others by the Abbot of Holy Cross, Waltham, to be his proctor at the Papal Curia and elsewhere).

Elemosinarius 29 Sep. 1416—6 Dec. 1417; 1418–9.

In expensis W. A....et aliorum equitancium usque Steuynton pro bladis diuersis et decimis intrandis tempore Autumpnali viˢ viiiᵈ 1408–9 (Richard II).

In expensis fratris W. A. una cum expensis duorum seruientium cum iii equis euntium ad diuersa monasteria pro pecunia mutuanda pro...abbate sancti Edmundi et priore Wygornie euntibus ad Constanciam ad concilium generale in ambassiata domini Regis et negociis totius ordinis, 1417 (*Mun.* 12396).

Defunctus 14 Jul. 1420 (Camden, *Reges,* &c.); nuper defunctus 1419–20 (Richard II).

Buried in the North Ambulatory outside the "Erasmus" Chapel under a large stone, the brass memorial of which is destroyed. The inscription was as follows, the spelling of his name being different from any that has been noted in the Muniments:—

Hic iacet frater Gulielmus Amundisham quondam monachus huius loci receptor nostri canonici[1]. Qui obiit anno Dom. 1420, mense Iulii die decimo quarto; cuius animae propitietur Deus. Amen. (Camden, *Reges,* &c.; J. Dart, *Westmonasterium,* II, 15.)

---

[1] I cannot assign any meaning to this phrase, and, if the authority were not Camden, should suspect an error in the copying of the inscription.

Coneham, Cofham, Coham, Cougham, Coueham, Cosham, Coucham, Henry.

Prima Missa 24 Nov. 1387—29 Sep. 1388 (Almoner); 1387–8 (Infirmarer; Sacrist).

Ad skillam 1397–8 (Infirmarer; Sacrist; Warden of the Churches; St Mary's Chapel).

Deleted from Q. Alianore 1403–4; not again in the manor-lists, and presumably away from the Convent, till 1407–8.

Collector of Abbey rents in Westminster and Wood Street, 1408–17.

Camerarius 1412–8.

Defunctus 1417–8 (Q. Alianore, $\frac{2}{5}$ share; so probably 1418); inter mortuos 1418–9 (Chamberlain).

Bassyngbourne, Bassyngborn, Bassingbourne, Basyngbourne, John.

Prima Missa 1388–9 (Sacrist; Warden of the Churches; St Mary's Chapel; probably Infirmarer).

Thesaurarius 1409–14.

Coquinarius 1409–14.

Not mentioned after 1413–4 (Q. Alianore); probably left the Convent.

Botkesham, Botkisham, Botkysham, Botekesham, Botesham, Bodesham, Bodsam, John.

Prima Missa 1388–9 (Sacrist; Warden of the Churches; Warden of St Mary's Chapel; probably Infirmarer).

Was deleted from Q. Alianore 1403–4 and not restored to the manor lists till 1412–3.

Et dat' fratri J. B. pro quodam musico instrumento emendando vi^s viii^d 1416–7 (Abbot's Treasurer).

Defunctus 1419–20 (Q. Alianore); nuper defunctus (Richard II; i.e. at the time of the audit); inter mortuos 1420–1 (Chamberlain).

Merston, Elymynus, Elminus, Elmig', E^s.

Of Hadleigh (Kal. Pap. Reg. v, 41).

Nuper professus 1387–8 (Q. Alianore).

Prima Missa 1388–9 (Sacrist; Warden of the Churches; St Mary's Chapel; probably Infirmarer).

Indult for plenary remission, 15 Mar. 1397 (Kal. Pap. Reg. v, 41).

Defunctus 1399–1400 (Infirmarer).

Sonewell, Sonewelle, Sonnewelle, Sonwelle, Sunwell, William,
= Delauale, W.

[W. Delauale appears at end of the Q. Alianore list 1387–8, but nowhere else; and is therefore assumed to be identical with William Sonewell who takes his place in the subsequent lists.]

Nuper professus 1387–8 (Q. Alianore).

Prima Missa 1388–9 (Sacrist; St Mary's Chapel; probably Infirmarer).

Pro medicinis fratris W. S. xxvi^s viii^d 1395–6 (Infirmarer).

Thesaurarius 1403–5; Ballivus 1409–10.

Coquinarius 1404–5.

Ad skillam 1405–6 (Warden of the Churches; St Mary's Chapel).

Custos ecclesiarum 1408–10.

Custos maner^m Regine Alianore 1408–10; Ricardi II et Anne 1408–9.

The collector of Westminster rents paid lix^s vii^d pro quadam summa pendente in lite inter R. Cretton et W. S. 1416–7 (*Mun.* 18560).

Granator 1418–23?+.

Refectorarius 1419–23; 1425–7 (Treasurer).

Custos tenementorum Episcopi Sarum [J. de Waltham], 1419–31.

Custos Novi Operis 29 Sep. 1420—16 Nov. 1421.

Celerarius 4 Apr. 1423 (*Mun.* 13405); 1430-1 (*Mun.* 18890).

Fecit capellam sancti Johannis Euangeliste (*Lib. Nig. Quat.* f. 92 b).

Pension x^s 1432-3 (St Mary's Chapel).

Defunctus 1432-3 (inter mortuos, Chamberlain).

1389-90

Lucas, John.

Prima Missa 1394-5 (Infirmarer; Almoner; Sacrist; Warden of the Churches).

Granator 1413-4 (Treasurer).

Thesaurarius et Coquinarius 1414-5.

Ad skillam 1416-7 (Infirmarer; Almoner; Cellarer; Warden of the Churches; St Mary's Chapel).

Thesaurarius maner^m Regine Alianore 1417-8.

? Prior de Sudbury 1417 (Q. Alianore). Omitted from the manor rolls after 29 Nov. 1420 (Q. Alianore).

Grant of xx^s pro debitis fratris J. L. defuncti, 1431-2 (Sacrist).

Woxebrigge, Woxebregg, Wuxbregge, Wuxbrigge, Wyxbrugge, Walter.

Prima Missa 1394-5 (Infirmarer; Almoner; Sacrist; Warden of the Churches).

Deleted from Q. Alianore 1401-2; probably left the Convent.

Birlyngham, Birlingham, Byrlyngham, Byrlingham, Richard.

Dominus Birlyngham fuit ultimus tunc in conventu Westmon' 1390 (*Lib. Nig. Quat.* f. 92, with reference to the year of Jubilee).

Prima Missa 1394-5 (Infirmarer; Almoner; Sacrist; Warden of the Churches).

In attendance on Abbot Colchester at the General Chapter of the Benedictines, Northampton, 6 Jul. 1411 (*Lib. Nig. Quat.* f. 90 b).

Serious illness Apr. 1412; had a nurse for 18 days and nights (Infirmarer).

Ad skillam 1412-3 (Infirmarer).

Custos capelle b. Marie 13 Apr. 1422 (*Mun.* 13957).

Elemosinarius 1423-7? +.

Granator 1428-33 (Treasurer).

Refectorarius 1433-4 (Treasurer).

Was admitted to a camera in the Infirmary (Kal. Pap. Reg. x. 590).

Pension xvi^s 1435 (St Mary's Chapel); xvi^s ad terminum vite 1435 (New Work); £1. 13s. 4d. 1436 (Treasurer, who in 1438-9 commuted the payment for 300 "fagetts" and some coal).

He was at Hendon for his health 1439-41 (Treasurer).

Defunctus (? Jan.) 1441 (Infirmarer). Sepultus in claustro (*Mun.* 33289 f. 3).

1392-3

Middleton, Middelton, Midelton, Middilton, Middylton, Myddilton, Myddylton, Benedict.

Prima Missa 1396-7 (Infirmarer; Almoner; Warden of the Churches; probably Sacrist).

Ad skillam, 1410-1 (Infirmarer, who entered him simply as fratri Benedicto; Almoner; Warden of the Churches).

Custos capelle b. Marie, 1416-8.

Precentor 1418-20 (Warden of the Churches).

Defunctus 1419-20 (Q. Alianore; Richard II, which says nuper defunctus, i.e. at the time of the audit); inter mortuos 1420-1 (Chamberlain).

Whaddon, Waddon, Edmund.
Prima Missa 1396–7 (Infirmarer; Almoner; Warden of the Churches; probably Sacrist[1]).
Studens Oxoñ (£10) 1395–1401 (Treasurer).
Defunctus 1400–1 (Infirmarer, who gives obit but no mention of illness; not entered in Q. Alianore after 1399–1400; perhaps died at Oxford).

1394-5

Sauereye, Saueray, Savery, Safferey, Saffery, Saffrey, John.
Prima Missa 1395–6 (Infirmarer; Sacrist; St Mary's Chapel; Warden of the Churches); 1396–7 (Almoner, apparently in another hand).
Ad skillam 1405–6 (Infirmarer; Cellarer; Warden of the Churches; St Mary's Chapel).
Camerarius 1410–12; 1418–9.
Receptor denariorum Abbatis [W. Colchester] 1413–4; Senescallus hospicii Abbatis 28 Sep.—18 Nov. 1413.
Elemosinarius 1414–15.
Scolaris studens Oxon. (£10) 1415–7 (Treasurer).
Prior de Hurley 1420–52 ? +.

Gedeney, Gedney, Walter.
Prima Missa 1396–7 (Infirmarer; Almoner; Warden of the Churches; probably Sacrist)..
Last mentioned in his usual place in the manor lists 1410–1; perhaps left the Convent.

1395-6

Fordham, John.
Prima Missa 1396–7 (Infirmarer; Almoner; Warden of the Churches; probably Sacrist).
Dispensation to him to hold a benefice with cure of souls 4 Feb. 1406 (Kal. Pap. Reg. vi. 74).
Last mentioned in his usual order in Q. Alianore, 1408–9; deleted, Richard II, that year.

Coggeshale, Coggysale, Coggyssall, Cogeshale, Cogishale, Coxale, Walter.
Prima Missa 1396–7 (Infirmarer; Almoner; Warden of the Churches; probably Sacrist).
Ad skillam 1409–10 (Infirmarer; Almoner; Warden of the Churches).
Thesaurarius maner^m Regine Alianore; Ricardi II et Anne; 1410–6; 1418–26.
Celerarius ? + 1416–7 ? +.
Granator 1416–8; as such he had a legal dispute (lis) with John Mylys, the Ashwell carrier, about eight quarters of barley, 1417–8.
Indult to choose confessor 8 Apr. 1421 (Kal. Pap. Reg. vii, 330).
Custos Novi Operis 16 Nov. 1421—29 Sep. 1422.
Collector of Abbey rents in Westminster and in Wood Street, 1427–32.
Reclusus 28 Sep.—24 Dec. 1435 (St Mary's Chapel, which paid him 1d. a day); 1434–5 (Treasurer); xii lbs. of candles and some coals 1440–1 (Sacrist); solut' fratri W. C. recluso Westm. ex precepto domini Abbatis x^s, 1442–3 (New Work).
Defunctus 1442–3 (Q. Alianore, half share; Henry V, $\frac{6}{7}$ share; so probably 1443).

[1] The Sacrist's roll 1396–7 allows 9s. 9d. (=1s. 7½d. × 6) for the Primae Missae of six Brethren not named,—probably Whaddon, Middleton, Gedney, Fordham, Coggeshale and Eston.

Eston, Estone, Eyston, John.

Prima Missa 1396–7 (Infirmarer; Almoner; Warden of the Churches; probably Sacrist).

In attendance on Abbot Colchester at the General Chapter of the Benedictines, Northampton, 6 Jul. 1411 (*Lib. Nig. Quat.* f. 90 b).

Defunctus 1433–4 (Richard II).

1397–8

Shiplake, Shyppelake, Schiplake, Schippelake, Schyplake, Reginald.

In Priest's orders 1398–9, when he was placed so high on the list, above R. Whatele (1386–7), that he may have been a Priest when he joined (Q. Alianore).

Ad skillam 8 Dec. 1400—29 Sep. 1401 (St Mary's Chapel); 1400–1 (Infirmarer; Chamberlain; Cellarer; Warden of the Churches); 1401–2 (Almoner).

Thesaurarius maner^m Regine Alianore 1401–3; 1426–7.

Refectorarius 1411–3 (Treasurer); 1414–7; 1427–8.

Custos capelle b. Marie 28 Sep.—24 Nov. 1420.

Infirmarius 1 Dec. 1420—28 Sep. 1421; 28 Sep.—21 Dec. 1436.

From 1443 onwards he was stagiarius infra Infirmariam (Sacrist), receiving an allowance of candles, &c.

Defunctus, circa horam octavam in nocte, 15 Dec. 1445. Sepultus in claustro juxta tumbam fratris Ricardi Byrlyngham (*Mun.* 33289, f. 3).

York, Yorke, Yoork, William.

In Priest's orders 1398–9 (Q. Alianore).

Defunctus 1419–20 (Q. Alianore); inter mortuos, 1420–1 (Chamberlain).

Dalby, Thomas.

Prima Missa 1401–2 (Infirmarer; Warden of the Churches).

Defunctus, 29 Sep.—21 Dec. 1436 (Infirmarer, *Mun.* 19418, which gives his obit and says that he was in the sick-room for 80 days from 29 Sep.; thus there is a presumption of his death c. 17 Dec.).

Ludlow, Lodelowe, Lodlowe, Ludelawe, Ludlowe, John.

Prima Missa 1402–3 (Infirmarer; Almoner; Warden of the Churches).

Scolaris studens Oxon. (£10) 1402–5 (Treasurer).

Defunctus, c. Oct. 1408 (Infirmarer).

Milton, Multon, Multone, Walter.

Defunctus c. Feb. 1400 (Infirmarer).

Kyngestone, Kingiston, Kigstone, John.

Priest's share 1398–9 (Q. Alianore).

Eodem anno J. K. fuit Ultimus in congregacione (1398–9, *Lib. Nig. Quat.* f. 92).

Mentioned in his usual place in the manor rolls 1410–1; was in the sick-room with a male nurse night and day for a fortnight in Apr. 1412; no mention of obit; no further appearance.

H A R W D E N, Harweden, Harewedene, Hareden, Harden, Harowdene, Richard.

Full priest's share 1398–9 (Q. Alianore). In 1397–8 he had received 6s. 8d. as against 5s. given to other novices.

Senescallus hospicii Domini [W. Colchester] 1406–7 (*Mun.* 24417).

Thesaurarius maner^m Regine Alianore 1403–5; custos 1410–6; 1418–20; Ricardi II et Anne 1410–6; 1418–20.

Camerarius 1408–10 (Treasurer; *Mun.* 18735, in which he and his successor settled their balances 2 Nov. 1410).

Thesaurarius; Ballivus; Custos ecclesiarum; 1410–6; 1418–20.

Custos Novi Operis 1413 (probably 1411)–1420. (For his association with Richard Whityngton and for his work on the triforium cf. R. B. Rackham, *Nave of Westminster*, pp. 13–16.)

Sacrista 1414–9 ?+ (Treasurer).

A visus compoti of 1420 shows that Harwden vacated his treasurerships 29 Nov. (*Mun.* 23769).

Custos infirmarie 28 Sep.—1 Dec. 1420.

Abbot Colchester as President of the General Chapter of the Benedictine Order paid him £10 pro bono labore suo pro certis negociis expediendis uersus dominum Regem, 1420 (*Mun.* 12397).

Abbas ? 29 Nov. 1420. (The royal licence to Prior Whatele and the Convent to elect a successor to Colchester was dated 12 Nov.; *Mun.* 5440. When the compotus of Henry V for 1419–20 was made up, he was already Electus and was therefore placed on the list next after the Prior.)

Confirmation of his election by Martin V 29 Mar. 1421 (Kal. Pap. Reg. VII, 191).

Indults to choose confessor and for portable altar 8, 10 Apr. 1421 (*ibid.* 333).

Superuisor nauis ecclesie Westm., facte per dominum Regem 1420–1 (New Work).

Henry V granted to the Convent the privilege of having its Abbots-elect confirmed in their office by a Bishop in England instead of going at ruinous expense to the Roman Court, 7 Jun. 1421 (*Mun.* 5439).

The Papal Chamberlain acknowledged receipt of 83 florins due to the clerks of the Papal Camera from the new Abbot 29 Mar. 1421 (*Mun.* 9449); and another sum of 125 florins, an instalment of what was due to various Papal familiares et officiales, was acknowledged 20 Nov. 1421 (*Mun.* 9463).

i pecia argentea cum cooperculo argenteo ex dono domini Ricardi Abbatis ponderante xiii uns' di., 1427–8 (Monk-Bailiff).

Resignauit 2 Apr. die Sabbati in septimana Pasche 1440 (*Mun.* 24436).

His pension of 200 marks from the Abbot's rents in Worcestershire was secured by royal confirmation 15 Mar. 1440; so the matter was evidently arranged in Chapter before his resignation (*Mun.* 5902). The Papal permission to Harwden to receive this pension spoke of him as adeo senio confractum, and acknowledged that he had been a good ruler, laudabiliter praefuisse; 20 Aug. 1440 (*Mun.* 5253).

The receiver of the money for Henry V's anniversary 1439–40 entered a "recreation" of xx⁸ paid fratri R. H. nuper Abbati (*Mun.* 24125); and it appears from the same account and from that of 1440–1 that Harwden had lent the fund £75, which was being repaid to him at the rate of £25 yearly. He received the second £25 "in part payment" 1440–1; but there is no record of the third.

Prior Essex entered in 1482 a receipt of 3s. 4d. xviii° die Junii pro obitu R. H. (*Mun.* 33289, f. 15).

Defunctus ? 18 Jun. 1441.

Karlill, Karlil, Karlell, Karlyle, Karlyll, Karlylle, Carlill, John.

Prima Missa 28 Sep.—13 Nov. 1401 (Cellarer); 1401–2 (Infirmarer; Warden of the Churches).

Ad skillam 1421–2 (Chamberlain; New Work; Almoner; Warden of the Churches).

Last appearance in, the manor-lists 1422–3 in his usual place, with full share; last appearance in Chamberlain's lists 1423–4, where he received the usual outfit, except panni nigri. Probably he left the Convent.

Wilton, Wylton, John.

Novice's share 1397–8 ; priest's share 1398–9 (Q. Alianore).

Ad skillam 1418–9 (Infirmarer ; Chamberlain ; Almoner ; Warden of the Churches).

Elemosinarius 22 Jul. 1420—29 Sep. 1423 ; 1428–30 ? +.

Thesaurarius maner^m Ricardi II et Anne 1435–45 ; custos 1437–40.

Indult for plenary remission 11 Mar. 1421 (Kal. Pap. Reg. vii, 329).

Thesaurarius maner^m Regine Alianore 19 Jun. 1438—29 Sep. 1446 ; custos 1438–40.

Supprior 1440 (*Mun.* 5414).

In *Mun.* 5414, which is a licence to John Cambridge [q.v.] to prosecute Alicia Peese, Wilton is described as supprior custos presidens siue gubernator Monasterii Westm....per Resignacionem reuerendi in Christo patris et domini domini Ricardi [Harwden]....As such he affixed the corporate seal to the document in the Chapter House 27 May 1440.

Custos feretri 1444–5 (Sacrist ; *Mun.* 33289, f. 3).

Auditor super compotum 1446–7 (Q. Alianore).

Infirmarius 1446–9.

Pension xx^s 1452–3 (New Work).

Defunctus 8 Mai. 1453 (*Mun.* 33289) ; 1452–3 (Q. Alianore ; Henry V ; ½ share). Sepultus in vigilia Ascensionis Domini in capella sancti Martini episcopi coram altari (*Mun.* 33289, f. 2).

Thetforde, Tetford, Thomas.

Was entered in Q. Alianore 1397–8 as if a novice, but in 1398–9 received at the rate of a priest and was entered with R. Fakenham next to E. Whaddon who said his first Mass 1396–7.

Defunctus 1402 (probably Jan. ; Infirmarer 1401–2 entered him as sick for 9 days that month, and his name was deleted and marked with a † in Q. Alianore).

Fakenham, Ralph.

[See under T. Thetforde.]

Last mention 1401–2 (Q. Alianore ; where he was entered at the end with a half share).

1398-9

Selby, Magister Ralph.

Prebendary of Driffield in York Minster 9 Dec. 1385, sub-dean in 1387 ; archdeacon of Buckingham, by exchange, 1 Jul. 1392 ; archdeacon of Norfolk 20 Nov. 1398, but the King's presentee, John Midleton, was actually admitted to this last, 28 Jan. 1399 (Le Neve, *Fasti*). Was one of the executors (*Mun.* 5262 A) of John de Waltham, Bishop of Salisbury, who preceded him in the subdeanery of York, 1384, and who was buried in St Edward's Chapel, Westminster Abbey, Sep. 1395. The Bishop's executors gave the Convent a red vestment costing £40 and a sum of 500 marks. Selby may have joined our Convent in this connexion.

In Q. Alianore 1398–9, and in Chamberlain 1399–1400 and following, he was placed next after the Prior ; at some anniversaries he received a double, or Prior's, share in the distribution.

16^s' worth of "fagetts" bought for him yearly 1399, &c. (Treasurer).

Indult to visit his Archdeaconry of Buckingham by deputy for life 14 Jul. 1399 (Kal. Pap. Reg. v, 202). There is a reference (*ibid.* p. 517), dated 13 Jun. 1402, to the fact that, being then a secular clerk, he had vacated the canonry and prebend of Netherburychurch (sc. Netherbury in Ecclesia) in Salisbury Cathedral on becoming a monk at Westminster in 1398.

Pension of £4 from 1402–3 (Treasurer).

Another sign of special privilege is the Infirmarer's gift to him of 20ˢ 1417–8, and 1418–9; in the former case there is an attempt to work this out as 11ˢ 6ᵈ for 46 meat-days (at 3ᵈ.) and 9ˢ 6ᵈ for 57 fish-days (at 2ᵈ.); but in the latter the arithmetic is dropped and it is said that he received the 20ˢ licet ibidem non existenti pro diuersis temporibus hoc anno.

Defunctus 29 Sep. 1420 (Camden, *Reges*, &c.); 28 Sep.—1 Dec. 1420 (Infirmarer); 1419–20 (Q. Alianore); 1420–1 (Chamberlain).

Buried in the South Ambulatory.

1399–1400

Surreys, Surreis, Sorreys, Sotheron, Sothron, Southeron, Southerne, Southerene, Sutherne, Suthren, William.

Prima Missa 1401–2 (Infirmarer; Warden of the Churches).

Scolaris studens Oxon. 1416–7 (Treasurer).

Elemosinarius 6 Dec. 1417—29 Sep. 1418.

Custos capelle b. Marie 1420–1.

Thesaurarius manerᵐ Regine Alianore 1427–31; Ricardi II et Anne 1427–9 ? +.

Refectorarius 1434–5.

Defunctus 1439–40 (Q. Alianore, ½ share; Henry V, ⅔ share).

1403–4

Wrotham, Wrottham, Wratham, de Rotham, John.

Diaconus 1404–5 (Richard II).

Prima Missa 1406–7 (Infirmarer; Almoner; Cellarer; Warden of the Churches).

Thesaurarius 1415–8; (et Ballivus) 1421—27 Jul. 1431.

Coquinarius 1415–6 (Treasurer).

Custos manerᵐ Regine Alianore 1416–8; 1420–31; Ricardi II et Anne 1416–7; 1420–9.

Et eidem [custodi] liˢ pro diuersis expensis factis in sepultura regis Henrici quinti hoc anno 1421–2 (Q. Alianore).

Custos ecclesiarum 1416–8; 1420—28 Jul. 1431.

Ad skillam 1418–9 (Infirmarer; Chamberlain; Almoner; Warden of the Churches).

Custos capelle b. Marie 1432–3.

Elemosinarius 1433–4.

Granator 1434–8 (Treasurer).

Defunctus 1438–9 (Q. Alianore; Chamberlain; Richard II, ⅖ share).

KIRTON, Kyrton, Edmund.

Diaconus 1404–5 (Richard II).

Scolaris studens Oxon. (£10) 1407–16; 1417–25 (Treasurer; Sacrist).

Prima Missa 1408–9 (Infirmarer; Almoner; Warden of the Churches).

In expensis fratris E. K. monachi Westm. cum duobus seruientibus equitantibus a Westm. usque Walden Bury et Norwyche per x dies pro negociis expediendis [for the General Chapter] 1420 (*Mun.* 12397).

There were frequent payments to him by the Treasurer for journeys to and from Oxford 1421–5, and in 1424–5 the £10 was continued to him, though the two customary students were also being paid at the same rate. This would follow upon his appointment as Prior of the Benedictine students at Oxford (Gloucester Hall, now Worcester College): soluᵗ E. K. priori studentium Oxoñ pro parte expensorum eiusdem ibidem xxˢ, 1425-6 (Treasurer). At the same time his exhibition of £10 was stopped and, apparently, deleted from the account.

Indults for a portable altar and to choose confessor 8 Apr. 1421 (Kal. Pap. Reg. vii, 332 f.).

Sacrista 1433—16 Dec. 1440.

Custos Novi Operis 1433-7 ?+ (cf. R. B. Rackham, *Nave of Westminster*, pp. 18-27).

Abbas 1440 (after 27 May, *Mun.* 5414; the Pope "provided" him to the Abbacy 3 Aug. 1440 and issued a faculty to him to be blessed as such by any Bishop 6 Aug. 1440; Kal. Pap. Reg. ix, 105).

Ad skillam, Abbas, 28 Sep.—16 Dec. 1440 (Sacrist); 1440-1 (Infirmarer; Almoner; Monk-Bailiff).

As Sacrist ("sexteyn") he mortgaged some plate with John Nankilly, citizen and draper, for £42. 19s. 3d.; among the items were "iiii saltsalere with a covercy¹ gylt and a senser gylt...a basyn and an ewer of syluer and gylt...a stondyng cuppe of syluer with a covercil thereto," 22 Dec. 1439 (*Mun.* 9481).

On a report from the Prior of Winchester and the Abbots of St John, Colchester, and Chertsey, Pope Eugenius IV issued a mandate for summoning and examining Kirton on a charge of being a fornicator, dilapidator, adulterer, simoniac, and guilty of other crimes, and for depriving him of his office, if the charges were proved, 24 Sep. 1446 (Kal. Pap. Reg. viii, 309).

Et in batyllag' Thome Cornewayle [q.v.] de Westm. usque London de London usque Bermyssey...de inde usque London et Westm....pro baculo pastorali domini Abbatis ibidem impignorato redimendo...xˡⁱ, 1447 (Abbot's Treasurer).

Received King Henry VI, when he came to the Abbey church to choose the place for his burial c. 1460 (*Mun.* 6389**).

Resigned the Abbotship in or about 1462-3; before 24 Nov. 1463 (*Mun.* 24279); Widmore (p. 115) says 23 Oct. 1462.

There is an indenture between him and his successor, G. Norwych, in which the latter acknowledged receipt of 120 lb. 3½ oz. (Troy weight) of silver plate, valued at 2s. 6d. per oz.; 13 Dec. 1463 (*Mun.* 5443).

He was granted a pension of 200 marks; his earliest surviving quarterly receipt is dated 19 Jan. 1464 (*Mun.* 5428).

When Abbot Norwych [q.v.] issued a commission to Millyng and others to administer the affairs of the convent, the commission was to continue quousque praefatum monasterium ab omni debito per nos seu Edmundum predecessorem nostrum causato penitus liberatum fuerit (*Mun.* 5432).

After his retirement the Abbot's Receiver 1464 paid domino E. K. ad diuersas vices viiiˡⁱ and the Abbot's Treasurer (1463-4) laid out xiiᵈ pro fagetts et talwode¹ pro Magistro E. K.

Defunctus 3 Oct. 1466 (Camden, *Reges*, &c.); buried in St Andrew's Chapel, the screen of which he had adorned.

Item rec' de Thoma More die obitus Dompni E. K. nuper Abbatis Westm. pro iiiiᵒʳ Tapr. xxᵈ (St Margaret, Westminster, churchwardens' accounts 1467-8).

1406-7

Norrys, Norreys, Norys, Noryssh, William.
    Novicius professus 1406-7 (Richard II).
    Novus sacerdos 1407-8 (Q. Alianore).

---

¹ Cf. Kitchin, *Obedientiary Rolls, Winchester*, p. 230, n. 2.

Prima Missa 1408–9 (Infirmarer; Almoner; Warden of the Churches).
Scolaris studens Oxon. (£10) 1412–5 (Treasurer).
Last payment from Q. Alianore in 1412–3; no further mention; perhaps he remained at Oxford.

London, John.
Novicius professus 1406–7 (Richard II).
Prima Missa 1408–9 (Infirmarer; Almoner; Warden of the Churches).
Novus sacerdos 1408–9 (Richard II; i.e. he received from the manors at the rate of half the payment made to the older priests).
Defunctus 1431 (Infirmarer, 1430–1, gives his obit and notes a ten weeks' illness towards the close of that year); inter mortuos, 1430–1 (Q. Alianore, full share).

Walden, John.
[? = John Walden, who was praepositus of the Abbot's manor of Pyrford up to Mich^s 1407; *Mun.* 27435.]
Novicius professus 1406–7 (Richard II).
Prima Missa 1408–9 (Infirmarer; Almoner; Warden of the Churches).
Novus sacerdos 1408–9 (Richard II).
Solut' fratri J. W. pro nouo libro organorum xx^s, 1415–6 (St Mary's Chapel).
Ad skillam 1417–8 (Almoner: primo ad skillam presidenti in Refectorio; Warden of the Churches).
Granator 1423–5 (Treasurer).
Last mention in the manor rolls 1426–7, at his usual place; was entered at end of Chamberlain 1428–9, who supplied foot-wear to him but no panni nigri. Probably he left the Convent.

1408-9

Mordon, Moredon, Nicholas.
Novicius junior 1408–9 (Richard II).
Prima Missa 1410–1 (Infirmarer; Almoner; Warden of the Churches).
Thesaurarius 1416–33; 19 Jun. 1438—29 Sep. 1442.
Coquinarius 1418–20 (Treasurer; Q. Alianore); 1441 (*Mun.* 33288, f. 36 b), when he gave the Prior a pair of gloves at Christmas.
Celerarius et Gardinarius ?+25 Dec. 1445 (*Mun.* 33289)—2 Feb. 1447 ?+.
Defunctus 1454 (Henry V, full share, Q. Alianore, $\frac{2}{3}$ share, Richard II, $\frac{1}{2}$ share, 1453–4); inter mortuos 1454–5 (Chamberlain).

Bryd, Bryde, Brid, Byrd, Geoffrey.
Novicius junior 1408–9 (Richard II).
Prima Missa 1412–3 (Infirmarer).
Refectorarius 1417–8.
Camerarius 1419–33.
Collector of Abbey rents in Westminster and Wood Street, 1417–32 (*Mun.* 18561–81).
Indult to choose confessor 11 Mar. 1421 (Kal. Pap. Reg. vii, 332).
Defunctus 1433 (Q. Alianore 1432–3 enters him at his usual place with a full share; but in Richard II he is entered separately with a note: non plus de cetero quia mortuus est; i.e. he must have died in the late autumn of 1433).

Massham, Masseham, Masham, Massam, Bartholomew.
= Selby, Bartholomew.
[The name Selby was twice corrected in another hand to Massam in

Infirmarer 1412–3, no doubt in order to avoid confusion with Ralph Selby, but was retained by an oversight when the exennia for First Mass were entered.]

Novicius junior 1408–9 (Richard II).

Prima Missa 1412–3 (Infirmarer).

Ad skillam 1443–4 (Infirmarer; Chamberlain; Almoner; Sacrist; Warden of the Churches; Treasurer).

Auditor super compotum 1446–7 (Q. Alianore).

Custos feretri 1446—12 Jun. 1450 (*Mun.* 33289, f. 3; Sacrist).

Thesaurarius maner^m Ricardi II et Anne 1445–50; Regine Alianore 1446–50.

Refectorarius (Christmas) 1438 (*Mun.* 33288, f. 38 b); 1448–9.

Defunctus c. 12 Jun. 1450 (when the Sacrist took on his duties as Custos feretri); inter mortuos 1449–50 (Chamberlain; ½ share, Q. Alianore, Richard II).

1410-1

Hatton, William.

Prima Missa 1415–6 (Warden of the Churches; St Mary's Chapel).

Last mention at end of Chamberlain 1424–5; last payment from the manors 1422–3 (Q. Alianore).

Broughton, Browton, Brotton, William.

Prima Missa 1414–5 (Almoner; Warden of the Churches; Q. Alianore for that year enters him as receiving 40s. and calls him sacerdoti de nouo ordinato; the full dividend was 50s.).

Defunctus c. Mar. 1417 (Infirmarer 1416–7, which gives his obit and says he was ill during March; Q. Alianore, ½ share, i.e. to the end of March).

1412-3

Southbroke, Southbrook, Sothbrok, Sowthbroke, Sudbroke, Richard.

[On his first appearance he was placed in the second grade above the novices (Q. Alianore, Richard II, 1412–3), receiving a priest's full share from the manors in 1414–5.]

Scolaris studens Oxon. (£10) 1417–20 (Treasurer).

Precentor 1420–38 ?+ (Warden of the Churches).

Magister 1444–5 (Treasurer; and *Mun.* 33289, f. 3).

Solut' Magistro R. S. pro quadam annuitate sibi concessa ad terminum vite p. ann. xx^s 1445–6 (New Work); gift of 10 lb. of candles, 1445–6 (Sacrist); pension x^s 1447–8 (St Mary's Chapel).

Reclusus 1445–6 (Sacrist).

Defunctus 1458–9 (Infirmarer); inter mortuos 1457–8 (Richard II: full share); 1458–9 (Henry V: ⅙ share).

Gedney, Gedneye, Geddeney, Gedeney, Gydeney, Thomas.

Prima Missa 1416–7 (Infirmarer; Almoner; Cellarer; Warden of the Churches; St Mary's Chapel).

Indult to choose confessor 11 Mar. 1421 (Kal. Pap. Reg. vii, 332).

Ad skillam 24 Nov. 1420—29 Sep. 1421 (St Mary's Chapel); 1420–1 (Chamberlain; Almoner; Warden of the Churches; New Work. From the last it is deleted, a note being added that it was not the custom of the Warden of the Novum Opus to give exennia. This probably refers to exennia for being promoted ad skillam, which do not seem to have been provided by this officer. But in the same year 1420–1 he started providing exennia for First Masses and maintained the practice for a few years).

In emendacione...organorum per fratrem T. G. xiii^s, 1422–3 (Sacrist).

Refectorarius 1423–5 (*Mun.* 19535; Treasurer).

Defunctus 1432–3 (name deleted from Q. Alianore and marked †).

Bodenham, Boddeham, Boddenham, Bodenam, Bodynham, Bodnam, Thomas.

Prima Missa 1416–7 (Infirmarer; Almoner; Cellarer; Warden of the Churches; St Mary's Chapel).

Defunctus 1419–20 (Q. Alianore); nuper defunctus (Richard II).

Symond, Simond, William.

Prima Missa 1416–7 (Infirmarer; Almoner; Cellarer; Warden of the Churches; St Mary's Chapel).

Ad skillam 1431–2 (Almoner; Cellarer; Sacrist; Warden of the Churches).

Thesaurarius 1433—17 Dec. 1435.

Coquinarius 1433–4 (Almoner).

Refectorarius 1435–7; 1437–9 (Treasurer; cf. *Mun.* 33288, f. 38 b).

Defunctus 1438–9 (Q. Alianore; Chamberlain. Probably 1439, as he received $\frac{4}{5}$ share, Richard II, and $\frac{1}{2}$ share, Henry V, 1438–9).

1415-6

Petham, Pettham, W.

Prima Missa 1417–8 (Almoner; St Mary's Chapel; Warden of the Churches).

Defunctus 28 Sep.—1 Dec. 1420 (Infirmarer); 1419–20 (Q. Alianore; Chamberlain; Richard II; in the last he is said to be nuper defunctus, i.e. at the time of the audit).

Stokes, Stoke, Stokys, Stookes, John.

[Is it possible that he was the Master Stokes who attended the Council of Constance (J. H. Wylie, *Council of Constance*, p. 156)?]

Prima Missa 1417–8 (Almoner; St Mary's Chapel).

Left the Convent 1421–2 (Q. Alianore) and returned 1436–7 (Chamberlain).

Refectorarius 1439–43.

Hennessey, *Repertorium Londinense*, p. 456, dates his appointment to a prebend of St Stephen's College 14 Sep. 1441 and identifies him with John Stokes who was vicar of St Martin in the Fields in 1406 and 1409, rector of St Ethelburga in 1426–7, and prebendary of Wildland in St Paul's Cathedral 1431–40. The last-mentioned is possibly the man in question, but it is hard to suppose that a monk who said his first Mass here in 1417–8 on admission to the priesthood could have been vicar of St Martin's ten years earlier.

"Master John Stokes" was tenant in 1441–2 of the Misbourne fishery at Denham (cf. R. H. Lathbury, *History of Denham*, p. 159).

Ad skillam 8 Nov. 1444—29 Sep. 1445 (Sacrist); 1444–5 (Infirmarer; Treasurer; St Mary's Chapel; Warden of the Churches).

Et solut pro debitis magistri J. S. de collegio sancti Stephani xx^s, 1450–1 (Infirmarer).

Defunctus 1450–1 (Infirmarer, which mentions his obit; Q. Alianore, $\frac{1}{8}$ share; Henry V, $\frac{3}{4}$ share; so probably 1450).

In 1449–50 he was granted a pension of £20 (Treasurer) and in 1450–1 one of £2. 13s. 4d. (Sacrist), each to be paid for five years. The payments were thus made for several years after his decease and were perhaps used to discharge his debts. A tattered page of Domesday, f. 654, refers to this pension.

Parker, Richard.

Prima Missa 28 Sep.—24 Nov. 1420 (St Mary's Chapel); 28 Sep.— 29 Nov. 1420 (Q. Alianore); 28 Sep.—1 Dec. 1420 (Infirmarer; Chamberlain); 1420–1 (Almoner; New Work; Warden of the Churches).

Ad skillam 1426–7 (Infirmarer; Almoner; Sacrist; Monk-Bailiff; St Mary's Chapel).

Custos capelle b. Marie 29 Sep. 1433—24 Dec. 1435.

Camerarius 1435–7.

Made up his compotus as Chamberlain for 1436–7 and was entered at his usual place in the manor lists of that year ; no further mention.

Freston, Frestoon, Freeston, Fryston, Thomas.

[The signature of the Granger's roll 1426–7 appears to be an autograph ; if so, he called himself T. ffryston.]

Prima Missa 1417–8 (Almoner; St Mary's Chapel; Warden of the Churches).

Indult to choose confessor 11 Mar. 1421 (Kal. Pap. Reg. vii, 332).

Ad skillam 1423–4 (Chamberlain; Almoner; Sacrist; Monk-Bailiff; Warden of the Churches).

Granator 1425–8.

Celerarius 1431–2.

Camerarius 1433–5 (Treasurer) ; 19 Jun.—29 Sep. 1438.

Elemosinarius 1434–5 ? +.

Custos maner^m Regine Alianore; Ricardi II et Anne; 1435–7.

Thesaurarius et Ballivus 17 Dec. 1435—19 Jun. 1438. (For his payments to the Kitchener for food, &c., see *Mun.* 18642).

Custos ecclesiarum 17 Dec. 1435—29 Sep. 1437.

Infirmarius ? + 1440–1 ; 28 Sep.—12 Oct. 1443 (*Mun.* 19420).

Gave to Prior Walsh as a Christmas gift, 1441, unam peciam paruam argenteam et deauratam (*Mun.* 33288, f. 37 b).

Sacrista 16 Dec. 1440—8 Nov. 1444.   After his election as such, drew up a visus compoti with a defence of his financial administration as Treasurer, saying that he had received his office ex unanimi concensu (*sic*) et assensu totius capituli (*Mun.* 23035).

Defunctus ? 1444–5 (not mentioned in any manor-rolls of 1445–6).

Solut' pro debitis T. F. nuper camerarii xxxviii^s ii^d 1443–4 (Chamberlain) ; xl^s 1447 (New Work); xl^s 1448–9 (Almoner).

The Custos feretri in 1520 had charge of "a quatre-foyle of sylver and gylt of the gyffte of Dan T. F." (*Mun.* 9485).

Whitton, Whytton, Witton, Wytton, William.

Prima Missa 1417–8 (Almoner; St Mary's Chapel; Warden of the Churches).

Last mention in manor-rolls of 1439–40 at end, as if deceased (Q. Alianore, ½ share ; Richard II, ⅘ share ; Henry V, ⅔ share ; so probably 1440 ; but there is neither obit nor illness entered by Infirmarer).

Tonley, Tonleye, Towneley, Tunley, Tonle, Tunle, Thomas. [R. (St Mary's Chapel).]

Prima Missa 1417–8 (Almoner; St Mary's Chapel; Warden of the Churches).

Defunctus 28 Sep.—1 Dec. 1420 (Infirmarer); nuper defunctus 1419–20 (Richard II); inter mortuos 1419–20 (Q. Alianore); 1420–1 (Chamberlain).

1416-7

WALSH, Walsch, Walssh, Walsshe, William.
De novo professus (Q. Alianore), nouicius (Richard II), 1416–7.
Prima Missa 28 Sep.—24 Nov. 1420 (St Mary's Chapel); 28 Sep.—
29 Nov. 1420 (Q. Alianore): 28 Sep.—1 Dec. 1420 (Infirmarer; Chamberlain); 1420–1 (Almoner; New Work; Warden of the Churches).
Ad skillam 1423–4 (Chamberlain; Almoner; Sacrist; Monk-Bailiff; Warden of the Churches).
Thesaurarius maner^m Regine Alianore; Ricardi II et Anne; 1431–3.
Custos capelle b. Marie 29 Sep. 1433—12 Mai. 1434.
Custos tenementorum constructorum ad sustentacionem Anniversarii domini Johannis Waltham nuper Episcopi Sar' 1431–41 (*Mun.* 24633–48).
Thesaurarius et Ballivus 19 Jun. 1438—26 Jan. 1440 (*Mun.* 23036).
Custos ecclesiarum 19 Jun. 1438 (*Mun.* 23385)—26 Jan. 1440 (*Mun.* 23036).
Celerarius 2 Feb. 1440 (*Mun.* 18891)—1441 (*Mun.* 33288, f. 34 b).
Prior 1441 (after 1 Sep., *Mun.* 24126)—1456 (Richard II 1455–6 places him next to the new Prior, John Flete; i.e. he resigned office[1]).
For notes of his receipts and expenditure as Prior see *Mun.* 33289.
For the Christmas presents received by the Prior 1441 see *Mun.* 33288, f. 37 b.
Custos Novi Operis 1444–5 (*Mun.* 19694).
Auditor super compotum 1446–7 (Q. Alianore).
Oneratus est frater W. W. per Abbatem Edmundum [Kirton] in presencia Johannis Flete tunc prioris...cum officio Infirmarii, 1 Mar. 1460 (*Mun.* 33288, f. 12).
Defunctus 1461–2 (Infirmarer; Henry V, $\frac{1}{8}$ share).
The new pair of organs made for the Choir in 1441–2 cost £6. 0s. 8d. over and above the 13s. 4d. given through the Prior (Sacrist, *Mun.* 19692).
As Prior, was instrumental in acquiring the Hospital of St James for the anniversary of Katharine of Valois, Queen of Henry V, 1448–9.
Prior Walsh's "costs" in bringing this matter to completion amounted to £7. 16s. 4d. The gifts included pike, rabbits, capons, partridges, quails, and larks, and four flagons of wine sent to the King at Belsize; pike and partridges to the Duke and Duchess of Suffolk; capons, rabbits, pigeons, three flagons of wine and "i potell de syrup," to Lord Saye, the King's Chamberlain, and to his Lady; 13s. 4d. to John Say[2], the Speaker of the Parliament, and others, on three occasions, and other 20s. to the Speaker pro expedicione materii (*sic*) sancti Jacobi; besides pike to the Lord Treasurer and "refreshers" to four other persons (*Mun.* 24134 B; and for further detail see Walsh's own entry in *Mun.* 33289, f. 64).
The various Convent offices came to Walsh's aid; e.g. there was a grant of £4 from Henry V's manors (1448–9) in parte expensorum factorum per dominum priorem...circa acquisicionem....

ASSHBY, Assheby, Asseby, Asthby, Asscheby, Nicholas.
[If the signature of the Treasurer's roll 1431 is his autograph, he signed himself N. Asscheby.]
De novo professus (Q. Alianore), nouicius (Richard II) 1416–7.
Prima Missa 1417–8 (Almoner; Warden of the Churches).

---

[1] This is now confirmed by the recent volume of the Papal Registers, from which it appears that a Papal mandate was issued to him granting him the camera in the Infirmary lately occupied by Richard Birlyngham (d. 1441); a parcel of ground in the monks' cemetery adjoining the camera; a weekly corrody; distributions at the rate allowed to senior monks; and a pension of £12; 10 Jun. 1452 (Kal. Pap. Reg. x. 590 f.). So he prepared for his resignation in advance.
[2] Cf. A. I. Dasent, *Speakers of the House of Commons*, 1911, p. 80.

Custos Novi Operis 1423–33.

Custos capelle b. Marie 1426–31 ?+.

Thesaurarius et Ballivus 27 Jul. 1431—17 Dec. 1435.

Custos ecclesiarum 27 Jul. 1431—(? 17 Dec.) 1435.

Custos maner^m Regine Alianore 1431–5; Ricardi II et Anne 1431–5.

Ad skillam, Prior, 17 Dec. 1435—29 Sep. 1436 (Warden of the Churches); 1435–6 (Chamberlain).

Prior 1435–41.

Mandate for his confirmation as Prior 2 Jul. 1438 (Kal. Pap. Reg. IX. 2).

The delay in issuing this confirmation is explained by a mandate, 7 Sep. 1436 (*ibid.* VIII, 587), which was given by Eugenius IV to the Bishop of London [? R. Gilbert], on the petition of the Abbot [R. Harwden], to summon Asshby and examine him on the following charge; namely, that whereas it was usual for the Abbot on a vacancy in the Priorship to nominate five, seven, nine or more brethren, out of whom the Convent should elect one with the Abbot's consent, Asshby pretended that he had been elected or nominated by way of scrutiny by some of the monks and had kept the Priorship improperly for about a year. If necessary, the Bishop was to declare the office void and the Abbot was to proceed to a fresh election in the usual way.

There appears to be no trace of this tragedy in the Muniments and Asshby seems to have been held in high esteem.

Bishop of Llandaff 24 May 1441 (Stubbs, *Registrum*, 2nd ed. p. 88).

In regardo facto domino Episcopo Landauensi nuper priori...xl^s 1440–1 (Henry V).

Officiated at the dedication of Henry V's altar, 1447–8: in expensis factis circa dedicacionem altaris Regis Henrici V^{ti} in honore beate Virginis Marie et Omnium Sanctorum, viz. in pane albo vino rubro et dulci pro domino Episcopo Landauensi et aliis confratrum et famulorum post laborem eorundem ...vii^s viii^d (Henry V, 1447–8).

Defunctus 1458 (Stubbs, *ibid.*).

1418-9

Frank, Franke, John.

Novicius ultimo professus 1418–9 (Q. Alianore).

Prima Missa 1420–1 (Chamberlain; Almoner; New Work; St Mary's Chapel; Warden of the Churches).

Custos Novi Operis ?+ 1442–3 ?+.

Defunctus 1444–5 (Infirmarer; obit, but no mention of illness); inter mortuos hoc anno 1444–5 (Richard II, ⅓ share; Henry V, full share); 1445–6 (Chamberlain).

West, William.

Novicius ultimo professus 1418–9 (Q. Alianore).

Prima Missa 1422–3 (Chamberlain; Almoner; Sacrist; Monk-Bailiff).

Refectorarius 1444–8.

Grant of 200 "fagetts" 1462–3 (Treasurer).

Defunctus c. Jan. 1464 (Infirmarer 1463–4 records that he was ill for over 15 weeks from Mich^s, and gives his obit).

Wale, Whale, John.

Novicius ultimo professus 1418–9 (Q. Alianore).

Defunctus 1419–20 (probably of the Plague; Q. Alianore).

Cambridge, Cambrigge, Cambreg, Cambrygge, Cambrugge, Caumbrygge, John.

Novicius ultimo professus 1418–9 (Q. Alianore).

Prima Missa 1420–1 (Chamberlain; New Work; Almoner; St Mary's Chapel; Warden of the Churches).

Ad skillam 1427–8 (Chamberlain; Sacrist; Monk-Bailiff; St Mary's Chapel; Warden of the Churches).

Granator 1433–4; 1438–9 (Treasurer).

Thesaurarius maner^m Regine Alianore; Ricardi II et Anne; 19 Jun. 1438—28 Sep. 1439.

Received the licence of the Convent to proceed in an action for slander—causa diffamacionis—in the Ecclesiastical Court against one Alicia Peese, a woman within the jurisdiction of the Abbot, 27 May 1440, during the vacancy caused by Abbot Harwden's resignation (*Mun.* 5414).

Elemosinarius 26 Feb. 1440—28 Sep. 1443?+ (cf. *Mun.* 33306, f. 8).

Infirmarius 12 Oct. 1443—27 Feb. 1446 (as he remained in this office till his death, he had the right to be buried in the Infirmary Chapel).

Defunctus circa x a.m. 27 Feb. in Dominica Quinquagesime, 1446.

Sepultus in capella sancte Katerine in sinistra parte chori...in die Cinerum (*Mun.* 33289, f. 3).

Bonnok, Bonnoke, Bonhok, Boonhok, Boonhoc, Bounhok, Boonnok, Bunnok, William.

Novicius ultimo professus 1418–9 (Q. Alianore).

Prima Missa 1420–1 (Chamberlain; Almoner; New Work; St Mary's Chapel; Warden of the Churches).

Scolaris studens Oxon. (£10) 1421–9 (Treasurer).

Defunctus 1429–30 (full share, Q. Alianore; so probably 1430); inter mortuos 1430–1 (Chamberlain).

1420–1

Kympton, Kempton, Kemton, John.

Nouicius 1420–1 (Richard II).

Prima Missa 1422–3 (Chamberlain; Almoner; Sacrist; Monk-Bailiff).

Ad skillam, die dominica in Ramis Palmarum, 1440 (*Mun.* 19419*); 26 Feb.—29 Sep. 1440 (Almoner); 2 Feb.—29 Sep. 1440 (Cellarer); 24 Dec. 1439—29 Sep. 1440 (St Mary's Chapel).

Precentor 1444–50 (Warden of the Churches).

Auditor super compotum 1446–7 (Q. Alianore).

Infirmarius 1450–9.

Defunctus 1459–60 (Q. Alianore, $\frac{1}{4}$ share; Henry V, $\frac{1}{2}$ share); inter mortuos 1460–1 (Chamberlain).

Stratford, Stretford, Stradford, Stratfyrd, John.

Nouicius 1420–1 (Richard II).

Prima Missa 1422–3 (Chamberlain; Almoner; Sacrist; Monk-Bailiff).

Defunctus 1432–3 (deleted and marked with a †, Q. Alianore).

FLETE, Fleet, John.

Nouicius 1420–1 (Richard II).

Prima Missa 1422–3 (Chamberlain; Almoner; Sacrist; Monk-Bailiff).

Ad skillam 16 Dec. 1435—29 Sep. 1436 (Monk-Bailiff; Warden of the Churches).

Elemosinarius ?+1436–8?+.

Receptor Abbatis 1438–40 (cf. *Mun.* 33306); 1444—29 Jan. 1447.

Archidiaconus 2 Apr. 1440 (*Mun.* 24436).

Camerarius 1438–45 (Treasurer).

Custos maner^m Regine Alianore; Ricardi II et Anne; 1443–56.

Receptor Anniversarii Henrici V 1 Sep. 1443—1 Sep. 1445; custos maner^m Henrici V 1445–56.

Compiled (1443) *De Fundatione ecclesiae Westmonasteriensis*, or *History of Westminster Abbey* (ed. J. Armitage Robinson, Camb. Press, 1909) ex diversis chronicis approbatis scriptisque authenticis, chartis regum summorumque pontificum bullis compilato, fratrum petitionibus intendens satisfacere.

During his wardenship of the royal manors there was compiled the first part of "Extenta Maneriorum" (Camb. Univ. Lib. Kk.5.29), viz. Territorium de Holme, &c. (cf. *Manuscripts of Westminster Abbey*, p. 102).

In expensis J. F. circa capturam seisine manerii de Letcombe et W. Bernell [q.v.] circa eandem materiam apud Offord Clune viii^{li} v^s x^d 1444–5] (Henry V).

Sacrista 8 Nov. 1444—5 Feb. 1447.

Custos Novi Operis 1445–6; 1456—25 Mar. 1457.

Auditor super compotum 1446–7 (Q. Alianore).

Custos ecclesiarum 1446–56.

Thesaurarius 4 Feb. 1447—3 Nov. 1456. As such, he collected money for, and himself superintended the rebuilding of, the Dormitory in 1449–50, after it had been set on fire by George Norwych [q.v.] (*Mun.* 23515; cf. R. B. Rackham, *Nave of Westminster*, pp. 24–5).

Ballivus 4 Feb. 1447—3 Nov. 1456.

In expensis fratris J. F. Ballivi Westm. euntis usque Batrycheseye ad diuersas vices pro manerio superuidendo stauro de Waltero Tynnok recipiendo et dicto stauro deliberando xii^s 1447 (Monk-Bailiff).

Celerarius et Gardinarius 1448–50?+.

Prior 1456–66.

"Priour Fleet's gyft" to the Lady Chapel was "a Chiseple and Awbe of whyte damaske garnyshed with Egles" (*Mun.* 23258).

"The gyfte of dan J. F. late priour" to St Edward's Shrine was "ii tuellys a chesepille a aube with stole and phanone[1] of blew damaske braudred with flours of gold" (*Mun.* 9477).

In the Granger's roll 1470–1 there is reference to a payment made ut ordinatum fuit per venerabilem nuper priorem J. F.

Defunctus 1465–6. (Probably 1466. He was nuper prior when the compotus of Henry V 1465–6 was made up; but he was given a ⅔ share, Henry V and Q. Alianore, as if he had lived till the spring of 1466.)

1421-2

Pomeray, Pomerey, Pumray, Thomas.

Nouicius 1422–3 (Richard II).

Scolaris studens Oxon. (£10), 1424–37 (Treasurer).

Prima Missa 1428–9 (Chamberlain; Almoner; Sacrist; Monk-Bailiff; St Mary's Chapel).

Dispensation to him as the son of a married nobleman and an unmarried woman to hold conventual dignities 8 Oct. 1437 (Kal. Pap. Reg. VIII, 640).

Celerarius ante 1440–1 (*Mun.* 33288, f. 34 b); ?+(Mich^s) 1463—(East^r) 1464.

Thesaurarius et Ballivus 26 Jan. 1440—29 Sep. 1446.

Custos ecclesiarum 1443–6.

Sacrista 5 Feb.—25 Dec. 1447 ?+(*Mun.* 33289, f. 4).

---

[1] Phanon or fanon was commonly used to designate the maniple; cf. Blunt, *Annotated B. C. P.* ed. 1884, p. 79; Bloxam, *Ecclesiastical Vestments*, p. 7.

In expensis fratris T. P. Sacryste Westm. et fratris Thome Cornewell Camerarii ibidem cum vi seruientibus in viii^{to} equis mense Junii...de London usque Feuersham causa visitacionis ibidem de Autoritate generalis capituli... per quinque dies et tot noctes lx^s iiii^d 1447 (Abbot's Treasurer).

Custos Novi Operis 25 Mar. 1447—28 Sep. 1451 ?+.

Camerarius 1448–50; 1450–4 (Treasurer).

Pension xx^s Christmas 1454 (St Mary's Chapel); xx^s 1445–6 (New Work).

Defunctus 1464. (In Infirmarer 1463–4 his obit is given next after that of William West [q.v.]. The payment of ½ share, Q. Alianore, Henry V, points to c. Mar. 1464.)

Redyng, Radyng, Robert.

Nouicius 1422–3 (Richard II).

Prima Missa 1423–4 (Chamberlain; Almoner; Sacrist; Richard II, where he is called sacerdos junior; Monk-Bailiff; Warden of the Churches).

He received from Q. Alianore's manors at the rate of a junior priest in 1432–3; but does not appear afterwards.

Breynt, Breynte, Brent, Braynt, Braynte, Brayntte, Richard.

Nouicius 1422–3 (Richard II).

Prima Missa 1428–9 (Chamberlain; Almoner; Sacrist; Monk-Bailiff; St Mary's Chapel).

Ad skillam 29 Sep. 1433—12 Mai. 1434 (St Mary's Chapel); 1433–4 (Sacrist; Monk-Bailiff; Warden of the Churches).

Thesaurarius maner^m Regine Alianore 1439–40; custos 1440–3; 1456–60.

Thesaurarius maner^m Ricardi II et Anne 1439–40; custos ?+ 1441–2?+; 1456–60.

Receptor anniversarii Henrici V, 1439–43; custos maner^m Henrici V, ?+ 1457–60.

Custos feretri 1440–1 (Sacrist).

Auditor super compotum 1446–7 (Q. Alianore).

Custos capelle b. Marie 1447–55; 24 Dec. 1460—29 Sep. 1468?+.

Thesaurarius 3 Nov. 1456—19 Jan. 1461; Ballivus 1456–61?+.

Custos ecclesiarum 1456–61.

Defunctus 1471–2 (Infirmarer; Chamberlain; Q. Alianore, full share; Richard II, ⅚ share; 1470–1; so probably 1471).

Barnell, Barnel, Barnhull, Barnhyll, Bernell, Bernhill, Bernhull, Benerl, William.

Nouicius 1422–3 (Richard II).

Prima Missa 1428–9 (Chamberlain; Almoner; Sacrist; Monk-Bailiff; St Mary's Chapel).

Ad skillam 17 Dec. 1435—29 Sep. 1436 (Monk-Bailiff; Warden of the Churches); 1435–6 (Chamberlain).

Indult to choose confessor 13 Feb. 1437 (Kal. Pap. Reg. VIII, 615).

Granator 1439–42?+.

Custos vestibuli 1440–2 (Sacrist).

Thesaurarius instrinsecus 1444–5; 1448–52 (*Mun.* 33289, f. 8).

Elemosinarius 1445–8.

Auditor super compotum 1446–7 (Q. Alianore).

In expensis W. B. equitanti (*sic*) circa le uppynge cignorum domini Abbatis una cum donis datis magistris cignorum domini Regis et pro le markynge dictorum cignorum et conductione equorum xi^s iiii^d 1447 (Abbot's Treasurer).

Supprior 1448 (*Mun.* 33289, f. 5).

Custos Novi Operis ?+ 1459–61.

Camerarius 1459 (*Mun.* 31786); 29 Sep.—25 Dec. 1462.
Infirmarius 1463—24 Jun. 1467.
Pension xvi⁸ viii^d 1474–5 (St Mary's Chapel).
Defunctus 1476 (Infirmarer 1475–6 implies that he died about 20 weeks after Mich⁸; i.e. in the middle of Feb. He had been continuously in the sick-room since Nov. 1467, with a pittance of a penny a day).

He was a member of the Guild of the Assumption connected with the church of St Margaret, Westminster, and in the accounts of the guild for 1474–7 is described as being xvi⁸ iii^d in arrear with his subscription.

Cornwayle, Cornewayle, Cornewaylle, Cornwayll, Cornwaile, Cornewell, Cornwell, Thomas.

Nouicius 1422–3 (Richard II).
Prima Missa 1428–9 (Chamberlain; Almoner; Sacrist; St Mary's Chapel; Monk-Bailiff).
Ad skillam 1436–7 (Almoner; Sacrist; Monk-Bailiff; Warden of the Churches).
Custos capelle b. Marie 24 Dec. 1439—25 Mar. 1444.
Camerarius 1445–8 (*Mun.* 33289, f. 4).
Auditor super compotum 1446–7 (Q. Alianore).
Receptor Abbatis [Ed. Kirton] 2 Feb. 1447—29 Sep. 1448.
Sacrista 1448–50.
Elemosinarius 1444–5 (Abbot's Treasurer); 1448–61.
Mentioned among the parishioners of Denham, 1451–2 (R. H. Lathbury, *History of Denham*, p. 160).
Solut' fratri T. C. pro conduccione hominum ad vigilandam et salvo custodiendam ecclesiam tempore turbido 1460–1 (New Work).
Solut' Rectori ecclesie sancti Clementis London pro debitis fratris T. C. ex precepto domini Abbatis 1464–5 (Chamberlain).
Defunctus 1461–2 (Infirmarer); inter mortuos (Chamberlain; Q. Alianore; Henry V).

Salisbury, Salesbury, Salesbery, Salysbery, Sarisbury, Surisbury, Nicholas.
= Thomer, N.
[In Chamberlain 1423–4 he was entered for exennia as "Salysbery" but in the list at the back of the roll as "Thomer." In 1425–6 "Salisbury" was substituted for "Thomer."]
Nouicius 1422–3 (Richard II: "N. Salesbury").
Prima Missa 1423–4 (Chamberlain; Almoner; Sacrist; Richard II, where he was called sacerdos junior; Monk-Bailiff; Warden of the Churches).
In Q. Alianore 1430–1 his name was deleted from his proper place and added at the end with these words: si videatur priori et conventui x⁸, as if his worthiness to receive a share were in question.
He received his habit (Chamberlain) and a junior priest's share from the manors (Q. Alianore, &c.) in 1432–3; but is not mentioned again.

1423-4
Knoll, Knolle, Thomas.
Nouicius 1423–4 (Richard II).
Prima Missa 1428–9 (Chamberlain; Almoner; Sacrist; Monk-Bailiff; St Mary's Chapel).
? Vicar of Datchet and a member of the (St Margaret's) Guild of the Assumption (cf. H. F. Westlake, *St Margaret's, Westminster*, p. 51).
Not mentioned after 1461–2 (Q. Alianore; Chamberlain).

Holborne, William.
Nouicius 1423–4 (Richard II).
Defunctus 1425–6 (entered in Infirmarer 1426–7, with note: omissum in compoto precedente; he was in the sick-room for 3 days just before Michaelmas, 1426).

Hyde, Hide, Adam.
Nouicius 1423–4 (Richard II).
Prima Missa 1428–9 (Chamberlain; Almoner; Sacrist; Monk-Bailiff).
Ad skillam 1434–5 (Almoner; Sacrist; Monk-Bailiff; Warden of the Churches).
His last appearance is in Chamberlain 1446–7; in Q. Alianore of that year his name was erased and he received no payment.

NORWYCH, Norwyche, Northwych, George.
Nouicius 1423–4 (Richard II).
Prima Missa 1428–9 (Chamberlain; Almoner, where it was inserted in another hand; Sacrist; Monk-Bailiff).
Ad skillam 16 Dec. 1435—29 Sep. 1436 (Monk-Bailiff); 1435–6 (Chamberlain; Warden of the Churches).
Custos capelle b. Marie 1445–6 (Sacrist).
Memorandum quod anno regni regis Henrici sexti xxvi° feria ivᵃ xxv° die mensis Octobris in festo sanctorum Crispini et Crispiniani circa horam novenam in nocte factum est incendium dormitorii per fratrem G. N. (*Mun.* 33289, f. 64 b; cf. J. Armitage Robinson, *Flete*, p. 2).
Refectorarius 1452 (*Mun.* 33289, f. 8)–1454 ?+.
Archidiaconus 1451 (*Mun.* 33289, f. 6); 1461 (cf. Whitaker, *History of Craven*, ed. 1878, p. 323 [Dr Scott]).
Abbas 1463–9. (Installed between 24 Nov. 1463 and 5 Feb. 1464; *Mun.* 24279).
On 13 Dec. 1463 he gave an acquittance to Edmund Kirton [q.v.] who handed over the silver plate (*Mun.* 5443).
In expensis domini Abbatis apud Kyngeston equitantis a Piriford usque Westm. ad exequias domini ducis Ebor' [Richard, d. 1460] eundo et redeundo xiiˢ 24 Nov. 1463—5 Feb. 1464 (*Mun.* 24279).
Petition of "the seniour and more part" of the Convent to the King for a visitation of the Abbey owing to the misgovernance of N. (n.d. *Mun.* 5429).
The Muniments contain a number of bonds for money lent to him (e.g. 28159–62; 28166–7). One mortgage (*Mun.* 9476), dated 15 Dec. 1467, three weeks after his demission, puts no less than 430 oz. of silver plate in pawn with a merchant against a loan of 300 marks. The plate consisted of olle argentee, long "cuppys," "spyce plates," silver spoons, a pixis, and a number of salt-cellars. The silver, much of which was gilt, was variously valued at 3s. 4d. and 3s. per oz.
A notarial instrument (*Mun.* 5456; Widmore, appendix VII, p. 191 ff.) was executed 24 Nov. 1467 in quadam bassa parlura ex parte australi infirmarie between Norwych of the one part and Prior Thomas Millyng and eleven other monks of the other part, by which Norwych agreed to retire from the active duties of his office and to nominate Prior Millyng, William Chertsey, and John Estney [q.v.] as commissarii Abbatis.
The brethren put in a cedula supplicacionis sive desideracionis in which they stated that Norwych had involved the convent in heavy debts under the convent seal, 2350 marks being still unpaid and other obligations bringing the total debt to 3037 marks, six shillings and eight pence.
They asked him to go and reside in some ancient monastery with a chaplain and a few retainers and to leave Pyrford, where the visits of gentry

and other guests would involve great expense. He was to resign all the abbatial estates and revenues to the management of his commissaries and was not to return to Westminster till payment in full had been made. He was to receive an annual allowance of 100 marks, paid by quarterly instalments.

It is evident that some of the trouble was due to misplaced trust in Brother Thomas Ruston (q.v.).

Defunctus 1469 (between 26 Aug., *Mun.* 1740, and 14 Nov., *Mun.* 5413).

Bowode, William.
Nouicius 1423–4 (Richard II).
Prima Missa 1429–30 (Chamberlain ; Almoner ; Monk-Bailiff ; Warden of the Churches).
Defunctus 1433–4 (Richard II).

1425-6

Spencer, Spenser, John.
Ultimo professus 1425–6 (Richard II).
Prima Missa 1426–7 (Infirmarer ; Almoner ; Sacrist ; Monk-Bailiff ; St Mary's Chapel).
Ad skillam 28 Sep. 1430—29 Jul. 1431 (St Mary's Chapel ; Warden of the Churches) ; 1430–1 (Infirmarer ; Chamberlain ; Almoner ; Sacrist ; Monk-Bailiff).
Defunctus 1433–4 (Richard II).

Henton, Hynton, John.
Ultimo professus 1425–6 (Richard II).
Prima Missa 1428–9 (Chamberlain ; Almoner ; Sacrist ; Monk-Bailiff ; St Mary's Chapel).
Thesaurarius 17 Dec. 1435—19 June 1438.
Coquinarius 1436–7 (*Mun.* 18642).
Precentor ? + 1443–4 (Warden of the Churches).
Defunctus c. 1450 (deleted, Q. Alianore 1450–1).

Woderowe, Woderue, Wodroue, Woderoue, Woderof, Woderoffe, Wode-rove, John.
Ultimo professus 1425–6 (Richard II).
Prima Missa 1429–30 (Chamberlain ; Almoner ; Monk-Bailiff ; Warden of the Churches).
Ad skillam 1434–5 (Almoner ; Sacrist ; Monk-Bailiff ; Warden of the Churches).
Defunctus 1440–1 (Infirmarer ; Henry V, full share).

Atherstone, Adereston, Athelstoon, Athelston, Adilston, Thomas.
Ultimo professus 1425–6 (Richard II).
Prima Missa 1429–30 (Chamberlain ; Almoner ; Warden of the Churches).
Defunctus c. 1434 (full share, Q. Alianore, Richard II, 1433–4 ; deleted, Q. Alianore, 1434–5).

Venour, John.
Ultimo professus 1425–6 (Richard II).
Prima Missa 1428–9 (Chamberlain ; Almoner ; Sacrist ; Monk-Bailiff ; St Mary's Chapel).
Thesaurarius maner^m Regine Alianore 1433–6 ; Ricardi II et Anne 1433–4 ? +.
Ad skillam 1436–7 (Almoner ; Sacrist ; Monk-Bailiff ; Warden of the Churches).
Elemosinarius 29 Sep. 1439—26 Feb. 1440.
Defunctus ? 26 Feb. 1440 (*Mun.* 19045 ; deleted, Q. Alianore 1438–9).

1428-9

Fynden, Fyndenne, Thomas.

Prima Missa 1429–30 (Chamberlain; Almoner; Monk-Bailiff; Warden of the Churches).

Defunctus ? 1430–1 (deleted from Q. Alianore).

Sporley, Sporle, Spurley, Spurle, Richard.

[In the Granator's roll 1460–1, which is not in the ordinary scrivener's hand and may be autograph, the name is written Sporle.]

Prima Missa 1431–2 (Almoner; Cellarer; Sacrist; Warden of the Churches).

Ad skillam 1438–9 (Chamberlain; Sacrist; Monk-Bailiff).

Granator 1445–6; 1453–63; 1470–1.

Compiled in `1450 a history of the Abbots, Priors, &c. of Westminster Abbey, mainly derived de quodam laudabili opere Johannis Flete (Brit. Mus. Cotton MS. Claud. A viii; cf. J. Armitage Robinson, *Flete*, p. 30, 31). "Sporley's extracts, comprising as they do the chief part of Flete's book, are frequently of value in controlling the text of the Westminster MS. when other evidence is lacking." His own contribution is "entirely worthless" (*ibid.*).

Supprior 1452 (*Mun.* 33289, f. 8).

Precentor 1464–6 ? + (Warden of the Churches).

Pension x^s 1474–5 (St Mary's Chapel); x^s 1479–80 (Domestic Treasurer); x^s 1480–1 (Almoner).

Defunctus 1490–1 (Infirmarer; probably early in 1491, as he received from Q. Alianore at the rate of 14 weeks from Michaelmas 1490).

Tedyngton, Todynton, Tydyngton, Richard.

Prima Missa 1431–2 (Almoner; Cellarer; Sacrist; Warden of the Churches).

Ad skillam 1443–4 (Infirmarer; Chamberlain; Almoner; Sacrist; Treasurer; Warden of the Churches).

Custos capelle b. Marie 1445–7 (Sacrist; *Mun.* 33289, f. 4).

Scolaris studens Oxon. (£6. 13s. 4d.) 1447–56 (Treasurer).

Supprior 1458–60 (*Mun.* 23838).

Thesaurarius 1463–71 ? +.

Was party to the resignation of Abbot Norwych 24 Nov. 1467 (*Mun.* 5456).

Thesaurarius maner^m Regine Alianore 1464–8; 1472–4; 1477–80.

Custos feretri 21 Dec. 1467 (*Mun.* 9477)—9 Oct. 1479 (*Mun.* 9478).

Custos maner^m Ricardi II et Anne ? + 1470–8.

Member of the Guild of the Assumption.

Pension xx^s 1479–80 (Almoner); xx^s 1480–1 (St Mary's Chapel); xiii^s iiii^d 1482–3 (Domestic Treasurer); xiii^s iiii^d 1484–5 (New Work); xiii^s iiii^d (Infirmarer 1479–80).

"Also the Tombe of Kyng Herry the Vth is complete with two teeth of golde on his hande Except iii hole flourid delice and ii middilpoynts of floure delice And ii lyons and an half. The Angels a Balle and a Crosse of silver and gilt A Septre and an Antelop also of Silver and gilt alle the which were stolen awey in the tyme of the seid Dan Richard Tedyngton." (Indenture 9 Oct. 1479; *Mun.* 9478.) This entry is not fair to Tedyngton, for the previous indenture 21 Dec. 1467 (*Mun.* 9477) says that all the above objects "were stole" as well as "ii tethe of gold hangyng by a wire apon the handde of the ymage of Kyng Harry the Vth,"—which apparently Tedyngton recovered and bequeathed to his successor. Cf. Sir W. H. St John Hope, *The Funeral, Monument, and Chantry Chapel of King Henry the Fifth*, 1914, p. 151.

Possessed the Flores Historiarum now in the Chetham Library, Manchester (cf. *Manuscripts of Westminster Abbey*, p. 25).

Defunctus 1487 (the Domestic Treasurer paid his pension to Xmas; ⅓ share Henry V, 1487–8).

Amondesham, Amondysham, Amundysham, Amodesham, Admundesham, Agmondesham, Amesham, Amersham, Ametsham, Amettesham, John.

Sacerdos 1429–30 (Q. Alianore).

Scolaris studens Oxon. (£10) ? + 1432–48 (Treasurer).

Prima Missa 1434–5 (Almoner; Sacrist; Monk-Bailiff; Warden of the Churches).

Et solut' fratri J. A. pro diuersis reparacionibus factis Oxonie lx⁸ (*Mun.* 33288, f. 18).

Et J. A. pro sermone in die parasceues una cum expensis eiusdem xx⁸ 1440–2; 1444–5 (Sacrist).

In regardo dato fratri J. A. laboranti in generali capitulo [at Northampton] pro domino Abbate [Ed. Kirton] 1447 (*Mun.* 24275).

Archidiaconus 1449 (*Mun.* 33289, f. 6).

Sacrista 1450–60 ? +.

Abbot's Receiver in the Western parts (Gloucestershire, &c.) 1456.

Pension xx⁸ 1462–3 (New Work: ex concessione domini Abbatis); vi⁸ viii⁴ 1473–4 (Richard II: ex concessu capituli).

Was party to the resignation of Abbot Norwych, 24 Nov. 1467 (*Mun.* 5456).

One John Amesham was presented to Alre (now Aller) juxta Langport, Somerset, by Margaret, Lady Hungerford, 3 Mar. 1475, after papal dispensation dated 3 Sep. 1472 (Bishop Stillington's Register, f. 95 b). [J. A. R.]

The Custos feretri of 1520 had charge of "an Agnus Dei gold with a salutacyon of oure ladye and xx⁴ᵗⁱ peryllys fyxed in the circuyte thereof that sometyme were Dane John Amershamys and afterwards assigned to the Shryne by Abbatt Estney" (*Mun.* 9485).

Defunctus 1481–2 (Infirmarer; Q. Alianore; Richard II, ⅙ share; Henry V, ⅔ share).

1429–30

Milton, Mylton, William.

Prima Missa 1431–2 (Almoner; Cellarer; Sacrist; Warden of the Churches).

Custos vestibuli 1444–5; at the time of Margaret of Anjou's Coronation (Sacrist).

Granator 1446–8.

Thesaurarius 4 Feb. 1447—19 Jan. 1461.

Infirmarius 1461–3.

Thesaurarius intrinsecus 25 Dec. 1461—29 Dec. 1463.

Member of the Guild of the Assumption.

Nuper coquinarius (Treasurer 1466–7).

Defunctus 1464–5 (probably before Christmas 1464; Q. Alianore; Chamberlain; Henry V).

1432–3

Walsingham, Walsyngham, Robert.

Nouicius 1432–3 (Richard II).

Prima Missa 1434–5 (Almoner; Sacrist; Monk-Bailiff; Warden of the Churches).

Ad skillam 1442–3 (Chamberlain; Almoner; Sacrist; Treasurer).
Granator 1443–4.
Camerarius 1454–5.
Defunctus 1457–8 (Infirmarer, where his was the last obit of seven that year; $\frac{1}{2}$ share, Richard II; $\frac{3}{4}$ share, Q. Alianore; full share, Henry V; so probably 1458).

Aston, Thomas.

Nouicius 1432–3 (Richard II).
Prima Missa 1434–5 (Almoner; Sacrist; Monk-Bailiff; Warden of the Churches).
Ad skillam 26 Feb.—29 Sep. 1440 (Almoner); 2 Feb.—29 Sep. 1440 (Cellarer); 24 Dec. 1439—29 Sep. 1440 (St Mary's Chapel).
In 1463–4 he was omitted from Q. Alianore and deleted from Henry V, without any share; no further mention.

1433–4

Whetnale, Whetnall, Whatnall, Wetnale, Thomas.

Sacerdos 1434–5 (Q. Alianore).
Defunctus 1445 (after four months' illness—Infirmarer 1444–5); inter mortuos hoc anno, 1444–5 ($\frac{1}{3}$ share Richard II; full share Henry V); inter mortuos 1445–6 (Chamberlain).

1434–5

Markus, Marchus, Markis, Markys, Mark, Marks, John.

Levita 1435–6 (Richard II).
Prima Missa 1436–7 (Almoner; Sacrist; Monk-Bailiff; Warden of the Churches).
Defunctus 1440–1 (Q. Alianore; was in the sick-room that year, but there is no obit for him in the Infirmarer's roll).

Ocle, Oclee, Octlee, John.

Levita 1435–6 (Richard II).
Prima Missa 1436–7 (Almoner; Sacrist; Monk-Bailiff; Warden of the Churches).
Reclusus 1445–6; pension of xx^s (New Work); 12lb. of candles bought for him as such by the Sacrist, 1445–6; 200 "fagetts" by the Treasurer 1447–8.
Defunctus 1448–9 (Infirmarer; $\frac{1}{3}$ share, Henry V).

1435–6

Witneye, Witteney, Wytney, Wytteneye, John.

Levita 1435–6 (Richard II).
Sacerdos 1436–7 (Q. Alianore).
Ad skillam 8 Nov. 1444—29 Sep. 1445 (Sacrist); 1444–5 (Treasurer; Warden of the Churches).
He was entered as if deceased in Q. Alianore 1447–8; but was mentioned in his usual place in Chamberlain 1448–9; no further appearance.

Ruston, Rustone, Thomas.

Nouicius 1435–6 (Richard II).
Prima Missa in die omnium sanctorum Innocentium 1440 (Sacrist); 1440–1 (Infirmarer; Almoner; Monk-Bailiff).
Scolaris studens Oxon. (£6. 13s. 4d.) 1448–56 (Treasurer).

Ad skillam 1455–6 (Infirmarer; Sacrist; Monk-Bailiff; Warden of the Churches).

Precentor 1457–60 (Warden of the Churches).

Camerarius 1460–1 [also 1461–2 (Treasurer)].

Custos Novi Operis 1461—24 Nov. 1467.

Sacrista 1462–7.

Celerarius Apr. 1464 (Treasurer)—1467.

Sequestratus et amotus ab omnibus et singulis officiis praedictis [sc. Warden of the New Work, Cellarer, and Sacrist] cuius negligentia ut concipitur omnia officia praedicta sunt in magno decasu 24 Nov. 1467 (cf. the notarial instrument for the deposition of Abbot Norwych, *Mun.* 5456).

The Brethren specified among other offences that as Custos vestibuli Ruston had raised money on a gold chalice which he had removed without the consent of the Prior and Seniors; they asked that he should be made responsible for the six or seven copes of divers colours lost from the vestry during his wardenship, and that in his next compotus he should make a full statement of all his debts. They also inserted a proviso that he should not be one of the appointed commissaries (*ibid.*).

Member of the Guild of the Assumption; but not regular in paying his subscription (cf. H. F. Westlake, *St Margaret's, Westminster*, p. 51).

Prior de Hurley 1468–80.

Daunt, Dawnt, Dawnte, John.

= London, John.

[The change of name from "London" to "Daunt" occurs in Q. Alianore and Richard II 1438–9.]

Nouicius 1435–6 (Richard II).

Prima Missa 28 Sep. 1439—26 Feb. 1440 (Almoner); 2 Feb.—29 Sep. 1440 (Cellarer); 24 Dec. 1439—29 Sep. 1440 (St Mary's Chapel); 28 Sep. 1439—24 Jan. 1440 (Treasurer).

Defunctus 1440–1 (Q. Alianore, full share); 1441–2 (Henry V, $\frac{2}{3}$ share).

Benet, Benett, Beneyt, Benyt, Thomas.

Nouicius 1435–6 (Richard II).

Prima Missa 28 Sep. 1439—26 Feb. 1440 (Almoner); 2 Feb.—29 Sep. 1440 (Cellarer); 28 Sep. 1439—24 Jan. 1440 (Treasurer).

Not mentioned after Q. Alianore, 1452–3; Henry V, 1453–4.

Costyng, Costyn, Robert.

Nouicius 1435–6 (Richard II).

Prima Missa 1438–9 (Chamberlain; Sacrist; Monk-Bailiff).

Not mentioned after 1440–1 (Q. Alianore).

Bedford, Bedeford, Paschal.

Nouicius 1435–6 (Richard II).

Prima Missa 1438–9 (Chamberlain; Sacrist; Monk-Bailiff).

Not mentioned after 1440–1 (Q. Alianore).

Martyn, Marten, John.

Nouicius 1435–6 (Richard II).

Prima Missa 1438–9 (Chamberlain; Sacrist; Monk-Bailiff).

Defunctus 1471–2 (Infirmarer; Chamberlain; Q. Alianore).

Huntyngdon, Huntingdon, Richard.

Nouicius 1435–6 (Richard II).

Prima Missa 1439–40 (Chamberlain; Sacrist; Monk-Bailiff).

Ad skillam 29 Sep. 1446—2 Feb. 1447 (Cellarer); 1446–7 (Infirmarer;

Chamberlain; Almoner; Warden of the Churches); 4 Feb.—29 Sep. 1447 (Monk-Bailiff).

Subelemosinarius 1445-6 (*Mun.* 33289, f. 3).

Defunctus 1479 (Q. Alianore, full share, Richard II, $\frac{17}{20}$ share, 1478-9; Henry V, $\frac{1}{8}$ share, 1479–80).

1438-9

Wellys, Welles, Wellis, William.

[In Chamberlain 1438-9. " Wellys J "; no outfit given to him that year.]

In his first year he received a $\frac{3}{4}$ share from Q. Alianore's manors and was probably above the average age; he received a full (priest's) share in 1439–40. But his first mention in the Richard II rolls is in 1443–4.

Thesaurarius intrinsecus 1446-7.

Auditor super compotum 1446-7 (Q. Alianore).

Archidiaconus 25 Dec. 1447 (*Mun.* 33289, f. 4).

Ad skillam 1452-3 (Sacrist; Monk-Bailiff; Warden of the Churches).

Defunctus 1454-5 (Q. Alianore, $\frac{1}{4}$ share; Henry V, $\frac{1}{2}$ share).

Mede, T.

Sacerdos 1439-40 (Q. Alianore).

He received a $\frac{1}{3}$ share, Q. Alianore 1440-1, his name standing in its ordinary place; not mentioned again.

1439-40

Chertsey, Chertesey, Cherteshey, Cherchesey, Chirchesty, Charsey, William.

Prima Missa 1442-3 (Chamberlain; Almoner; Sacrist; Treasurer); 28 Sep. 1443—25 Mar. 1444 (St Mary's Chapel).

Ad skillam 1445-6 (Chamberlain; Almoner; Sacrist; Monk-Bailiff; Warden of the Churches).

Subsacrista 1445-6 (*Mun.* 33289, f. 3).

Subelemosinarius 1448-55 (*ibid.* f. 5–12).

Custos capelle b. Marie ?+ 24 Jun. 1458—24 Dec. 1460.

Custos maner^m Regine Alianore; Ricardi II et Anne; Henrici V; 1460-82.

Thesaurarius 19 Jan. 1461—18 Jan. 1483 (fourteen rolls missing).

Custos ecclesiarum 28 Sep. 1461—18 Jan. 1483.

Celerarius ?+ 1468-82 (only three rolls—1468-9; 1471-2; 1481-2).

Ballivus 1465-70; ?+ 1482—18 Jan. 1483.

Was party to the resignation of Abbot Norwych 24 Nov. 1467 and was nominated one of his three commissaries (cf. Widmore, p. 191 ff.).

Pension xx^s 1481-2 (Richard II); xx^s (St Mary's Chapel), xl^s (Almoner) 1482-3; xx^s 25 Mar. 1483 (Domestic Treasurer).

Member of the Guild of the Assumption.

" A Mantell for the ymage of our lady " was " Dan William Chirchestys gyft " to St Mary's Chapel before 1 Oct. 1485 (*Mun.* 23258).

Defunctus 1487 (Domestic Treasurer paid his pension to Christmas).

ARUNDEL, Arundell, Thomas.

Prima Missa 1442-3 (Chamberlain; Almoner; Sacrist; Treasurer); 28 Sep. 1443—25 Mar. 1444 (St Mary's Chapel).

Ad skillam 1448-9 (Infirmarer; Chamberlain; Almoner; Cellarer; Sacrist; St Mary's Chapel; Monk-Bailiff; Warden of the Churches).

Tertius Prior 1449 (*Mun.* 33289, f. 6).

Precentor 1450-7; 1460-4; 1470-1?+ (Warden of the Churches).

Custos Novi Operis 25 Mar. 1457—28 Sep. 1458? +.

Custos feretri ?—21 Dec. 1467 (*Mun.* 9477).

Was party to the resignation of Abbot Norwych 24 Nov. 1467 (*Mun.* 5456).

Custos capelle b. Marie ? + 1470–7.

Member of the Guild of the Assumption (entered 1475–8).

Prior 1474 (after 29 Nov. *Mun.* 5410)–1482 (when he resigned, before 30 Sep.; *Mun.* 33289, f. 15).

Pension xx^s 1481–2 (Richard II); xx^s 1482–3 (Almoner); xx^s, afterwards lx^s, from 24 Jun. 1483 (Domestic Treasurer). He continued to receive a Prior's share on Henry V's Anniversary (Treasurer, 1486–7) and on John Blokley's Anniversary (Domestic Treasurer 1494–5).

The Custos feretri in 1520 had charge of "a crosse of golde blakk enamylyd and a bell hangyng therby an ymage on the one syde and an ymage of oure lady on the other syde of Dane Thomas Arundells gyffte" (*Mun.* 9485).

Defunctus 1495–6 (Infirmarer: pro anima fratris T. A. quondam prioris huius loci; Q. Alianore; Henry V); inter mortuos 1496–7 (Chamberlain).

ESTNEY, Esteney, John.

Prima Missa 1442–3 (Chamberlain; Almoner; Sacrist; Treasurer; Monk-Bailiff; St Mary's Chapel; Warden of the Churches).

Ad skillam 1448–9 (Infirmarer; Chamberlain; Almoner; Sacrist).

Quartus Prior 1449 (*Mun.* 33289, f. 6).

Custos feretri 1450–7.

Thesaurarius maner^m Regine Alianore 1450–7.

Custos maner^m Ricardi II et Anne 1450–8 ? +.

Elemosinarius 25 Mar. 1463—29 Sep. 1465? +.

Camerarius 1462–70.

Infirmarius 13 Jul. 1467—29 Sep. 1470.

Was party to the resignation of Abbot Norwych 24 Nov. 1467 and was nominated one of his three commissaries (cf. Widmore, p. 191 ff.).

Prior 1470 (by 10 Aug. *Mun.* 17802)–1474.

Sacrista ? + 1470–97.

Thesaurarius intrinsecus 1470–85 : 1490–4.

Custos Novi Operis 1471–97. [For the progress made during his long tenure of this office cf. R. B. Rackham, *Nave of Westminster*, pp. 34–44.]

Abbas 1474 (? + 29 Nov. *Mun.* 5410)—24 Mai. 1498.

There was a payment of £30 to Giovanni de Barde, of London, for the Papal bull confirming his election 14 Apr. 1475 (Mun. 5452).

The Custos feretri in 1520 had charge of "a mandrake roote in fasshion of a crosse with the ymage of our lorde annexyd to the same crusified of the Abbott Estneis gyffte" (*Mun.* 9485).

Kept Christmas 1492 at "Cheynynggate" [the Abbot's mansion] with the Prior [G. Fascet] and the whole Convent (*Mun.* 33290, f. 2).

He and the Convent received permission from the Abbot of Abingdon as Papal Nuncio to choose a confessor, on condition of sending a large contribution (competens quantitas) from their income in aid of the operations by sea and land against the Turks 17 Feb. 1477 (*Mun.* 6659; another licence (*Mun.* 6652 A) is dated 27 Mar. 1498).

He also received the Papal Indulgence permitting Abbots-elect of Westminster to dispense with the visit to the Roman Court for confirmation, on payment of 100 florins to the Papal Collector in England; 13 Aug. 1478 (*Mun.* 5419; cf. 6652 A, B).

He received from Richard III, by the hands of Richard Redman, Bishop of St Asaph, and Thomas Langton, Bishop-elect of St Davids, "An egle of gold garnysshed with perles and precious stones in which is closed the precious Relique called the Ampulle,"—for inclusion among the Regalia 7 Jul. 1483 (*Mun.* 9482).

Item...potecario pro lozengis cordialibus pro domino Abbate ii^s iiii^d 11 Jun. 1496 (*Mun.* 33291, f. 5 b).

During the last few months of his life the Abbey was engaged in the effort to procure the translation of the body of Henry VI from Windsor; petition to the Crown (*Mun.* 6389*); judgment at Greenwich in favour of the Abbey, 5 Mar. 1498; depositions of witnesses (*Mun.* 6389**).

His Treasurer bought books for him, e.g. Allexander (*sic*) de Anima v^s, Johannes Canonicus iv^s 25 Jan. 1498 (*Mun.* 33291, f. 19).

For an account of his life by Brother John Felix (Brit. Mus. Cotton MS. Claudius A viii), see under that name, 1525–6.

Defunctus 24 Mai. 1498 (vicesimo quarto die instantis mensis viam universe carnis ingressus est, *Mun.* 5459).

Buried in the Chapel of St John the Evangelist, where his tomb, the brass of which was afterwards removed to the North Ambulatory, formed part of the screen separating the Ambulatory from the Chapel.

"His body was not long since, upon breaking up a Grave, discover'd lying in a Chest quilted with yellow Satten, he had on a Gown of Crimson Silk girded to him with a black Girdle; on his legs were white Silk Stockings, and over his Face, which was black, a clean Napkin doubled up and laid Cornerwise; the Legs and other Parts of the Body firm and plump. This I think is the exact account I had from that good-natur'd communicative Gentleman, Mr *Battley*[1], late Register of this Church." Dart, *Westmonasterium*, 1723, ii, xxxiii.

Note.—Brayley (1823), ii, 195 gives the date of this opening as 17 Aug. 1706 and says the tomb was again opened in the summer of 1772 when the foundation of General Wolfe's monument was being made; on this occasion "the head was found separated from the shoulders."

Aleyn, Ralph.

Prima Missa 1442–3 (Chamberlain; Almoner; Sacrist; Treasurer); 28 Sep. 1443—25 Mar. 1444, St Mary's Chapel).
Ad skillam 1452–3 (Sacrist).
Defunctus 1464–5 (Q. Alianore; Chamberlain).

Aylmer, John.

Sacerdos 1443–4 (Q. Alianore).
Defunctus 1443–4 (Sacrist: in v cereis conductis in exequiis fratris J. A. defuncti cum vast (= the waste) hoc anno. Last dividend from the manors 1442–3).

Thornwerke, Gervase.

Prima Missa 1443–4 (Infirmarer; Chamberlain; Almoner; Sacrist; Treasurer; Warden of the Churches).
Frequently laid aside by illness (Infirmarer).
Defunctus (before 24 Jun.) 1467 (Infirmarer); inter mortuos 1466–7 (Chamberlain; Q. Alianore; Henry V).

Frampton, Thomas.

Prima Missa 1443–4 (Infirmarer; Chamberlain; Almoner; Sacrist; Treasurer; Warden of the Churches).
Ad skillam 1454–5 (Chamberlain; St Mary's Chapel).

---

[1] Cf. Chester, *Westminster Abbey Registers*, p. 69 n.

Granator 1465–6 ; 1480–3 ? +.

Was party to the resignation of Abbot Norwych 24 Nov. 1467 (*Mun.* 5456).

Camerarius 1470–2.

Refectorarius 1475–7.

Defunctus 1483 (Infirmarer 1482–3, which contains his obit, and shows that he was in the sick-room three times during the latter part of the year).

Wenlock, Wenlocke, Wenlok, Robert.

Prima Missa 1442–3 (Chamberlain ; Almoner ; Sacrist ; Treasurer) ; 28 Sep. 1443—25 Mar. 1444 (St Mary's Chapel).

Defunctus, 1448–9 (Infirmarer ; Henry V).

1440–1

Downe, Doune, Edmund.

Sacerdos 1440–1 (Q. Alianore).

Thesaurarius 1442–6.

Custos capelle b. Marie 1444–5 (Sacrist).

Archidiaconus 1454 (*Mun.* 33289, f. 11).

Custos Novi Operis ? + 1455–6.

Camerarius 1455–6 (Treasurer) ; 29 Sep. 1456—24 Mar. 1459.

Prior de Hurley 25 Jun. 1459 (*Mun.* 18761 dors.)–? 1467.

Member of the Guild of the Assumption (cf. H. F. Westlake, *St Margaret's, Westminster,* p. 51).

Solut' pro debitis E. D. x^s (Infirmarer) ; xx^s (Chamberlain) ; xx^s (Almoner) 1467–8.

1441–2

Ellyngton, Elyngton, Illington, Yllyngton, Richard.

Sacerdos 1443–4 (Q. Alianore ; Richard II).

Granator 1448–50.

Ad skillam 1450–1 (Infirmarer ; Sacrist ; Monk-Bailiff).

Defunctus 1 Dec. 1469 (after being a confirmed invalid for several years, Infirmarer) ; inter mortuos 1469–70 (Chamberlain).

Ramsey, John.

Prima Missa 1445–6 (Chamberlain ; Almoner ; Sacrist ; Monk-Bailiff ; Warden of the Churches) ; 1446–7 (Infirmarer ; but deleted).

Ad skillam 1452–3 (Monk-Bailiff ; Warden of the Churches).

Thesaurarius maner^m Regine Alianore 1457–62.

Custos maner^m Ricardi II et Anne 1459–61 ? +.

Thesaurarius 19 Jan.—29 Sep. 1461.

Elemosinarius ? + 29 Sep. 1462—25 Mar. 1463.

Infirmarius 1473–94.

For his loan of 20 marks sterling to a tailor and for the plate which he received in pledge, 20 Apr. 1490, cf. *Mun.* 5921.

Pittance of one penny a day 1494–1500 (Infirmarer).

Pension x^s (Almoner), vi^s viii^d (Cellarer), xiii^s iiii^d (Domestic Treasurer) 1494–5 ; xiii^s iiii^d (Warden of the Churches) 1495–6 ; xx^s (St Mary's Chapel) 1496–7.

Was present at Islip's election as Abbot 27 Oct. 1500, being then senior monk, but was apparently too infirm to propose the name of the new Abbot (cf. J. Armitage Robinson, *Ch. Quart. Rev.* April 1907, p. 69 ; Widmore, p. 236).

Defunctus 1501 (about Lady-Day ; the Almoner 1500–1 paid his pension ut pro dimidio anno) ; inter mortuos 1500–1 (Chamberlain).

Wycombe, Wycome, Wycumbe, Weycam, Wicombe, William.

Prima Missa 1445–6 (Chamberlain ; Almoner ; Sacrist ; Monk-Bailiff ; Warden of the Churches) ; 1446–7 (Infirmarer ; but deleted).

Ad skillam 1455–6 (Infirmarer ; Sacrist ; Monk-Bailiff ; Warden of the Churches).

Archidiaconus 8 Jan. 1468 (*Mun.* 5983).

Camerarius 1472–4 ? +.

Refectorarius 1477–9.

Pension x^s (Almoner), x^s (St Mary's Chapel) 1489–90 ; x^s (Domestic Treasurer) 1490–1.

Defunctus 1492 (the Warden of St Mary's Chapel paid his pension to Xmas) ; inter mortuos 1492–3 (Chamberlain).

1443–4

Bury, Bery, Byry, J.

Sacerdos 1443–4 (Richard II).

Defunctus 11 Mar., dominica medie Quadragesime, 1453 (*Mun.* 33289, f. 3) ; 1452–3 (Q. Alianore ; Henry V).

Chinnor, Chynnore, William.

Sacerdos 1443–4 (Richard II).

Ad skillam 1450–1 (Infirmarer ; Sacrist ; Monk-Bailiff).

Refectorarius 1458–66 ; 1470–2.

Was party to the resignation of Abbot Norwych 24 Nov. 1467 (*Mun.* 5456).

Elemosinarius ? + 1467–9 ? +.

Infirmarius 1470–2.

Granator 1473–4 ; 1479–80.

Member of the Guild of the Assumption.

Gave to the Refectory a ciphus murrenus weighing 7$\frac{1}{2}$ oz. (*Mun.* 19583).

Defunctus 1480–1 (Infirmarer ; Q. Alianore ; Henry V).

Bovington, Bovyngton, William.

Defunctus, 1444–5 (Infirmarer ; Q. Alianore) ; inter mortuos hoc anno, 1444–5 (Richard II ; Henry V ; no payment).

Northampton, Thomas.

Prima Missa 1447–8 (Infirmarer ; Almoner ; St Mary's Chapel ; Monk-Bailiff ; Warden of the Churches, who in his first draft wrongly entered primo ad skillam).

Gave to the Refectory a ciphus murrenus weighing 4$\frac{3}{4}$ oz. (*Mun.* 19583).

Defunctus 1473–4 (Infirmarer ; Q. Alianore ; Henry V).

1444–5

Fynden, Thomas.

Sacerdos 1445–6 (Q. Alianore).

Succentor 1448–9 (*Mun.* 33289, f. 5).

Revestiarius 1451 (*ibid.* f. 6).

Refectorarius 1456–8.

Two long illnesses 1458–9 (Infirmarer).

Defunctus 1460 (Q. Alianore, half-share ; Richard II, $\frac{1}{3}$ share ; Henry V, $\frac{2}{3}$ share, 1459–60).

1445–6

Crosse, Thomas.

Sacerdos 1448–9 (Q. Alianore).

Prima Missa 1451–2 (Almoner ; Sacrist ; Monk-Bailiff ; Warden of the Churches).

Scolaris studens Oxon. (£6. 13s. 4d.) 1456–63 (Treasurer).

Pro sermonibus in die Palmarum et Parasceues vi^s viii^d, 1462–3 (Sacrist).

Ad skillam Apr. 1463 (Warden of the Churches); 1462–3 (Infirmarer; Chamberlain; Sacrist; New Work); 25 Mar.—29 Sep. 1463 (Almoner).

Granator 1464–5; 1466–70.

Was party to the resignation of Abbot Norwych 24 Nov. 1467 (*Mun.* 5456).

Thesaurarius maner^m Regine Alianore 1468–72; 1474–7.

Custos Novi Operis 1470–1.

Elemosinarius 1470–9.

Refectorarius 1479–80.

Supprior et Camerarius 1483 (*Mun.* 33289, f. 17).

Defunctus 1483 (1482–3 Infirmarer; Q. Alianore, Henry V, full share; Richard II, $\frac{2}{3}$ share; Prior Essex paid him 13s. 4d. at Christmas 1483; so he must have died at the end of the calendar year, probably while the Infirmarer's compotus was being made up).

Bukland, Buklond, Bokeland, Bokelond, Bokelande, Bokyllond, Buclond, William.

Prima Missa 1447–8 (Infirmarer; Almoner; St Mary's Chapel; Monk-Bailiff; Warden of the Churches, who in his first draft wrongly entered primo ad skillam).

Ad skillam 1457–8 (Infirmarer); 1458–9 (Monk-Bailiff; Warden of the Churches).

Last mentioned in 1461–2 (Q. Alianore, $\frac{3}{4}$ share; so he probably died or left in 1462).

Ellerton, Ellyrton, Elerton, Illerton, Elderton, Eldyrton, J.

Prima Missa 1452–3 (Sacrist; Monk-Bailiff; Warden of the Churches).

Defunctus 1454–5 (Q. Alianore, Richard II, half-share; Henry V, $\frac{2}{3}$ share; so probably 1455).

Selly, Richard.

= Petworth, Petteworth, R.

[The change from "Petworth" to "Selly" was made in Q. Alianore 1447–8 and in Richard II 1448–9; in Q. Alianore 1448–9 it was written "Selby."]

Prima Missa 1451–2 (Almoner; Sacrist; Monk-Bailiff; Warden of the Churches).

Defunctus 1459–60 (Q. Alianore; probably during the time of the compotus, 1460).

Baanes, Banes, Banys, Thomas.

Prima Missa 1452–3 (Sacrist; Monk-Bailiff; Warden of the Churches).

He received a full share from the manors up to Michaelmas 1458 and was not mentioned thereafter.

MILLYNG, Milling, Myllyng, Melling, Mellyng, Thomas.

Prima Missa 1450–1 (Infirmarer; Sacrist; Monk-Bailiff).

Scolaris studens Oxon. (£6. 13s. 4d.) 1456–63; (£5) 1464–6 (Treasurer).

Pro sermonibus in die Palmarum et Parasceues vi^s viii^d 1462–3; xiii^s iiii^d, 1463–5; (as Prior) 1465–6; (as Bishop of Hereford) 1475–6 (Sacrist).

Placed next to the Prior 1464–5 (Henry V).

Ad skillam, Prior, mense Martii 1466 (Monk-Bailiff; Warden of the Churches); 1465–6 (Chamberlain; Sacrist; St Mary's Chapel).

Prior 1466–9.

Solut' domino priori ex concessione conventus durante tempore prioratus sui xl^s (Q. Alianore); £12 (Treasurer) 1465–6.

Thesaurarius intrinsecus 1466–70.

Custos Novi Operis 25 Dec. 1467—29 Sep. 1470.

Was party to the resignation of Abbot Norwych 24 Nov. 1467 and, as Prior, was nominated one of his three commissaries (*Mun.* 5432, 5456).

Abbas 1469 (described as Abbot-elect 14 Nov.; *Mun.* 5413)-1474; cf. R. B. Rackham, *The Nave of Westminster*, p. 29.

For Millyng's part in the "new work" and his efforts to raise money cf. *ibid.* pp. 30–34.

S.T.P. Gloucester Hall, Oxford. Incorporated at Cambridge 1470-1 (p. 28).

Received Elizabeth Woodville, Queen of Edward IV, on 1 Oct. 1470, when she took sanctuary at Westminster, into the Abbot's house, where her son Edward V was born on 2 or 3 Nov. Millyng, together with Estney the Prior, stood Godfather to the boy at his baptism in the Abbey church.

Was made a Privy Councillor by Edward IV and was consecrated as Bishop of Hereford in the Lady Chapel, 21 Aug. 1474 (Stubbs, *Registrum*, 2 ed. p. 92).

Et in recreacionibus factis domino Episcopo Hereford in diebus Ramis Palmarum et Parasceues vii^s ix^d 1475-6 (Sacrist), when he was invited once more to preach the Passion-tide sermons.

Was a member of the Guild of the Assumption and so remained after his promotion (cf. H. F. Westlake, *St Margaret's, Westminster*, p. 51).

Died at Hereford Mar. 1492; buried at the Abbey in the chapel of St John Baptist (in medio sacelli, Camden); the stone coffin with the Hereford cross-fleury on it being afterwards removed from the centre of the chapel and placed upon Abbot Fascet's tomb.

[Cf. Camden, *Reges*, &c.; Mrs Murray Smith, *Westminster Abbey*, p. 111; do. *Roll-Call*, p. 78; A. P. Stanley, *Memorials*, 3rd ed. p. 392.]

1447-8

Hertford, Herteford, Herford, Edward.

Not mentioned after 1451-2, when he received $\frac{1}{6}$ share, Q. Alianore, $\frac{1}{3}$ share, Richard II.

Chesterfield, Chesterfeld, Chestyrfeld, Richard [Robert (Almoner 1451-2)].

Prima Missa 1451-2 (Almoner; Sacrist; Monk-Bailiff; Warden of the Churches).

Defunctus 1457-8 (Infirmarer; Q. Alianore and Richard II, $\frac{1}{2}$ share; Henry V, $\frac{2}{3}$ share; so probably 1458).

Alby, Henry.

Prima Missa 1450-1 (Infirmarer; Sacrist; Monk-Bailiff).

Defunctus 1467-8 (Infirmarer; Chamberlain; Q. Alianore).

1450-1

Westminster, Richard.

Sacerdos 1451-2 (Richard II).

Scolaris studens Oxon. (£6. 13s. 4d.) 1456-60 (Treasurer).

Ad skillam 1459-60 (*Mun.* 33288, f. 12); 24 Dec. 1460—28 Sep. 1461 (St Mary's Chapel); 1460-1 (Chamberlain).

Granator 1463-4.

Senescallus hospicii Abbatis [Kirton] 1463 (13 Apr.—14 Nov.).

Receptor Abbatis [Norwych] 24 Nov. 1463—5 Feb. 1464.

Refectorarius 1466-7.

Was party to the resignation of Abbot Norwych 24 Nov. 1467 (*Mun.* 5456).

Defunctus 1470-1 (Infirmarer; Chamberlain; Q. Alianore; Richard II).

1451-2

Clare, Richard.

Prima Missa 1455–6 (Infirmarer; Sacrist; Monk-Bailiff; Warden of the Churches).

Defunctus 1458 (Q. Alianore and Richard II, $\frac{1}{2}$ share; Henry V, $\frac{2}{3}$ share, 1457–8; obit, Infirmarer 1457–8).

Lynne, Thomas.

= Myldenale, T.

[Entered as "Myldenale" at his first appearance in Q. Alianore; Richard II; Henry V; the change to "Lynne" occurs first in 1456–7 (Q. Alianore). The Chamberlain only uses "Lynne."]

Prima Missa 1455–6 (Infirmarer; Sacrist; Monk-Bailiff; Warden of the Churches).

Ad skillam. Sep. 1465 (Warden of the Churches); 1464–5 (Chamberlain; New Work; Almoner; Sacrist; St Mary's Chapel).

Item rec' de dompno T. L. monacho die sepulture matris sue pro iiii^{or} Tapr'. xvi^d (St Margaret, Westminster, churchwardens' accounts 1466–7).

In St Edward's Shrine 21 Dec. 1467 there were "a walannce of ble weluet braudryd with flours of gold and a ymage of Seint Edward and Seint John Euangelist of Dan T. L. gift" (*Mun.* 9477). The valance was "to hong above the shryne" (*Mun.* 9478). By 1479 "the same Dan T." had added "a creste of tymbre and broñ (= burnished) gold to stonde above ye Awter" (*ibid.*; cf. *Mun.* 9485, which shows that these gifts survived till 1520).

Refectorarius 1472–4.

Defunctus 1473–4 (Infirmarer, which enters an illness towards the end of that year; Q. Alianore, full share; Richard II, $\frac{2}{3}$ share; so probably 1474).

Ashford, Assheford, John.

Prima Missa 1455–6 (Infirmarer; Sacrist; Monk-Bailiff; Warden of the Churches).

Ad skillam 29 Sep. 1466—24 Jun. 1467 (Infirmarer); 1466–7 (New Work; Chamberlain; Sacrist; Monk-Bailiff; St Mary's Chapel).

Defunctus 1473–4 (Infirmarer; he was ill for two months at the beginning of that year; so probably died in the autumn of 1473).

ESSEX, Robert.

Prima Missa 1454–5 (Chamberlain); 1455–6 (Infirmarer); Sacrist; Monk-Bailiff; Warden of the Churches).

Thesaurarius 1461–3.

Thesaurarius maner^m Regine Alianore 1462–4.

Custos maner^m Ricardi II et Anne 1462–3 ?+.

Ad skillam Apr. 1463 (Warden of the Churches); 25 Mar.—29 Sep. 1463 (Almoner); 1462–3 (Infirmarer; Chamberlain; New Work; Sacrist).

Camerarius ?+1477–82. *Mun.* 33292 is a leaf of his ledger as such, showing that he had to defend an action for trespass at Guildhall 5 Oct. no year.

Nuper coquinarius 1483 (Treasurer). He gave the kitchen "a posnet of brasse" (*Mun.* 6647).

Prior 30 Sep. 1482 (*Mun.* 33289, f. 15)–1491.

Supervisor operum voltorum (*sic* for voltarum, the vaulting of the new Nave) 23 Mar. 1482—11 Mai. 1483 (*Mun.* 23557; R. B. Rackham, *Nave of Westminster*, pp. 39–40).

Thesaurarius intrinsecus 1485–90.

Mun. 6225 is an undated petition from him, apparently to Edward IV, as follows:—

To the Kyng our soueraigne Lord, Please it your most noble grace to calle unto your goode remembraunce how that your frames ordaigned and made for the making of Sylkes stondith as nowe unoccupied within your monastery of Westm' and that in consideracion thereof it wolde like your good grace to graunte the said frames with theire instruments thereunto necessarily belongyng unto yor faithfull oratour Dompnus R. E. and he shall ordaigne workmen toccupie the same in the place there as they be at his costs and charges....

Into the note-book (*Mun.* 33289) in which Prior Walsh kept an account of burials of the Brethren, and of various Prior's receipts and payments, Prior Essex inserted his own receipts and payments, headed by the following record of his appointment, the date of which would be otherwise unknown :—

Memorandum quod anno regni regis E. iiii^{ti} xxii^o ultimo die Sept' R. E. monachus monasterii beati Petri Westm' electus erat per Abbatem eiusdem loci et totum conuentum in prioratum eiusdem loci Deo gratias.

Defunctus, Prior, 1490–1 (Infirmarer; Q. Alianore, $\frac{5}{6}$ share; Henry V, full share; so probably in summer of 1491. This agrees with the entries in his note-book which continued till 25 Jun., *Mun.* 33289, f. 52).

Billingburgh, Billyngburgh, Billyngborowe, Byllingborow, Byllyng-borugh, Byllyngborth, John.

Prima Missa 1455–6 (Infirmarer; Sacrist; Monk-Bailiff; Warden of the Churches).

Ad skillam Sep. 1465 (Warden of the Churches); 1464–5 (Chamberlain; New Work; Almoner; Sacrist; St Mary's Chapel).

The Custos feretri in 1520 had charge of "a trefoile of syluer and gylt with an ymage off y^e trynyte fyxed in the myddys off J. B.'s gyffte" (*Mun.* 9485).

Defunctus 1484–5 (Infirmarer; Chamberlain; Q. Alianore, full share; Richard II, $\frac{4}{5}$ share; so probably 1485).

1455–6

Bryssey, Byrsey, William.

Spent about ten weeks in the Infirmary 1455–6.
Defunctus 1455–6 (Infirmarer; Richard II, $\frac{1}{4}$ share).

Lamborne, Langborne, Langbourne, Langebourne, J.

Defunctus 1457–8 (Infirmarer; Henry V, $\frac{1}{6}$ share; so probably 1457).

Lowth, Lowthe, R.

= Benet, Robert.

[The name "Lowth" is given in Chamberlain 1456–7 and is used at his first appearance in Q. Alianore; Richard II; and Henry V; 1455–6. The Chamberlain changes to "Benet" in 1460–1.]

Prima Missa in dominica media Quadragesime 1459 (St Mary's Chapel); 1458–9 (Infirmarer; Chamberlain; Sacrist; Monk-Bailiff; Warden of the Churches).

Ad skillam 1474–5 (Infirmarer; New Work; Almoner; Sacrist; St Mary's Chapel).

Not mentioned after the manorial lists of 1474–5 in which he received a full share.

Prymer, Prymmer, Primer, Premer, Thomas.

Prima Missa dominica in passione 1459 (St Mary's Chapel); 1458–9 (Infirmarer; Chamberlain; Sacrist; Monk-Bailiff; Warden of the Churches).

Defunctus 1479 (Q. Alianore, full share; Richard II, $\frac{17}{20}$ share; 1478–9; Henry V, $\frac{1}{6}$ share; 1479–80).

1456-7

Appulton, Appilton, Appylton, Apulton, Peter.
Prima Missa Mar. 1460 (*Mun.* 33288, f. 12); 1459-60 (Almoner; Sacrist; Monk-Bailiff; Warden of the Churches).
Two brief illnesses, May and Jul. 1460 (*Mun.* 33288, f. 12).
No later mention.

Lambard, Lambarde, Lamberd, Lambert, William [John (Monk-Bailiff 1459- 60; Almoner 1464-5)].
Prima Missa dominica in passione Domini 1460 (*Mun.* 33288, f. 12); 1459-60 (Almoner; Sacrist; Monk-Bailiff; Warden of the Churches).
Scolaris Oxon. (£5) 1465-8 ? + (Treasurer).
Ad skillam Nov. 1464 (Warden of the Churches); 1464-5 (Chamberlain; New Work; Almoner; Sacrist; St Mary's Chapel).
Custos maner^{m} Ricardi II et Anne 1479-80.
Supprior 1483 (*Mun.* 33289, f. 15).
Archidiaconus 1483-4 (*ibid.*).
Pension x^s 1490-1 (Almoner); x^s 1490-1, afterwards xiii^s iiii^d (Domestic Treasurer); xx^s 1494-5 (Infirmarer); iii^s iiii^d 1497-8, vi^s viii^d 1498-9 (Richard II); vi^s viii^d 1499-1500 (Q. Alianore).
Proctor at the election of George Fascet as Abbot 9 Jul. 1498 (*Mun.* 5459).
Proposed the election of John Islip as Abbot 27 Oct. 1500 (Widmore, p. 240).
Refectorarius 1503-5.
Defunctus 1513 (the Domestic Treasurer's Roll and that of Q. Alianore 1513-4 omit his pension).

Harding, Hardyng, Herdyng, Christopher.
Defunctus 1457-8 (Infirmarer. He had been for five days in the sick-room, being entered in the list simply as Brother Christopher. Received $\frac{1}{6}$ share, Henry V, 1457-8; so probably died in 1457).

Everton, Evyrton, Euerton, J.
Defunctus 1457 (received $\frac{1}{6}$ share, Richard II; Henry V; 1457-8).

1458-9

Pawnton, Paunton, Robert.
Prima Missa 1461-2 (Infirmarer; New Work; Cellarer; St Mary's Chapel; Warden of the Churches).
No appearance after Q. Alianore 1476-7.

Bayndon, Baynton, John.
Scolaris Oxon. (£6. 13s. 4d.) 1461-5.
Prima Missa Mar. 1464 (Almoner; Chamberlain; Warden of the Churches); 29 Sep. 1463—1 Apr. 1464 (Cellarer); 1463-4 (Infirmarer; New Work; Sacrist; St Mary's Chapel).
Defunctus 1467-8 (Infirmarer; Chamberlain; Q. Alianore).

Marlowe, Merlowe, Merlawe, John.
Prima Missa 1461-2 (Infirmarer; Cellarer; New Work; St Mary's Chapel; Warden of the Churches).
Ad skillam 29 Sep.—25 Dec. 1467 (New Work); 1467-8 (Infirmarer; Chamberlain; Almoner; St Mary's Chapel).
Last payment from the manors 1471-2; the Chamberlain entered him for a habit, &c. 1472-3, 1473-4, but deleted the latter entry.

Kingston, Kingeston, Kyngeston, John.

Prima Missa Jan. 1463 (Warden of the Churches); 29 Sep. 1462—25 Mar. 1463 (Almoner); 1462-3 (Infirmarer; Chamberlain; New Work; Sacrist).

Defunctus 1464 (his obit is in Infirmarer 1463-4 after that of N. Whaplode [q.v.]).

Hampton, John.

Prima Missa Oct. 1463 (Almoner; Chamberlain); 29 Sep. 1463—Apr. 1464 (Cellarer); 1463-4 (Infirmarer; New Work; Sacrist; St Mary's Chapel).

Refectorarius 1474-5; 1480-1? +.

Ad skillam 1480-1 (Infirmarer; Chamberlain; New Work; Almoner; St Mary's Chapel).

Camerarius 1484-5? +.

Coquinarius 1484-5 (*Mun.* 23045).

Custos maner^m Regine Alianore; Ricardi II et Anne; Henrici V, 1485 (before Mich^s)-1486.

Ballivus 1485-6 (Refectorer).

Thesaurarius et Custos ecclesiarum 1485-6 (*Mun.* 23045-6).

Precentor 1491-2 (*Mun.* 23047).

Proclaimed the election of Fascet as Abbot 9 Jul. 1498 (*Mun.* 5459).

Last payment from the manors, Michaelmas 1498 (Q. Alianore).

Prior de Hurley ? 1498-1501? +.

Tudbery, Tutbery, Tutbury, Tuttebury, Humphrey.

Prima Missa 1461-2 (Infirmarer; New Work; Cellarer; St Mary's Chapel; Warden of the Churches).

Defunctus c. 1464 (full payment, Q. Alianore 1463-4); inter mortuos 1464-5 (Chamberlain).

1460-1

Stokeley, Stokley, Robert.

Prima Missa Jun. 1464 (Chamberlain); Jul. (Warden of the Churches); 1463-4 (Infirmarer; New Work; Almoner; Sacrist; St Mary's Chapel).

Defunctus 1464 (his obit is in Infirmarer 1463-4 after that of W. Pavor [q.v.]).

Charing, Charyng, Charringe, Charryng, Richard.

[John (Infirmarer 1463-4; probably by interchange with Waterden).]

Prima Missa Jun. 1464 (Chamberlain; Warden of the Churches); 1463-4 (Infirmarer; New Work; Sacrist; Almoner; St Mary's Chapel).

Ad skillam 1473-4 (Infirmarer; New Work; Almoner; Sacrist; St Mary's Chapel).

Granator ? + 1484-5.

Subsacrista 1483-4 (*Mun.* 33289, f. 16).

Refectorarius 1485-7.

Coquinarius 1487—16 Dec. 1491 (*Mun.* 6647, an inventory of the goods of the Kitchen); 1498-1501 (Treasurer).

Camerarius ? + 1499-1507.

Chosen proctor, along with William Lambard, to announce to John Islip his election as Abbot 27 Oct. 1500 (*Mun.* 5444); the senior of the five monks who met the Abbot-elect, when he entered the church, 25 Nov. 1500 (*Mun.* 5454).

Pension or recreacio vi^s viii^d (Q. Alianore); vi^s viii^d (Richard II); xiii^s iiii^d (St Mary's Chapel); vi^s viii^d 1510-1; xiii^s iiii^d 1513-4 (Domestic Treasurer); vi^s viii^d 1509-10 (Chamberlain).

Infirmarius 1518–9 ; 1523-4.

Defunctus 1524 (Domestic Treasurer 1524–5 paid his pension ; full share, Henry V, Q. Alianore [and pension], Richard II, 1523–4 ; the last put a † against his name as if dead and did not pay his pension.   Charing was still alive at compotus time in the autumn of 1524, for his own account as Infirmarer was then made up and contained no mention of his decease or even his illness).

1461-2

Waterden, Waterdene, Watyrden, John [Richard (Infirmarer 1463–4)].

Prima Missa mense Junii 1464 (Chamberlain ; Warden of the Churches) ; 1463–4 (Infirmarer ; New Work ; Almoner ; Sacrist ; St Mary's Chapel).

Ad skillam 1477–8 (Infirmarer ; New Work ; Almoner ; Sacrist ; St Mary's Chapel).

Custos maner^m Ricardi II et Anne 1478–9.

Custos feretri 9 Oct. 1479 (*Mun.* 9478)—? 1481 (Sacrist).

Precentor ? + 1483–91 ; 1493–4 (cf. *Manuscripts of Westminster Abbey*, p. 2).

Custos capelle b. Marie 1485–9 ; "newe made keper of our lady Chapell" 1 Oct. 1485 (*Mun.* 23258).

Infirmarius 1494–1505 (was Infirmarius at Fascet's election 9 Jul. 1498 and Islip's election 27 Oct. 1500; *Mun.* 5444; and on 25 Nov. 1500 he handed to Islip the schedule containing the Abbot's oath on admission to office ; cf. J. Armitage Robinson, Ch. Quart. Rev. April 1907, p. 70 ; *Mun.* 5454).

The Custos feretri in 1520 had charge of " a coffre of syluer and gylte with this scripture in the bottom Ex dono fratris Johannis Waterden " (*Mun.* 9485).

Pension x^s 1491–2 (Almoner) ; x^s (Domestic Treasurer) ; iii^s iiii^d, 1494–5 (Cellarer).   Pittance of i^d a day from 1494–5 (Infirmarer).

Gave iii^s iiii^d for the repair of the " Seyny bookes " c. 1492 (*Manuscripts of Westminster Abbey*, p. 9).

Witnessed in St Katharine's Chapel within the Infirmary the appointment of William Cornysshe (who officiated at Islip's election) to be a Notary, Tabellion, and Judge in Ordinary 23 Feb. 1497 (*Mun.* 6538).

Defunctus 1505 (Infirmarer 1505–6, where the entry of his pittance ceases) ; inter mortuos 1504–5 (Q. Alianore ; Richard II ; full share) ; 1505–6 (Chamberlain ; Henry V, full share).

Hilston, Hylston, Hilleston, Hyllyston, Helleston, Helston, Elston, John.

Prima Missa Jun. 1464 (Chamberlain ; Warden of the Churches) ; 1463–4 (Infirmarer ; New Work ; Almoner ; Sacrist ; St Mary's Chapel).

Ad skillam 1474–5 (Infirmarer ; New Work ; Almoner ; Sacrist ; St Mary's Chapel).

" The gyft of Dan J. H." to St Edward's Shrine c. 1479 was " a cappe of purpull velvet for ye child of Isrell " (*Mun.* 9478).   It was still there in 1520 (*Mun.* 9485).

Nuper Coquinarius 1483 (Treasurer).

Prior de Hurley (? 1482) 1487–97 (cf. F. T. Wethered, *Last Days of Hurley Priory*, p. 11).   He received his last payment from the manors 1481–2, and his appointment to Hurley, *vice* T. Ruston, probably dated from that time.

In 1496–7 proceedings arose between him and the Convent of Westminster.   Islip as Abbot's Treasurer of that year entered (*Mun.* 24281 B) a "regard" paid secretario matris domini Regis [i.e. the Lady Margaret,

Countess of Richmond] pro sua beneuolencia c⁸ and the large sum of £66. 13s. 4d. domino Cardinali [?Morton] pro sua amicitia in materia predicta; also Magistro Warham [afterwards Archbishop of Canterbury] pro batillagio suo, x⁸.

Hilston was alive 16 Sep. 1497 (*Mun.* 3666).

1462-3

Pavor, Pavour, William.

Defunctus 1464 (his obit is in Infirmarer 1463–4 after that of William West [q.v.]).

Drope, Droppe, John.

Prima Missa mense Junii 1466 (Monk-Bailiff; Warden of the Churches); 1465–6 (Chamberlain; Sacrist; St Mary's Chapel).

Vestiarius 1483–4 (*Mun.* 33289, f. 16).

Ad skillam 1485–6 (Infirmarer; Cellarer; St Mary's Chapel).

Refectorarius 1490–8 (and so at Fascet's election, 9 Jul. 1498, *Mun.* 5459).

Gave iii⁸ iiii^d for repairing the "Seyny bookes," c. 1492 (*Manuscripts of Westminster Abbey*, p. 10).

Pension x⁸ 1498–9 (Almoner); xiii⁸ iiii^d 1499–1500 (St Mary's Chapel).

Defunctus 1500 (Q. Alianore); the Almoner of 1499–1500 paid three-quarters of his pension; 1499–1500 (Infirmarer; Chamberlain; Richard II, full share).

Ashby, Asshby, John.

Defunctus 1464 (his obit is in Infirmarer 1463–4 after that of J. Kingston [q.v.]. He had had three short illnesses during the year).

Stanes, Stanys, John.

Prima Missa mense Junii 1466 (Monk-Bailiff; Warden of the Churches); 1465–6 (Chamberlain; Sacrist; St Mary's Chapel).

Scolaris Oxonie (£6. 13s. 4d.) ?+1470–1?+ (Treasurer).

Custos capelle b. Marie 1483–5 (*Mun.* 9479; 33289, f. 16).

Subelemosinarius 1483–4 (*Mun.* 33289, f. 16).

Defunctus 1485 (reference to his recent "decees," 1 Oct. 1485; St Mary's Chapel); 1484–5 (Infirmarer; Chamberlain; Q. Alianore; Richard II).

Whaplode, Waplot, Waplott, Nicholas.

Defunctus 1464 (his obit is in Infirmarer 1463–4 after that of R. Stokeley [q.v.]. Eight monks out of 51 died that year).

Clifford, Clyfford, Thomas.

Scolaris Oxon. (£5) 1465–8?+ (Treasurer).

Prima Missa mense Maii 1467 (Monk-Bailiff); 28 Sep. 1466—24 Jun. 1467 (Infirmarer); 1466–7 (Chamberlain; New Work; St Mary's Chapel); 1470–1 (Infirmarer, apparently by error for ad skillam).

Custos capelle b. Marie 1477—1483 (*Mun.* 9479).

In denariis missis T. C. existenti Rome vi^{li} xiii⁸ iiii^d 1477–8 (*Mun.* 23253).

Elemosinarius 1479–83.

Custos maner^m Regine Alianore; Ricardi II et Anne; Henrici V; 1482–5.

Celerarius 1482–3.

Thesaurarius et Ballivus; Custos ecclesiarum; 18 Jan. 1483—29 Sep. 1484?+.

In expensis domini prioris [R. Essex] et T. C. Ballivi cum suis seruientibus et equis equitantium usque Westerham et Echelesford [Ashford, Midx.] pro reparacione ibidem superintendenda xv⁸ 1483–4 (Treasurer).

Gave to the Refectory a ciphus murrenus weighing 6½ oz. (*Mun.* 19583).

The Custos feretri of 1520 had charge of "two Agnus (*sic*) Dei of syluer and gylt one of them iiii square with stones the othere round with a Crosse standyng upon hit of the gyfte of Dane T. C." (*Mun.* 9485).

The rubricated title of the *Liber Niger Quaternus* states that the volume was re-written at the cost of Thomas dominus Clifforde vir honorabilis ac huius monasterii beati Petri Westm. quondam monachus, and by permission of Abbot Estney. Possibly, fifth son of Thomas, Lord Clifford, slain at St Albans 1455 (cf. *Manuscripts of Westminster Abbey*, p. 97 f.).

Defunctus c. 29 Sep. 1485 (*Mun.* 23045); 1484–5 (Infirmarer; Chamberlain; Q. Alianore; Richard II). *Mun.* 23045 is a visus compoti subscriptus immediate post decessum fratris T. C. qui non computauit....

Hervy, Nicholas.
Defunctus 1464 (his obit is in Infirmarer 1463–4 after that of T. Pomeray [q.v.]).

1465-6

Brewode, Brewood, William.
Prima Missa 1468–9 (Infirmarer; New Work; Chamberlain; Almoner; Cellarer).

Ad skillam 1476–7 (Infirmarer; New Work; Almoner; Sacrist; St Mary's Chapel).

Refectorarius 1483–5.

Tertius Prior 1484 (*Mun.* 33289, f. 16).

Celerarius 1484–96; 1500–1.

Camerarius ? + 1491–8 ? + (at Fascet's election 9 Jul. 1498, *Mun.* 5459).

Gave ii⁸ iiii^d towards the repair of the "Seyny bookes" c. 1492 (*Manuscripts of Westminster Abbey*, p. 10).

Thesaurarius 1499–1501; Ballivus 1499–1500. [Described as Thesaurarius et Celerarius at Islip's election 27 Oct. 1500; cf. Widmore, p. 235.]

Custos maner^m Regine Alianore; Ricardi II et Anne, 1499–1500.

Custos ecclesiarum 1499–1500.

Custos capelle b. Marie 1503–14.

Infirmarius ? + 1512–3 ? +.

Defunctus 1514–5 (Q. Alianore, Richard II, Henry V, full share; so probably 1515); inter mortuos 1515–6 (Chamberlain).

Langley, Langeley, Ralph.
Prima Missa mense Maii 1471 (Warden of the Churches); 1470–1 (Chamberlain; New Work; Almoner; Sacrist; St Mary's Chapel).

Palm Sunday and Good Friday preacher 1477 and 1478 (Sacrist).

Thesaurarius maner^m Regine Alianore; Ricardi II et Anne 1480–1.

Custos feretri 1481–2 (Sacrist).

Refectorarius 1482–3.

Ad skillam 18 Jan.—29 Sep. 1483 (Monk-Bailiff); 1482–3 (Infirmarer; New Work; Almoner; Cellarer; St Mary's Chapel).

Elemosinarius 1483–5 ? +.

Coquinarius 1485–7 (Treasurer; *Mun.* 33289, f. 20).

Solut' pro debitis fratris R. L. per voluntatem et consensum domini Abbatis prioris et seniorum xl⁸ (New Work); lx⁸ (Sacrist) 1487–8.

Granator 1490–2.

Gave ii⁸ towards repairing the "Seyny bookes" c. 1492 (cf. *Manuscripts of Westminster Abbey*, p. 9).

Pension x⁸ (Almoner); x⁸ (St Mary's Chapel); 1498–9.

"Infirm" at the date of Fascet's election 9 Jul. 1498 (*Mun.* 5459).

Along with W. Lokyngton, W. Borow, and W. Grene [q.v.] he made an inventory of the ornaments of St Andrew's Chapel, 1497–8 (*Mun.* 6605).

Defunctus 1501 (Almoner 1500–1 paid his pension to Lady-Day); inter mortuos, 1500–1 (Chamberlain); 1499–1500 (Richard II).

Graunt, Graunte, Grawnt, Grawnte, Grawntte, Grannte, William. [John (New Work 1468–9).]

Prima Missa 1468–9 (Infirmarer; Chamberlain; New Work; Cellarer; Almoner).

Ad skillam 1479–80 (Infirmarer; New Work; Almoner).

Quartus Prior 1483 (*Mun.* 33289, f. 16).

Granator 1485–8?+.

Gave iii^s iiii^d towards repairing the "Seyny bookes" c. 1492 (*Manuscripts of Westminster Abbey*, p. 10).

Coquinarius 1497–1500 (*Mun.* 33318; 33321; at Fascet's election, 9 Jul. 1498, *Mun.* 5459); 1501–3.

Refectorarius 1498–1501 (and so at Islip's election 27 Oct. 1500; *Mun.* 5444).

Custos capelle b. Marie 1501–3 (*Mun.* 30470).

Prior de Hurley 1504–10.

Faringdon, Faryngdon, Faryndon, Walter.

Prima Missa 1468–9 (Infirmarer; Chamberlain; New Work; Almoner; Cellarer).

His last regular payment from the manors was a full share Q. Alianore 1475–6, to which was added in 1476–7 xl^s paid W. F. nuper confratri nostro qui recessit ad ordinem Cartusiensem (*Mun.* 23868).

Ware, John.

Prima Missa 1468–9 (Infirmarer; Chamberlain; New Work; Almoner; Cellarer).

Defunctus 1479 (obit, Infirmarer, 1478–9, which enters him as sick towards the end of the year; Q. Alianore, full share; Richard II, $\frac{4}{5}$ share).

Bridgewater, Briggewater, Bregewater, Brygewater, Edward.

Prima Missa 1468–9 (Infirmarer; Chamberlain; New Work; Almoner; Cellarer).

Defunctus 1471–2 (Infirmarer, which shows that he had a 3 weeks' illness at the beginning of the year; Chamberlain; Q. Alianore, full share; Richard II, $\frac{5}{6}$ share, 1470–1; so probably 1471).

Camden (*Reges*, &c.) records the burial in the Chapel of St Blaise of Edwardus monachus Westmonasteriensis, son of Owen Tudor by Queen Katharine, widow of Henry V; brother of Edmund Earl of Richmond, who married the Lady Margaret; and uncle of Henry VII. The only other Edward on our list at this period is Edward Boteler [q.v.], who was transferred to St Milburga's Priory at Wenlock; so we are left with the option of identifying Edward Bridgewater with Camden's Edward Tudor.

Stanley (*Memorials*, 3rd ed. 1869, pp. 170 n.; 395; 412) thrice repeats a statement, taken from Sandford, *Geneal. Hist.* ed. 1677, p. 285, that Owen, son of Owen Tudor, became a Westminster monk, and this statement has been reproduced by subsequent writers. On p. 170 n. he gives a reference to Crull, *Antiquities*, p. 233 (3rd ed. I. 251), who has correctly taken the name Edward from Camden.

Knight, Richard.

Prima Missa 1468–9 (Infirmarer; Chamberlain; New Work; Almoner; Cellarer).

Probably an old servant of the Abbey to whom payments were made through the Succentor.

Defunctus ? 1472–3. (His last payment from the manors, 1471–2, Q. Alianore; entered for his habit by Chamberlain 1472–3; entered but deleted 1473–4.)

Selly, Selley, John.

Prima Missa mense Maii 1471 (Warden of the Churches); 1470–1 (Infirmarer; Chamberlain; New Work; Almoner; Sacrist; St Mary's Chapel).

Defunctus 1478–9 (Infirmarer, his being the last obit of the year; Q. Alianore, Richard II, full share, 1478–9; so probably 1479).

1468–9

Holand, Holond; Holonde, John.

Prima Missa 1471–2 (Infirmarer; Chamberlain; New Work; Sacrist; Cellarer; St Mary's Chapel).

Thesaurarius maner^m Regine Alianore 1481–8.

Custos maner^m Ricardi II et Anne 1481–7.

Custos feretri 1482–8 (Sacrist).

Thesaurarius 18 Jan. 1483—29 Sep. 1488.

Elemosinarius 29 Sep. 1486—7 Dec. 1491.

Granator 1492–3.

Gave iii^s iiii^d towards the repair of the "Seyny bookes" c. 1492 (*Manuscripts of Westminster Abbey*, p. 10).

Ad skillam 1493–4 (Infirmarer; New Work; Almoner; Sacrist; Treasurer; Warden of the Churches).

Sub-prior at Fascet's election, 9 Jul. 1498 (*Mun.* 5459) and at Islip's election 27 Oct. 1500 (*Mun.* 5444; cf. Widmore, p. 235).

Pension x^s 25 Mar. 1502 (St Mary's Chapel); iii^s iiii^d (Almoner); iii^s iiii^d (Domestic Treasurer) 1501–2.

Defunctus 1503 (Almoner 1502–3 paid his pension pro dimidio Anni).

Sion College (Arc. L. 40) possesses a manuscript Gospel of Nicodemus, &c. in English verse which is inscribed: pertinet fratri Joh. holonde monacho Westm. (cf. *Manuscripts of Westminster Abbey*, p. 24).

The Custos feretri of 1520 possessed "one corporas and i case of blewe tyssue of Dan John Holandys gyfte" (*Mun.* 9485).

Westow, Westowe, Westhowe, Wystowe, Thomas.
= **Nicoll, Nicholl, T.**

[The name "Nicoll" appears in the Manor-lists up to 1473–4 and is changed to "Westow" in Q. Alianore 1474–5 and after.]

Prima Missa 1474–5 (Infirmarer; New Work; Almoner; Sacrist; St Mary's Chapel).

Defunctus 1478–9 (Infirmarer; Q. Alianore and Henry V, full share; Richard II, $\frac{17}{20}$ share; so probably 1479).

1469–70

Purcell, Pursell, Robert.

Prima Missa 1476–7 (Infirmarer; New Work; Sacrist; St Mary's Chapel).

Defunctus 1478–9 (Infirmarer; Q. Alianore, full share, Richard II, $\frac{4}{5}$ share, 1478–9; so probably 1479; Henry V, $\frac{1}{8}$ share, 1479–80).

Boteler, Botiller, Butler, Buteler, Butteler, Edward.
Prima Missa 1474–5 (Infirmarer; New Work; Almoner; Sacrist; St Mary's Chapel).
Ad skillam 1486–7 (Infirmarer; New Work; Almoner; Sacrist; St Mary's Chapel).
Debts paid by Almoner xxvi^s viii^d; by Sacrist vi^s viii^d; 1487–8.
Received from Abbot Estney a dimissory letter to Prior Richard Synger in order that he might join the Cluniac priory of St Milburga, Wenlock. The letter (*Register* A, f. 30 b) stated that he was of "competent lernyng and understondyng," and could "syng bothe playn song and prikked song," and was moreover "a faire writer, a florissher and maker of capitall letters," 9 Apr. 1489 (cf. *Manuscripts of Westminster Abbey*, p. 12).
His last payment from the manors was in 1487–8.

Maynell, William.
Prima Missa 1476–7 (Infirmarer; New Work; Almoner; Sacrist; St Mary's Chapel).
Gave to the Refectory a ciphus murrenus weighing 5½ oz. (*Mun.* 19583).
Defunctus 1482–3 (Q. Alianore, full share, Richard II, ¾ share; so probably 1483; Henry V, ¼ share, 1483–4).

Eton, Nicholas.
Prima Missa 1476–7 (Infirmarer; New Work; Sacrist; St Mary's Chapel).
Defunctus 1481–2 (Infirmarer; Q. Alianore; Richard II; Henry V).

Flete, Flett, Thomas.
Prima Missa 1471–2 (Infirmarer; Chamberlain; New Work; Sacrist; Cellarer; Monk-Bailiff; St Mary's Chapel).
Ad skillam 1483–4 (Infirmarer; Almoner; Sacrist; Warden of the Churches).
Quartus Prior 1484 (*Mun.* 33289, f. 15).
Archidiaconus 1484–5 (*ibid.* f. 20).
Custos capelle b. Marie 1489–98 (and so at Fascet's election 9 Jul. 1498, *Mun.* 5459).
Coquinarius 16 Dec. 1491 (*Mun.* 6647)—28 Sep. 1493 (*Mun.* 33317). He gave the Kitchen "a grete panne of brasse newe and ii byrde spytts" (*Mun.* 6647).
For his help towards repairing the "Seyny bookes" c. 1492 cf. *Manuscripts of Westminster Abbey*, p. 10.
Was appointed by Abbot Fascet to be Prior of St Bartholomew, Sudbury, 29 Jul. 1499 (*Mun.* 20887); the appointment was ad terminum vite, and its purpose was ut tuis strenuis laboribus aliqualem requiem ex speciali gracia prouiderimus.

1472-3

F A S C E T, Fasset, Fassett, Facet, Facett, George.
[The first form is that used in the legal record of his election as Abbot; *Mun.* 5459. His motto was Geras te facete, *Mun.* 33601, f. 20.]
Prima Missa 1478–9 (Infirmarer; Sacrist; New Work; Almoner).
Thesaurarius et Ballivus 1486–92.
Custos ecclesiarum ?+ 1489–90 ?+ (*Mun.* 6647).
Custos maner^m Regine Alianore; Ricardi II et Anne; Henrici V 1486–92.
Prior ?+ 29 Sep. 1491—9 July 1498.
Ad skillam, Prior, 1490–1 (Infirmarer; Almoner; New Work; Sacrist).

11—2

Thesaurarius intrinsecus 1494–1500.

Custos Novi Operis 1497–1500.

G. F. "priour payeth for the byndyng of the ii (Seyny) bookes," c. 1492 (*Mun.* 9326; cf. *Manuscripts of Westminster Abbey*, p. 9).

The Custos feretri of 1520 had charge of "a small caskett of syluer and gylt with rosys redde and whyte of Dane G. F.'s gyffte" (*Mun.* 9485).

For his generosity towards the New Work cf. R. B. Rackham, *Nave of Westminster*, pp. 44–5, and the following sentence from the Novum Opus roll of 1497–8 : Que summa [viz. Estney's deficit of £599. 9s. 2d. = roughly, £7000 of our money] perdonatur ex mero motu domini nunc Abbatis pro anima pie memorie domini Johannis Estney nuper Abbatis predecessoris sui cui predicta debita pertinebant et sic hic predictus computans recessit nunc quietus.

Sacrista 1497–1500.

Abbas 9 Jul. 1498 (*Mun.* 5459). He at first pleaded that he was not equal to the task, but assented on 10 Jul.

Assigned the house in the Infirmary which was built by William Chertsey [q.v.] as a Dormitorium Infirmorum...pro infirmis fratribus causa egritudinis illuc venientibus et sanitate recepta in claustrum iterum redeuntibus, 2 Aug. 1499 (*Mun.* 6213).

Defunctus 1500. (Late in the summer. The Abbot's Receiver's roll 29 Sep. 1498—?29 Sep. 1500 [*Mun.* 24283] speaks of him as nuper Abbas. He may have been failing for some time, as *Mun.* 25321* appears to reproduce a power of attorney to John Islip, Prior, to act for him.)

Buried in the Chapel of St John Baptist.

Ely, Elye, Elie, Thomas.

Prima Missa 1478–9 (Infirmarer; New Work; Sacrist; Almoner).

Ad skillam 1484–5 (Infirmarer; Chamberlain; Almoner; Sacrist).

Quartus Prior 1484 (*Mun.* 33289, f. 19).

Gave iii^s ,iiii^d towards the repair of the "Seyny bookes" c. 1492 (cf. *Manuscripts of Westminster Abbey*, p. 10).

Tertius prior et vestibularius 1498 (so at Fascet's election 9 Jul., *Mun.* 5459).

Thesaurarius maner^m Regine Alianore 1499–1500.

Custos maner^m Ricardi II et Anne 1498–1500.

Custos feretri 1498–1501 (Sacrist; and so at Islip's election 27 Oct. 1500; *Mun.* 5444; cf. Widmore, p. 235).

Thesaurarius 1498–1500.

Ballivus et Custos ecclesiarum 1499 (*Mun.* 23051–2).

Defunctus 1503–4 (Infirmarer; early in the year. He was dead before the compotus of Q. Alianore 1502–3 was made up. So probably 1503).

Barker, Berker, Baker, Thomas.

Prima Missa 1478–9 (Infirmarer; New Work; Almoner; Sacrist).

Defunctus 1478–9 (Infirmarer; probably 1478).

1473-4

Newbery, Newebury, Nubery, Richard.

Prima Missa 1477–8 (Infirmarer; New Work; Chamberlain; Almoner; Sacrist; St Mary's Chapel).

Capellanus 1484–5 (*Mun.* 33289, f. 19).

Refectorarius 1487 (*Mun.* 19583)–1490.

Custos feretri 1492–8 (Sacrist; and so at Fascet's election 9 Jul. 1498; *Mun.* 5459).

Thesaurarius 1492–8.

Mun. 33291 is his account-book, apparently as Abbot's Treasurer, or general factotum, 1496–8.

Gave iiiˢ iiiiᵈ towards the repair of the "Seyny bookes" c. 1492 (cf. *Manuscripts of Westminster Abbey*, p. 10).

Custos manerᵐ Ricardi II et Anne 1492–8.

Thesaurarius manerᵐ Regine Alianore 1493–9.

Custos capelle b. Marie 1498–9.

Subelemosinarius 27 Oct. 1500 (at Islip's election; cf. Widmore, p. 235).

Celerarius 1501–6.

Defunctus 1506 (Q. Alianore, Richard II, full share; 1505–6); inter mortuos 1506–7 (Chamberlain).

Norton, John.

Prima Missa 1476–7 (Infirmarer; New Work; Sacrist; Almoner; St Mary's Chapel).

Ad skillam 29 Sep.—7 Dec. 1491 (Almoner); 1491–2 (Treasurer).

Gave iiˢ towards repairing the "Seyny bookes" c. 1492 (cf. *Manuscripts of Westminster Abbey*, p. 10).

Tertius Prior 27 Oct. 1500 (at Islip's election; cf. Widmore, p. 235).

Refectorarius 1501–3.

In regardo dato fratri J. N. causa debilitatis hac vice tantum iiijˢ iiijᵈ 1501–2 (Q. Alianore).

Defunctus 1502–3 (Q. Alianore; Henry V).

Preston, George [Gilbert (Richard II, 1473–4)].

Last mentioned in 1475–6 (deleted from Q. Alianore 1476–7).

Caston, Caxston, Richard.

Prima Missa 1478–9 (Infirmarer; New Work; Almoner; Sacrist).

Ad skillam 1487–8 (New Work; Almoner; Sacrist).

Gave iiˢ towards the repair of the "Seyny bookes" c. 1492 (cf. *Manuscripts of Westminster Abbey*, p. 10).

Quartus Prior 1498 (at Fascet's election, 9 Jul., *Mun.* 5459).

Custos manerᵐ Ricardi II et Anne 1501–2.

Thesaurarius manerᵐ Regine Alianore 1501–3.

Among the stuff in the hands of the Custos feretri 10 Nov. 1520 was "an awtere clothe of whyte damaske with flouris golde and the armys of saynte Edwarde in the myddys of the gyffte of Dan R. C." (*Mun.* 9485).

Magister noviciorum et vestibularius 1500 (at Islip's election 27 Oct.; *Mun.* 5444; cf. Widmore, p. 235).

Thesaurarius 1501–3.

Custos feretri 1501–4 (Sacrist).

Defunctus 1504 (custos feretri pro dimidio anno, 1503–4 Sacrist; Infirmarer; Q. Alianore; Richard II).

Lokyngton, William.

Prima Missa 18 Jan.—29 Sep. 1483 (Monk-Bailiff); 1482–3 (Infirmarer; New Work; Almoner; Cellarer; St Mary's Chapel).

Ad skillam 1492–3 (Chamberlain; St Mary's Chapel; Monk-Bailiff; Warden of the Churches); 1491–2 (Treasurer).

For his help towards the repair of the "Seyny bookes," c. 1492, cf. *Manuscripts of Westminster Abbey*, p. 10.

Defunctus 1499–1500 (deleted and marked with a †, Richard II).

Litlington, Letlyngton, Lytlyngton, Humfrey.

Prima Missa 1478–9 (Infirmarer; New Work; Almoner; Sacrist).

Ad skillam 1488–9 (Sacrist).

In 1501 and up to his death was assisting Prior Mane in his financial management (*Mun.* 33288, f. 20, 21).

Defunctus 17 Apr. 1502 (*Mun.* 33288, f. 21); 1501-2 (Infirmarer; Q. Alianore, Richard II, Henry V, full share).

1476-7

BLAKE, Roger.

Prima Missa 1481-2 (Infirmarer; Chamberlain; New Work; Sacrist).

Scolaris Oxon. ? + 1483—Jul. 1491 (Treasurer).

Solut' fratribus Ricardo (*sic*) Blake et H. Duffeld scolaribus Oxoñ pro reparacionibus mansionis eorundem scolarium in Oxon. lx^s 1487-8 (Treasurer).

Palm Sunday and Good Friday preacher 1488-91 (Sacrist).

Prior 1491. (Apparently for a few weeks only. R. Essex [q.v.] lived till 25 Jun. and the students, Blake included, were brought up for the election in July. G. Fascet was Prior by Mich^s.)

Ad skillam, Prior, 1490-1 (Infirmarer; New Work; Almoner; Sacrist).

Defunctus (as Prior) 1490-1 (Infirmarer; Q. Alianore, Richard II, $\frac{5}{6}$ share; Henry V, full share).

MANE, William.

Prima Missa 1481-2 (Infirmarer; Chamberlain; New Work; Sacrist; Cellarer).

Custos maner^m Ricardi II et Anne 1487-92.

Thesaurarius maner^m Regine Alianore 1488-93.

Thesaurarius 1488-92; Ballivus et Custos ecclesiarum 1492 (*Mun.* 23048).

Custos feretri 1488-92.

Elemosinarius 7 Dec. 1491—1501 (and so at Fascet's election 9 Jul. 1498 (*Mun.* 5459) and at Islip's election 27 Oct. 1500; cf. Widmore, p. 235).

Gave iii^s iiii^d towards repairing the "Seyny bookes" c. 1492 (cf. *Manuscripts of Westminster Abbey*, p. 10).

Prior 1501-28.

Ad skillam, Prior, 1500-1 (Chamberlain; New Work; Almoner; Sacrist; Treasurer; St Mary's Chapel).

Thesaurarius intrinsecus 1501-27; as such he paid to himself as Prior a pension of xl^s, 1501-2, and in 1518-9 paid to himself as Prior £17. 5s. 11½d., being the balance of the Domestic Treasurer's account, ex discrecione domini Abbatis et seniorum ad maiorem sustentacionem domini Prioris hoc anno.

Defunctus 4 Mai. 1528 (1527-8, Infirmarer; Q. Alianore; Richard II; Henry V,—full share of each. The date 4 May is derived from the back of the Treasurers' roll 1506-7, where it is written that Prior Mane died that day together with two conversi and thirteen familiares; no year is stated and only the Christian names of the others are given; *Mun.* 23003, dors.).

1479-80

Duffeld, Henry.

Scolaris Oxon. (£6. 13s. 4d.) 1483-93 (Treasurer).

Prima Missa 1485-6 (Infirmarer; Cellarer; St Mary's Chapel).

In regardo dato fratri H. D. predicanti in ecclesia dominica Passionis, x^s, 1490;...predicanti hoc anno tempore quadragesimali, iii^s iiii^d, 1491; 1492 (Sacrist).

Defunctus apud Oxon. 16 Feb. 1493 (*Mun.* 30457; Treasurer).

Mun. 30457 is a mutilated paper giving John Islip's receipts as Treasurer pro fratre H. D. post mortem dicti Henrici videlicet a xvi^o die Februarii anno regni regis H. vii^l viii^o usque. The figures are torn off, but the items include gifts due to him in respect of Richard II's and other anniversaries, and Item inueniebantur in Bursa dicti Henrici tempore mo[rtis].......

Beauford, Beford, Beuford, Bewford, Beweford, John.

Prima Missa 1483–4 (Infirmarer; Almoner; Sacrist; Warden of the Churches; Monk-Bailiff).

Defunctus 1484–5 (Infirmarer; Chamberlain; Q. Alianore, full share; Richard II, $\frac{4}{5}$ share; so probably 1485).

Mulsham, Mulsam, Thomas.

Prima Missa 1485–6 (Infirmarer; Cellarer; St Mary's Chapel).

Defunctus 1492 (Q. Alianore, Henry V, $\frac{5}{6}$ share, 1491–2; so probably in 1492); inter mortuos, 1492–3 (Chamberlain).

ISLIP, Islipp, Iselep, Iseleep, Iselepp, Iselipp, Iselyppe, Islepe, Isselippe, Isselyppe, Yslyp, Istlip, Istelyp, Isthlyp, John.

Born 10 Jun. 1464; entered religion on St Benedict's day in Lent, 21 Mar. 1480 (*Mun.* 33290, f. 1).

Prima Missa 1 Jan. 1486 (*ibid.*); 1485–6 (Infirmarer; Cellarer; St Mary's Chapel).

Item in pitanc̄ ffris J. I. existent̄ it̄m p xxxix dies carnm̄ et
xxvi dies piscm̄   xiiii^s iiii^d
           (Infirmarer 1480–1.)

In pitanc̄ ffris J. I. ex̄ ibm̄ p xxi dies carnm̄ v^s iii^d et xxiiii dies
piscm̄ iiii^s ix^s iii^d
           (Infirmarer 1482–3.)

In pitanc̄ ffris J. I. ex̄ it̄m p xiiii dies carnm̄ iii^s vi^d et x dies
piscm̄ xx^d v^s ii^d
           (Infirmarer 1483–4.)

...x dies...viii dies.   (Infirmarer 1483–4.)

Capellanus Abbatis [Estney] 1487–92, et subelemosinarius, ?—1492 (*Mun.* 33290, f. 1).

Thesaurarius; Ballivus; Custos ecclesiarum 12 Oct. 1492—28 Sep. 1499 (*Mun.* 23050; 33290; and so at Fascet's election 9 Jul. 1498; *Mun.* 5459).

Custos maner^m Regine Alianore; Ricardi II, 12 Oct. 1492–9; Henrici V 1492–8?+ (see also *Mun.* 33286).

For his journey through the manors Jul. 1493 see *Mun.* 33290, f. 5.

Celerarius 1496–9 ?+.

Receptor Abbatis [Estney] 23 Oct. 1496—5 Nov. 1497.

His expenses in the matter of the sepulture of Henry VI 10 Feb. &c. 1498 (*Mun.* 33290, f. 16).

Prior (after 9 Jul.) 1498—27 Oct. 1500.

Received delegation of Fascet's powers for the purpose of an investigation into the affairs of the Abbey and of the church of St Martin-le-Grand (*Mun.* 25321*; no date).

Ad skillam, Prior, 1497–8 (Infirmarer; New Work; Almoner; Cellarer; Sacrist; Treasurer; St Mary's Chapel; Monk-Bailiff; Warden of the Churches).

Abbas 27 Oct. 1500 (*Mun.* 5444; Widmore, pp. 234–44).

For the procession at his installation 25 Nov. see *Mun.* 5454.

The Abbot, the Prior, the Monk-Bailiff and all the Convent spent Christmas "with my seyd Lord Abbott at his manor of Neyte" (*Mun.* 33320, f. 8 b).

Custos Novi Operis 1500–32. (For his work on the west end of the church, &c. cf. Rackham, *Nave of Westminster Abbey*, pp. 45–50).

"The Kyngs grace [Henry VII] dyned at Cheynygate" Friday 11 Jun. 1501 (*Mun.* 33320, f. 35).

Sacrista 1500–32.

Custos maner^m Henrici VII, 1502–24 ? +.

Drew up statutes for the college of St Martin-le-Grand, then annexed and united to the Convent of Westminster c. 1502 (*Mun.* 13188). The copy of the royal order for the Abbey to take possession of St Martin's is dated 23 Jul. 1503 (*Mun.* 13193).

In a certificate of a proctorial visit ad limina, 1506, he is called Joannes de Pacientia, abbas exempti monasterii Beati Petri apostoli Westm. La necte [? Neyte] uulgariter nuncupati (*Mun.* 9462).

Received from Cardinal Wolsey official notice of a visitation of the Abbey to take place on 10 Jan. 1519, and replied that he and his Brethren, of whom he gave a list, would then present themselves in the Chapter House (*Mun.* 12789; 12790).

For notice of Wolsey's visitation 30 May 1525 and its acknowledgment by Islip see *Mun.* 12788.

Being present, as appears from a draft copy (*Mun.* 22950) of a notarial record, at a Chapter of the Prior and Convent of Greater Malvern, he read a protestation that his presence there in order to receive the professions of certain monks must not be taken to impair in any way the ancient arrangement by which the monks of that Priory must make their profession at Westminster before the Abbot, 1529.

Defunctus 12 Mai. 1532. [duodecimo die instantis mensis maii viam uniuerse carnis est ingressus, *Mun.* 5458.]

His death took place at his manor house of La Neyte on a Sunday. For a full description in English of the funeral ceremonies, cf. Widmore, pp. 206–10; J. Armitage Robinson, *The Benedictine Abbey of Westminster*, Ch. Quart. Rev. Apr. 1907, pp. 75–6.

The famous Islip Roll was the Brief in which his decease was to be announced to other monasteries (*ibid.*).

Mun. 6325 is a bill of "Parcells layde oute by me Taylor aboute my lordes byryall"; it deals with the materials for making up the "blake clothe for hangynge in the quere my lords chapell and other places" and clearly refers to Islip, though it does not name him.

Among the "ornaments delyvered by Mr North, threasorer of the King's Maties augmentacons,...from the late monastery of Westminster" were "ij riche aulter fruntts of cloth of golde powdred with...scutcheons of tharmes of Abbott Islyp, and tharmes of the place,...a coope of fyne cloth of golde with a riche orphras enbraudred with Islyppes and other imagry" (Exchequer MSS. $\frac{833}{32}$).

The Islip chapel or chantry, which he built, consisted of the "Jhesus Chapell beneath" and the "Jhesus Chapell above," the latter having "a payer of Organys with a corten of lynen cloth to cover them" (*ibid.*); cf. J. Armitage Robinson, *op. cit.* p. 75, and *Mun.* 33303, f. 3, which is John Fulwell's [q.v.] account for the painting and furnishing of this chapel and of the one made by Islip in the Abbot's mansion; Feb. 1530.

Barker, Barkar, Berker, Thomas.

First Mass 1487–8 (New Work; Almoner).

Defunctus 1495–6 (Infirmarer; Q. Alianore, $\frac{3}{4}$ share; Richard II, Henry V, full share; so probably 1496); inter mortuos 1496–7 (Chamberlain).

Brice, Bryce, Brise, John.

Prima Missa 1487–8 (New Work; Almoner; Sacrist).

Gave x^s towards the repair of the "Seyny bookes" c. 1492 (*Manuscripts of Westminster Abbey*, p. 10).

Ad skillam 1499–1500 (Infirmarer ; New Work ; Chamberlain ; Almoner ; Sacrist ; Treasurer ; Monk-Bailiff ; St Mary's Chapel).

Subelemosinarius 1498 (at Fascet's election, 9 Jul.; *Mun.* 5459).

Quartus Prior 1500 (at Islip's election, 27 Oct.; *Mun.* 5444).

Defunctus 1499–1500 (ill in the sick-room late in that year, Infirmarer ; marked with a †, and given a full dividend, Richard II, 1499–1500 ; inter mortuos, 1500–1, Chamberlain ; so probably 1500).

More, Moore, John.

Prima Missa 1486–7 (Infirmarer ; New Work ; Almoner ; Sacrist ; St Mary's Chapel).

Studens Oxon. 1490–2 (Treasurer). Along with R. Blake, H. Duffeld, and W. Borow, he received 12s. for their joint expenses in riding from Oxford in Feb. 1491, for the sermons ; 6s. 8d. for returning thither in May ; and 16s. 8d. for another visit to the convent in July for the election of the Prior (R. Blake), videlicet in eundo morando et redeundo (*Mun.* 19987).

...predicanti hoc anno in ecclesia tempore quadragesimali iii^s iiii^d 1491 (Sacrist).

There is no mention of him after the entry of his £10 scholarship in the Treasurers' roll 1491–2 ; he appears at the end of Q. Alianore and Richard II with full share 1490–1, as if deceased ; but he may have left the convent.

Borow, Borowe, Borrow, Burgh, Burghe, William.

Prima Missa 1485–6 (Infirmarer ; Cellarer ; St Mary's Chapel).

Scolaris Oxon. (£6. 13s. 4d.) 1486–96 (Treasurer). *Mun.* 23047 has : student' in collegio Glous' apud uniuersitatem Oxon.

...predicanti in ecclesia hoc anno tempore quadragesimali iii^s iiii^d 1491–3 (Sacrist ; the Treasurer added viii^s viii^d).

He, H. Duffeld, and J. Warde received 13s. 4d. for their expenses in coming from Oxford, Dec. 1492, and returning thither, Jan. 1493 ; in February he returned to the Convent circa mortem H. Duffeld [q.v.] going back to Oxford in May (Treasurer 1492–3).

Archidiaconus 9 Jul. 1498 (at Fascet's election, *Mun.* 5459) and 27 Oct. 1500 (at Islip's election, *Mun.* 5444).

He was the preacher at Fascet's election, cuius thema erat Constituamus nobis ducem [Num. 14. 4].

Thesaurarius 1500–4 ; Ballivus 1501–4.

Custos maner^m Regine Alianore ; Ricardi II et Anne ; 1501–4 ; Henrici V 1501–3 ? +.

Custos ecclesiarum 1501–3.

Last mentioned at the head of the Treasurers' roll of 1503–4, when his colleague was Robert Humfrey. As after this there was only one Treasurer, it appears that Borow died during his year of office ; and this is supported by the roll of Q. Alianore of the same year, where Borow began the year and Humfrey was described as successiue occupans dictum officium.

1482-3

Ashley, Assheley, Asley, John.

Prima Missa 1485–6 (Infirmarer ; Cellarer ; St Mary's Chapel).

Precentor 1486 (Treasurer, *Mun.* 19980).

Ad skillam 1492–3 (Chamberlain ; New Work ; Almoner ; Sacrist ; Warden of the Churches ; Monk-Bailiff).

Gave iii^s iiii^d towards the repair of the "Seyny bookes" c. 1492 (*Manuscripts of Westminster Abbey*, p. 10).

Scrutator 1498 (at Fascet's election 9 Jul. ; *Mun.* 5459).

Granator 1500–1 (and so at Islip's election 27 Oct. 1500; *Mun.* 5444).

Priest of King Henry VII's foundation (£5 yearly) 1502 (*Mun.* 24236).

Coquinarius 1503–4 ? + (Treasurer).

Pension 1507–8 x^s (New Work), xx^s (Almoner), xx^s (Sacrist); 1509–10 xx^s (Cellarer).

Solut' J. A. nuper coquinario per manus Edwardi Assheley aurifabri pro denariis sibi debitis xxv^{li} 1506–7 (Treasurer).

Refectorarius 1515–6 (Treasurer).

Defunctus 1522–3 (Q. Alianore); inter mortuos 1523–4 (Chamberlain).

Adam, Adams, John.

Prima Missa 1487–8 (New Work; Sacrist).

Defunctus 1490–1 (Infirmarer, where his is the first sick case and the first among the obits of the year; so probably 1490; Q. Alianore, full share, Richard II, $\frac{2}{3}$ share, 1489–90; Henry V, $\frac{1}{2}$ share, 1490–1).

Redyng, William [John (Infirmarer 1486–7)].

Prima Missa 1486–7 (Infirmarer; New Work; Almoner; Sacrist; St Mary's Chapel).

Defunctus 1493–4 (Q. Alianore, $\frac{3}{4}$ share; Henry V, $\frac{5}{8}$ share); inter mortuos 1494–5 (Chamberlain).

Jones, Joones, Jonys, Joyns, Johns, Henry.

Prima Missa 1487–8 (New Work; Almoner; Sacrist).

Gave iii^s iiii^d towards the repair of the "Seyny bookes," c. 1492 (cf. *Manuscripts of Westminster Abbey*, p. 10).

Ad skillam 1499–1500 (Infirmarer; New Work; Chamberlain; Almoner; Sacrist; Treasurer; Monk-Bailiff; St Mary's Chapel).

Scrutator 27 Oct. 1500 (at Islip's election; *Mun.* 5444; cf. Widmore, p. 235).

Priest on King Henry VII's foundation, £5 yearly, 1502 (*Mun.* 24236).

Coquinarius 1506–7 (*Mun.* 33322 gives his accounts 22 Oct. 1506—28 Nov. 1507).

Elemosinarius 1514–31.

One of the four monks to whom Islip granted authority to challenge, examine, and receive clerks committed to "le Conuicthous" 1528 (*Mun.* 6113).

Supprior 1528 (at Thomas Jaye's election as Prior 6 May; *Mun.* 9501).

Defunctus 1531–2 (Infirmarer; Q. Alianore, Henry V, full share).

Wellys, Welles, Robert.

Not yet a priest in 1487–8 (Q. Alianore); ? in 1488–9.

Last mentioned 1488–9, when he was entered at end of Q. Alianore, with a half share.

Warde, John.

Prima Missa 1487–8 (New Work; Almoner; Sacrist).

Gave iii^s iiii^d towards the repair of the "Seyny bookes" c. 1492 (cf. *Manuscripts of Westminster Abbey*, p. 10).

Scolaris Oxon. (£6. 13s. 4d.) 1492–4 (Treasurer); *Mun.* 23047 describes him and his two fellows as studentes in Collegio Glous' apud uniuersitatem Oxon.

Mun. 30457 contains a mutilated statement of the expenditure made on his behalf by John Islip as Treasurer during the year 1493. The figures remain, amounting to £7. 12s. 4d., but the details of the items are mostly torn away. There is a payment of £2. 14s. 1d. mancipio Collegii Gloc' apud Oxoniam ix° die Januarii...ut pro Batillagio dicti Johannis, and there is what looks like a fee of five shillings pro lectura.

Precentor 1494–1510 (Treasurer; Warden of the Churches; and so at

Fascet's election 9 Jul. 1498, *Mun.* 5459, and at Islip's election 27 Oct. 1500 *Mun.* 5444).

For his debts to John Islip 1496–9 and the method of payment see *Mun.* 33290, f. 14.

Defunctus 1509–10 (Chamberlain; he was alive at Henry V's anniversary 31 Aug. 1510; *Mun.* 33297, f. 5 b, 6).

Walsh, Walssh, Simon.
Three periods in the sick-room during his first and only year.

Defunctus 1482–3 (Infirmarer; Q. Alianore, $\frac{1}{12}$ share; Richard II, Henry V, $\frac{1}{8}$ share).

1484-5

Grove, William [N. (Richard II)].
Prima Missa 1486–7 (Infirmarer; New Work; Almoner; Sacrist; St Mary's Chapel).

Last mentioned 1492–3 (Q. Alianore, $\frac{3}{4}$ share; deleted, Henry V, 1493–4).

1485-6

Champney, Champeney, Champnay, Thomas [William (Infirmarer 1489–90)].
= **Chapman, T.** (Q. Alianore 1485–6).

Prima Missa 1489–90 (Infirmarer; New Work; Almoner; Sacrist; St Mary's Chapel).

Ad skillam 1501–2 (Infirmarer; New Work; Cellarer; Sacrist; Treasurer; St Mary's Chapel).

Owner of MS. of "Innocent de Contemptu Mundi," &c., now in British Museum (Royal D. xxi; cf. *Manuscripts of Westminster Abbey*, p. 24).

Defunctus 1501–2 (Infirmarer; Q. Alianore, Richard II, Henry V, full share; so probably 1502).

Nevill, Thomas.
Defunctus 1491 (1490–1, Infirmarer, where his obit is after those of R. Essex and R. Blake, who certainly died in 1491).

Sall, Sale, Salle, Thomas.
Prima Missa 7 Dec. 1491—29 Sep. 1492 (Almoner); 1491–2 (New Work; Sacrist; Treasurer).

Ad skillam 1503–4 (Infirmarer; New Work; Sacrist; Treasurer; St Mary's Chapel).

Refectorarius 1505–6.

Gave ii^s towards the repair of the "Seyny bookes," c. 1492 (cf. *Manuscripts of Westminster Abbey*, p. 10).

Defunctus 1522–3 (Q. Alianore; Richard II; Henry V).

Albon, Albone, John.
Prima Missa 7 Dec. 1491—29 Sep. 1492 (Almoner); 1491–2 (New Work; Sacrist; Treasurer).

Gave iii^s iiii^d towards the repair of the "Seyny bookes," c. 1492 (*Manuscripts of Westminster Abbey*, p. 10).

Defunctus 1501–2 (Infirmarer, who entered two long illnesses and put his last among the obits; Q. Alianore, Richard II, full share; so probably 1502).

Brown, Browne, Thomas.
Prima Missa 7 Dec. 1491—29 Sep. 1492 (Almoner); 1491–2 (New Work; Sacrist; Treasurer).

Gave iii^s iiii^d towards the repair of the "Seyny bookes," c. 1492 (cf. *Manuscripts of Westminster Abbey*, p. 10).

For J. Islip's account of his debts 21 Dec. 1496 see *Mun.* 33290, f. 13.

Supervisor pauperum Domini Regis (Henry VII) 1503.

Infirmarius 1505–6 ? +.

Mun. 33293 is his note-book (38 ff.) of his expenditure as Abbot's Treasurer or general factotum in officio sacristie et noui operis 1505–9.

Camerarius 1507–8 ? +.

"Southamoner" (subelemosinarius) ?—1509 (*Mun.* 6597); cf. p. 177.

Custos maner^m Regine Alianore [deputatus et assignatus vice fratris Roberti Humfrey defuncti nuper custodis] 1508–13.

Celerarius 1509–13 (cf. *Mun.* 18921).

Thesaurarius et Ballivus 1509–13.

Custos maner^m Ricardi II et Anne 1508–13; Henrici V 1508–10 ? +.

Custos ecclesiarum 1509–13.

Custos capelle b. Marie 1511–2 (*Mun.* 31823).

Defunctus 1513–4 (Q. Alianore, Richard II, Henry V, full share, with mention of his death at head of the roll); inter mortuos 1513–4 (Chamberlain).

Buried beside R. Humfrey at the entrance to the North Ambulatory, the stone having once borne the inscription recorded in Camden, *Reges, &c.*

The records of the Guild of the Assumption in St Margaret's parish for Henry VII 20–23 have several entries "for the obite of Maister Browns moder monk xx^d"; so that he must himself have been a member of the guild.

Humfrey, Humffrey, Umfray, Umfrey, Robert.

Prima Missa 7 Dec. 1491—29 Sep. 1492 (Almoner); 1491–2 (New Work; Sacrist; Treasurer).

Gave iii^s iiii^d towards the repair of the "Seyny bookes" c. 1492 (cf. *Manuscripts of Westminster Abbey*, p. 10).

Granator 1493–8 ? + (and so at Fascet's election, 9 Jul. 1498, *Mun.* 5459).

Custos capelle b. Marie 1499–1501 (at Islip's election 27 Oct. 1500).

Priest on King Henry VII's foundation (£5 yearly) 1502 (*Mun.* 24236).

Elemosinarius ? + 1502–5 ? +.

Thesaurarius et custos maner^m Regine Alianore 1503–8.

Custos maner^m Ricardi II et Anne 1503–9; Henrici V, ? + 1504–9.

Thesaurarius 1503–8 ? +; Ballivus 1504–8 ? +.

Custos ecclesiarum 1504–8 ? +.

Celerarius ? + 1507–8 ? +.

Defunctus 13 Feb. 1509 (Camden, *Reges*).

Buried beside the place afterwards occupied by Thomas Brown at the entrance to the North Ambulatory. The first line of the inscription Robertus Monachus iacet hic Humfrey vocitatus was read by Camden to imply that his name was Humfrey Roberts, and the mistake has been repeated by Camden's imitators.

Prior Jaye's copy of Distinctiones Mauricii (Bodleian MS. 46) came to him ex dono eiusdem confratris egregii uiri d. R. H. cuius anime, &c. (cf. *Manuscripts of Westminster Abbey*, p. 24).

Hill, John.

Defunctus 1486–7 (Infirmarer; Q. Alianore; Henry V, ⅙ share; Richard II, ⅙ share; so probably before Christmas 1486).

Grene, William.

Prima Missa 7 Dec. 1491—29 Sep. 1492 (Almoner); 1491–2 (New Work; Sacrist; Treasurer).

Gave ii^s towards the repair of the "Seyny bookes," c. 1492 (cf. *Manuscripts of Westminster Abbey*, p. 10).

Ad skillam 1503–4 (Infirmarer; New Work; Sacrist; Treasurer; St Mary's Chapel).

Custos feretri 1513–20 (Sacrist). *Mun.* 9485 is an indenture of the relics delivered by him on 10 Nov. 1520 to Henry Winchester [q.v.].

His own gift to the Shrine was "a lytle oche [= ouche; cf. Exodus 39. 6] of syluer lyke a rose garnisshyd with peryll and stones" (*Mun.* 9485).

Pension vi⁸ viii^d (Chamberlain); vi⁸ viii^d (Domestic Treasurer); iii⁸ iiii^d (Richard II) 1526–7; x⁸ (St Mary's Chapel) 1527–8.

An elector of Thomas Jaye to the Priorship 6 May 1528 (*Mun.* 9501).

Defunctus 1530 (St Mary's Chapel pension paid to Lady Day); 1529–30 (Infirmarer; Q. Alianore; Henry V, full share).

1487-8

Chamber, Chambre, Christopher.
Prima Missa 1491–2 (Treasurer).

Gave ii⁸ towards the repair of the "Seyny bookes," c. 1492 (cf. *Manuscripts of Westminster Abbey*, p. 10).

Ad skillam 1500–1 (Chamberlain; New Work; Almoner; Sacrist; Treasurer; St Mary's Chapel).

Defunctus 1503–4 (Infirmarer; Q. Alianore, Richard II, full share. Inter mortuos 1504–5, Chamberlain; Henry V, full share. So probably 1504).

Davers, Robert.
Prima Missa 29 Sep.—7 Dec. 1491 (Almoner); 1491–2 (Treasurer).

Ad skillam 1492–3 (Almoner; St Mary's Chapel; Monk-Bailiff; Warden of the Churches).

Gave ii⁸ towards the repair of the "Seyny bookes" c. 1492 (cf. *Manuscripts of Westminster Abbey*, p. 10).

Succentor 27 Oct. 1500 (at Islip's election; cf. Widmore, p. 235).

Elemosinarius ? + 1507–8 ? +; 1532–3.

Precentor 1510–24 (Treasurer; Warden of the Churches).

Infirmarius 1525–33.

Supervisor pauperum regis Henrici VII (xl⁸)[1] 1515–7 ? +; 1523–4; 1532–3.

An elector of Thomas Jaye to the Priorship 6 May 1528 (*Mun.* 9501). He was one of the three nominated to the Abbot by the Convent.

Defunctus 1532–3 (Q. Alianore, Richard II, full share); inter mortuos 1533–4 (Chamberlain).

Hertford, R.
Defunctus 1491–2 (Q. Alianore, $\frac{5}{12}$ share; Richard II, $\frac{1}{3}$ share; Henry V, $\frac{1}{6}$ share); inter mortuos 1492–3 (Chamberlain).

James, Jamys, Martin.
[In *Mun.* 33290, f. 15, J. Islip calls him Jacobus Marten; on f. 15 b as above; and so he appears in the lists.]

Prima Missa 7 Dec. 1491—29 Sep. 1492 (Almoner); 1491–2 (New Work; Treasurer; Sacrist).

Gave iii⁸ iiii^d towards the repair of the "Seyny bookes" c. 1492 (cf. *Manuscripts of Westminster Abbey*, p. 10).

For his debts to J. Islip 1493–7 see *Mun.* 33290 f. 15.

Succentor 1498 (and so at Fascet's election 9 Jul. *Mun.* 5459).

Granator 1502–3 ? +.

Custos feretri Mar.—Sep. 1504 (Sacrist).

Defunctus 1504–5 (Infirmarer; Chamberlain; Q. Alianore, Richard II, Henry V, full share).

---

[1] When the Abbot took oath to observe the directions of Henry VII's bequest, he promised to "Depute and Ordeigne a *sad* and *discrete Monke*...to have Rewle and Governance of the said xiii Pore Men," and to pay him 40s. yearly (Rymer, *Foed.* xiv, 461).

Barnewell, Bernwell, John.
Prima Missa 1489–90 (Infirmarer; New Work; Almoner; Sacrist; St Mary's Chapel).
Defunctus 1490–1 (Q. Alianore, full share; Richard II, $\frac{2}{3}$ share; so probably 1491); inter mortuos 1492–3 (Chamberlain).

1491–2

Redmayne, Redemayne, Redmane, Redeman, John.
Prima Missa 1492–3 (Chamberlain; New Work; Almoner; Sacrist; St Mary's Chapel; Monk-Bailiff; Warden of the Churches).
Gave ii^s towards the repair of the "Seyny bookes," c. 1492 (cf. *Manuscripts of Westminster Abbey*, p. 10).
? Prior of Totnes 1499 (cf. Dugdale, *Monast.* iv, 629). Received his year's outfit from the Chamberlain 1499–1500. No further mention.

Worsley, Worseley, Wursley, Ralph.
Prima Missa 1492–3 (Chamberlain; New Work; Almoner; Sacrist; St Mary's Chapel; Monk-Bailiff; Warden of the Churches).
Gave ii^s towards the repair of the "Seyny bookes," c. 1492 (cf. *Manuscripts of Westminster Abbey*, p. 10).
Ad skillam 1503–4 (Infirmarer; New Work; Sacrist; St Mary's Chapel).
Defunctus 1510 (before Michaelmas; was alive at Henry V's anniversary 31 Aug.; *Mun.* 33297, f. 6).

Romney, Rumney, Rumpney, Rumpnay, Ralph.
Prima Missa 1492–3 (Chamberlain; New Work; Almoner; Sacrist; St Mary's Chapel; Monk-Bailiff; Warden of the Churches).
Gave ii^s towards the repair of the "Seyny bookes" c. 1492 (cf. *Manuscripts of Westminster Abbey*, p. 10).
Ad skillam 1503–4 (Infirmarer; New Work; Sacrist; St Mary's Chapel).
Defunctus 1507–8 (Chamberlain; Q. Alianore, Richard II, Henry V, full share; so probably 1508).

Southwell, Sowthwell, Sothwell, Suthwell, William.
Prima Missa 1492–3 (Chamberlain; New Work; Almoner; Sacrist; St Mary's Chapel; Monk-Bailiff; Warden of the Churches).
Gave ii^s towards the repair of the "Seyny bookes" c. 1492 (cf. *Manuscripts of Westminster Abbey*, p. 10).
Scolaris studens Oxon. (£6. 13s. 4d.) 1497–1504 (Treasurer); B.D. 24 Feb. 1506 (Foster, *Al. Oxon.*).
Ad skillam 1505–6 (Infirmarer; Chamberlain; New Work; Cellarer; Sacrist; Monk-Bailiff; St Mary's Chapel).
Coquinarius 23 Dec. 1507—13 Oct. 1509 (*Mun.* 33323 is his ledger, 71 ff.).
Elemosinarius 1511–4.
Prior de Hurley ? 1513 (he disappeared from the lists of the manors in 1513–4 and ceased to be Almoner)–1536 (when the Priory was dissolved).

1493–4

Fenne, William.
Scolaris studens Oxon. (£6. 13s. 4d.) 1497–1504 ? + (Treasurer). Studens Oxon. et Cantebrig. 1499–1501 (*ibid*).
Prima Missa 1498–9 (Infirmarer; Almoner; Cellarer; Treasurer; St Mary's Chapel; Monk-Bailiff; cf. *Mun.* 33286, f. 84).

Custos maner^m Regine Alianore; Ricardi II et Anne; 1504–6; Henrici V; 1504–5.

Elemosinarius 1510–1.

Granator 1511–2.

Defunctus 1512–3 (Infirmarer, who did not enter him as a patient that year; Q. Alianore, Richard II, full share; so probably 1513); inter mortuos 1513–4 (Chamberlain).

Cornehill, Cornehyll, Vincent [entered in Henry V 1493–4 as "J. Vincent"].

Defunctus 1494–5 (was in the sick-room for eight days on a fish diet early in this year—Infirmarer; Chamberlain; Q. Alianore, $\frac{1}{2}$ share; Henry V, $\frac{1}{3}$ share; Richard II, $\frac{2}{3}$ share).

Alen, Aleyn, Alyn, John.

Prima Missa 1497–8 (Infirmarer; New Work; Almoner; Cellarer; Sacrist; Treasurer; St Mary's Chapel; Monk-Bailiff; Warden of the Churches).

Defunctus 1499–1500 (Q. Alianore, $\frac{3}{4}$ share; Richard II, full share; inter mortuos, Chamberlain).

Gardener, Gardyner, Thomas.

Scolaris studens Oxon. (£6. 13s. 4d.) 1497–9 ; studens Oxon. et Cantebrig. 1499–(Christmas) 1500 (Treasurer).

Prima Missa 1500–1 (Chamberlain; New Work; Almoner; Sacrist; Treasurer; St Mary's Chapel).

Was receiving and making payments for Prior Mane Jul. 1502 (*Mun.* 33288, f. 21 b).

His name occurs in the Flores Historiarum MS. (Chetham Library, Manchester); cf. *Manuscripts of Westminster Abbey*, p. 25.

In the list presented by Abbot Islip to Cardinal Wolsey 31 Dec. 1518 his name appeared much lower down, between George Abyndon (1502–3) and Nicholas Lindesey (1503–4); *Mun.* 12790.

His name dropped out of our manorial lists after 1505–6, as on 20 May 1507 he was appointed Prior of Blythe by the Crown acting through the Duchy of Lancaster. He resigned this office before 16 Jul. 1511, returned to Westminster and was given a $\frac{2}{3}$ share from the Manors 1511–12 (Dugdale, *Monast.* IV, 621).

Ad skillam 1520–1 (New Work; Almoner; Cellarer; Sacrist; St Mary's Chapel; Monk-Bailiff; Warden of the Churches).

Coquinarius 1521–2 ? + (*Mun.* 33330).

Camerarius 1528–9 [nuper camerarius 24 Jun. 1530; *Mun.* 18821].

He received a double share of outfit in 1528–9, being himself Chamberlain; but was not afterwards mentioned, except as above.

Breynt, Brent, Brente, William.

For J. Islip's expenses in fitting him out as a novice, 12 Nov. 1493, see *Mun.* 33290 f. 18.

Prima Missa 1498–9 (Infirmarer; New Work; Cellarer; Sacrist; Treasurer; Monk-Bailiff; cf. *Mun.* 33286 f. 84).

Scolaris studens Oxon. (£6. 13s. 4d.) 1501–8 ? + (Treasurer); B.D. 1507 (Foster, *Al. Oxon.*).

Pro reparacione domus W. B. [and two other] studentium hoc anno Oxon. vii^s viii^d 1502–3 (Treasurer). In 1506–7 Breynt and the others came to the Convent in May for the visitation and Breynt came again alone in September.

Defunctus 1507–8 (Chamberlain; Q. Alianore, Richard II, Henry V, full share; so probably 1508).

Stanley, Staynle, Robert.
Prima Missa 1497–8 (Infirmarer; New Work; Almoner; Cellarer; Sacrist; Monk-Bailiff; Warden of the Churches; Treasurer; St Mary's Chapel).
Ad skillam 1505–6 (Chamberlain; New Work; Cellarer; Sacrist; Monk-Bailiff; St Mary's Chapel).
Defunctus 1507–8 (Chamberlain; Q. Alianore, Richard II, full share; so probably 1508).

Elfrede, Elfred, Elfride, Elfryde, Thomas.
Born at Langton [Launton], Oxon. (Hennessey, *Repertorium*, clxxii).
Took part in Fascet's election 9 Jul. 1498 (*Mun.* 5459).
Prima Missa 1498–9 (Infirmarer; New Work; Sacrist; Treasurer; Monk-Bailiff [*Mun.* 33286 f. 84]; Cellarer; Almoner; St Mary's Chapel).
Took part in Islip's election 27 Oct. 1500 (*Mun.* 5444).
Ad skillam 1506–7 (Chamberlain; Sacrist; Treasurer; Monk-Bailiff; St Mary's Chapel).
Refectorarius 1506–9. As such he received into the Refectory the body of the Lady Margaret, Countess of Richmond, who died at Cheynygates, the Abbot's mansion, 29 Jun. 1509. The body lay in the Refectory from 3 to 9 Jul., when it was removed to the Abbey church (*Mun.* 19606).
Coquinarius 1509–10 (Treasurer).
Signed the deed of Surrender 16 Jan. 1540.
Installed as ninth Prebendary of the Abbey 17 Dec. 1540. "To have [yearly] xxviii^{li} v^s" (*Mun.* 6478, f. 2).
"Mr Elfride to be vice-deane," 15 Dec. 1545 (Acts of Dean and Chapter, f. 28 a). Last attendance at Chapter 20 Mar. 1546 (*ibid.* f. 30 a). His will was dated 8 Jun. and proved 12 Nov. 1546; he desired to be buried against the south door in what was "sometyme the processione way" (Consist. Ct Reg. "Thirlby," f. 96 b).

Westminster, Westmyster, William.
Prima Missa 1498–9 (Infirmarer; New Work; Sacrist; Cellarer; Almoner; Monk-Bailiff; Treasurer; St Mary's Chapel).
Ad skillam 1507–8 (Chamberlain; New Work; Almoner; Cellarer; Sacrist; Treasurer; Monk-Bailiff).
Custos feretri 1508–13 (Sacrist).
Camerarius 1509–28.
Custos capelle b. Marie 1528–31.
An elector of Thomas Jaye to the Priorship 6 May 1528 (*Mun.* 9501).
Defunctus 1532–3 (Infirmarer; Q. Alianore; Richard II; Henry V; Chamberlain).

1494–5

London, Robert [William (Almoner; Sacrist; 1497–8)].
Prima Missa 1497–8 (Infirmarer; New Work; Almoner; Cellarer; Sacrist; Treasurer; St Mary's Chapel; Monk-Bailiff; Warden of the Churches).
Defunctus 1503–4 (Infirmarer; Q. Alianore, Richard II, full share; so probably 1504); inter mortuos 1504–5 (Chamberlain).

Benwell, Benewell, Thomas.
The junior of the chapter which elected Fascet as Abbot, 9 Jul. 1498, by which time he must have been a priest, though he only received a $\frac{5}{6}$ share, Q. Alianore, and a $\frac{2}{3}$ share, Richard II, for that year.
Defunctus 1499–1500 (Infirmarer; Q. Alianore, $\frac{1}{2}$ share; Richard II, $\frac{2}{3}$ share; Chamberlain; so probably 1500).

1498-9

Barton, Thomas.

Studens Oxon. (Henry VII; £10), 1502-6 ? +.

Prima Missa 1505-6 (Infirmarer; Chamberlain; New Work; Cellarer; Sacrist).

Studens Oxon. (Easter) 1515-22 ? + (Treasurer; *Mun.* 15212); B.D. 1512; D.D. 1516 (Foster, *Al. Oxon.*).

In diuersis reparacionibus hoc anno factis super domum studentium Oxon. ut in quibusdam caminis edificatis et tegulis renouatis ceteribusque defectibus in dicta domo reparatis, cˢ 1517-8 (Treasurer).

A note in his handwriting (*Mun.* 15212) shows how he and his fellows kept the Feast of St Edward :—Thys byll testyfythe yᵗ we v scolars [the other four were presumably D. Dalianns, A. Dunston, J. Laurence and R. Benet] wᵗʰ other v wᵗʰ us of yᵉ bretheren of Glossetʳ colege hathe expendyd in yᵉ obseruance of holy Saint Edwards our patronys seruisse kept at yslype in hys chappell & of yᵉ dyryge & masses kept there in yᵉ paryshe churche for yᵉ sowlys of yᵉ parents of oʳ most worshypfull spirituall father in God yᵉ abotte of Westm the summe of xˢ the yere of oʳ lord a mccccxxii the xvᵗʰ day next after mykylmas day [14 Oct. 1522]. By me rudely wryten Dan Thomas Barton Monk of Westminster.

Prior of the students at Gloucester College 25 Oct. 1522 (*Mun.* 15703). Not mentioned after the manorial lists of 1521-2.

Knolle, Knolles, Knollys, John.

Prima Missa 1502-3 (New Work; Almoner; Cellarer; Treasurer).

Ad skillam 1509-10 (Chamberlain; New Work; Cellarer; Sacrist; Treasurer; Monk-Bailiff; St Mary's Chapel).

Pension iiiˢ iiiiᵈ (Richard II); viˢ viiiᵈ (Domestic Treasurer) 1526-7; xˢ 1527-8 (St Mary's Chapel).

Defunctus 1529-30 (Infirmarer; his St Mary's Chapel pension was paid to Lady-Day 1530).

March, Marisshe, Marsh, Marsshe, Merssh, Mersshe, William.

Prima Missa 1501-2 (Infirmarer; New Work; Cellarer; Sacrist; Treasurer; St Mary's Chapel).

"Southamoner (= subelemosinarius) and Corderer" in succession to Thomas Brown 3 Nov. 1509 (*Mun.* 6597, which is an inventory of "the stuff belonging to the misericorde and aumerie").

Coquinarius 1511-6 (Treasurer).

Defunctus 1516-7 (Q. Alianore, Richard II, Henry V, full share): inter mortuos 1517-8 (Chamberlain).

Stowell, Thomas.

Prima Missa 1500-1 (Chamberlain; New Work; Almoner; Sacrist; Treasurer; St Mary's Chapel).

His receipts and payments for Prior Mane Jul. 1502 (*Mun.* 33288 f. 22).

Ad skillam 1509-10 (Chamberlain; Cellarer; Treasurer; Monk-Bailiff; St Mary's Chapel).

Last mentioned as receiving his outfit from the Chamberlain 1515-6.

Fyttz, Fyttez, Fittes, Fyte, Fitt, William.

Prima Missa 1500-1 (Chamberlain; New Work; Almoner; Sacrist; Treasurer; St Mary's Chapel).

Granator ? + 1506-7 ? +.

Studens Oxon. (£6. 13s. 4d.) ? + 1509—(Christmas) 1511 (Treasurer).

Subelemosinarius 1512–3 (*Mun.* 32306; 33301 ff. 1–3 b).

Defunctus 1512–3 (Q. Alianore; Richard II; Henry V); inter mortuos 1513–4 (Chamberlain).

1501-2

JAYE, Jay, Thomas.

A mutilated paper (*Mun.* 12890 v) records his profession and vow of obedience 17 —— 1501. His age was given, but the figure has gone.

Studens Oxon. (Henry VII; £10), 1502–6 ? +.

Prima Missa 1508–9 (New Work; Sacrist; St Mary's Chapel).

B.D. Oxon. 28 Mar. 1512 (Foster, *Al. Oxon.*).

Thesaurarius et Ballivus 1514–28.

Custos ecclesiarum 1514–28.

Custos maner^m Regine Alianore; Ricardi II et Anne; Henrici V; 1514–28.

Celerarius 1515–28.

Prior 6 Mai. 1528.

The notarial instrument of his election (*Mun.* 9501) shows that two days after 4 May 1528, when William Mane died, the Convent assembled in the Chapter House with a legal assessor and two notaries public. The Abbot nominated seven senior monks,—H. Jones, W. Grene, R. Davers, W. Westminster, Thomas Jaye, J. Langham, and R. Calowe,—who were to retire by themselves and choose three monks from among whom the Abbot might select one. In due course H. Jones, the Sub-Prior, reported that their choice had fallen on R. Davers, the Infirmarer, Thomas Jaye, the Treasurer, and Dionysius Dalyannce, the Precentor. Thereupon the Abbot, with the consent of the Convent and of R. Davers and D. Dalyannce, appointed Thomas Jaye to be Prior. They then left the Chapter House, reciting the accustomed canticles, psalms, and prayers, and Thomas Jaye was installed as Prior in the choir, on the left-hand side of it.

Ad skillam, Prior, 1528 (1527–8, Infirmarer; Chamberlain; New Work; Almoner; Cellarer; Sacrist; Treasurer; St Mary's Chapel).

Thesaurarius intrinsecus 1528–34 ? +.

Muniments, Book 3, a folio parchment of 94 pages, recording the Appropriations of the churches belonging to the Abbey, is described (p. 3) as ex sumptibus Fratris Thome Jay quondam Thesaurarii (*Manuscripts of Westminster Abbey*, p. 98).

He was alive at the anniversary of Abbot Colchester, Oct. 1534 (*Mun.* 5262 B) and at the anniversary of Henry Merston in April of the 26th of Henry VIII, but the day of this anniversary is not known; so this year may be 1534 or 1535 (*Mun.* 5255*). The Chamberlain of 1535–6 entered him as Prior and supplied his outfit.

Downes, Downys, Downe, Robert.

Professus 17 —— 1501, an. aet. XVII (*Mun.* 12890 v).

Prima Missa 1506–7 (Chamberlain; Sacrist; Treasurer; Monk-Bailiff; St Mary's Chapel).

His last payment from the manors was in 1522–3 (Q. Alianore); but the Chamberlain entered his outfit in his usual place up to 1524–5.

Marshall, Marchall, John.

Professus 17 —— 1501, an. aet. XXI (*Mun.* 12890 v).

Prima Missa 1502–3 (New Work; Almoner; Cellarer; Treasurer).

Ad skillam 1514–5 (Chamberlain; New Work; Almoner; Cellarer; Sacrist; Warden of the Churches).

His last payment from the manors was in 1520–1 (Q. Alianore); the Chamberlain entered him for an outfit, except panni nigri, in 1521–2; so he may have joined another Order.

Eles, Elis, Elyce, Elys, Elice, Elles, Ellys, William.

Professus 17 —— 1501, an. aet. xix (*Mun.* 12890 v).

Prima Missa 1504–5 (Infirmarer; New Work; Almoner; Cellarer; Sacrist; Monk-Bailiff).

Ad skillam 1516–7 (New Work; Almoner; Cellarer; Sacrist; St Mary's Chapel; Monk-Bailiff; Warden of the Churches).

Refectorarius 1530–4.

Signed the deed of Surrender 16 Jan. 1540.

Flete, Flet, Flett, Edward.

Studens Oxon. (£6. 13s. 4d.) 1506–8 ? + (Treasurer).

Prima Missa 1508–9 (New Work; Sacrist; St Mary's Chapel).

Was entered as if deceased in Q. Alianore 1511–2 with full payment, but by the Chamberlain of that year in his usual place. No further mention.

Callowe, Callow, Calowe, Calho, Karowe, Robert.

Prima Missa 1504–5 (Infirmarer; New Work; Almoner; Cellarer; Sacrist; Monk-Bailiff).

Ad skillam 1516–7 (Almoner ["William Karowe"]; Cellarer; St Mary's Chapel; Monk-Bailiff; Warden of the Churches).

Coquinarius 1516–20 (Treasurer ["William Callow" 1516–7; "Robert Calowe" 1517–8]; 1523–33 (and so at Prior Jaye's election 6 May 1528, *Mun.* 9501); cf. *Mun.* 32279.

Was alive at Abbot Colchester's anniversary Oct. 1534 (*Mun.* 5262 B).

Inter mortuos 1533–4 (Q. Alianore; Richard II); 1534–5 (Henry V); 1535–6 (Chamberlain).

Langham, John.

Prima Missa 1504–5 (Infirmarer; New Work; Almoner; Cellarer; Sacrist; Monk-Bailiff).

Custos feretri 1528 (at Prior Jaye's election 6 May; *Mun.* 9501).

Alive 1534–5 (Henry V; and Colchester's anniversary Oct. 1534); but not entered in the Chamberlain's list 1535–6.

Overton, Ouerton, William.

Prima Missa 1504–5 (Infirmarer; New Work; Almoner; Cellarer; Sacrist; Monk-Bailiff).

Ad skillam 1515–6 (New Work; Almoner; Cellarer; St Mary's Chapel; Monk-Bailiff; Warden of the Churches).

Coquinarius 1520–1 (*Mun.* 33329).

Subsacrista ? + 1523–31 ? +.

Refectorarius 1525–30.

Elemosinarius 1531–2.

Camerarius ? + 1531–6.

Infirmarius 1533–4.

Not mentioned after 1536 when he was in the sick-room on meat diet for three days (Infirmarer 1536–7).

Fulwell, John.

Appears at the end of Q. Alianore, Richard II and Henry V (inter mortuos) in 1501–2 with a full share in each case. No other appearance. Rackham suggested that John Brice (1479–80) = John Fulwell; but Brice appears at end of Richard II, 1499–1500 (inter mortuos); Chamberlain, 1500–1. Another John Fulwell entered the Convent in 1503–4. It seems therefore that the above John Fulwell died within his first year, having entered the Convent as a fully ordained priest.

Bothe, Boothe, Bouth, William.
Studens Oxon. (Henry VII; £10), 1502–6? +.
Defunctus 1507–8 (Chamberlain; Q. Alianore, ½ share; Richard II, ⅔ share; so probably 1508).

1502–3

Cornysshe, John [William (New Work; Sacrist; 1504–5)].
Prima Missa 1504–5 (Infirmarer; New Work; Almoner; Cellarer; Sacrist; Monk-Bailiff).
Ad skillam 1519–20 (Chamberlain; New Work; Cellarer; Sacrist; Monk-Bailiff; Warden of the Churches).
Supervisor pauperum Henrici VII (*Mun.* 32249).
Last mentioned in Henry V, 1534–5, and in *Mun.* 5255* (Apr. ? 1535); alive at Abbot Colchester's anniversary Oct. 1534 (*Mun.* 5262 B).

Bedford, Bedforde, Beddeford, John.
Prima Missa 1506–7 (Chamberlain; Sacrist; Treasurer; Monk-Bailiff; St Mary's Chapel).
Granator 1512–4.
Celerarius 1513–5.
"Misericorderer and Southamner" (= Keeper of the Misericorde and Sub-almoner) 1514 (*Mun.* 33301 f. 4 b).
Custos maner^m Regine Alianore; Ricardi II et Anne; Henrici V; 1513–4 (perhaps he merely drew up the compotus vice T. Brown, deceased).
Supervisor pauperum regis Henrici VII (xl^s) 1518–9 (*Mun.* 24248).
Defunctus 1519–20 (Q. Alianore; Richard II); inter mortuos 1520–1 (Chamberlain).
Mun. 31839 is an undated account for camphor and other drugs supplied to him amounting to 4s.

Abyndon, Abyngton, Abyngdon, Abendon, George.
Prima Missa 1506–7 (Chamberlain; Sacrist; Treasurer; Monk-Bailiff; St Mary's Chapel).
Defunctus 1521–2 (Q. Alianore; Richard II; Henry V).

1503–4

Campion, Campyon, John.
Prima Missa 1508–9 (New Work; Sacrist; St Mary's Chapel).
? Coquinarius 29 Sep. 1516—24 Jun. 1517 (*Mun.* 33327 is a Kitchener's ledger of 29 ff. which bears this date and his name, but does not call him Kitchener).
Defunctus 1515–6 (Q. Alianore; Henry V; full share); inter mortuos 1516–7 (Chamberlain).

Lindesey, Lyndesey, Lynsey, Lynzeye, Nicholas.
Prima Missa 1508–9 (New Work; Sacrist; St Mary's Chapel).
Studens Oxon. (£6. 13s. 4d.) ? + 1509–17 (Treasurer). Received £10 (Henry VII) on proceeding to the degree of Bachelor 1516–7; 5 Nov. 1516 (Foster, *Al. Oxon.*).
Defunctus 1523–4 (Infirmarer); inter mortuos 1522–3 (Q. Alianore; Richard II); 1523–4 (Henry V).

Ledgold, Lydegold, Lydgold, Thomas.

Prima Missa 1508–9 (New Work ; Sacrist ; St Mary's Chapel).
Ad skillam 1521–2 (New Work ; Sacrist ; St Mary's Chapel).
Alive at Abbot Colchester's anniversary Oct. 1534 (*Mun.* 5262 B).

Fulwell, John.

Prima Missa 1508–9 (New Work ; Sacrist ; St Mary's Chapel).
Granator 1514–25 ? + (probably to 1528).
Subelemosinarius ? + 14 Oct. 1520—29 Sep. 1521 ? + (*Mun.* 33301 ff. 6–9).
Deputatus domini Abbatis in officio custodis capelle b. Marie 1514–25 ; custos 1525–8. Pro factura corone virginis beate Marie nuper furate ac pro deauracione eiusdem iiii^{li} xvi^{s}...pro xii unc' argenti ad idem...xlviii^{s}, 1527–8 (St Mary's Chapel).
Thesaurarius et Ballivus 1528–35. (As such, he made payments for the decoration of the Jesus [= Islip] Chapel ; cf. J. Armitage Robinson, *Benedictine Abbey of Westminster*, Ch. Quart. Rev. Ap. 1907, p. 75.)
As Treasurer he held Courts at the different manors and *Mun.* 9544 shows his itinerary for this purpose in 1531. Leaving Westminster after the feast of St Peter and St Paul, he sat at Aldenham, Herts., 30 Jun. ; at Launton, Oxon., 3 Jul. ; at Turweston, Bucks., 4th ; at Knolle, Warwickshire, 6th ; at Oakham, Rutland, 10th ; at Offord Cluny, Hunts., 12th ; at Ashwell, Herts., 14th ; at Birdbrook, Essex, 17th ; at Fering, 18th ; at Kelvedon and at Moulsham, 19th ; and at Benfleet, 21st ; returning to Westminster, 22nd.
Custos ecclesiarum 1528–35.
Celerarius 1528–35.
Archidiaconus 18 Aug. 1528 (when he conducted an inquiry into the boundaries of the parish of St Botolph, Aldersgate ; *Mun.* 13530).
Custos maner^{m} Regine Alianore 1528–34 ; Ricardi II et Anne 1528–34 ; Henrici V, 1528–35.
Deputatus custos maner^{m} Henrici VII 1531–3 (*Mun.* 28043 A, B).
Coquinarius 1533 (Treasurer).
As Islip's chaplain he was much concerned with the furnishing of Henry VII's Chapel ; e.g. Benedetto da Rovezzano, the sculptor, received through him a payment, "on account," of £11. 5s., being one third of the price of Our Lady's Altar, 22 Aug. 1526 (*Mun.* 30626).
Together with Thos. Jaye and D. Dalianns he was chosen to make to Henry VIII the official notification of Islip's death (*Mun.* 5458).
Defunctus 1535–6 (Chamberlain ; he was alive 27 Aug. 1535, *Mun.* 8731).
In a letter from John Gostwyk to Cromwell, 26 Aug. 1535, it was stated that Richard Gresham [presumably the Lord Mayor and father of the founder of the Royal Exchange] desires Cromwell's favour for J. F., monk-bailly of Westminster, to be Prior of Worcester. Gresham will give £100 to Cromwell to buy a saddle and £20 to Gostwyk for his procurement in the matter (*Lett. and Pap. Foreign and Domestic*, IX, no. 184). Apparently F.'s death disposed of the project ; but the priory of Worcester did not fall vacant till early in 1536 (Dugdale, *Monast.* I. 581).

Algood, Algode, Algude, Allgood, Allgoode, William.

Prima Missa 1510–11 (Chamberlain ; New Work ; Almoner ; Sacrist ; Monk-Bailiff ; St Mary's Chapel).
Ad skillam 1524–5 (New Work ; Almoner ; Cellarer ; Sacrist ; Treasurer, on behalf of the Monk-Bailiff and the Warden of the Churches ; St Mary's Chapel).
Defunctus 1531–2 (Infirmarer ; Q. Alianore ; Henry V ; full share) ; inter mortuos 1532–3 (Chamberlain).

Evsam, Evsham, Evesham, Ipsam, Ipsham, Ypsam, William.

Prima Missa 1510–11 (Chamberlain; New Work; Almoner; Sacrist; Monk-Bailiff; St Mary's Chapel).

Last mention 1534–5 (Henry V, in his usual place in the list; alive Apr. ? 1535, *Mun.* 5255*).

Hendon, Nicholas.

Studens Oxon. (£6. 13s. 4d.) 1506—Apr. 1512 (Treasurer).

Prima Missa 1510–11 (Chamberlain; New Work; Almoner; Sacrist; Monk-Bailiff; St Mary's Chapel).

No mention after 1511–12, when he was entered as usual by the Chamberlain, but at the end of Q. Alianore without payment; at end of Richard II, full payment, 1510–1. Perhaps he left the Convent.

1506–7

Winchester, Wynchester, Henry.

Prima Missa 1510–11 (Chamberlain; New Work; Almoner; Sacrist; Monk-Bailiff; St Mary's Chapel).

Studens Oxon. (Henry VII; £10) ? + 1515–6. Received £10 (Henry VII) on proceeding to the degree of B.D., 1516–7; 2 Apr. 1517 (Foster, *Al. Oxon.*).

Custos feretri 1520–1 (*Mun.* 9485).

Defunctus 1520–1 (Q. Alianore; Richard II; Henry V); inter mortuos 1521–2 (Chamberlain).

Malvern, Malverne, John.

Prima Missa 1512–3 (Infirmarer; New Work; Sacrist; St Mary's Chapel).

Granator 1528–34.

Signed the deed of Surrender 16 Jan. 1540.

Installed as tenth Prebendary of the Abbey 17 Dec. 1540; £28. 5s. yearly (*Mun.* 6478, f. 2).

Died 1541 (Hennessey, *Repertorium*, p. 446).

Holand, Holonde, Hollond, William.

Defunctus 1509–10 (Q. Alianore; Richard II; he was alive at Henry V's anniversary 31 Aug. 1510; *Mun.* 33297 f. 6); inter mortuos 1510–11 (Chamberlain).

Godehappes, Godeapes, Godeapis, Godhappes, Goodhappes, Goodhappez, Goodehappys, Goodhappys, Goodhoppys, Gudhappys, Christopher.

Prima Missa 1510–1 (Chamberlain; Almoner; Sacrist; Monk-Bailiff; St Mary's Chapel).

Ad skillam 1527–8 (Infirmarer; Chamberlain; New Work; Almoner; Cellarer; Sacrist; Treasurer, for the Monk-Bailiff and the Warden of the Churches; St Mary's Chapel).

The Custos feretri of 1520 had charge of "a relyke of Saint Christopher syluer and parcell gylte like the son [sun] of Dan C. G. gyfte" (*Mun.* 9485).

Signed the deed of Surrender 16 Jan. 1540.

1509–10

Vertue, Vertu, William.

Studens Oxon. (£6. 13s. 4d.) 1512—Apr. 1515 (Treasurer).

Prima Missa 1514–5 (Chamberlain; New Work; Cellarer; Almoner; Warden of the Churches; probably Monk-Bailiff).

Ad skillam 1531–2 (Infirmarer; New Work; Sacrist; Cellarer; Almoner).

Granator 1534–5.

Custos capelle b. Marie 1534–6.

Refectorarius, deputatus Abbatis, 1535–6.

Master of the Novices 1535 (*Mun.* 32042 B).

For his expenses on clothing and boots for the novices see *Mun.* 32275–9.

Mun. 22904 is a paper account from his shoe-maker for goods supplied to "Mr Vertue," "Mr Veryte," "Mr Patyens" and "Mr Cryshostome." His own part of the account is as follows :—

Item a payre shoys solynge for your selfe

Item a payre of buskyns makynge for your selfe

Item a payre of shous for your larderere

sū—xviii^d.

He was entered as usual in the last Chamberlain's list 1535–6 and was alive Apr. ? 1535 (*Mun.* 5255*).

Stanley (*Memorials*, p. 342) says that George Vertue, the sculptor, being related to him, was buried near him in the West Cloister.

Thornton, Thorneton, George.

Prima Missa 1514–5 (Chamberlain ; New Work ; Almoner ; Cellarer ; Sacrist ; Warden of the Churches ; ? Monk-Bailiff).

Last appearance in the manor lists, 1522–3 ; received an outfit, except panni nigri, from Chamberlain 1524–5 ; no further mention.

Springwell, Spryngwell, George.

Prima Missa 1514–5 (Chamberlain ; New Work ; Sacrist ; Cellarer ; Almoner ; Warden of the Churches ; ? Monk-Bailiff).

Ad skillam 1529–30 (Infirmarer ; New Work ; Almoner ; Sacrist ; Treasurer ; St Mary's Chapel ; repeated in New Work 1530–1 ; Almoner 1532–3).

Was in the sick-room for 15 days on fish diet in 1536–7, the last year of which the Infirmarer-roll survives.

DALIANNS, Dalyans, Dalyannce, Dalyaunnce, Daliannse, Dolyans, Dolyon, Daliane, Dalyane, Dalions, Dionisius, or Dyonysse, or Dennis, or Denys.

[*Mun.* 30818 is signed "By me dane dyonysse Dalyons chauntt^r of Westm."]

Studens Oxon. (£6. 13s. 4d.) 1512–22 ? + (Treasurer) ; studens (£10) 1515 (Henry VII). B.D. 4 Jun. 1522 (Foster *Al. Oxon.*).

Prima Missa 1514–5 (Chamberlain ; New Work ; Almoner ; Cellarer ; Sacrist ; probably Monk-Bailiff).

Precentor ? + 1528 (*Mun.* 9501)—Oct. 1534 (*Mun.* 30818 ; 5262 B).

One of three monks nominated by the Convent to the Abbot for election to the Priorship, 6 May 1528 (*Mun.* 9501).

Elemosinarius 1533–6.

Prior c. 29 Sep. 1536 (Chamberlain).

Signed the deed of Surrender as Prior 16 Jan. 1540.

Installed as sixth Prebendary of the Abbey 17 Dec. 1540 ; " to abate xx^li of his penson and to be a Prebendary"; £28. 5s. yearly (*Mun.* 6478, f. 2).

Died Apr. 1543 ; his will being proved 12 Apr. (Consistory Court of Westminster "Thirlby" f. 23 b).

Rawlyns, Rawlins, William.

Prima Missa 1514–5 (Chamberlain ; New Work ; Almoner ; Cellarer ; Sacrist ; Warden of the Churches ; probably Monk-Bailiff).

Defunctus 1516–7 (Q. Alianore ;. Richard II ; Henry V) ; inter mortuos 1517–8 (Chamberlain).

Harlewes, Harlewis, Harlewys, Harlews, Harleus, Harleux, Harles, Herleus, Herlewes, Michael.

Prima Missa 1514–5 (Chamberlain; New Work; Almoner; Cellarer; Sacrist; Warden of the Churches; ?Monk-Bailiff).

Defunctus 1529–30 (Infirmarer; Q. Alianore, Henry V, full share).

1511–12

Dunston, Dunstane, Anthony [Thomas (Henry VII) 1515–6].

Studens Oxon. (Henry VII; £10), ?+ 1515–24?+.

First Mass 1516–7 (New Work; Almoner; Cellarer; St Mary's Chapel; Monk-Bailiff; Warden of the Churches; probably Sacrist).

Deleted from the manor lists 1512–3, and thereafter omitted, perhaps because he had already gone to Oxford; but was entered in his usual place in the Chamberlain's lists up to 1528–9.

B.D. Oxon. 1525; D.D. 29 Jul. 1538 at the same time as Humfrey Charite [q.v.] (Foster, *Al. Oxon.*).

Prior of Gloucester College, Oxford, 1526.

Abbot of Eynsham 1532; signed the deed of Surrender there 4 Dec. 1539.

Bishop of Llandaff as "Antony Kitchin or Dunstan"; consecrated 3 May 1545 in Westminster Abbey by Thomas Thirlby, Bishop of Westminster, and two others (cf. Stubbs, *Registrum*, pp. 103, 240).

Died 31 Oct. 1563.

Laurence, Lawrans, Lawrens, Lawrence, John.

Studens Oxon. (£6. 13s. 4d.) 1517–25 (Treasurer)[1].

Prima Missa 1520–1 (New Work; Almoner; Cellarer; Sacrist; St Mary's Chapel; Monk-Bailiff; Warden of the Churches).

Ad skillam 1528–9 (Infirmarer; Chamberlain; New Work; Almoner; Cellarer; Sacrist; Treasurer; St Mary's Chapel).

Refectorarius 1536–7.

Signed the deed of Surrender 16 Jan. 1540.

Benet, Benett, Bennett, Robert.

Prima Missa 1516–7 (New Work; Almoner; Cellarer; ?Sacrist; St Mary's Chapel; Monk-Bailiff; Warden of the Churches).

Studens Oxon. (Henry VII; £10), 1516–24?+.

B.D. 8 Jul. 1523; D.D. 22 Nov. 1527 (Foster, *Al. Oxon.*)[2].

Deputatus custos maner^m Henrici VII, 1531–2.

Archidiaconus 19 Oct. 1528 (*Mun.* 6113, which is a grant from Abbot Islip to him and Henry Jones, John Fulwell, and Thomas Gardener [q.v.] to challenge, examine and receive clerks convicted and imprisoned in the Abbot's prison, called "le Convicthous").

Last mention 1535–6 (Chamberlain).

1513–4

Forster, Foster, John.

Prima Missa 1515–6 (New Work; Almoner; Cellarer; St Mary's Chapel; Monk-Bailiff; Warden of the Churches).

Studens Oxon. (Henry VII; £10) 1532. Studens 1533–4; 1535–6 (Chamberlain).

---

[1] For the difficulty of separating his academic career from that of another of the same name, see Foster, *Al. Oxon.*

[2] Is he identical with Robert Benyt or Benett, who proceeded B.D. at Cambridge 1523–4; D.D. 1532–3 (Camb. *Grace Book* Γ pp. 213, 274)?

Signed the deed of Surrender 16 Jan. 1540.

The fourth on the list of those who were " Bretheren of Westmonasterie " under Abbot Feckenham was " Mr Foster " (*Mun.* 9327).

Gregory, William.

Prima Missa 1519–20 (Chamberlain; New Work; Cellarer; Sacrist; Monk-Bailiff; Warden of the Churches).

Ad skillam 1533–4 (Infirmarer; Chamberlain; New Work; Almoner; Cellarer; Treasurer; St Mary's Chapel).

"Presydent" at Abbot Colchester's anniversary, Oct. 1534 (*Mun.* 5262 B).

Alive Apr. ? 1535 (*Mun.* 9255*).

Byrte, Byrtt, Byrtte, Birt, Bryght, Bryt, Brytt, William.

Prima Missa 1519–20 (Chamberlain; New Work; Cellarer; Sacrist; Monk-Bailiff; Warden of the Churches).

Defunctus 1533 (Infirmarer 1532–3, who gives his obit, says he was ill for 14 weeks from Mich^s 1532).

Essex, Thomas.

Prima Missa 1515–6 (New Work; Almoner; Cellarer; St Mary's Chapel; Monk-Bailiff; Warden of the Churches).

Studens Oxon. (Henry VII; £10) ?+ 1523–4 ?+.

B.D. 27 May 1522 (Foster, *Al. Oxon.*).

Custos capelle b. Marie 1533–4.

Signed the deed of Surrender 16 Jan. 1540.

Installed as eighth Prebendary of the Abbey, 17 Dec. 1540; £28. 5s. yearly (*Mun.* 6478, f. 2).

Died before 3 Mar. 1543 (Acts of Dean and Chapter, f. 10 a).

Denys, Deuenysh, Devenysshe, Dyonyse, James.

Prima Missa 1520–1 (New Work; Almoner; Cellarer; Sacrist; St Mary's Chapel: Monk-Bailiff; Warden of the Churches).

Defunctus 1533 (Infirmarer 1532–3 enters his obit after W. Byrte's); inter mortuos 1532–3 (Chamberlain).

Albright, Albryght, Christopher.

Defunctus 1515–6 (Q. Alianore, Richard II, Henry V, full share); inter mortuos 1516–7 (Chamberlain).

1517-8

Charyte, Cheryte, Cherite, Cheritie, Humfrey.
= Perkins, Perkyns, Parkins, Humfrey.

Prima Missa 1523–4 (Infirmarer; New Work; Cellarer; Sacrist; Treasurer).

Studens Oxon. (£6. 13s. 4d.) 1525—Jun. 1530 (Treasurer); studens (£10) 1532–3 (Henry VII); studens 1533–4; 1535–6 (Chamberlain). B.D. 1 Jul. 1535; D.D. 29 Jul. 1538 (Foster, *Al. Oxon.*).

Deputatus domini Abbatis in officio Elemosinarii 1536–7.

Signed the deed of Surrender 16 Jan. 1540.

Installed as seventh Prebendary of the Abbey 17 Dec. 1540, holding the office till c. Mar. 1553; £28. 5s. yearly (*Mun.* 6478, f. 2).

" M^r dr. Perkyns to be ye tresorer for this yere to take ye money of ye receyuer and se ye laying of it up in the cheste therto apointed " 20 Jan. 1545 (Acts of Dean and Chapter, f. 22).

Had a brother, John Pekyns or Pekyngs, who was sixth Prebendary 3 May 1543—c. Apr. 1554 (*Mun.* 6608).

Admitted to benefice of St Margaret, New Fish Street, on nomination of Bishop Thirlby 31 Dec. 1548; deprived 1554; reinstated by the Bishop of London [Bonner], after Apr. 1556 (Newcourt, *Repertorium*, I, 406).

Vicar of Staines on nomination of Henry VIII, 20 Jul. 1540—(before) 6 Dec. 1550.

"It is decreede by Mr deane [Hugh Weston] and the chapiter that the greate orcharde latly belongyng to Mr docter Perkyns shalbe equally deuydyd betwene Mr doctor Cole Mr Pye and Mr Alphonsus [de Salinas]" 13 May 1554 (Acts, f. 88 b).

Involved in a suit for the restitution of the rectory of Islip 18 Aug. 1559 (*Mun.* 15185).

Installed as second Prebendary of the Abbey 21 May 1560 (cf. Hennessey, *Repertorium*, s.v.).

Subdecanus 24 Mar. 1561 (*Mun.* 13473); nuper subdecanus 1 Jun. 1565 (*Mun.* 33222). From Jul. 1576 onwards he could only witness the minutes of Chapter with "Mr dr Perkines marke †"; his last attendance was on 23 Mar. 1577 (Acts, f. 164 a).

Defunctus 16 Nov. 1577 (*Mun.* 6495).

Mannyngham, Manyngham, John.
Prima Missa 1520–1 (New Work; Cellarer; Sacrist; St Mary's Chapel; Monk-Bailiff; Warden of the Churches).

Defunctus 1527–8 (Infirmarer; Q. Alianore, Henry V, full share); inter mortuos 1528–9 (Chamberlain).

Lovewell, Lovwell, Lowell, Thomas [John (Infirmarer 1523–4)].
Prima Missa 1523–4 (Infirmarer; New Work; Cellarer; Sacrist; Treasurer).

Studens Oxon. (£6. 13s. 4d.) 1525–30 (Treasurer); (£10) 1532–3 (Henry VII). Studens 1533–4; 1535–6 (Chamberlain).

Signed the deed of Surrender 16 Jan. 1540.

The first of four of "the monkes there" who were retained among the "xii Petycanones to syng in the Quere" and "to have xˡⁱ" yearly (*Mun.* 6478, f. 3 b).

Martyn, Marten, Hugh.
Defunctus 1523–4 (Infirmarer; Henry V); 1522–3 (Q. Alianore; Richard II).

Brice, Bryce, Edmund [John (Infirmarer 1523–4)].
Prima Missa 1523–4 (Infirmarer; New Work; Cellarer; Sacrist; Treasurer).

Studens Oxon. (£6. 13s. 4d.) ? + 1530–1 (Treasurer).

Alive in Apr. ? 1535 (*Mun.* 5255*).

Philip, Phillip, Phelyp, Phelyppe, Phyllyp, Phyllype, Thomas.
Prima Missa 1523–4 (Infirmarer; New Work; Cellarer; Sacrist; Treasurer).

Alive in Apr. ? 1535 (*Mun.* 5255*).

1519-20

Austen, Awsten, Austyn, J.
Alive in Apr. ? 1535 (*Mun.* 5255*).

Whethamsted, Whethamstede, Whetehamsted, Wethampsted, John.
Prima Missa 1524–5 (New Work; Almoner; Cellarer; Sacrist; Treasurer, on behalf of the Monk-Bailiff and Warden of the Churches; St Mary's Chapel).

Studens Oxon. (£6. 13s. 4d.) Mar. 1527–33 (Treasurer). Supplicat for a degree Jun. 1533 (Foster, *Al. Oxon.*).

Signed the deed of Surrender 16 Jan. 1540.

Petty Canon (*Mun.* 6478, f. 3 b).

Godeluke, Goodluck, Goodlucke, Goodloke, Goodlook, Goodlooke, Goodluk, Gooluk, Gudluck, John.

Prima Missa 1523–4 (Infirmarer; New Work; Cellarer; Sacrist; Treasurer).

Studens Oxon. (£6. 13s. 4d.) 1531–3 (Treasurer).

Signed the deed of Surrender 16 Jan. 1540.

Among those who were "Bretheren of Westmonasterie" under Abbot Feckenham was "Mr Goodlook" (*Mun.* 9327).

1521-2

Randall, Randoll, Randolle, Rendoll, John.

His First Mass is not recorded, but he received a priest's share from the manors in and after 1523–4.

Subsacrista 1527–37 (*Mun.* 33302).

Was ill for 3 months 1533–4 (Infirmarer), but was still living 29 Aug. 1537 (*Mun.* 33302, f. 80 b).

1523-4

Hurley, Horley, Armell, or Armigill, or Armigell, or Armygill.

Prima Missa 1525–6 (Infirmarer; New Work; Almoner; Cellarer; Sacrist; St Mary's Chapel).

Signed the deed of Surrender 16 Jan. 1540.

Petty Canon (*Mun.* 6478, f. 3 b).

Henley, Richard.

Defunctus 1527–8 (Infirmarer; Q. Alianore; Henry V); inter mortuos 1528–9 (Chamberlain).

Jerame, Jheram, Jherom, Jerome, Jerom, Richard.

Prima Missa 1528–9 (Infirmarer; New Work; Chamberlain; Almoner; Cellarer; Sacrist; Treasurer; St Mary's Chapel).

Defunctus 1529–30 (Infirmarer; Q. Alianore; Henry V).

Ambrose, William.

Defunctus 1527–8 (Infirmarer; Q. Alianore; Henry V); inter mortuos 1528–9 (Chamberlain).

Grace, John.

Prima Missa 1528–9 (Infirmarer; Chamberlain; New Work; Almoner; Cellarer; Sacrist; Treasurer; St Mary's Chapel).

Mun. 31819 is the account of a bootmaker for goods supplied to him amounting to 14s. 8d. The goods consisted chiefly of items such as "a payer of shouys ffor yower shelfe ixd" and "a payer of shouys for mary goldeys sone vd."

Was ill for about 9 weeks towards the end of 1533–4 (Infirmarer), but was still alive Apr. ?1535 (*Mun.* 5255*).

Chamberlayne, Chamberlayn, Chamberleyn, Thomas.

Prima Missa 1528–9 (Infirmarer; Chamberlain; New Work; Almoner; Cellarer; Sacrist; Treasurer; St Mary's Chapel).

Last mention 1536–7 (Infirmarer).

Windesore, Wyndesor, Wyndsor, Wyndsore, Wyndesore, Wynsor, Wynsore, Richard [Robert (Infirmarer; Almoner; 1526–7)].
>Prima Missa 1526–7 (Infirmarer; New Work; Almoner; Cellarer; Sacrist).
>Defunctus 1529–30 (Infirmarer; Q. Alianore; Henry V).

Cheseman, Chesman, Cheysman, Robert.
>Prima Missa 1526–7 (Infirmarer; New Work; Almoner; Cellarer; Sacrist).
>Studens Oxon. 1531–3 (Treasurer).
>Studens Cantabrigie 1533–4 (Treasurer); Oct. 1534 (*Mun.* 5262 b).
>Last mention 1534–5 (Henry V).

1525–6

Felix, Felex, Felyx, Felyxe, John.
>Prima Missa 1528–9 (Chamberlain; New Work; Sacrist); 1529–30 (Infirmarer; Cellarer; Treasurer).
>Wrote an account of Abbot John Estney (Brit. Mus. Cotton MS. Claud. A. viii, f. 64 b), including an elegiac poem (printed by Widmore, p. 204 f.). The writer added (f. 65): Oro orate pro me Jhone Felix huius sancti cenobii Westm. monacho (cf. *Flete*, ed. J. Armitage Robinson, p. 31).
>Alive Mich^s 1535 (Henry V).

Faith, Fayth, Feith, Feyth, William.
> = Harvey, Hervy.
>Prima Missa 1528–9 (Infirmarer; Chamberlain; New Work; Almoner; Cellarer; Sacrist; Treasurer; St Mary's Chapel).
>Signed the deed of Surrender 16 Jan. 1540.
>Installed as eleventh Prebendary of the Abbey 17 Dec. 1540; £28. 5s. yearly (*Mun.* 6478, f. 2).
>Died before 1 Feb. 1544[5] (Widmore, p. 223).

Hope, Hoope, Hooppe, Hoppe, William.
>Prima Missa 1530–1 (Infirmarer; Almoner; Cellarer; Treasurer, for himself and Warden of the Churches; St Mary's Chapel).
>*Mun.* 32280 is a bootmaker's account for goods supplied to him amounting to 6s. It includes "Item a payer of shewe ffor yower ffather...x^d."
>Alive Apr. ? 1535 (*Mun.* 5255*).

1530–1

Penne, Panne, Pend, William.
>Prima Missa 1534–5 (Cellarer; St Mary's Chapel).
>Grant of pardon for all felonies committed by him and Anthony Pen yeoman of Westminster within the Abbey church or precincts, Jun. 1538 (Record Office, Grant 39).

Tamworth, Tameworth, Richard.
>Studens 1533–4 (Chamberlain).
>Studens Cantabrigie 1533–4 (Treasurer); Oct. 1534 (*Mun.* 5262 b).
>Alive Mich^s 1535 (Henry V).

Crome, Cromem, Crowham, Robert [Richard (Almoner 1532–3)].
>Prima Missa in Dominica 6 Oct. 1532 (*Mun.* 23025*, f. 8); 1531–2 (Treasurer; Cellarer; repeated in their next year's rolls); 1532–3 (Infirmarer; New Work; Almoner).

Signed the deed of Surrender 16 Jan. 1540.

Petty Canon; £28. 5s. yearly (*Mun.* 6478, f. 2).

Appointed by the Dean and Chapter to be "Sexten" [= Sacrist] 15 Dec. 1547 (Acts, f. 40 b); re-elected yearly up to and including 11 Nov. 1552 (*ibid.* f. 73 b).

Empson, Richard.

Prima Missa 1532–3 (Infirmarer; New Work; Cellarer).

Alive Mich[s] 1535 (Henry V).

Alen, Aleyn, Alyn, John.

Prima Missa Oct. 1532 (*Mun.* 23025*, f. 8 b); 1531–2 (Treasurer; Cellarer; repeated in their next year's rolls); 1532–3 (Infirmarer; New Work; Almoner).

Studens Cantabrigie 1533–4 (Treasurer); Oct. 1534 (*Mun.* 5262 B).

Alive Mich[s] 1535 (Henry V).

Darby, Derby, Robert [John (Treasurer 1531–2)].

Prima Missa 1531–2 (Treasurer).

Defunctus 1533 (Infirmarer 1532–3 enters his obit after that of J. Denys [q.v.]. Darby had several long illnesses in the course of 1532).

1531–2

Lyncolne, Robert.

Not mentioned in Richard II or Henry V rolls. The mention in Q. Alianore 1531–2 implies that he was already a priest.

Defunctus 1533 (Infirmarer).

1532–3

Boston, William.

= Benson, William.

[Perhaps because Boston was his birth-place and Benson was his family name, which he used as Dean.]

Was not a monk of this house and so was the first man to be made Abbot from outside since William Humez was appointed in 1214. Generally supposed, on the "finding" of Widmore (p. 126), to have been Abbot of Burton-on-Trent, "and therefore is called John erroneously, in the catalogue of the Abbots of that place" (*ibid.*). But Boston's account book (*Mun.* 33313) is concerned with properties belonging to the great monastery at Peterborough, which must thus be substituted for Burton as the place from which he was translated (cf. J. Armitage Robinson, *The Benedictine Abbey of Westminster*, Ch. Quart. Rev. Apr. 1907, p. 78).

Mun. 33313, f. 7, 8 contains a statement of his expenses "for my commensmentt of the Doctorshipp" at Cambridge 20 Henry VIII, 1528–9 (*Grace Bk* B. II, 149). The fees, &c. (£14. 0s. 7½d.) included:

Item ye same daye to y[e] vicechancellere for hys dwtye as that daye and y[e] Presento[ur] and to the Bedells — xiiii[s]

Item to y[e] Proctors for theire Bonetts — vi[s] viii[d]

Item to the uniuersytie huttches [? = chest] — vi[li] xiii[s] iiii[d]

Item paid on the daye in the tyme of disputacion to xviii doctors every doctor iiii[d] — vi[s]

Date of appointment as Abbot uncertain; took the oath to perform the duties of Henry VII's foundation in the Court of Chancery 12 May 1533 between 9 and 10 a.m. super sacrosancta Dei Evangelia (Rymer, *Foed.* xiv, 459).   *Mun.* 30635, f. 2 implies that he was in authority before Easter 1533. The fact that he rendered the accounts of the New Work as from Michaelmas 1532 is inconclusive.

Custos Novi Operis 1532–4.

Celerarius 1535–6.

Custos capelle b. Marie 1535–6.

Thesaurarius intrinsecus ? + 1536–7.

Agreed to two quite disadvantageous exchanges of land with Henry VIII, by which the Convent received Hurley Priory and certain lands in Berkshire, and parted with the London manors of Hyde, Neyte, &c. and other land at Covent Garden 3 Jul. 1536 (*Mun.* 2226).

Mun. 12787 is a confirmation by the King, dated 30 Jul. 1536, of orders already issued to Abbot Boston by Thomas Cromwell as vicar-general.   These are concerned with the granting by the Abbot of permission to the Brethren to be absent from the monastery ad honestam animi et corporis sui recreationem.   Noble and honourable women with their attendants de quibus nulla viget sinistra fama vel suspitio may be welcomed from time to time at the Abbot's table, but the privilege must not descend into a daily habit, lest the weaker brethren should be caused to stumble.   The Abbot and Convent were not bound to attend or to read a Divinity lecture on the great festivals or on the days of the royal anniversaries.

Arranged with John Whyt and John Saunders of Reading " for the new castyng of ii bells of the Rynge of the said monastery," the 3rd and the 5th, at a cost of £9. 10s., 3 Nov. 1539 (*Mun.* 25103).

Signed the deed of Surrender 16 Jan. 1540.

Installed as Dean 17 Dec. 1540.   *Mun.* 6478, f. 2, enters "The Deane there Wyllyam Boston late Abbot there to have [yearly] ccxxxii^li x^s."

Died Sep. 1549.

1533–4

Barnards, Barnard, Barnarde, Bernard, Robert.

His and the six following names appear in the 1533–4 roll of Richard II's manors at the foot of the list after the entry of R. Callow deceased, in a different script.   Each received iii^s iiii^d as against xx^s to each of the rest; whereas the duplicate of the same roll duly inserts the names in the usual place and is in the same hand throughout.

Prima Missa 1536–7 (Infirmarer).

Signed the deed of Surrender 16 Jan. 1540.

"The Kinges newe College at Westm." maintained twenty students, of whom four had been monks there.   R. B. was the first of these.   The yearly allowance was increased from £6. 13s. 4d. to £8. 6s. 8d. (*Mun.* 6478, f. 3).

Chrysostome, Crysostome, R.

Alive Apr. ? 1535 (*Mun.* 5255*).

Ambrose, John.

Prima Missa 1536–7 (Infirmarer).

Student under the new foundation; £8. 6s. 8d. (*Mun.* 6478, f. 3).

Patyence, J.

Alive Apr. ? 1535 (*Mun.* 5255*).

Veryty, Verytee, Verite, T.

Defunctus 1535–6 (Chamberlain).

Jerome, Jherome, R.
    Alive Apr. ? 1535 (*Mun.* 5255*).

Mercye, R.
    Alive Apr. ? 1535 (*Mun.* 5255*).

1535-6

Mylton, Melton, Milton, William.
    Granator 1536–7.
    Custos capelle b. Marie 1536–7.
    Signed the deed of Surrender 16 Jan. 1540

1536-7

Clerke, John.
    Infirmarius 1536–7.
    John Clarke, of Cambridge, Benedictine, was incorporated as D.D. 13 Jul.
    1538 (Foster, *Al. Oxon.*).
    Bishop Latimer recommended Clerke and Gortton [q.v.] to Cromwell as
    suitable men to be sent to the Priory of Coventry (Brit. Mus. Cotton MS.
    Cleop. E. IV, 139; Dugdale, *Monast.* III, 184).

Rolston, John.
    Sole mention in Infirmarer 1536–7, which records that he had two illnesses
    that year, one of them being of over nine weeks' duration.

Yslyp, John.
    Sole mention in Infirmarer 1536–7.

Underwood, Symon.
    Signed the deed of Surrender 16 Jan. 1540.
    Student under the new foundation; £8. 6s. 8d. (*Mun.* 6478, f. 3).

Lathbury, John.
    Signed the deed of Surrender 16 Jan. 1540.
    Student under the new foundation; £8. 6s. 8d. (*Mun.* 6478, f. 3).
    " Agreede...that ser John Lathbury shall have the advouson of the vicarage
    of Chatysley [Chaddesley, Worcs.] wyche ser John Smythe now hathe," 1 Feb.
    1550 (Acts of Dean and Chapter, f. 62 a).

Romayne, John.
    Sole mention in Infirmarer 1536–7.

Mekenes, Thomas.
    Sole mention in Infirmarer 1536–7.

1538-9

Gortton, Richard.
    Elemosinarius 1538–9.
    For Latimer's recommendation of him to Cromwell see Clerke, John,
    1536–7.
    B.A. 1518; B.D. 27 Feb. 1528; D.D. 29 Jul. 1538 (Foster, *Al. Oxon.*).
    Vicar of Staines on the nomination of Dean Benson 23 Mar. 1540.
    Died the same year (Hennessey, *Repertorium*, p. 403) and was succeeded
    by Humphrey Charite or Perkins [q.v.].

1540

Morton, Richard,
> Signed the deed of Surrender 16 Jan. 1540 (fourth, after Humphrey Charite).

Byrd, William.

Latham, William.

Huse, William.

Vernon, John.

Sole mention at the end of the signatures to the deed of Surrender 16 Jan. 1540.

Thacksted, Henry.
> Mentioned in *Mun.* 6478, f. 3, as " one of the monkes there " who became students under the new foundation ; £8. 6s. 8d.

Style, Henry.
> *Mun.* 38945 is an acquittance to George Burden, Receiver, for £6. 13s. 4d., " the fyrst payment dewe by obligacion " to H. S. late monk of Westm. 1 Nov. 1570.

THE ABBOTS, PRIORS, AND OBEDIENTIARIES OF THE CONVENT OF WESTMINSTER, 1049–1540.

ABBOTS

Domini Abbates

[For a list of the earlier Abbots up to Litlington and for valuable notes on their dates see J. Armitage Robinson, *Flete*, pp. 139 ff.]

1049–1071 (12 June)	Edwin
c. 1071–5	Geoffrey
1076–85 (19 June)	Vitalis
1085–1117 (6 Dec.)	Gilbert Crispin
1121 (Jan.)—?1136 (3 Sep.)	Herbert
?1137–57?	Gervase
?1158–73 (Apr. 11)	Laurence
1175 (July)—1190 (27 Sep.)	Walter
1191 (9 Oct.)—1200 (?4 May)	William Postard
1200 (30 Nov.)—1214 (23 Jan.)	Ralph de Arundel
1214 (4 May)—1222 (20 Apr.)	William Humez
1222 (20 Apr.-7 July)—1246 (23 Nov.) ...	Richard de Berking
1246 (?16 Dec.)—1258 (17 Feb.)	Richard de Crokesley
1258 (Aug.—Oct.)	Philip de Lewesham
1258 (Dec.)—1283 (8 Dec.)	Richard de Ware
1283 (31 Dec.)—1307 (25 Dec.)	Walter de Wenlok
1308 (26 Jan.)—1315 (9 Apr.)	Richard de Kedyngton
1315 (24 Apr.)—1333 (11 Sep.)	William de Curtlington
1333 (Sep.)—1344 (29 Oct.)	Thomas de Henle
1344 (10 Nov.)—1349 (15 May)	Simon de Bircheston
1349 (27 May)—1362 (20 Mar.)	Simon Langham
1362 (7–14 Apr.)—1386 (29 Nov.) ...	Nicholas de Litlington
1386 (10 Dec.)—1420 (?Oct.)	William Colchester
1420 (?29 Nov.)—1440 (2 Apr.)	Richard Harwden
1440 (27 May +)—1462	Edmund Kirton
1463–9 (+ 14 Nov.)	George Norwych
1469 (+ 14 Nov.)—1474 (21 Aug.) ...	Thomas Millyng
1474 (+ 29 Nov.)—1498 (24 May) ...	John Estney
1498 (9 July)—1500 (?Aug.)	George Fascet
1500 (27 Oct.)—1532 (12 May)	John Islip
1533 (?before Easter)—1540 (16 Jan.) ...	William Boston or Benson

PRIORS

Domini Priores

c. 1085	Robert
?+ 1121–3 (?) ; 1134–9	Osbert de Clare
c. 1121	Eadwye
+ 1157	Hugh
c. 1157 ... ...˙	Elias
c. 1158–73	Alquin
c. 1175–90	Richard
?—1191 (9 Oct.)	William Postard
c. 1189–97	Robert de Molesham
+ 1219 (June)—1222 (Apr.)...	Richard de Berking
+ 1246	Peter
c. 1246	Maurice
?+ 1253 (11 June)—1258 (Aug.)	Philip de Lewesham
c. 1258–83	Elias
c. 1266...	John de Sancto Paulo
?+ 1283 (31 Dec.)—1291 (11 July)? + (1295, Widmore)	John de Coleworth
? 1298—1305 (23 Feb.? +)	William de Huntingdon
1305 (+ 14 July)—1318 ? + ...	Reginald de Hadham
?+ 1325 (25 June)–27	John de Wanetyng
1327–8	R.
?+ 1334–46	Simon Warewik
1346 (?+ 13 Dec.)—1349	Simon de Haumodesham
1349 (10 Apr.—27 May)	Simon Langham
1349 (27 May +)—1350 (+ 18 Nov.) ...	Benedict de Cherteseye
1350 (+ 18 Nov.)—1362	Nicholas de Litlington
1362 (c. Apr.)—1376? + ...	Richard de Merston
1377–82	Richard Excestr'
1382—1407	John de Wratting
1407–35	Robert Whatele
1435–41	Nicholas Asshby
1441–56	William Walsh
1456–66	John Flete
1466–9	Thomas Millyng
1470 (+ 10 Aug.)—1474	John Estney
1474 (29 Nov. +)—1482 (+ 30 Sep.) ...	Thomas Arundel
1482 (30 Sep.)—1491 (c. 25 June) ...	Robert Essex
1491 (July)	Roger Blake
1491–8 (9 July)	George Fascet
1498 (9 July +)—1500 (27 Oct.)... ...	John Islip
1501–28 (4 May)	William Mane
1528 (6 May)—1535 ? + ...	Thomas Jaye
1536 (c. 29 Sep.)—1540 (16 Jan.) ...	Dionisius Dalianns

SUB-PRIORS

Suppriores

[Hen. III]	Henry de Colecestr'
„ „	William de Haseley

1286	...	...	...	...	..	... William de Hanyngton
1304	...	...	...	...	...	... Jordan de Wratting
1307	...	...	...	...	...	... Henry Payn
1318	...	...	...	...	...	... William de Chalk
1351–2	...	...	...	...	...	... John de Mordon
1387–8	...	...	...	...	...	... John Canterbery
+ 1419–20	...	...	...	...	...	... Thomas Peuerell
1440	...	...	...	...	...	... John Wilton
1458–60	...	...	...	...	...	... Richard Tedyngton
1483	...	...	...	...	...	... Thomas Crosse; William Lambard
1498	...	...	...	...	...	... John Holand

WARDENS OF ST MARY'S CHAPEL

Custodes capelle beate Marie

+ 1189	...	...	...	...	...	Robert de Molesham
1240–7 ?+	...	...	...	...	...	Ralph de Glovernia
[Hen. III]	...	...	...	...	...	Henry de Colecestr'
"	...	...	...	...	...	Stephen de London
"	...	...	...	...	...	Walter de Hurley
"	...	...	...	...	...	Ralph de Wautone
"	...	...	...	...	...	Walter de Baunc
c. 1266	...	...	...	...	...	John de Sancto Paulo
1278	...	...	...	...	...	Alexander de Neuporte
+ 1298	...	...	...	...	...	Thomas de Chicelden
1298 (30 Nov.)—1301 (30 Sept.)	...	...	Robert de Bures
1299—1300	...	...	...	...	Gilbert Rauel
1303	...	...	...	...	...	John de Butterle
?—1304 (c. 11 June)	...	...	...	Reginald de Hadham
1304 (c. 11 June)—1305	...	...	...	Henry de la Rye
1325	...	...	...	...	...	William de Harleston
1328	...	...	...	...	...	John de Ashwelle
1335	...	...	...	...	...	John de Mordon
1336; 1344	...	...	...	...	...	Adam de Campeden
1346–7	...	...	...	...	...	Thomas de Combroke
1348–51	...	...	...	...	...	Richard de Redyng
1351 (29 Sep.)—1352 (8 Apr.)	...	...	William de Flete
1356–8	...	...	...	...	...	John de Walingford
1359–61	...	...	...	...	...	John Bampton
1362 (17 Apr.)—1364 (29 Sep.)	...	...	John de London
?—1369	...	...	...	...	...	John Bokenhull
1369–70	...	...	...	...	...	Richard Honyngton
1373–4	...	...	...	...	...	William Zepeswych
?	...	...	...	...	...	John Holbech
1376	...	...	...	...	...	Robert Wynewyk
?	...	...	...	...	...	John Stowe
1382–3	...	...	...	...	...	Richard Circestr'
1384–7 (23 Nov.)	...	...	...	...	William Cleangre
1387–9 (25 Nov.)	...	...	...	...	William Litlington
1389 (25 Nov.)—1391 (9 Dec.)	...	...	William Cleangre
1391 (9 Dec.)—1392	...	...	...	John Enston
1392–3	...	...	...	...	...	Richard Merlawe
1393–4	...	...	...	...	...	William Cleangre

1395–8	Peter Coumbe
1398—1400 (8 Dec.)	Robert Hermodesworth
1400 (8 Dec.)–1401	John Enston
1401–3	Peter Coumbe
1403–7	John Feryng
1407–8 ; 1410	Peter Coumbe
1411–6	Ralph Toneworth
1416–8	Benedict Middleton
1420 (28 Sep.—24 Nov.)	Reginald Shiplake
1420–1	William Surreys
1422	Richard Birlyngham
1426–31	Nicholas Asshby
1432–3	John Wrotham
1433–4 (12 May)	William Walsh
1433–5 (24 Dec.)	Richard Parker
1439 (24 Dec.)—1444 (25 Mar.)	Thomas Cornwayle
1445–6	George Norwych
1445–7	Richard Tedyngton
1447–55	Richard Breynt
1458 (24 June)—1460 (24 Dec.)	William Chertsey
1460 (24 Dec.)—1468	Richard Breynt
1470–7	Thomas Arundel
1477–83	Thomas Clifford
1483–5	John Stanes
1485–9	John Waterden
1489–98	Thomas Flete
1498–9	Richard Newbery
1499—1501	Robert Humfrey
1501–3	William Graunt
1503–14	William Brewode
1511–2	Thomas Brown
1514–28	John Fulwell
1528–31	William Westminster
1533–4	Thomas Essex
1534–6	William Vertue
1535–6	William Boston
1536–7	William Milton

SACRISTS

SACRISTE

c. 1161	Walter
1247	William de Bedeford
1257 + ...	William Tailard
[Hen. III]	Godfrey
1266	John de Sutton
1267	Gilbert Rauel
1278	John de Coleworth
1282–7	John de Sutton
1288	Alexander de Persore
1297 (1 Jan.)—1299 (21 Nov.); 1301; 1302	Reymund de Wenlok
1303 (24 Feb.—29 Sep.)	Adam de Warfeld
1303 (29 Sep.)—1305 (24 June)	Reginald de Hadham

1305 ; 1306	Henry Payn
1307 (25 Nov.)—1308 (29 Sep.)	John de Witteneie
1311	Thomas de Dene
1317 (30 Sep.)—1318 (10 Dec.)	Henry de Bircheston
1318 (10 Dec.)—1320 (14 Oct.) ? + ...	John de Witteneie
+ 1338	Robert de Hampslap
? —1338 (17 Feb.)	John de Tothale
1338 (17 Feb.—29 Sep.)	Robert de Curtlington
1341 ; 1344	John de Mordon
+ 1346	Hugh de Shenegeyze
1346–7	John de Crendon
1351–5 ? + ...	John de Mordon
1356 (31 July)—1360 (29 Sep.)	William de Lakyngheth
1361–2	John Bokenhull
1362–3	William Bromle
1363 (June 23)—1364 (28 Sep.)	Walter de Warfeld
1364–5 ? + ...	John de Somerton
1370–1 (30 Oct.)	William de Zepeswych
1372–7 (30 Nov.)	William de Mordon
1377 (30 Nov.)—1383	Richard Honyngton
1383–4	William Colchester
1384 (28 Sep.)—1385 (17 Nov.)	William de Mordon
1385 (17 Nov.)—1399 (25 Nov.)	Peter Coumbe
1399 (25 Nov.)—1411 (22 Nov.)	Ralph Toneworth
1411–3	Peter Coumbe
1413–4	William Amondesham
1414–9 ? + ...	Richard Harwden
? +1422–33	Roger Cretton
1433–40 (16 Dec.)	Edmund Kirton
1440 (16 Dec.)—1444 (8 Nov.)	Thomas Freston
1444 (8 Nov.)—1447 (5 Feb.)	John Flete
1447 (5 Feb.—25 Dec.) ? + ...	Thomas Pomeray
1448–50	Thomas Cornwayle
1450–60 ? + ...	John Amondesham
1462–7...	Thomas Ruston
? +1470–97	John Estney
1497—1500	George Fascet
1500–32	John Islip

CHAMBERLAINS

CAMERARII

1065	Ralph
1193	Geoffrey
[Hen. III]	Walter de Bureford
1275	Henry de London
1277 ; 1278	John de Sutton
1286	Henry de Waledene
1296	Jordan de Wratting
1298—1304 (24 June)	Simon de Henle
1304 (24 June)—1305 (24 June)	Henry de Bircheston
1306–7	Walter de Arkesdene
1307 (25 Nov.)—1308 (24 June)	John de Butterle

1308 ; 1311	Ralph de Salopia
1312–4	Simon de Henle
1316 (20 Mar.—6 July)	John de Wygornia
1326–7	William de Harleston
1328–31	Michael de Bridbroke
+ 1338	Robert de Hampslap
1338 (16 Feb.)—1339 (16 Feb.)	Thomas de Wenlok
1339–43	Richard de Redyng
1344 (31 May)—1345 (31 May); 1346	
(20 Dec.)—1347 (29 Sep.)	Hugh de Shenegeyze
+ 1346–7	Benedict de Cherteseye
1350–1	John de Walingford
1355–7 ; 1359–61	John de Wratting
1362–4	John de Somerton
1364–5 ; 1366–71 ?+	William de Mordon
1372–4	John Stowe
1375–9	John Holbech
1379–80 ; 1382–7 ; 1389	Richard de Merlawe
1380–1	Robert Adelard
1389–97	William Litlington
1397—1400	John Enston
1400–1 (5 Aug.)	Richard de Merlawe
1401–4	William Amondesham
1404–8	John Feryng
1408–10	Richard Harwden
1410–12	John Sauereye
1412–8	Henry Coneham
1418–9	John Sauereye
1419–33	Geoffrey Bryd
1433–5	Thomas Freston
1435–7	Richard Parker
1438 (19 June—29 Sep.)	Thomas Freston
1438–45	John Flete
1445–8	Thomas Cornwayle
1448–54	Thomas Pomeray
1454–5	Robert Walsingham
1455–9 (24 Mar.)	Edmund Downe
1459	William Barnell
1460–2	Thomas Ruston
1462 (29 Sep.—25 Dec.)	William Barnell
1462–70	John Estney
1470–2	Thomas Frampton
1472–4 ?+	William Wycombe
?+1477–82	Robert Essex
1483	Thomas Crosse
1484–5 ?+	John Hampton
?+1491–8 ?+	William Brewode
?+1499—1507	Richard Charing
1507–8 ?+	Thomas Brown
1509–28	William Westminster
1528–9	Thomas Gardener
1531–6	William Overton

ALMONERS

Elemosinarii

+ 1121	Herbert
+ 1246	Peter
+ 1267	John de Lyra
[Hen. III]	Gregory de Tayleboys
”	Bacinus
+ 1293	Richard de Fanelore
1293 (c. 14 Feb.)—1294 (18 Jan.) ...	Alexander de Persore
1294 (18 June)—1305 (24 June) ...	Reginald de Hadham
1301 ; 1305–7	John de Wenlok
+ 1317	Thomas de Dene
1317 (17 June)—1319	John de Wygornia
1319–20	Richard Atte Heyg
1320–1	John de Biburi
1321–2	William de Chalk
1325	John de Biburi
1328 (31 May)—1329 (23 Feb.) ...	William de Harleston
1335–6	Robert de Beby
?—1339 (31 May)	John de Ashwelle
1339 (31 May)—1342 (28 Oct.) ...	William de Staunton
1342 (21 Oct.)—1344 (29 Sep.) ? +	William de Dumbeltone
1349 (24 June—28 Sep.) ; 1351–2	John de Ashwelle
?—1355 (5 Apr.)	John de London
1355 (5 Apr.)—1361	Walter de Warfeld
1361–3	Walter de Moredon
1363–8 ? + ...	William de Hervyngton
1370–1	John de Somerton
1371–5	Richard Honyngton
1382–5 ; 1387 (28 Sep.—24 Nov.) ...	William de Mordon
1387 (24 Nov.)—1411 (20 Nov.) ...	John Stowe
1411–4	Roger Cretton
1414–5	John Sauereye
1416–7 (6 Dec.)	William Amondesham
1417 (6 Dec.)—1418	William Surreys
1418–9	William Amondesham
1420 (22 July)—1423	John Wilton
1423–7 ? + ...	Richard Birlyngham
1428–30 ? + ...	John Wilton
1431–3	Roger Cretton
1433–4	John Wrotham
1434–5 ? + ...	Thomas Freston
?+1436–8 ? + ...	John Flete
1439–40 (26 Feb.)	John Venour
1440 (26 Feb.)—1443	John Cambridge
1444–5	Thomas Cornwayle
1445–8	William Barnell
1448–61	Thomas Cornwayle
?+1462–3 (25 Mar.)	John Ramsey
1463 (25 Mar.)—1465 ? + ...	John Estney
?+1467–9 ? + ...	William Chinnor
1470–9	Thomas Crosse
1479–83	Thomas Clifford

1483–5 ? + ...	Ralph Langley
1486–91 (7 Dec.)	John Holand
1491 (7 Dec.)—1501	William Mane
?+1502–5 ? + ...	Robert Humfrey
?+1507–8 ? + ...	Robert Davers
1510–1	William Fenne
1511–4	William Southwell
1514–31	Henry Jones
1531–2	William Overton
1532–3	Robert Davers
1533–6	Dionisius Dalianns
1536–7	Humfrey Charyte
1538–9	Richard Gortton

CELLARERS

CELERARII

c. 1161	Thomas
1199	James
+1239	Hugh de Sancto Albano
+1239	Reginald de Hermodesworthe
1246	John de Lyra
1281 (19 Apr.)—1282 ; 1284–5	Philip de Sutton
1331–3	Simon de Bircheston
1334–7 ; 1343–4	Simon de Pireford
1346–7 ; 1348–9 (25 Mar.)	William de Staunton
1349 (25 Mar.—28 Sep.)	Benedict de Cherteseye
1349–51	Thomas de Combroke
1351–2 (1 Aug.)	Richard de Colecestr'
1353 (1 Aug.)—1354	John de Redyng
1354–5	Richard de Redyng
1355–61 ? + ...	John de Ashwelle
?+1362–77 ? + ...	Walter de Warfeld
?+1379–82	John Canterbery
1382–7	John Lakyngheth
1387–93 ? + ...	Richard Honyngton
1396–7 (11 Nov.)	Richard de Merlawe
1397 (11 Nov.)—1400 (15 Aug.) ...	John Canterbery
1400–1 (13 Nov.)	John Borewell
1401 (13 Nov.)—1406	Roger Cretton
1406–8	John Borewell
1410 (25 June)	Roger Cretton
?+1416–7 ? + ...	Walter Coggeshale
1423 ; 1430–1	William Sonewell
1431–2	Thomas Freston
+1440	Thomas Pomeray
1440 (2 Feb.)—1441	William Walsh
1445 (25 Dec.)—1447 (2 Feb.)	Nicholas Mordon
1448–50 ? + ...	John Flete
?+1463–4 (Easter)	Thomas Pomeray
1464 (Easter)—1467	Thomas Ruston
?+1468–82	William Chertsey
1482–3	Thomas Clifford
1484–96	William Brewode

1496–9 ?+	John Islip
1500–1	William Brewode
1501–6	Richard Newbery
?+1507–8 ?+	Robert Humfrey
1509–13	Thomas Brown
1513–5	John Bedford
1515–28	Thomas Jaye
1528–35	John Fulwell
1535–6	William Boston

INFIRMARERS

Infirmarii

?1161	Roger
[Hen. III]	William
,, ...	Simon de Sancta Katerina
1286	William de Pharindon
1297–8	Richard de Fanelore
1305–6	Philip de Sutton
1309–11	Henry de Bircheston
1320–1; 1322–3	John de Wanetyng
1333–5; 1339–41; 1344; 1347–8	John de Ryngstede
1350–3	John de Redyng
1354–7	John de Ashwelle
1357–79 (25 Jan.)	John de Mordon
1379 (25 Jan.)—1383	Walter de Warfeld
1383–7	John Canterbery
1387—1391 (19 Aug.)	William Mordon
1391 (19 Aug.—28 Sep.)	William Litlington
1391–7	John Canterbery
1397—1413	William Litlington
1416–7 (12 Dec.)	Roger Cretton
1418–9	Ralph Toneworth
1420 (28 Sep.—1 Dec.)	Richard Harwden
1420 (1 Dec.)—1421 (28 Sep.)	Reginald Shiplake
1421–31	John Feryng
1436 (28 Sep.—21 Dec.)	Reginald Shiplake
1440–1; 1443 (28 Sep.—12 Oct.) ...	Thomas Freston
1443 (12 Oct.)—1446 (27 Feb.)	John Cambridge
1446–9	John Wilton
1450–9	John Kympton
1460 (1 Mar.)	William Walsh
1461–3	William Milton
1463–7 (24 June)	William Barnell
1467 (13 July)—1470	John Estney
1470–2	William Chinnor
1473–94	John Ramsey
1494—1505	John Waterden
1505–6	Thomas Brown
1512–3	William Brewode
1518–9; 1523–4	Richard Charing
1525–33	Robert Davers
1533–4	William Overton
1536–7	John Clerke

REFECTORERS

Refectorarii

1270; 1278	Roger de Waleden
1303 (24 Feb.—29 Sep.)	Reginald de Hadham
?+1304–5	Henry de la Rye
?—1327	John de Tothale
1327–8	Hugh de Northalle
?—1344 (17 Oct.)	John de Ashwelle
1344 (17 Oct.)—1345 (25 Mar.) ...	William de Staunton
1345 (25 Mar.—29 Sep.)	Adam de Campeden
1359–60	Geoffrey Paxton
1360–1	John de Redyng
1361–3	Geoffrey Paxton
1363–7	John de London
1368–70?+	Richard Honyngton
1372–3	John de Somerton
1373–6?+	William Litlington
1380–1	John Borw
1383–4	John Canterbery
1384–5	John Farnago
1385–7	John Borw
1387–91	Richard Circestr'
1391–2	William Sudbury
1392–4	Richard de Merlawe
1395–8	Richard Circestr'
1398—1400	John Sandon
1400–11	William Sudbury
1411–13	Reginald Shiplake
1413–4	William Asshwell
1414–7	Reginald Shiplake
1417–8	Geoffrey Bryd
1418–9	John Feryng
1419–23	William Sonewell
1423–5	Thomas Gedney
1425–7	William Sonewell
1427–8	Reginald Shiplake
1433–4	Richard Birlyngham
1434–5	William Surreys
1435–9	William Symond
1438 (Christmas)	Bartholomew Massham
1439–43	John Stokes
1444–8	William West
1448–9	Bartholomew Massham
1452–4?+	George Norwych
1456–8	Thomas Fynden
1458–66	William Chinnor
1466–7	Richard Westminster
1470–2	William Chinnor
1472–4	Thomas Lynne
1474–5	John Hampton
1475–7	Thomas Frampton
1477–9	William Wycombe
1479–80	Thomas Crosse

1480–1?+	...	...	...	...	John Hampton
1482–3	...	...	...	...	Ralph Langley
1483–5	...	...	...	...	William Brewode
1485–7	...	...	...	...	Richard Charing
1487–90	...	...	...	...	Richard Newbery
1490–8	...	...	...	...	John Drope
1498—1501	...	...	...	...	William Graunt
1501–3	...	...	...	...	John Norton
1503–5	...	...	...	...	William Lambard
1505–6	...	...	...	...	Thomas Sall
1506–9	...	...	...	...	Thomas Elfrede
1515–6	...	...	...	...	John Ashley
1525–30	...	...	...	...	William Overton
1530–4	...	...	...	...	William Eles
1535–6	...	...	...	...	William Vertue
1536–7	...	...	...	...	John Laurence

PRECENTORS OR CHANTERS

PRECENTORES VEL CANTORES

c. 1189	...	...	...	...	Robert de Molesham
?—1246	...	...	...	...	Maurice
1266	...	...	...	...	William de Pharindon
1277	...	...	...	...	Adam de Wycumbe
1278	...	...	...	...	William de Lokeleya
1297–8; 1304	...	...	...	...	Laurence de Benflet
1311	...	...	...	...	Alexander de Persore
1318	...	...	...	...	John de Butterle
1332	...	...	...	...	Robert de Hampslap
1341	...	...	...	...	John de Torinton
1346	...	...	...	...	Robert de Lake
1349	...	...	...	...	John de Mordon
1360–1	...	...	...	...	John Bokenhull
1361–4	...	...	...	...	William de Flete
1364–7?+	...	...	...	...	William de Zepeswych
1368–9?+; 1372–4	...	...	...	...	John Bokenhull
1374–6	...	...	...	...	Richard Circestr'
1376–82	...	...	...	...	William Witlesford
1382–4	...	...	...	...	Robert de Hereford
1384–7	...	...	...	...	William Litlington
1387–1418	...	...	...	...	John Borw
1418–20	...	...	...	...	Benedict Middleton
1420–38?+	...	...	...	...	Richard Southbroke
?+1443–4	...	...	...	...	John Henton
1444–50	...	...	...	...	John Kympton
1450–7	...	...	...	...	Thomas Arundel
1457–60	...	...	...	...	Thomas Ruston
1460–4	...	...	...	...	Thomas Arundel
1464–6	...	...	...	...	Richard Sporley
1470–1?+	...	...	...	...	Thomas Arundel
?+1483–91	...	...	...	...	John Waterden
1491–2	...	...	...	...	John Hampton
1493–4	...	...	...	...	John Waterden
1494—1510	...	...	...	...	John Warde

1510–24 ?+	...	...	...	...	...	Robert Davers
?+1528—1534	...	...	...	...	...	Dionisius Dalianns

KITCHENERS

Coquinarii

+1335	...	...	...	...	...	John de Ashwelle
+1335	...	...	...	...	...	Robert de Arderne
1350–2	...	...	...	...	...	William de Tourseie
1353–4	...	...	...	...	...	Walter de Warfeld
1356–7	...	...	...	...	...	John de Ashwelle; Thomas Pik; William de Flete
1359–60	...	...	...	...	...	William Bromle
1360–1	...	...	...	...	...	John de London
1375–6	...	...	...	...	...	William Colchester
1378–9	...	...	...	...	...	John Witlesford
1380–5	...	...	...	...	...	Peter Coumbe
1385–7	...	...	...	...	...	John Enston
1389	...	...	...	...	...	William Cleangre
1391–3	...	...	...	...	...	John Braynt
1399—1400	...	...	...	...	...	Roger Cretton
1404–5	...	...	...	...	...	William Sonewell
1405–9	...	...	...	...	...	John Borewell
1409–14	...	...	...	...	...	John Bassyngbourne
1415–6	...	...	...	...	...	John Wrotham
1418–20	...	...	...	...	...	Nicholas Mordon
1433–4	...	...	...	...	...	William Symond
1436–7	...	...	...	...	...	John Henton
1441	...	...	...	...	...	Nicholas Mordon
+1483	...	...	...	...	...	John Hilston
1484–5	...	...	...	...	...	John Hampton
1485–7	...	...	...	...	...	Ralph Langley
1487–91 (16 Dec.)	...	...	...	...	...	Richard Charing
1491 (16 Dec.)—1493	...	...	...	...	Thomas Flete
1497—1500; 1501–3	...	...	...	...	William Graunt
1503–4	...	...	...	...	...	John Ashley
1506–7	...	...	...	...	...	Henry Jones
1507 (23 Dec.)—1509 (13 Oct.)	...	...	...	William Southwell
1509–10	...	...	...	...	...	Thomas Elfrede
1511–6	...	...	...	...	...	William March
1516–7 (24 June)	...	...	...	...	John Campion
1516–20	...	...	...	...	...	William Callowe
1520–1	...	...	...	...	...	William Overton
1521–2	...	...	...	...	...	Thomas Gardener
1523–33	...	...	...	...	...	William Callowe
1533	...	...	...	...	...	John Fulwell

WARDENS OF THE CHURCHES

Custodes Ecclesie de Ocham

+1286	...	...	...	...	...	Roger de Waleden
1320	...	...	...	...	...	John de Wanetyng; William de Harleston
1321–9	...	...	...	..	...	Robert de Beby
1329–33	...	...	...	...	...	Walter de Woxebrugge

CUSTODES ECCLESIARUM DE ASHWELLE, STANES ET OKEHAM

1334–43	John de Ashwelle
1349–50	Nicholas de Litlington
1353–4	Richard de Merston
1366–7	John de Wratting
1372–7	John Lakyngheth
1377–81	Peter Coumbe
1381–3	John Lakyngheth
1383–7	Richard Honyngton
1387–92	John Lakyngheth
1392–3	John Borewell
1393–7	Richard de Merlawe
1397–9	John Borewell
1399—1401	Peter Coumbe
1401–3	John Borewell
1403–8	Roger Cretton
1408–10	William Sonewell
1410–6	Richard Harwden
1416–8	John Wrotham
1418–20	Richard Harwden
1420–31 (28 July)	John Wrotham
1431 (27 July)—1435	Nicholas Asshby
1435 (17 Dec.)—1437	Thomas Freston
1438 (19 June)—1440 (26 Jan.)	William Walsh
1443–6	Thomas Pomeray
1446–56	John Flete
1456–61	Richard Breynt
1461–83 (18 Jan.)	William Chertsey
1483 (18 Jan.)—1484	Thomas Clifford
1485–6	John Hampton
1489–90	George Fascet
1492	William Mane
1492–9	John Islip
1499	Thomas Ely
1499—1500	William Brewode
1501–3	William Borow
1504–8	Robert Humfrey
1509–13	Thomas Brown
1514–28	Thomas Jaye
1528–35	John Fulwell

WARDENS AND TREASURERS OF QUEEN ALIANORE'S MANORS

CUSTODES ET THESAURARII MANERIORUM REGINE ALIANORE

1297	Alexander de Neuporte
1301 (30 Nov.)—1302 (29 May)	Reginald de Hadham
1302 (28 May)—1305 (17 Apr.)	William de Chalk
1305 ; 1306	Jordan de Wratting
1309–10	Henry de Bircheston
1315 (25 Mar.)—1319 (30 Nov.)	John de Witteneie

1318 (8 Dec.)—1334 (7 Dec.)			Henry de Bircheston
1334 (8 Dec.)—1344			Simon de Bircheston
1334–7			John Payn ; Robert de Hamslap
1339–42			,, ,, ; John de Mordon
1349 (15 Apr.)—1350			Nicholas de Litlington
1351			William de Tourseie
1357–62	Richard de Merston	...	John Bokenhull
1369–70	John de Wratting ...	...	John Stowe
1372–5	John Lakyngheth ...	...	John de London
1375–7	,, ,, ...	...	John Witlesford
1378–80	,, ,, ...	...	Peter Coumbe
1380–3	,, ,, ...	...	John Farnago
1383–7	,, ,, ...	..	Robert Adelard
1387–8	,, ,, ...	...	William Halle
1388–90	,, ,, ...	...	John London
1390–1	,, ,, ...	...	John Enston
1391–2	,, ,, ...	...	John London
1392–3	William de Sudbury...	...	,, ,,
1393–9	John Borewell ...	...	John Braynt
1399—1400	Peter Coumbe ...	...	,, ,,
1400–1	John Borewell ...	...	,, ,,
1401–3	,, ,, ...	...	Reginald Shiplake
1403–5	Roger Cretton ...	...	Richard Harwden
1405–8	,, ,, · ...	...	Robert Hermodesworth
1408–10	William Sonewell ...	...	,, ,,
1410–6	Richard Harwden ...	...	Walter Coggeshale
1416–7	John Wrotham ...	...	John Feryng
1417–8	,, ,, ...	...	John Lucas
1418–20	Richard Harwden ...	...	Walter Coggeshale
1420–6	John Wrotham ...	...	,, ,,
1426–7	,, ,, ...	...	Reginald Shiplake
1427–31	,, ,, ...	...	William Surreys
1431–3	Nicholas Asshby ...	...	William Walsh
1433–5	,, ,, ...	...	John Venour
1435–7	Thomas Freston ...	...	,, ,,
1438 (19 June)—1439	John Wilton ...		John Cambridge
1439–40	John Wilton ...	...	Richard Breynt
1440–3	Richard Breynt ...	...	John Wilton
1443–6	John Flete	...	,, ,,
1446–50	,, ,, ...	...	Bartholomew Massham
1450–6	,, ,, ...	...	John Estney
1456–7	Richard Breynt ...	...	,, ,,
1457–60	,, ,, ...	...	John Ramsey
1460–2	William Chertsey ...	...	,, ,,
1462–4	,, ,, ...	...	Robert Essex
1464–8	,, ,, · ·	...	Richard Tedyngton
1468–72	,, ,, ...	...	Thomas Crosse
1472–4	,, ,, ...	...	Richard Tedyngton
1474–7	,, ,, ...	...	Thomas Crosse
1477–80	,, ,, ...	...	Richard Tedyngton
1480–1	,, ,, ...	...	Ralph Langley
1481–2	,, ,, ...	...	John Holand
1482–5	Thomas Clifford ...	...	,, ,,
1485–6	John Hampton ...	...	,, ,,
1486–8	George Fascet ...	...	,, ,,

1488–92	George Fascet	William Mane
1492 (12 Oct.)—1493	John Islip •••	,, ,,
1493–9	,, ,, ...	Richard Newbery
1499—1500	William Brewode	Thomas Ely
1501–3	William Borow	Richard Caston
1503–4	,, ,, ••• ...	Robert Humfrey
1504–6	Robert Humfrey	William Fenne
1506–8	,, ,, ...	
1508–13	Thomas Brown	
1513–4	John Bedford ... •••	
1514–28	Thomas Jaye	
1528–34	John Fulwell	

[The monks in this list up to and including Simon de Bircheston are named
Wardens, and in 1334–42 there are two additional officers called Treasurers.
From 1357 to 1443 both are called Treasurers, the first being mainly responsible
and sometimes called Wardens. From 1443 onwards both are frequently called
Wardens. The titles, in fact, are interchangeable. It may be assumed that the
same officers acted as Wardens and Treasurers of the other royal foundations of
Richard II and Queen Anne, and of Henry V.]

PITTANCERS

PITANCIARII

1267 ...	... ...	Reginald de Stanes
1278 ...	... ... ••• ...	William de Pharindon
1286 ...	... ... •••	Roger de Waleden
1301 ...	... ...	Jordan de Wratting ; Reginald de Hadham
1343 ...	... ...	John de Ashwelle

GRANGERS

GRANATORES

1297–8 ; 1303 (24 Feb.)—1304 (24 June)	Jordan de Wratting
1304–5	John de Witteneie
1307–8 ; 1310–1	Guido de Asshewelle
1327–8	John de Witteneie ; William de Logardin
1338–41 •••	William de Dumbeltone
1346–7	Richard de Redyng
1349–50 ... ... ••• ...	Nicholas de Litlington
1350–1	Thomas de Combroke ; Richard de Merston
1351–3 (1 Aug.)	Richard de Colcestr'
1355–9 ; 1360–1 •••	John de Ashwelle
1361–71 ... ••• ... ••• ...	Walter de Warfeld
1378–80	John Canterbery
1380–2	William Colchester
1382–6	John Lakyngheth
1386–90 ; 1391–4 ... ... ••• ...	Richard Honyngton
1394–7 ... •••	Richard de Merlawe

1397—1400	John Canterbery
1399—1401	John Borewell
1402–3	Roger Cretton
1404–9	John Borewell
1409–13 (19 Nov.)	Roger Cretton
1413–4	John Lucas
1416–8	Walter Coggeshale
1418–23	William Sonewell
1423–5	John Walden
1425–8	Thomas Freston
1428–33	Richard Birlyngham
1433–4	John Cambridge
1434–8	John Wrotham
1438–9	John Cambridge
1439–42	William Barnell
1443–4	Robert Walsingham
1445–6	Richard Sporley
1446–8	William Milton
1448–50	Richard Ellyngton
1453–4 ; 1458–63	Richard Sporley
1463–4	Richard Westminster
1464–5	Thomas Crosse
1465–6	Thomas Frampton
1466–70	Thomas Crosse
1470–1	Richard Sporley
1473–4 ; 1479–80	William Chinnor
1480–3	Thomas Frampton
1484–5	Richard Charing
1485–8	William Graunt
1490–2	Ralph Langley
1492–3	John Holand
1493–8	Robert Humfrey
1500–1	John Ashley
1502–3	Martin James
1506–7	William Fyttz
1511–2	William Fenne
1512–4	John Bedford
1514–25	John Fulwell
1528–34	John Malvern
1534–5	William Vertue
1536–7	William Mylton

WARDENS OF THE NEW WORK

Custodes Novi Operis

1341–4	Simon de Bircheston: John de Mordon
1344 (Apr.—Nov.); 1349–65 ; 1377 ...	John de Mordon
1387–99 (25 Nov.)	Peter Coumbe
1400—1411 (22 Nov.)	Ralph Toneworth
1413–20	Richard Harwden
1420–1 (16 Nov.)	William Sonewell
1421 (16 Nov.)—1422	Walter Coggeshale

1423–33	... ...	Nicholas Asshby
1433–7	... ...	Edmund Kirton
1442–3	... ...	John Frank
1444–5	... ...	William Walsh
1445–6	... ...	John Flete
1447 (25 Mar.)—1451	... ...	Thomas Pomeray
1455–6	... ...	Edmund Downe
1456–7 (25 Mar.)	... ...	John Flete
1457 (25 Mar.)—1458	... ...	Thomas Arundel
1459–61	... ...	William Barnell
1461–7 (24 Nov.)	... ...	Thomas Ruston
1467 (25 Dec.)—1470	... ...	Thomas Millyng
1470–1	... ...	Thomas Crosse
1471–97	... ...	John Estney
1497—1500	... ...	George Fascet
1500–32	... ...	John Islip
1532–4	... ...	William Boston

TREASURERS

Thesaurarii

1293–5?+	Richard de Fanelore (?)
1297–9	Henry de Wantyng; William de Watford
1299; 1301; 1302	Walter de Arkesdene
1299; 1301	Thomas de Dene
1301; 1302	Jordan [de Wratting]
1303 (24 Feb.)—1304 (24 June)	Jordan de Wratting; Roger de Aldenham
1304 (24 June)—1305 (24 June)	Roger de Aldenham; Henry Payn
1306–7	John de Witteneie; Richard de Coleworth
1307 (25 Nov.)—1308 (29 Sep.); 1310 (29 Sep.)—1311 (4 Apr.)	Philip de Sutton
1311–3	Guido de Asshewelle
1311–2	Ranulph de Salopia
1313	John de Butterle; John de Witteneie
1316	William de Harleston; John de Wygornia
1318; 1319	,, ,, ,, John de Wanetyng
1321	,, ,, ,, John de Wygornia
1327–8	R. de Brackele; Walter de Woxebrugge
1329–33	Walter de Woxebrugge
1330–33	Thomas de Henle
1333	Hugh de Papworth
1337–40	Robert de Curtlington
1337–8	Simon de Pireford
1343	John de Ashwelle
1344–5	Simon de Pireford; Nicholas de Litlington
1346	William de Staunton; Robert de Lake
1350–1	Nicholas de Litlington; Thomas de Combroke; Richard de Merston
1351 (29 Sep.)—1352 (1 Aug.)	Richard de Merston; John de Mordon
1353 (1 Aug.)—1354	John de Redyng; Richard de Merston

1356–7	...	...	•••	...	John de Mordon ; Walter de Warfeld
1357–62	...	...	...	•••	Richard de Merston ; ,, ,, ,,
1362–71	...	...	...	...	John de Wratting ; ,, ,, ,,
1371–2	...	...	...	...	John Lakyngheth ; ,, ,, ,,
1375–6	•••	...	...	...	,, ,, William Colchester
1378–9	...	...	...	...	,, ,, John Witlesford
1380–1	...	...	...	...	,, ,, Peter Coumbe
1382–3	...	...	...	...	,, ,,
1383–5	...	...	...	...	Richard Honyngton ; Peter Coumbe
1385–7	...	...	...	...	,, ,, John Enston
1387–8	...	...	...	...	John Lakyngheth ; William Cleangre
1391–2	...	...	...	...	,, ,, John Braynt
1392–3	...	...	•••	...	William Sudbury ; ,, ,,
1393–7	...	...	...	•••	John Borewell ; Richard de Merlawe
1397–8	...	...	...	...	,, ,, William Pulburgh
1399—1401	...	...	...		Peter Coumbe ; Roger Cretton
1401–3	...	•••	...	...	John Borewell ; ,, ,,
1403–5	...	...	...	...	Roger Cretton ; William Sonewell
1405–8	...	...	...	...	,, ,, John Borewell
1408–9	...	•••	...	...	William Sonewell ; ,,
1409–10	...	...	...	•••	,. ,, John Bassyngbourne
1410–4	...	...	...	...	Richard Harwden ; ,, ,,
1414–5	...	...	...	...	,, ,, John Lucas
1415–6	...	...	...	...	,, ,, John Wrotham
1416–8	...	...	•••	...	John Wrotham ; Nicholas Mordon
1418–20	...	...	...	...	Richard Harwden ; ,, ,,
1421–31 (27 July)		...	...		John Wrotham ; ,, ,,
1431 (27 July)—1433		...	...		Nicholas Asshby ; ,, ,,
1433–5 (17 Dec.) ...		...	...		,, ,, William Symond
1435 (17 Dec.)—1438 (19 June)					Thomas Freston ; John Henton
1438 (19 June)—1440 (26 Jan.)					William Walsh ; Nicholas Mordon
1440 (26 Jan.)—1442		...	...		Thomas Pomeray ; ,, ,,
1442–6	...	...	...	•••	,, ,, Edmund Downe
1447 (4 Feb.)—1456 (3 Nov.) ...					John Flete ; William Milton
1456 (3 Nov.)—1461 (19 Jan.)					Richard Breynt ; ,, ,,
1461 (19 Jan.–29 Sep.) ...		...			William Chertsey ; John Ramsey
1461–3	...	...	..	...	,, ,, Robert Essex
1463–83 (18 Jan.)		...	...		,, ,,
1463–71 ?+		...	...	...	Richard Tedyngton
1483 (18 Jan.)—1484 ?+ ...		...			Thomas Clifford ; John Holand
1485–6	...	...	...	...	John Hampton ; ,, ,,
1486–8	...	...	...	...	George Fascet ; ,, ,,
1488–92	...	•••	...	...	,, ,, William Mane
1492 (12 Oct.)—1498		...	...		John Islip ; Richard Newbery
1498–9	...	...	•••	...	,, ,, Thomas Ely
1499—1500		...	...	...	William Brewode ; Thomas Ely
1500–1	...	...	...	...	,, ,, William Borow
1501–3	...	...	...	...	William Borow ; Richard Caston
1503–4	...	...	...	...	,, ,, Robert Humfrey
1504–8 ?+ ...		...	...	...	Robert Humfrey
1509–13	...	...	...	...	Thomas Brown
1514–28	...	...	...	•••	Thomas Jaye
1528–35	...	...	...	...	John Fulwell

MONK-BAILIFFS

Ballivi

1260 (?); 1269	John de Sutton
1271	Walter de London
1303 (24 Feb.)—1305 (24 June)	Reymund [de Wenlok]
1307; 1312; 1318; 1319	Philip de Sutton
1322; 1323; 1326–7	Ralph de Westbury
1339; 1340; 1343–5	Richard de Wynton
1345–7	John de Mordon
1350–1	Thomas de Combroke
1352–56	Richard de Merston
1365–71	John de Wratting
1373–83	John Lakyngheth
1383–7	Richard Honyngton
1387–92	John Lakyngheth
1393–8; 1401–3; 1405–9	John Borewell
1399—1401	Peter Coumbe
1404	Roger Cretton
1409–10	William Sonewell
1410–20	Richard Harwden
1421–31 (27 July)	John Wrotham
1431 (27 July)—1435	Nicholas Asshby
1435 (17 Dec.)—1438 (19 June)	Thomas Freston
1438 (19 June)—1440 (26 Jan.)	William Walsh
1440 (26 Jan.)—1446	Thomas Pomeray
1447 (4 Feb.)–56 (3 Nov.)	John Flete
1456 (3 Nov.)–61	Richard Breynt
1465–70; 1482–3 (18 Jan.)	William Chertsey
1483 (18 Jan.)—1484	Thomas Clifford
1485–6	John Hampton
1492	William Mane
1492 (12 Oct.)—1499	John Islip
1499	Thomas Ely
1499—1501	William Brewode
1501–4	William Borow
1504–8	Robert Humfrey
1509–13	Thomas Browne
1514–28	Thomas Jaye
1528 35	John Fulwell

DOMESTIC TREASURERS

Thesaurarii Intrinsecus et Collectores Reddituum;

vel

Custodes communis Thesauri

1444–5	William Barnell
1446–7	William Wellys
1448–52	William Barnell
1461 (25 Dec.)—1463 (29 Dec.)	William Milton
1466–70	Thomas Millyng

1470–85	...	...	...	...	John Estney
1485–90	...	...	...	...	Robert Essex
1490–4	...	...	...	...	John Estney
1494—1500	...	...	...	...	George Fascet
1501–27	...	...	...	...	William Mane
1528–34	...	...	...	...	Thomas Jaye
1536–7	...	...	...	...	William Boston

ARCHDEACONS

ARCHIDIACONI

?—1246 (16 Dec.)		Richard de Crokesley
1260 (2 Apr.)		Thomas de Marleberge
1278 (21 Mar.)—1288 (c. 21 Sep.) ...		Adam de Wycumbe
1290		Walter de Huntyndon
+ 1293		Roger de Bures
1311 (24 Aug.)		Alexander de Persore
1324 (7 May); 1325 (20 May)		Robert
1366 (19 Oct.); 1367 (2 Mar.); prob. 1370 (25 Jan.)		William de Zepeswych
1372 (Apr.); 1373 (12 Oct.)		Thomas Pik
1382		William Colchester
1383 (27 Mar.)		Peter Coumbe
1386 (9 Nov.)		William Colchester
1388 (24 June)		John Stowe
1391 (Oct.); 1393 (12 July)		John Borewell
1414 (6 Nov.)		William Amondesham
1417–8		? Ralph Toneworth ?
1440 (2 Apr.)		John Flete
1447 (25 Dec.)		William Wellys
1449		John Amondesham
1451		George Norwych
1454		Edmund Downe
1461		George Norwych
1468 (8 Jan.)		William Wycombe
1483–4		William Lambard
1484–5		Thomas Flete
1498 (9 July); 1500 (27 Oct.)		William Borow
1528 (18 Aug.)		John Fulwell
1528 (19 Oct.)		Robert Benet

ABBOT'S RECEIVERS OR TREASURERS

RECEPTORES VEL THESAURARII ABBATIS

1288–9		John de Henle
1296 (June)—1298 (May)		Alexander de Persore ; Richard de Fanelore
1305 (13 Dec.)—1307 (24 Dec.)		Henry Payn
1341 (22 Jan.)—1342 (17 Nov.)		John de Henle
1343 (25 Dec.)—1344 (4 Apr.)		John de Crendon
1363–4 ; 1371		John Lakyngheth
1413–4		John Sauereye

1416–8	Roger Cretton
1438–40 ; 1444–7 (29 Jan.)	John Flete
1447 (2 Feb.)—1448	Thomas Cornwayle
1463 (24 Nov.)—1464 (5 Feb.)	Richard Westminster
1496 (23 Oct.)—1497 (5 Nov.)	John Islip

WARDENS OF THE ABBOT'S MANSION

CUSTODES HOSPICII ABBATIS

1288 (29 Sep.)—1289 (20 Mar.)	Ralph de Mordon
1289–90	Alexander de Persore
1362–71 (26 Oct.)	John Lakyngheth
1373–4 ? + ...	William Colchester

ABBOT'S STEWARDS

SENESCALLI [HOSPICII] ABBATIS

+ 1246	Juhele
1289–92	Thomas de Lenton
1298–9	Adam de Warfeld
1380–3 ; 1387 (29 Dec.)—1390 (16 Nov.) ...	Richard de Merlawe
1390 (16 Nov.)—1391	John Canterbery
1400–2	John Feryng
1406–7	Richard Harwden
1413 (28 Sep.—18 Nov.)	John Sauereye
1463 (13 Apr.—14 Nov.)	Richard Westminster

APPENDIX.

THE BENEDICTINES UNDER QUEEN MARY.

The restoration by Mary Tudor of a Benedictine establishment to Westminster Abbey[1] lies outside the limits of our present investigation. Nor, by comparison with the period before the Dissolution, have we any appreciable wealth of material for reconstructing the daily life of the place during this brief revival. There are grants of leases by John Feckenham, the Abbot, and Este, the Prior, in fair numbers. There is also a cancelled bond[2], "datum in capitulari nostra domo," 20 Mar. 1557, whereby the Abbot acknowledged that the Convent was indebted to Alphonsus de Salinas in the sum of £300. This divine, who had been appointed to the seventh Prebend of the new foundation 12 May 1554[3], and who is called in the document Alonso de Salines, was to receive "thirtie poundes yerelie at fowr termes in the yere" during his "naturall lyfe"; in other words, he purchased from the Abbey an annuity of £30. Or again there are directions about the management of rural property, such as those contained in a letter[4], signed by the Abbot, "to oʳ trustie and welbeloued ffarmer Thomas Pollye oʳ farmer of oʳ parsonage of Shoram," giving his lordship's "will and charge" as to the disposal of the "profettes."

But there is no series of obedientiary rolls to claim succession to the annual stock-takings of the former time. Feckenham's public record can be sought elsewhere, and when it leaps to light, he is in no way shamed. But as to his colleagues there has been little but rumour. Widmore[5] himself can do no more than assert, without references, that the new Abbot brought with him "fourteen monks, four of which (*sic*) formerly belonged to Glastenbury," and he disposes of the revival in a couple of pages, largely occupied with Feckenham's career.

Widmore's statement about the "fourteen monks" may arise from the record of Machyn[6], that on St Clement's Eve "the Lord Abbot with the Convent, thirteen monks shorn in, went in procession after the old fashion." I can find no document of ours to confirm it. But we possess a paper[7] which purports to give a list of the Convent and its servants and which, though it does not mention Feckenham by name, unquestionably belongs to his period. So it may be well to print it in full:—

THE NAMES OF THE BRETHEREN OF WESTMONASTERIE.

Dominˢ	Mʳ Foster
Abbas	Mʳ Goodlook
Mʳ Este prior	Mʳ Adthelstane
Mʳ Edon	Mʳ Newte
Mʳ Redborne	Mʳ Frewell

[1] 7 Sep. 1556. [2] *Mun.* 5927. [3] Widmore, p. 221.
[4] *Mun.* 14354. [5] p. 137.
[6] *Diary*, 21 Nov. 1556 (ed. Camd. Soc. p. 118 f.). [7] *Mun.* 9327.

Mr Coventri
Mr Bayli
Mr Aulton
Mr Philipps
Mr Vowell
Mr Bowcer
Mr Wooseter

Mr Adthelwolde
Mr Filde
Mr Legge
Mr Langdon
Mr Cook
Mr Strotforde

THE NAMES OF THOSE THAT SHALBE RELIGIUS AND BE NOWE IN COMONS.

Mr Lucie
Mr Bramsgrove
Mr Vlborne[1]
Selbe
Prince
Johnsone
Groundie

Wayte
Andersone
Lovewell
Mr Phagane
George Marshall
Kyngsewoode
Cley

THE NAMES OF MY LORDE ABBAT MEN.

Bosegrove marshall
Castlonde gentleman vssher
Willington of my lordes chamber
Hubbott of my lordes chamber
Bragden common cat' [? caterer]
Wilton vssher of the hall
Miles buttler

Morgayne butler
Thomas my Lordes cooke
William vnder cooke
and ij Skullayns
Masone porter
Culpaper poore man
Nune sub amner

THE NAMES OF THE COMMON SERVANTES.

Ralphe Ridell common tayler
West common Tayler
Roseter common buttler
Raynolde Tue the bell ryngar
Temple port'
Erle servant to the subcelerer
Ambrose Mr Celerers man
fayre servant to Mr Archedecon
Este servant to Mr Prior

Towe keper of the garnerde
Too common barbars
Vpthomas servant to Mr Redborne
The shomaker
Too Cookes for the Covent
One olde man to make clene the vessell
Robert bocher slawterman
Robert the bel ringar

THE CHAPPELL MEN AND CHILDERNE THAT BE IN COMMONS.

Boorne
Cavell
vi Choristars
iii brotherers

ii Gardiners
Mr Chanter
Mr Chelton
Mr Whatelie

There is no date to this document, and so it is possible that the list of the actual Brethren represents the Convent in the greater completeness to which Feckenham brought it after a while. But it will be noticed that there are twenty monks besides the Abbot and the Prior; and that there is a second class, preparing to enter religion, fourteen in number, of whom four are perhaps more advanced in their preparation than the rest, for they are described as "M^r." Besides these there is the Abbot's retinue, consisting of fifteen persons, and the

---

[1] "Slyngsbe" has been deleted.

staff of the Convent, numbering nineteen. Lastly, the gentlemen of the choir
and the singing children are in a group of sixteen along with gardeners and
"brotherers." Thus we have a Convent of 36 monks and postulants for admission,
and a staff of 50 retainers of various kinds.

Confining ourselves to the monks, we notice Widmore's statement that four
of the alleged fourteen "had formerly belonged to Glastonbury." He is no doubt
thinking of the letter, printed by Dugdale[1], which was addressed by four of
Feckenham's monks to Queen Mary's Lord Chamberlain, praying for the restoration
of Glastonbury and referring to the efforts already made by the Abbot to that
end. The letter is signed

John Phagan
John Neott
Will[m] Adelwold
Will[m] Kentwyne.

We may identify three of these with men on our list,—John Neott with
"M[r] Newte" and Will[m] Adelwold with "M[r] Adthelwolde," while John Phagan
who signs above them is represented by "M[r] Phagane," who stands eleventh
among the fourteen "that shalbe religius" but are not yet in full membership.
Of Will[m] Kentwyne we have no record, unless he stands for "Kyngsewoode."

The letter of the four monks bears no date, except in so far as it refers to
Philip and Mary, but the fact that Phagane heads the signatures, as if he were as
much a monk of Westminster as the other three, may be taken for what it is
worth as an implication that the Feckenham list belongs to an early date in the
history of the revival, and so is perhaps what it looks like, a list of those whom
the new Abbot proposed as his first set of colleagues.

We have seen reason[2] to suppose that "M[r] Foster" and "M[r] Goodlook,"
whose names occur together, were formerly Brethren of the Abbey of Westminster.
The publication here of all the names may lead to the identification of some of the
rest. What we miss is the ancient distribution of the offices. There is still a
Cellarer, and there is still an Archdeacon; for a servant is attached to each; but
the Archdeacon cannot be identified by name. "M[r] Edon" is referred to in
twelve documents[3] as Cellarer; in one he witnesses a bond for £200 given by the
Abbot and Convent to a citizen of London 17 April 1557 "in presentia magistri
Ricardi Edom Cellararii monasterii predicti"; in another he signs an acquittance
to John Moulton, the Receiver General of the Abbey, for the arrears of his account
16 Feb. 1557. We have also a reference to George Marshall or Marchal (who
stands last but two among the postulants) as the Treasurer of the Convent. He
similarly gives an acquittance[4] to the same Receiver. The two receipts taken
together are an indication that the old system of monk obedientiaries has been
replaced by a secular administration. The Abbot now trusts affairs not to his
Brethren but to laymen. The Receiver and the Auditor are the important factors
in the management of the House. So we may end our brief note on the revival
with a letter[5] which clearly belongs to its closing days, and which the anxious
Receiver, unwillingly pent up in Westminster, wrote to the apparently less anxious
Auditor, who was at his country house with his family and, what was of more
consequence at the moment, with some of the Abbey books:—

M[r] Audytor I commende me vnto yo[u] and my lorde Abbot wellyd me to wryte
to yo[u] to be here at Westm[r] with alle spede for he lokyth euery daye ffor the

---

[1] *Monast.* i. 9. 10; Harleian MS. 3881 f. 38 b, which is said in a note to the 1817 edition
to be "in the handwriting of Sir William Dugdale."

[2] pp. 185, 187.   [3] *Mun.* 13207; 33203; &c.

[4] *Mun.* 33204; 22 Feb. 1559.   [5] *Mun.* 33199.

house to be desoluyd praying you^u to bryng with yo^u suche bokes as ye thynke conuenyent I would ffayne ffor my parte to be in the contrey but I can not awaye I praye yo^u fayle not to come for y^t ys mete ffor vs bothe nowe attend And thus fare yo well with my hartye commendacions to M^{tres} Bolland Scrybelyd in hast this mornyng the xixth day of June

by yor assured louyng ffrend John moulton receyuer there

To my vearey louyng ffrend Mr Humfrey Bolland audytor at Westm^r
be this delyuyred at his house in
Essex with spede.

INDEX OF MONKS

NOTE. *The date after each name is that of the year under which the monk's record is to be found. The figures in italics represent the pages on which any other reference is made to him.*

Abindon, Nicholas de 1334–5
Abindon, Richard de 1318
Abyndon, George 1502–3
Adam c. 1191
Adam, J. 1482–3
Adelard, R. 1369
Ægelward 1122
Æiric +1141
Alanus +1283
Albon, J. 1485–6
Albright, C. 1513–4
Alby, H. 1447–8
Aldenham, R. de 1297–8 *3, 15, 63, 68, 73, 77*
Alen, John 1493–4
Alen, John 1530–1
Alexander 1175
Aleyn, R. 1439–40
Algood, W. 1503–4
Almaly, W. de 1303 *71, 73*
Alquin c. 1158 *45*
Alwold +1049
Ambrose, John 1533–4
Ambrose, William 1523–4
Amondesham, John 1428–9
Amondesham, William 1387–8 *5*
Ansgode c. 1137
Appulton, P. 1456–7
Arderne, R. de 1328–9
Arkesdene, W. de 1297–8 *73*
Arundel, John 1356–7
Arundel [Papilon], Ralph de +1173 *46*
Arundel, Thomas 1439–40 *25 n., 33*
Ashby, J. 1462–3
Ashford, J. 1451–2
Ashley, J. 1482–3
Ashwelle, John de 1318–9 *22, 92*
Asshby, N. 1416–7
Asshewelle, Guido de 1297–8 *73, 77*
Asshwell, William 1375
Aston, T. 1432–3
Atherstone, T. 1425–6
Atte Heyg, Richard ? +1319–20

Austen, J. 1519–20
Aylmer, J. 1439–40
Ayswelle, T. de 1235

Baanes, T. 1445–6
Bacinus Hen. III *52*
Bampton, J. 1354–5
Barker, Thomas 1472–3
Barker, Thomas 1479–80
Barnards, R. 1533–4
Barnell, W. 1421–2 *8, 138*
Barnewell, J. 1487–8
Barton, Robert 1383–4
Barton, Thomas 1498–9
Bassyngbourne, J. 1387–8
Baunc, Walter de Hen. III
Bayndon, J. 1458–9
Beauford, J. 1479–80
Beby, R. de 1297–8 *12, 70, 73, 79, 82, 83, 88*
Bedeford, William de +1246
Bedford, John 1502–3
Bedford, Paschal 1435–6
Belden, W. 1384–5
Benet, Robert 1511–2 *177*
Benet, Thomas 1435–6
Benflet, L. de 1297–8
Benwell, T. 1494–5
Beremundeshe, R. de +1288
Berking, Jordan de 1291–2
Berking, Richard de +1219 *13, 30, 49, 50, 102, 109*
Biburi, J. de ? +1314–5
Billingburgh, J. 1451–2
Bircheston, Henry de 1297–8 *61, 65, 73, 77, 82, 83*
Bircheston, Simon de 1328–9 *6, 76, 79, 81, 82, 85, 87, 88, 90, 92, 94*
Biritone, R. de 1346–7
Birlyngham, R. 1389–90 *126, 135 n.*
Bissea, R. de c. 1148–57
Blake, R. 1476–7 *4, 28, 169*
Blaston, R. de 1344–5

GENERAL INDEX

NOTE. *A number of entries will be found under the heads of "London," " Westminster," and " Westminster Abbey."*

Abingdon, 61
  Abbot of, 148
Ædric, Prior of Chertsey, 43
Aldebrandi, Dando, of Siena, 54
Aldenham, Herts, church and manor of, 5, 52 f., 74, 104, 181
  Gilbert de, 70
Alexander III, Pope, 42, 44
Alexander IV, Pope, 49, 65
Alianore of Castile, Queen, wife of Edward I, 15
  Abbot Wenlok, her Treasurer, 59 f.
  Candles for her tomb, 17, 114
  Manors of, and the distribution of their proceeds, 15 ff., 22, 25, 33 n., 55 f., 61 f., 67, 74, 77, 81, 83, 93, 110 n., 140
  Confirmation of charter, 78
  Warden, 16, 23, 29 f., 169, 172
  Wardens and Treasurers, list of, 205 f.
Aller-juxta-Langport, Somerset, benefice of, 144
Amalric, brother of Abbot Gervase, 42
Ampulla, the, golden eagle for, 149
Amwell, Herts, manor of, 60, 65
Anagni, 42, 44
Anne of Bohemia, Queen, wife of Richard 1I, 18
  Anniversary of, 18, 104, 109
Anselm, Archbishop of Canterbury, 40
Antwerp, the Virgin's girdle taken to, 72 n., 79
Apothecaries, 60, 63, 80, 105, 149
Armour of Abbots and Monks, 86, 104, 107
Arnald, Bishop of Sorra, 92
Ashford (Echelesford), Midx, 159
Ashwell, Herts, church and manor of, 5, 49, 79, 125, 181
Asserio, Rigaud de, Bishop of Winchester, 75
Assheley, Edward, goldsmith, 170
Avignon, 27, 63, 65, 70, 71, 73, 74, 75, 77, 79, 80, 81, 84, 85, 89, 92, 93, 94, 95, 97, 102, 103, 108

Balsham, Hugo de, Bishop of Ely, 56
Barde, Giovanni de, banker, 148
Baron, the Chief, 105
Bath and Wells, Bishops of, 48, 144
Battely, Charles, Receiver and Register of Westminster Abbey, 149
Battersea, church and manor of, 10, 44, 56, 138
Bec, Abbey of, 40 f.
Belsize, Hampstead, manor of, 83, 135
Benedict XII, Pope, 84
Benedictines, General Chapter of, 26, 28, 61, 63, 65, 84, 92, 103, 104, 105, 113, 117, 119, 122, 124, 126, 127, 129, 139, 144
  Statutes of the Order, 49, 84
Benfleet, South, Essex, 85, 181
Bermondsey, 130
Bernay, Abbey of, 40
Bidek, Thomas, of the manor of Finchley, 92
Biggleswade, Beds, manor of, 19
Birchurst, Abbot Wenlok's houses at, 65
Birdbrook, Essex, manor of, 15, 61, 83, 181
Bird-spits in the Convent Kitchen, 163
Birlingham, Worcs, manor of, 52, 86
Blanket, cloth bought for slippers, 14
Blokley, John, anniversary of at Westminster, 107, 148
Blyth, Priory of, 175
Bolland, Humfrey, Auditor of the Abbey under Feckenham, 216 f.
Bonner, Edmund, Bishop of London, 186
Boat-hire, 105, 108, 130, 159
Boniface VIII, Pope, 3, 55
Bonaventura, 56
Bononia, Peter of, Bishop of Corbavia 78
Bosco, Ralph de, 53
Boston, Lincs, 189
Bourton, Gloucs, 58
Boy-bishop of St Nicholas, 85
Brabazon, Roger le, Chief Justice, 63
Brademoor, John, surgeon, 114
Bray, Magister W. de, 65
Brazur, Thomas le, 52

CAMBRIDGE: PRINTED BY J. B. PEACE, M.A., AT THE UNIVERSITY PRESS